THE COGNITIVE SCIENCE  ON

Scientific Studies of Religion: Inquiry and Explanation

SERIES EDITORS: LUTHER H. MARTIN, DONALD WIEBE, WILLIAM W. MCCORKLE JR., D. JASON SLONE AND RADEK KUNDT

Scientific Studies of Religion: Inquiry and Explanation publishes cutting-edge research in the new and growing field of scientific studies in religion. Its aim is to publish empirical, experimental, historical, and ethnographic research on religious thought, behaviour, and institutional structures. The series works with a broad notion of scientific that includes innovative work on understanding religion(s), both past and present. With an emphasis on cognitive science of religion, the series includes complementary approaches to the study of religion, such as psychology and computer modelling of religious data. Titles seek to provide explanatory accounts for the religious behaviors under review, both past and present.

THE ATTRACTION OF RELIGION
edited by D. Jason Slone and James A. Van Slyke

CONTEMPORARY EVOLUTIONARY THEORIES OF CULTURE AND THE
   STUDY OF RELIGION
Radek Kundt

DEATH ANXIETY AND RELIGIOUS BELIEF
Jonathan Jong and Jamin Halberstadt

THE MIND OF MITHRAISTS
Luther H. Martin

NEW PATTERNS FOR COMPARATIVE RELIGION
William E. Paden

PHILOSOPHICAL FOUNDATIONS OF THE COGNITIVE SCIENCE OF
   RELIGION
Robert N. McCauley with E. Thomas Lawson

RELIGION EXPLAINED?
edited by Luther H. Martin and Donald Wiebe

RELIGION IN SCIENCE FICTION
Steven Hrotic

RELIGIOUS EVOLUTION AND THE AXIAL AGE
Stephen K. Sanderson

THE ROMAN MITHRAS CULT
Olympia Panagiotidou with Roger Beck

THE COGNITIVE SCIENCE OF RELIGION

A METHODOLOGICAL INTRODUCTION TO KEY EMPIRICAL STUDIES

Edited by
D. Jason Slone and William W. McCorkle Jr.

BLOOMSBURY ACADEMIC

LONDON • NEW YORK • OXFORD • NEW DELHI • SYDNEY

BLOOMSBURY ACADEMIC
Bloomsbury Publishing Plc
50 Bedford Square, London, WC1B 3DP, UK

BLOOMSBURY, BLOOMSBURY ACADEMIC and the Diana logo are trademarks
of Bloomsbury Publishing Plc

First published in Great Britain 2019

A catalogue record for this book is available from the British Library.

A catalog record for this book is available from the Library of Congress.

ISBN: HB: 978-1-3500-3369-6
PB: 978-1-3500-3368-9
ePDF: 978-1-3500-3371-9
eBook: 978-1-3500-3370-2

Series: Scientific Studies of Religion: Inquiry and Explanation | SSR

Typeset by Newgen KnowledgeWorks Pvt. Ltd., Chennai, India
Printed and bound in Great Britain

We dedicate this volume to our teacher, E. Thomas Lawson.

CONTENTS

Contents

ILLUSTRATIONS

Figures

Illustrations

Tables

ACKNOWLEDGMENTS

We thank Ken Ball, Klayton Cook, Dickson Hagan, Lucy Hutcheson, India Jones, Jordan Kendall, Tony Olorode, and Kathyrn Youngblood for providing comments on chapter drafts.

We thank Monique Bos for providing developmental edits to chapter drafts.

We thank Dr. Karin Fry and the Department of Philosophy and Religious Studies at Georgia Southern University for support for this volume.

CONTRIBUTORS

Quentin Atkinson—Quentin Atkinson is a research associate at the Max Planck Institute for the Science of Human History in Jena, Germany, and an associate professor in the School of Psychology at the University of Auckland in Auckland, New Zealand.

Justin Barrett—Justin Barrett is the Thrive Professor of Developmental Science and program chair for the PhD in psychological science at Fuller Theological Seminary in Pasadena, California, USA.

Jesse Bering—Jesse Bering is an award-winning science writer and associate professor in the Centre for Science Communication at the University of Otago in Dunedin, Otago, New Zealand.

Joseph Bulbulia—Joseph Bulbulia is a professor in the School of Humanities at the University of Auckland in Auckland, New Zealand.

Russell Gray—Russell Gray is a professor in the School of Psychology at the University of Auckland in Auckland, New Zealand.

Richard Grove—Richard Grove is a doctoral student in the social psychology area of the general/experimental psychology program at the University of North Dakota in Grand Forks, North Dakota, USA.

Deborah Hall—Deborah L. Hall is an assistant professor in the School of Social and Behavioral Sciences at Arizona State University in Tempe, Arizona, USA.

K. Mitch Hodge—Mitch Hodge is an associate lecturer at the Institute of Cognition and Culture at Queen's University in Belfast, Northern Ireland.

Danijela Jerotijević—Danijela Jerotijević is an assistant professor on the faculty of social and economic sciences at Comenius University in Bratislava, Slovakia.

Jan Krátký—Jan Krátký is a PhD candidate at LEVYNA: Laboratory for the Experimental Research of Religion at Masaryk University in Brno, Czech Republic.

Justin E. Lane—Justin Lane is a postdoctoral fellow at the Institute for the Bio-Cultural Study of Religion in Boston, Massachusetts, USA, and a research associate at LEVYNA: Laboratory for the Experimental Research of Religion at Masaryk University in Brno, Czech Republic.

Martin Lang—Martin Lang is a postdoctoral researcher in the Department of Human Evolutionary Biology at Harvard University in Cambridge, Massachusetts, USA, and a research associate at LEVYNA: Laboratory for the Experimental Research of Religion at Masaryk University in Brno, Czech Republic.

Kristin Laurin—Kristin Laurin is an assistant professor in the Department of Psychology at the University of British Columbia in Vancouver, British Columbia, Canada.

Kirsten Lesage—Kirsten Lesage is a doctoral candidate in the Department of Psychology at the University of California, Riverside, in Riverside, California, USA.

Rita Anne McNamara—Rita Anne McNamara is a lecturer in cross-cultural psychology in the School of Psychology and fellow of the Center for Cross-Cultural Research at the Victoria University of Wellington in Wellington, New Zealand.

Brian Malley—Brian Malley is a lecturer in the Department of Psychology at the University of Michigan in Ann Arbor, Michigan, USA.

William McCorkle—William McCorkle is a senior research associate and the former director at LEVYNA: Laboratory for the Experimental Research of Religion at Masaryk University in Brno, Czech Republic.

Kristoffer Nielbo—Kristoffer L. Nielbo is an associate professor in the School of Culture and Society—Interacting Minds Centre at Aarhus University in Aarhus, Denmark.

Ara Norenzayan—Ara Norenzayan is director of the Centre for Human Evolution, Cognition, and Culture and a professor in the Department of Psychology at the University of British Columbia in Vancouver, British Columbia, Canada.

Erik Porter—Erik Porter is a graduate student in the master of science in psychology program at Arizona State University in Tempe, Arizona, USA.

Michaela Porubanova—Michaela Porubanova is an assistant professor in the Department of Psychology at Farmingdale State College in Farmingdale, New York, USA.

Benjamin Purzycki—Benjamin Purzycki is a senior research associate at the Max Planck Institute for Evolutionary Anthropology in Jena, Germany.

Rebekah Richert—Rebekah Richert is an associate professor in the Department of Psychology at the University of California, Riverside, in Riverside, California, USA.

Uffe Schjoedt—Uffe Schjoedt is an associate professor in the School of Culture and Society—Department of the Study of Religion at Aarhus University in Aarhus, Denmark.

Azim Shariff—Azim Shariff is director of the Culture and Morality Lab and an associate professor in the Department of Psychology at the University of California, Riverside, in Riverside, California, USA.

John Shaver—John Shaver is an assistant professor in the religious studies program at the University of Otago in Dunedin, Otago, New Zealand.

Oliver Sheehan—Oliver Sheehan is a researcher at the Max Planck Institute for the Science of Human History in Jena, Germany, and a doctoral student in the School of Psychology at the University of Auckland in Auckland, New Zealand.

F. LeRon Shults—LeRon Shults is a professor of theology and philosophy in the Institute for Religion, Philosophy and History at the University of Agder in Kristiansand, Norway, and a senior research associate at the Institute for the Bio-Cultural Study of Religion in Boston, Massachusetts, USA.

Edward Slingerland—Edward Slingerland is a Distinguished University Scholar and professor of Asian studies at the University of British Columbia in Vancouver, British Columbia, Canada.

Jason Slone—Jason Slone is a professor in the Department of Philosophy and Religious Studies at Georgia Southern University in Statesboro, Georgia, USA.

Jesper Sorensen—Jesper Sorensen is a research program director and associate professor in the School of Culture and Society—Department of the Study of Religion at Aarhus University in Aarhus, Denmark.

Richard Sosis—Richard Sosis is James Barnett Professor of Humanistic Anthropology in the Department of Anthropology at the University of Connecticut in Mansfield, Connecticut, USA.

Paulo Sousa—Paulo Sousa is director of the Institute of Cognition and Culture (ICC) and senior lecturer in cognitive anthropology at Queen's University in Belfast, Northern Ireland.

Ryan Tweney—Ryan Tweney is an emeritus professor in the Department of Psychology at Bowling Green State University in Bowling Green, Ohio, USA.

Joseph Watts—Joseph Watts is a postdoctoral researcher in the Department of Linguistic and Cultural Evolution at the Max Planck Institute for the Science of Human History in Jena, Germany, and a postdoctoral research fellow in the Social and Evolutionary Neuroscience Research Group at the University of Oxford in Oxford, UK.

Claire White—Claire White is an associate professor in the Department of Religious Studies at the California State University, Northridge, in Northridge, California, USA.

Dimitris Xygalatas—Dimitris Xygalatas is an assistant professor in the Department of Anthropology at the University of Connecticut in Mansfield, Connecticut, USA.

STUDENT INTRODUCTION
Jason Slone and William McCorkle

It is a curious fact, and a scientific puzzle, that the types of concepts and behaviors that we call "religion" are found in all human cultures, past and present. It is also a curious fact that despite obvious surface-level differences between religions (Christianity and Buddhism, for example), at a structural level these concepts and behaviors are strikingly similar. These facts beg the question: *Why*? Why do similar types of god concepts recur across cultures with regularity? Why do people believe that supernatural agents, which they can't see, cause events in the world? Why do religious organizations have similar types of membership requirements? Why do people do similar types of rituals, such as making offerings to gods and burying their dead in ceremonial ways? Why do religious organizations promote similar types of morality, yet at times permit or even encourage violence against others? Why do religious organizations try to control sexual behavior, like promoting the "family values" of getting (and staying) married and having children?

These are some of the interesting questions that scholars in the recently emerged field known as *cognitive science of religion* (CSR) have tried to answer over the last few decades. The main theory in CSR is that religious systems have similar types of concepts and behaviors across cultures because religious concepts and behaviors are produced by human minds (hence, *cognitive* science of religion, as those in the cognitive sciences study how human minds work), and human minds, or more accurately human *brains*, are basically the same across cultures because we all belong to the same species.

More accurately, those in CSR argue that the types of religious systems that recur across cultures exist because they have been *culturally selected for*, meaning that there have been lots of religious concepts and behaviors that have been invented by people throughout history . . . but only a few have grown into the "world religions" that dominate the religious market. Today, roughly 75 percent of humanity practices just four religions: Christianity (2 billion people), Islam (1.5 billion), Hinduism (1 billion), and Buddhism (500 million).

According to scholars in CSR, religious systems that have concepts and behaviors that fit well with our cognitive biases (which presumably evolved for other purposes) are the types of systems that will attract people and be "selected for" culturally. And, of course, those that don't . . . don't. (For a readable overview of the main theories in CSR, we encourage you to read *Religion Explained: The Evolutionary Origins of Religious Thought* (2001) by Pascal Boyer.)

The purpose of this book is to introduce readers to this fascinating new field via readable summaries and discussions of empirical studies that have been conducted by CSR scholars over the past few decades. One of the exciting features of CSR is that unlike most other approaches and paradigms in the academic study of religion, it offers not only interesting theories for why similar types of religious concepts and behaviors recur across cultures but also fascinating and powerful *methods* for testing those theories scientifically—methods borrowed from fields like evolutionary biology, cultural anthropology, cognitive and developmental psychology, and even computer science. Having nearly forty years of combined teaching experience between us, we have learned that the best way for those interested in studying a new scientific field is to be *shown* studies, not just *told* theories.

Importantly, this book is an *introduction* to CSR via readable discussions of studies. We did this so that you can learn about these studies, and their importance, without having to read difficult, jargon-filled, and statistics-heavy articles in technical journals. However, you can certainly supplement your readings from this volume with those articles. Furthermore, the collection of studies in this book is by no means exhaustive. There are lots of other interesting and important studies that have been done, and we encourage you to read those, too. Indeed, one of the goals of this book is to get you so excited by how those in CSR conduct research that you'll be motivated to explore—and conduct!—more studies. Enjoy!

INSTRUCTOR'S INTRODUCTION
William McCorkle and Jason Slone

This book is different from most books in the study of religion. For one, it is meant to be used as a teaching resource, not a work of original scholarship. And two, this book—in contrast to most books in the study of religion—reviews empirical studies that test hypotheses rather than just presenting yet another theory or interpretation. Our belief is that *showing* students will get them more excited about the material than just *telling* them.

Of course, empirical studies such as those discussed in this book are designed to test hypotheses (and, by extension, theories), so as an instructor it will help if you familiarize yourself with the basics of key theories and hypotheses in cognitive science of religion (CSR). To help, the following is a very brief history of the field.

A Very Brief History of the Cognitive Science of Religion

Several decades ago, a small group of scholars became interested in explaining why certain types of concepts and behaviors that we call "religion" recur across cultures, and they formulated theories drawn from the recently emerged interdisciplinary field of the cognitive sciences. Early pioneers in CSR such as E. Thomas Lawson, Robert McCauley, Stewart Guthrie, Pascal Boyer, and Harvey Whitehouse used their extensive specialized knowledge and expertise to tease out how such a field might proceed. Over time, they established CSR by combining theories and findings from the history of religions and anthropology with the cognitive sciences. The end result was a dynamic new paradigm for studying religion that offered not only new theories that could explain recurrent features of religion but also new *methods* for testing hypotheses drawn from those theories. In our view, offering new methods for studying religion is certainly one of the most important contributions that CSR has made to the study of religion—for despite much talk about theory *and* method, the academic study of religion is drowning in theory but starved for actual methods.

In addition, scholars working on theory and method have pointed out, in our opinion a bit exhaustively at times, that religion is a "social construction" rather than a natural kind with ontological existence. Though we don't like the term "social construction" (because "society" itself is a construction, not a natural kind, and so "society" cannot construct anything—better, in our view, to use "cognitive construction"), we agree with the spirit of this point. Religion is a (cognitive) construction that we use as a scholarly category to describe a suite of cross-culturally recurrent types of concepts (which are produced by people's minds), artifacts likes texts and paintings (which are produced by people's minds), and behaviors (which are produced by people's minds). And this is the main theory offered by CSR: "religion" is a product of human minds. So to study religion, one can—and should—study the cognitive system(s) that produces it.

Additionally, it is important to note that scholars in CSR have always been interested in *explaining* religion. CSR benefited greatly from the fact that one of the field's pioneers, Robert McCauley, is a philosopher of science who provided a sound meta-theoretical framework for the project. McCauley argued that scholars can explain religion by reducing it by one level of analysis from culture to cognition—because "culture" is produced by minds (for more on this, see Lawson & McCauley 1990 and/or Boyer 2001). This is precisely what the latest generation of CSR scholars has done over the last decade or so—formulated testable hypotheses drawn from key theories in CSR and then designed empirical studies to test those hypotheses. The studies are fascinating and are moving the field forward with rapidity. And, we believe, they provide an excellent way to get students excited about studying CSR.

How to Read and Teach This Volume

This volume is meant to provide students with an introduction to the field via accessible discussions of empirical studies that have been conducted over the past few decades in CSR. The volume is by no means exhaustive. There are many more fascinating studies that have been conducted, and we encourage you and your students to read those. Importantly, the chapters in this volume are written in such a way that students should not need any background in cognitive science, methods, or statistics to understand what the studies were testing, why the authors wanted to test in that way, and what the findings suggest. Also, the chapter topics are relatively independent of each other and so you can read and teach them in any order.

It is our hope that by introducing students to the field via *studies* rather than just theories, the volume will excite students (and scholars new to the field) and inspire them to study more. Obviously, we encourage you, as the instructor, to familiarize yourself with the original studies that the chapters discuss as well as key papers and monographs in the field so that you can answer questions that students may have.

CHAPTER 1
WHY DO WE SEE SUPERNATURAL SIGNS IN NATURAL EVENTS?
Jesse Bering

Introduction

Shortly after my mother died, I began to experience certain events that challenged my otherwise skeptical beliefs about the afterlife. To any objective observer, these events wouldn't seem particularly profound; some were in fact so subtle and mundane that they likely wouldn't have even registered in my consciousness under normal circumstances. But in the wake of my loss, my mind freighted with grief, these banal happenings took on special significance. It was as though my mom—or rather, her spirit—was attempting to part the veil between this world and the next, intent on communicating with me, her stubbornly atheistic child, by delivering ambiguous messages from beyond the grave.

The morning after she passed, for instance, I awakened to the faint, melodious sounds of the wind chimes that hung from a tree branch just beneath her bedroom window. It was a still morning, but surely a breeze must have stirred it. My knee-jerk thought was not at all in keeping with my beliefs. "That's her," I said instinctively to myself. "She telling me she's okay."

One evening, as I lay reading in bed, I heard a loud crash—the sound of broken glass. Rushing downstairs to see what had caused it, I found that a stained glass window, an extraction from an old church that I'd propped up decoratively on a shelf, had somehow fallen and shattered on the concrete floor. My mind raced to find an explanation. The cat, perhaps? But the cat had been sleeping soundly at the foot of my bed and had jumped at the sudden noise just as I had. I still can't be certain, but in all probability, I'd merely left it leaning precariously on the shelf, with an eventual disastrous tumble being inevitable.

Yet just as with the wind chimes, it wasn't the logical explanation that first leapt to my mind. Rather, it was a supernatural one. My mother hated that stained glass window. "It's not for me," I recalled her saying when I first eyed it at an antique shop in Louisiana a few years prior. "But go on, get it if you like it." And now there it was in a thousand broken pieces on the floor. I should add, this also happened on her birthday—the first since her death—and she'd been occupying my thoughts that whole somber day. In any event, the rationalist in me rejected any such supernatural attributions out of hand. Still, it certainly *felt* like a sign.

There were also the conversations we'd had on her deathbed. A secular Jew, she was agnostic about the afterlife. We enjoyed speaking openly about it, however. "Who knows," she'd muse. "But it's you I'd come back to . . . your brother and sister, they already believe.

They wouldn't need any proof. If I can, I'll give you a sign." So, was I just being dense now? The thought of my kind, gentle mother trying desperately to get my attention from the other side was emotionally evocative, and guiltily I began to feel like one of those stereotypical hardheaded—and hardhearted—science types who refuse to open their minds and acknowledge the numinous.

Ultimately, it's a philosophical question, whether such things have a paranormal element to them. I didn't believe they did then and I don't believe they do now. But what does it matter what people say they believe? (See also Gendler 2008.) The fact that my mind so naturally gravitated toward seeing such events *as if* they were signs fascinated me. And as a cognitive psychologist, I wanted to get to the bottom of these strange subjective phenomena (see also Bloom 2007). What is it about the human mind that so effortlessly translates natural events into messages from another realm—even despite our best attempts to deny that there's any message in them at all?

Inspired by my mom's ostensible phantom presence, this was the question I sought to answer in a study I published a few years after her death, conducted when I was still an assistant psychology professor at the University of Arkansas. My colleague Becky Parker and I started off with a simple premise: seeing meaning in natural events (colloquially, what most people would call signs or omens) requires a special form of human social intelligence (Bering & Parker 2006). The technical term for the psychological capacity in question is called *theory of mind*.

In the everyday social world, we use our theory of mind constantly, and it's especially easy to grasp the concept when applied to other people's unexpected behaviors. Let's say, for example, that you're out for a stroll at the park one sunny day, minding your own business, when you notice a naked man staggering out from behind some bushes ahead of you. He's now heading your way. Now, consider the dilemma. Does this person need help—perhaps he's the victim of a crime or is caught in the grip of a psychotic episode— or is his strange appearance and behavior more sinister? What you see is a body with all its sinews and muscles and eyes darting this way and that. What you don't see, what you *can't* see, is the mind that stirs behind those eyes, causing the curious body before you to behave the way it is.

After all, mental states are abstractions that cannot be directly perceived; similar to other causal properties such as gravity and mass, they're just theoretical constructs. Intuitively, your theory of mind kicks in, and probably frantically in this case, with you trying to infer what's going on in that head of his. Essentially, this social cognitive capacity allows you to think about what others are thinking. (In case you're wondering, I've no idea why this man was naked in the bushes and is making a beeline in your direction; I'll leave that mystery to you.) Hopefully you get the idea. With a theory of mind, we're better able to explain and predict other people's actions because we're putting ourselves in their shoes (or bare feet) and trying to see the world from their perspective. We may get it wrong—we might assume he's a pervert when in fact he's the subject of a cruel prank—but the fact that, all day long, we're busily trying to decipher unobservable mental states such as emotions, intentions, and beliefs is why the evolutionary scholar Nicholas Humphrey referred to our species as the animal kingdom's "natural psychologists" (Humphrey 1976).

What does all of this have to do with the human habit of seeing meaningful signs in natural events? Becky and I suspected that theory of mind strikes at the heart of it. It's perhaps not a *sine qua non*, but a common feature of most supernatural agents, be they God or ghosts, is the presumed presence of a consciousness without a physical body. And since they lack bodies, we can't reason about what's on their mind by inferring things from their overt behaviors, facial expressions, or words. Instead, we perceive them as communicating with us through symbolic events. In the absence of a theory of mind, wind chimes are just wind chimes, and the rude cacophony of glass suddenly breaking is, well, just that. But with it, when the emotional climate is just right, these types of things can take on special significance. They seem to be *about* the communicative intent of an immaterial being. They jumpstart our psychological theorizing. "What is she trying to tell me?" we may find ourselves asking. "What does she mean by this?"

To investigate, we decided to take a developmental approach to the issue, building on previous research showing that theory of mind emerges cumulatively over the course of childhood (see Newman et al. 2010). Whereas children younger than about four years of age struggle to understand that others have beliefs differing from their own, older kids are increasingly able to take opposing, and often complex, recursive perspectives (Perner & Howes 1992). At what age, then, are children cognitively advanced enough to be superstitious in the ways I've been referring to, attributing deeper meaning to anomalous occurrences that trigger their theory of mind?

In an attempt to map out these unknown age patterns, I decided to invite my mother's "ghost" into my research lab at Arkansas and introduce her to a bunch of kids.

Methodology

We didn't refer to her as a ghost, of course. Our intention certainly wasn't to scare small children. The whole thing was quite innocuous. I'll get to that shortly. For now, let me explain the basics of how it all worked. After getting ethics approval, we used advertisements in the local newspapers and parental word of mouth and recruiting from nearby schools to rustle up about 150 kids ranging from three to nine years of age.

Based on what we knew going in about the development of theory-of-mind skills (that they get increasingly sophisticated), we divided the sample into three distinct age groups. The "youngest" group consisted of the three- to four-year-olds, the "middle" group was represented by the five- to six-year-olds, and the "oldest" group was the seven- to nine-year-olds.

Each child was tested separately in a kid-friendly lab, typically while their mom or dad watched the session live on CCTV from an adjacent room. After a brief warm-up period in which the friendly experimenter (Becky) got to know the child—chatting about family or pets, playing together with blocks, drawing pictures on the blackboard—they were asked if they'd like to play a fun game. If they said "yes," and of course they all did, they were led to the front of the room, where on a table before them sat two large blue boxes side by side. The tops of the boxes were hinged, such that they could be flipped open front to back, revealing the contents by looking down into them. Becky stood on the side of the table facing the front of the boxes, and the child on the opposite side.

Playing the game

"Now," Becky said. "Two rules, OK? First, you have to stay on that side of the table. And second, only I can open the boxes." Once the child agreed, she went on. "See this?" Becky asked while holding up a red plastic ball. "I'm going to hide this ball inside one of these two boxes. While I'm hiding it, you're going to go to the corner and face the wall so that you don't see where I put it. Then you're going to come back and guess where the ball is by placing your hand on top of the box that you think it's inside—like this." Becky demonstrated by placing a flattened palm on the top of one of the two closed boxes. "Now, if you change your mind," she added, "you can move your hand to the other box. So, let's say at first you think the ball is in this box, and then you think, no, maybe it's in this other box, then you can move your hand, like this." Again, she demonstrated accordingly, moving her hand from the top of one closed box to the other. "You can change your mind as many times as you want. But wherever your hand is when I say 'Time's up!' is your final choice. If you get it right, then you get to pick a cool sticker. [Every experimenter worth their salt knows that stickers are basically heroin for grade-schoolers.] But if you get it wrong, you don't get a sticker that time."

Each kid then got a practice run at the game, just to make sure they understood the ground rules. "Now go hide in the corner," Becky would say. "And remember, no peeking!" While they were doing that, and after a few seconds of loudly opening and closing both of the lids—just to throw off some of the cleverer little ones who might try to localize the sound—she'd say, "Okay, pick whichever box you think the ball's in!" Once the child put their hand on one of the boxes, Becky started her timer and stared down at the ticking clock for fifteen seconds, offering them no help. "Time's up!" she'd announce. "Let's see where the ball is!" She'd then ceremoniously open the box that they *didn't* pick. "Aw, it was in here this time, look," she'd say, inviting them to have a peek inside. All the while, she kept the other box—the one they'd actually selected—closed.

A rigged system

Here's the secret. There were in fact two identical balls, so that each of the boxes contained a ball at all times. The kids didn't know it, but the game was totally rigged. After the practice trial, each child got a total of four tries at the game, but we'd decided in advance whether they'd get each attempt "right" or "wrong." Furthermore, on a random half of the test trials, something unexpected or surprising (from the child's perspective, at least) happened in the room as soon as their hand first made contact with one of the boxes.

There were two varieties of these "unexpected events," as we referred to them in the study. In one case, a desk lamp behind Becky would switch on and off a few times. We didn't need Industrial Light & Magic to pull this off, just a remote control operated by a research assistant in that adjacent room with the parents. In the other case, a picture hanging on the back of the door to the lab would come crashing to the floor. This was made possible by the research assistant simply lifting a magnet on the other side. By contrast, for the other two trials—the "nonevent trials"—nothing surprising happened.

To keep up morale, everyone was told they guessed correctly on these two nonevent trials. But to win that coveted sticker prize for the two unexpected-event trials, the child's hand had to end up on the opposite box from the one they'd first chosen.

Introducing Princess Alice

That was the basic setup. Now comes the interesting part. Each child had also been randomly assigned to either the control condition or the experimental condition. The former played the game just as I've described. Those in the latter condition, however, got some additional information: someone very special, they were told, would be helping them.

"See this picture?" we asked half of the kids, pointing at a portrait hanging from the back of the door (the same one I mentioned before) of a friendly, smiling woman bedecked in jewels and a crown. If you're trying to visualize the scene, she bore an uncanny resemblance to a certain Disney character, including being two-dimensional. So, not exactly the stuff of nightmares. "This is a picture of Princess Alice," said Becky. "Isn't she pretty? Princess Alice is a magic princess. Do you know what she can do? She can make herself *invisible*. Do you know what invisible means? It means you can't see her, even though she's there." For those who needed a bit of clarification on the matter, Becky would then wave her hand in front of her, passing it through thin air as if to capture the concept of invisibility. "And guess what else?" she'd continue. "Princess Alice is in the room with us right now. Where do you think she is? Do you think she's there?" she'd ask playfully, pointing to one corner and then the next. "Or maybe over there? Remember, we can't see her."

Once the introductions had been made, we told the child why Princess Alice had stopped by. "Princess Alice really likes you," Becky explained. "So she's going to help you play the game. She's going to tell you when you pick the wrong box. I don't know how she's going to tell you," said Becky. "But somehow, she's going to tell you when you pick the *wrong* box."

If you're thinking like an experimental psychologist, you can see the purpose of this study design. Moving their hand to the other box after experiencing the light flickering on and off, or upon the picture falling to the floor, should reveal children's thinking that Princess Alice is communicating a message to them; namely, that the unexpected event is "about" their choice, and that she's trying to tell them (using the symbolic guise of a natural occurrence) to pick the other box. Compared to children in the control condition, anyway, those who were told about an invisible coconspirator in the room with them should be significantly more likely on these two unexpected-event trials to end up with their hand on the box opposite from where it started.

Also, just to unpack their reasoning further, at the end of the study we asked each child to reflect back and to tell us why those weird things occurred. "Hey, you remember before, when the light flashed on and off? Why do you think that happened?"

Results and Analysis

There were two main aspects of the data that we were most interested in. First, compared to those in the control group, were kids in the Princess Alice condition more likely to move their hand to the other box (and to keep it there) on the unexpected-event trials? And second, we wanted to know if these children's verbal explanations for the two unexpected events betrayed their reasoning that the invisible woman was trying to communicate with them through signs in their environment.

Moving hands and changing minds

Let's look at the behavioral responses first. As predicted, children in the experimental condition (those who'd heard about Princess Alice) were significantly more likely than those in the control group to display what Becky and I termed "receptive responding"—which is to say, after the light flashed or the picture fell, they immediately moved their hand to the opposite box as if they had "received" these events as messages from the invisible woman about the location of the ball. However, this effect panned out only for the oldest children (the seven- to nine-year-olds). For those children in both the youngest age group (three- to four-year-olds) and the middle age group (five- to six-year-olds), by contrast, it didn't matter whether they'd heard about Princess Alice or not; those in the experimental condition were no more or less likely to move their hand to the other box (again, to respond "receptively") when the surprising events transpired than were those who'd been randomly assigned to the control condition (see Figure 1.1).

Crunching the numbers further, we were able to rule out more simplistic accounts, for example that the oldest kids—or those in the experimental group—were simply more likely to move their hands overall. Rather, the effect was specific: only the seven- to nine-year-olds reliably moved their hand to the other box, and they did this only for the flashing-light and picture-falling trials. This tells us that it's only at about that age that children begin to perceive unexpected events in the environment as messages from supernatural agents. Prior to this, a light flashing is just a light flashing. A picture falling is just, well, a picture falling.

Explaining the unexpected

Next, for those in the experimental condition, we investigated if verbal judgments of the unexpected events showed clear evidence that kids were seeing these surprise happenings as communicative messages from Princess Alice. If so, then not only should

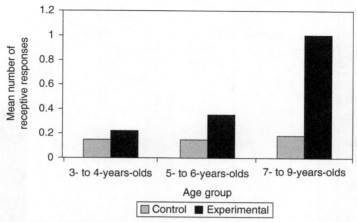

Figure 1.1 Behavioral change. Condition and age-group comparison of mean number of receptive responses (i.e., moved hand to the box opposite the first selection following the occurrence of either random event) on unexpected event trials. "Youngest": three- to four-year-olds; "middle": five- to six-year-olds; "oldest": seven- to nine-year-olds.

they move their hand, but they should also tell us that these events were in fact Princess Alice trying to reach out to them, helping them to find the ball.

Upon coding the full range of spoken answers, three general categories of verbal judgments for the unexpected events emerged. Moreover, these answer types were strongly associated with the three age groups. For instance, when we asked kids "Why did the picture fall off the door?" the youngest children gave largely *nonagentive* verbal judgments. Most of the time, these involved straightforward physical faults. "Because it wasn't sticking very well," said one four-year-old. They didn't see Princess Alice as being involved at all, in other words.

Those in the middle age group, by contrast, saw Princess Alice as clearly being involved, but they didn't associate the surprising events with the game. "Princess Alice took it off [the door]," a five-year-old told Becky. "Why?" Becky prodded. "Because she thought it would look better in another place," the child explained. In other words, children in this middle age group favored *intentional agentive* explanations for the unexpected events. Princess Alice caused these weird things to happen, but only because she "wanted to"—like a mischievous poltergeist, they saw her as an invisible woman intentionally making things happen in the room, but not because she was trying to tell them anything.

Finally, the most common type of verbal judgment among the oldest kids was of the kind we labeled *declarative agentive*. Explanations of this variety implied that the child perceived the event as Princess Alice communicating with them, using the picture falling (or the light flashing) to "declare" her knowledge about the ball's location. "Because she was telling me it was the wrong one," said one seven-year-old. Another stated, "It's another way of her not speaking, so she doesn't have to tell me that it's wrong." (See Figure 1.2.)

11

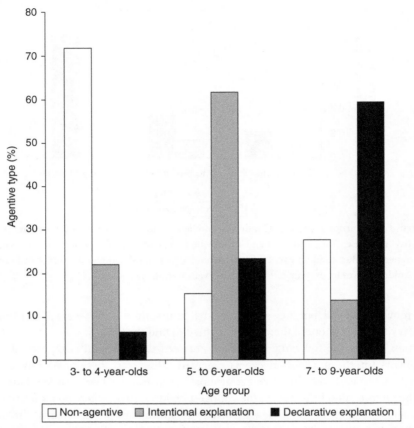

Figure 1.2 Verbal judgment. Age-group comparison of agentive explanatory types. Percentages do not include data from the control group. "Youngest": three- to four-year-olds; "middle": five- to six-year-olds; "oldest": seven- to nine-year-olds.

Discussion

Does everything happen for a reason? Of course! Why else would we be doing science? Science is reductionistic; our mission is to drill down incrementally into fundamental causal reasons for natural phenomena. But that's not what most people tend to mean when they ask this kind of question. Rather, it's not about scientific mechanisms for them; it's about creative design (Bloom 2007). They want to know if things are happening because there's an immaterial mind at work behind the scenes, causing the events in our lives *intentionally*. In the religious or spiritual realms, the question of meaning involves addressing "why" things happen rather than "how" they happen.

I've revealed my own existential prejudices already; I believe the "why" question is actually a nonquestion, one triggered by our species' overactive theory of mind spilling into a mindless domain. Ultimately, though, it's up to each of us to determine if our personal experiences (especially those that deviate from our expectations) are orchestrated by invisible supernatural beings trying to give us signs from the other side. But whether the world is brimming over with covert messages or is a big empty pit of meaninglessness, the findings from our study suggest that it's not until they're in about the second grade that children have the psychological capacity to even think in such meaning-laden terms.

Specifically, Becky and I argued that you need a "second-order theory of mind" to subjectively occupy a demon-haunted world. Whereas a basic (first-order) theory of mind allows us to think about what others are thinking ("He thinks that x"), a second-order one enables us to think about what others are thinking about our own thoughts ("He thinks that I think that x"). Perceiving a message in the picture falling, for instance, requires you to put yourself in Princess Alice's shoes as she's watching you pick the wrong box. You putting your hand on that box means that you think, falsely, that the ball is inside of it. Therefore, the picture falling is *about* your false belief. Whereas seven-year-olds could do this without any trouble at all, five-year-olds (limited to a more basic theory of mind) saw her as a sort of paranormal jokester. Sure, she did it. On purpose. She did it because she wanted to.

Meanwhile, the youngest kids didn't implicate Princess Alice at all. Another way to look at it, then, is that the preschoolers were the best scientists of the bunch. It's only with increasing age that people think irrationally by imbuing the world, and their experiences within it, with hidden meaning. In fact, some of the oldest kids saw Princess Alice attempting to give them messages in ways that we hadn't even anticipated. One little boy told us that the bell tolling in the university clock tower was Princess Alice "talking" to him; an eight-year-old girl likewise saw Princess Alice's guiding hand in a spider spinning its web in the corner.

From an adult psychiatric point of view, this type of thinking can get really, erm, insane. People suffering from schizophrenia, for instance, often display debilitating *apophenia*—which is basically seeing patterns of meaningful connections in completely unconnected events. "Theistic and philosophical phenomena populate their hallucinations," writes the psychiatrist Jonathan Burns of those with this disorder, "while the frantic search for, and misattribution of, intentionality . . . lie at the heart of symptoms such as thought insertion, ideas of reference and paranoid delusions" (Burns 2004: 840).

Yet most of us—atheist and believer alike—have at some point in our lives succumbed to this form of superstitious reasoning (Heywood & Bering 2014). It's typically harmless enough. Sure, we can dismiss such thoughts as silly, but sometimes, it's cognitively effortful to refrain from it. A flat tire on the way to the airport or a pigeon defecating on our shoulder as we're walking to a job interview can seem to be the universe's way of helping us to avert disaster. It's only when people begin stitching their own warped view of morality into the cosmic fabric that we run into serious trouble at the societal level, with religious fanatics preaching to gullible acolytes that, say, a devastating earthquake is "about" God's discontent over gay marriage.

A final note about our study. Despite our earnest attempts to debrief every child who participated—explaining to them that Princess Alice was just make-believe, and even showing them how we made the light flash on and off and the picture fall—she nonetheless "stuck" for many kids in the experimental condition. That is, they appeared to take her home with them. For years, in fact, parents would report to us how strange events in the house were being blamed on Princess Alice by these children (see also Piazza, Bering, & Ingram 2011; Woolley, Boerger, & Markman 2004).

Whether they were facetious attributions or not I cannot say. Still, not that I want to add any more haze to our species' already cloudy representation of reality, but I admit it's not displeasing to contemplate the idea that, somewhere in the Ozarks, a clandestine cell of twenty-somethings gathers at the altar of a powerful invisible princess. I can picture my mom, Alice, smiling upon such a scene, too.

CHAPTER 2
WHAT DO WE THINK ABOUT GOD WHEN WE AREN'T CAREFUL?

Justin L. Barrett

Introduction

As someone who grew up in a Christian home and is familiar with sermons, hymns, and general conversation about God, I have long been curious about the various images used for representing God. The Bible variously depicts God as a fortress and a rock, as having a face and hands, and as compared to a mother hen. A reasonably educated Christian would likely say that because God is so importantly different from humans, we have to use metaphors and images to think and talk about God, but we should not take such images to be actual descriptors of God. If that is so, I reasoned, then how a person thinks about and relates to God might predictably vary with the metaphors and images they use for God. As an undergraduate I began trying to research how metaphors for God impacted people's conceptions of God, but I quickly came across a challenge: How do I measure a conception of God that does not simply rely on the words that a person uses to describe God, including the metaphors? For example, discovering that people exposed to the hymn "A Mighty Fortress Is Our God" tend to describe God as a "fortress" would not be terribly interesting, but how could I get around this problem?

As a first-year graduate student at Cornell University, I made efforts to measure God concepts without just asking people to say what they thought God was like. I was part of the cognitive-developmental lab group that psychologists Frank Keil and Elizabeth Spelke led, and I would bring my challenges to the group for discussion. In one conversation, someone (Ann Phillips, I believe) suggested using memory intrusions as an indirect method to measure God concepts. Memory intrusions had received considerable study in the 1970s and 1980s (e.g., Bransford & McCarrell 1974). The basic idea is that when we recall a story or scene, what we expect to happen fills in the gaps that are present in the story's telling or in our perception of the event. We cannot possibly remember everything, and a story cannot possibly tell all of the details necessary to make it flow as a cohesive whole, so our minds do the rest of the work for us. In some cases, this "filling in the gaps" leads us to misremember something from a story or scene that was not actually there. For instance, if I am told about someone at a baseball game whose drink was hit and spilled by a foul ball, I may later remember that in the story a foul ball spilled a man's beer, even if the original story never specified that the person was a man or was drinking beer. Why? My mental picture of baseball games — my schema — may lead me to expect that most fans are men drinking beer. When I hear the story, my imagination fills in these details, and the later result is a false memory of what was actually in the story. Based upon this general rationale, then, I could use intrusion errors to indirectly measure how people conceptualize God. (See the Theory section for an explanation of how this would work.)

Though my original motivation was to study how metaphors might impact how people conceived of or understood God, I also recognized in my own experience and in my fellow Christians a certain tension in thinking about God. We know in some important sense that God is not remotely like a human being, but we very happily sing songs about God that use language about God's eyes, hands, heart, feelings, and so on that seem to depict God as very humanlike. That is, we anthropomorphize God. We make God in a human image. The Bible is full of such anthropomorphic imagery. Furthermore, the central claim of Christianity is that God self-anthropomorphized in the person of a first-century Jewish man, Jesus of Nazareth. That is, God became a human being in order for humans to better understand and form a loving relationship with God. Could this be because humans are rather poor at relating deeply to someone who is not humanlike? Religions all over the world and throughout history have deities that are very humanlike. Perhaps this fact says something about the psychological capacities that humans use to think about God and other deities. Maybe thinking anthropomorphically is conceptually easier or more natural in some respects than trying to comprehend wholly immaterial, immortal, superpowerful, all-knowing, and all-perceiving beings that are also everywhere at one time (or nowhere in space and time). Could it be demonstrated that anthropomorphism is conceptually easier than the theologically sophisticated and proper descriptions of gods?

The project that led to Barrett and Keil (1996), then, was motivated by two research questions and armed with one methodological insight. The two research questions were (1) is thinking of God in terms of humanlike traits conceptually simpler than the more common, theologically accurate alternatives and (2) to what degree does anthropomorphic thought about God vary with exposure to humanlike metaphors and images of God? Barrett and Keil (1996) primarily focused on the first question. Barrett and VanOrman (1996) took up the second question using similar methods. The methodological insight was that we could indirectly access people's God concepts by asking them to read, understand, and recall a story that included God. Intrusion errors could tell us something about the conception of God they brought to the task. Instead of reflecting on their understanding of God, then, we asked adult participants in this study to put their understanding of God to use.

Theory

In the course of designing and conducting the experiments reported in Barrett and Keil (1996), I became familiar with the theoretical work of Stewart Guthrie and Pascal Boyer. Both of these anthropologists provided reason to suspect that the mental representations of God that ordinary people use in day-to-day life, prayer, and worship would be very humanlike, even if the theological experts of their tradition construe crudely human traits as only metaphorical, or even if these people found themselves, in more reflective moments, rejecting humanlike traits as being true of God.

Guthrie (1980, 1993) has proposed that humans have a pervasive conceptual tendency to perceive and understand things of the world in terms of human properties. Our understanding of humans—including our thoughts, feelings, behaviors, social arrangements, biological needs, and physical properties—is so important to our interactions with each other and the world around us that human traits have become a "go-to" repository for thinking about even nonhuman aspects of the world. Guthrie terms this tendency "anthropomorphism" and sees it at play in many forms of thought and cultural expression, not just those that contemporary Westerners might regard as "religious." When anthropomorphic thinking is applied to the natural world and its processes, as it almost inevitably will be on Guthrie's account, the foundation has been laid for religious thought and concepts of gods. Because at its core all religious thought is a product of anthropomorphism, says Guthrie, his theory predicts that people will find the attribution of human properties to God very difficult to resist.

Boyer's cognitive approach to the study of religious thought, which was beginning to be published in the early 1990s (1992, 1994), offered another pathway to largely humanlike attributions to deities. Building upon cognitive linguistic and developmental studies, including those of my advisor and collaborator Keil (1979, 1989), Boyer observed that some ways of conceptualizing things in the world appear to develop early in our lives and with a strong degree of regularity across cultural groups, much like Guthrie's idea of anthropomorphism. Where Boyer departed from Guthrie was in suggesting that instead of one conceptual scheme (anthropomorphism) doing all of the work, humans appear to have a handful of different conceptual schemes for thinking about the various things in the world, and we can even combine these schemes in creative ways to come up with novel cultural concepts. Drawing upon the work of Dan Sperber (1985), Boyer further observed that good candidates for cultural concepts, including God concepts, tend to track very closely with these ordinary, typical conceptual foundations; otherwise they become too difficult to understand and communicate to others. If you cannot communicate an idea effectively, it stands a greatly reduced chance of becoming widespread enough to be "cultural" or "religious." For this perspective, then, God concepts that are simply too deviant from ordinary "intuitive" thought will be harder to think and communicate. If that is correct, we might expect that the massively counterintuitive theological concepts about God's wholly nonnatural properties (e.g., being intangible and invisible; lacking a location; being immortal, powerful, and all-knowing) are difficult to use on the fly. That is, behind a mask of theologically correct-sounding platitudes, we may expect that most believers have to use a simpler God concept to think and talk about God. This God concept may prove to be highly anthropomorphic.

In slightly different ways, then, both Guthrie's and Boyer's theoretical accounts encourage the prediction that at least the concepts of God that people use to make sense of stories will tend to have many human properties. Hence, if we present stories in which some of God's properties are deliberately made ambiguous, then readers will readily

17

insert human properties into those conceptual gaps—intrusion errors. These God concepts that people use to comprehend stories would likely deviate importantly from their stated theological beliefs about God's properties.

Methodology

The key to these studies was to create space for readers' concepts to do some work filling in gaps and ambiguities. The first step was to create a set of short stories that would do the job. I wrote eight such stories. All involved God as a character. Importantly, in all the stories, God needed to be able to play the described role without having specific human properties, such as being in only a single location at a time, only being able to pay attention to one thing at a time, requiring vision or hearing to know things, and so on. That is, even if one had a very non-humanlike understanding of God, the stories still had to make sense. Of course, some properties that God and humans share had to be assumed. These properties included that God can think, know, and pay attention and that God can act in the world, such as to move things. God is an intentional agent, even if not a human. The stories also needed enough detail about God's involvement and other features that some of the details could be left for readers to fill in, creating space for their memory intrusions. One such story was the following:

> A woman was exploring a cave when she got lost. The woman was terrified. She was alone in a dark, small, damp cave. There was not even enough room for her to stand upright. The walls had a bumpy texture with patches of fungus. Out of fear she started praying aloud for someone to come help her. As she prayed, her voice echoed mockingly in the cave. She then fell asleep. God responded by pushing a large stone from behind the woman to reveal a tunnel out of the cave. When she awoke, she saw no one, but the rock had been moved. She left the cave.

Notice that the story does not specify numerous assumptions we might make if we thought of God anthropomorphically (as like a human). If God were like a human and required hearing or seeing to know things, then we might assume that God literally heard the prayer (and needed to) and then responded. If God were like a human and must be in the presence of an object in order to act upon it, then God presumably came to the cave and moved the large stone. If God were visible like a human, then if God were still present when the woman awoke, God would have been visible to her. Stories like this one, then, allowed for a test of whether participants remembered various human traits as part of the story, even if those traits were not necessary for understanding the story and were not necessarily part of a "theologically correct" God concept.[1]

Barrett and Keil (1996) reported on three studies, all using these stories and the same basic rationale. Studies 1 and 2 both used questions to probe for intrusion errors. To illustrate, in the story about the woman in the cave, we asked participants, "Which of the following pieces of information were included in the story?" and gave eight yes/no items, for instance, "The woman cried when she discovered she was lost." If you think women in distress are likely to cry, you might answer "yes" to this item, even though the story never said that the woman cried. Likewise, if a person's God concept is highly humanlike, they may be inclined to answer affirmatively to this item: "When the woman awoke, God had already left but the rock was moved." The story never said God came or left. Some items also simply checked for the bare facts of the story, such as, "There was fungus on the walls of the cave" (yes) and "God responded to the woman's prayer by moving a rock" (yes). In Study 1, participants answered the questions after a brief delay and with very little time (approximately two seconds) to decide their answer. In Study 2, participants could answer the questions at their own pace and even reference the stories if they wished. Study 3 used four of the eight stories but did not use recall items. Rather, we asked participants to paraphrase the stories and then scored these paraphrases for whether they included new information that emphasized either God's humanlikeness or non-humanlikeness.

Studies 1 and 2 each had multiple conditions. Study 1 had three conditions. We randomly assigned roughly one-third of the participants to complete the story task first and then answer questions more reflectively about their concept of God. Another third of the participants answered the reflective questions first and then completed the story task, because we wondered whether first answering the more reflective questions about a participant's concept of God would trigger less anthropomorphism in the story task, because the participant would have been reminded of their theology just before the task. The third condition of Study 1 was the same story task, except that we replaced God with a fictitious supercomputer named Uncomp. We read participants a description of Uncomp twice and asked them to answer comprehension questions about it before starting the story task. Uncomp was Frank Keil's invention, and we used it to check whether any detected anthropomorphism was merely a product of the task demands and whether anthropomorphism is broadly and spontaneously used even when the entity in question is decidedly not human and has never been presented as human. Uncomp was described as a system of microscopic disks that record information and act. As far as possible, Uncomp was attributed godlike properties relevant to the stories.[2]

Study 2 had five conditions. Like Study 1, there was a condition in which participants first completed the story task and then a questionnaire about God's properties, and also a condition with the reverse order. This questionnaire was much more specific about the divine properties that distinguish God from humans than the questionnaire from Study 1, and we hoped that pointedly having participants think about God's superproperties would reduce anthropomorphism, thereby showing that the task alone was not driving all of the anthropomorphism. In the third condition, we merely encouraged participants to think about God as "very different from humans" while they performed the story task. The fourth condition substituted Superman for God in the stories in an effort to see how a fully anthropomorphic superbeing would be treated. The final condition introduced superhuman space aliens to fill God's role in the stories—we described Mog, Beebo, and Swek before the story task, and they took turns appearing in the stories.

In Study 3, participants did not answer items about the four stories but paraphrased them instead. These paraphrases were then coded. We instructed participants to "rewrite the story in your own words" and gave them permission to add or omit details to clarify and preserve the meaning of the original.

The sample for these studies consisted entirely of Cornell University students, and almost entirely of undergraduates. The typical participant was nineteen or twenty years old. The majority identified as Christian (Protestant or Catholic), but the sample also included participants who identified with Bahaism, Buddhism, Hinduism, Islam, and Judaism, as well as atheists and agnostics. Across the three studies, 145 young adults participated.

Results and Analysis

Studies 1 and 2

In Studies 1 and 2, we indexed participants' tendency to make anthropomorphic intrusion errors by calculating how frequently participants claimed that humanlike limitations were included in the story (the "God items"), divided by their accuracy on the other items ("base items"). In this way, generally sloppy performance was not accidentally construed as anthropomorphizing God (or Uncomp, Mog, Beebo, and Swek). We found no correlation in performance on these two sets of items, suggesting that something different was happening conceptually between the two types of items, rather than that one set merely was more difficult than the other. Dividing the God item accuracy by the base item accuracy, then, was the primary measure of how humanlike God concepts (or Uncomp concepts, etc.) were, or anthropomorphism.

Across all conditions of Studies 1 and 2, evidence of anthropomorphism was present, but it varied in degree. Participants anthropomorphized Uncomp less than God in Study 1, and asking participants to reflect on God's nonhuman properties before completing the story task reduced anthropomorphism in both Studies 1 and 2. The least anthropomorphized superbeings were Mog, Beebo, and Swek, showing very little evidence that participants unnecessarily attributed human traits to them. Superman had the greatest average degree of anthropomorphism but, interestingly, was not significantly different than any of the God conditions except for the one in Study 2, in which we first asked participants questions about God's non-humanlike properties. Importantly, across both studies, participants almost universally rejected humanlike limitations (e.g., having to be near something to see it, having just one location in space) on God when directly asked about these properties on questionnaires, even if they appeared to use these properties to comprehend the stories.

To summarize, Studies 1 and 2 showed that when people were in a reflective mode answering questions about God's properties, they answered very similarly to theologians: God does not have humanlike limitations. In contrast, in the story tasks, participants reported that the story said things entailing that God was near an object if God was perceiving it, God's perception could be blocked, God could only attend to one thing at a time, God could be in only one place at a time, and so forth. This tendency was reduced if we reminded participants of God's non-humanlike properties before the story task or if another superbeing that was not humanlike (Uncomp or Mog, Beebo, and Swek) replaced God.

Study 3

Study 3 supported the idea that people very easily anthropomorphize God and that this tendency was independent of any comprehension questions that might nudge them toward humanlike qualities. Of the fifty-two paraphrases (four from each of thirteen participants), half showed anthropomorphic intrusions, and only two included extra details to make clearer God's difference from humans. For instance, one story concluded this way:

> While God was listening to the birds, a large jet landed. It was extremely loud: the birds couldn't even hear each other. The air was full of fumes. God listened to the jet until it turned off its engines. God finished listening to the birds.

Though one could understand this story as God listening to the birds, then the jet and the birds simultaneously, and then just the birds again until they stopped singing to each other, one participant wrote:

> God was listening to two birds singing in a tall tree next to an airport. When a large jet landed, God listened to it because he could no longer hear the birds. Then he listened to the birds again.

Discussion

Validity

Before drawing conclusions about whether God concepts are tethered to ordinary conceptual systems that make us prone to anthropomorphism, we need to be confident that anthropomorphism was validly measured in this study. That is, apart from the particular demands introduced by these stories and/or the comprehension items, does poorer accuracy on the "God items" divided by accuracy on the "base items" indicate a more humanlike concept of God in the individual who is responding? Does the task approximate what happens psychologically in some real-world settings, such as when people are listening to accounts of God's activities, worshipping, and discussing God informally? Several pieces of evidence suggest that the measure of anthropomorphism is generally valid. First, as we've noted, answers on the God items did not correlate with the base items, and accuracy rates were much poorer, suggesting that the items were conceptually very different from each other. That is, variability in performance on the God items was independent of variability on the other items—people with great memory or reading comprehension were not necessarily better on both sets of items. Second, the less humanlike the being in question, the fewer intrusions on the God items, and hence, the higher the accuracy. So, in Study 1, Uncomp was less anthropomorphized than God; in Study 2, Mog, Beebo, and Swek were less anthropomorphized than God, who was less anthropomorphized than Superman (in one condition). If task demands were completely driving the anthropomorphism scores, we would be unlikely to find such a pattern. Third, when participants were reminded of God's specific non-humanlike properties prior to the story task, they made fewer intrusion errors. This finding is consistent with the idea that the easiest thing for participants to do is to think very anthropomorphically but that they can resist the impulse. For example, the story task does not coerce people into thinking anthropomorphically about the superhuman characters. Along these lines, when participants could respond slowly and reference the text (in Study 2) and were asked to think in terms of novel superhumans (Mog, Beebo, and Swek) with many theologically correct godlike properties, their anthropomorphism almost entirely went away: 92.5 percent adjusted accuracy, with 100 percent indicating no intrusion errors. For these reasons, the story comprehension task, particularly the written version in Study 2, appears to be a valid measure of anthropomorphism in God concepts. The paraphrase task in Study 3 seems to reveal even less prompted anthropomorphism.

Nevertheless, there are two minor pieces of evidence that may suggest the task added to or exaggerated the degree of anthropomorphism in the concepts that participants were carrying around in their minds. First, simply reminding participants to think of God as very non-humanlike during the story task failed to reduce the degree of anthropomorphism (Study 2). It may be, however, that the instructions were too nonspecific. Participants may have thought that they were being asked to understand God's greater goodness or power in comparison to humans, rather than the nature of God's perception, attention, or location. More importantly, in no condition did the anthropomorphism entirely go away (i.e., reach 100 percent for an adjusted score). This fact could be interpreted as the stories or their comprehension items gently seducing participants toward anthropomorphism.[3] Alternatively, however, this could merely indicate that once we attribute to an intentional being certain mental states, such as perception, knowledge, and attention, and the ability to act, we automatically find ourselves drawn to think of that being in at least somewhat humanlike terms in other regards. Perhaps, for instance, we are so accustomed to thinking that seeing something requires physical proximity that once we know that someone can see something, we assume that they need to be near things to see them. Likewise, perhaps the concept of attention automatically triggers the idea of attending to one thing at the expense of others; attending generally to everything may be a violation of our intuitive sense of what attention is. Consequently, the inability to completely eliminate anthropomorphism in this task may actually be due to the power of anthropomorphism in our thinking about all minded beings.

Implications

Accepting that the task does validly measure the tendency to anthropomorphize God (or other minded beings), what do these results tell us about how people conceptualize God? To start with, these studies suggest that there may be something slightly misleading in talking about a person's God concept. Rather, in each individual we may have multiple concepts of God or a very flexible concept of God that adapts to particular contexts. We may use one concept when reflecting on what God's properties are and doing theological, analytical work and use a different concept or concepts when we are more reflexively and less self-consciously thinking about God. Similarly, it may be that the God that we reason about is different than the God we relate to. This distinction between faster, more intuitive, less conscious religious thought and slower, more counterintuitive, conscious theological thought has been part of the legacy of these studies (e.g., Barrett 2011; McCauley 2011; Slone 2004). Furthermore, the notion that different, seemingly incompatible cultural and religious concepts may be triggered in some situations but not others has been supported by other studies in cognitive science of religion (e.g., Astuti & Harris 2008; Bek & Lock 2011; Cohen & Barrett 2008).

So it appears that people carry around multiple concepts of God (and maybe other religious and cultural ideas) simultaneously, but what is the easy version for use in day-to-day, informal thought? These studies suggest that the easy concept of God for adults is very humanlike or anthropomorphic. Care is needed in interpreting this claim, however. These studies specifically considered traits that humans and other nonhuman entities may share and that God is often said to not share. These properties include limited attention, a particular location in time and space, and the need to use sensory perception to know about things. Just because our most easily activated concept of God assumes these traits does not mean it assumes that God has a tangible physical body, is mortal, has body hair and fingernails, and so on. These studies and their measures do not address such possibilities. These studies also concerned young adult concepts of God and not those of children or older adults. In both the narrative comprehension task and others, evidence suggests that children may have an easier time with some counterintuitive concepts than adults, especially older adults (Barrett 1998; Gregory & Greenway 2017). It may be, then, that some aspects of anthropomorphism are a product of aging and/or enculturation (Barrett 2012; Chilcott & Paloutzian 2016).

The results of Barrett and Keil (1996) make the ability to ascribe certain "beliefs" and belief-like states to a person or an entire cultural group very difficult (Knight & Astuti 2008). For example, individuals and even entire communities may verbally report having concepts of a deity that do not map onto the apparent concepts that guide the bulk of their actions concerning that deity, as in saying that God is attending to everything at once but then feeling compelled to direct God's attention to a particular event as if it went unnoticed. Further still, people may be entirely unaware of the inconsistency. Likewise, the ease of using the more intuitive concept(s) may subtly distort the theological claims that people think they affirm, leading even to a difference between the stated theology of ordinary people and that of theological specialists (Slone 2004; see also Cohen & Barrett 2008).

Criticisms

In addition to the concern about some (but likely not all) of the intrusion errors being a product of the tasks more than the concepts that participants bring to the tasks, several criticisms could be leveled at the original studies. Some of these criticisms have been remedied, but others have not.

The original sample sizes were fairly small, and the sample was likely importantly nonrepresentative of both religious people and people in general. Undergraduates at an Ivy League university, even though drawn from many different nations, are not representative of the general population in terms of age, socioeconomic status, education, and cognitive skills, among other potentially relevant factors. Though we have no particular reason to think socioeconomic status would bear on these results, cognitive skills and education may. Also, as we've seen, age has proven to bear on these findings, with older people appearing to show more anthropomorphism than younger people (Barrett 1998; Chilcott & Paloutzian 2016). These two studies were both set in India and concerned concepts of Hindu deities (e.g., Vishnu and Krishna), with importantly similar findings. Hence, the original findings have been somewhat broadened. Barrett and Keil (1996) included people who identified with many different faith traditions and those who identified with none at all, but the sample sizes were too small to investigate differences among them.

Perhaps more importantly, the story comprehension and paraphrase tasks do not necessarily represent a broad range of contexts and ways in which people use God concepts. For instance, when people pray to God, sing worship songs, or conduct rituals and sacraments, do they similarly substitute humanlike traits for more conceptually challenging ones? Though suggestive, these studies cannot answer that question with any confidence.

Suggestions for further studies

Replication and extension in other cultural and religious contexts would be valuable in this area of study. The use of new methods that more strongly mirror other settings in which people may think about God or other deities would be helpful to better discern the generality of anthropomorphizing tendencies. As suggested above, examination of a broader range of age groups would also contribute insights regarding whether anthropomorphism detected here reflects the emergence of early developing cognitive biases and predilections ("developmental defaults") or whether this anthropomorphism is the result of enculturation (e.g., through seeing lots of anthropomorphic images of gods) or some other developmental factors. Of course, this general methodology—contrasting stated beliefs concerning a concept with features of the used concept—could be put to work to explore other cultural concepts, such as ghosts, spirits, and the afterlife.

CHAPTER 3
WHAT DO PEOPLE THINK OMNISCIENT AGENTS KNOW?

Benjamin Purzycki and Richard Sosis

Introduction

Would an all-knowing being know the color of the socks you are wearing? (Without looking, do you?) Clearly, a being who knows the answer to every question would know this information. Such a being is equally likely to know your deepest, darkest secrets as well as things that transpire on the other side of the globe. People often think of the Abrahamic god (i.e., the god of Jews, Christians, and Muslims) as having an infinite mind; God is omniscient. But gods are not the only entities to which we attribute omniscience. For example, we perceive the creepy government in George Orwell's *Nineteen Eighty-Four* ([1949] 2003), which monitors Winston Smith even while he does mundane things like brushing his teeth, to be omniscient.

There are reasons, however, to think that even though we might say an omniscient being knows everything, such a statement is fairly superficial. In other words, while we might claim that "God knows everything" and such an idea might be encoded in our minds, it might not be all that salient when we think about God. In other words, certain kinds of information about God might be more accessible in our minds than other kinds of information. We therefore might not reason consistently as though God is all-knowing. The study we discuss here (Purzycki et al. 2012) explored this.

For a long time, scholars have recognized our curious propensity to talk and think as though many things have intentions, personalities, and perceptions (Dennett 1987; Guthrie 1995). From machines (e.g., "my car refuses to function properly") and human organizations (e.g., "the government is watching you!") to features of the natural world (e.g., "this storm wants me to turn the car around"), humans undoubtedly excel at detecting minds even where they are not present. Researchers refer to this ability to make sense of other minds by a variety of names, including "theory of mind," "mentalizing," "hyper-sensitive agency detection," and "anthropomorphism." Cognitive scientists have proposed a variety of cognitive devices that are responsible for detecting other minds—even when those minds do not necessarily exist (Baron-Cohen 1995; Barrett & Keil 1996; Guthrie 1980). Such devices, scientists argue, make thinking about other real minds possible, but these devices also likely help us reason about and detect supernatural minds. In other words, our ability to think about other minds makes it possible—and perhaps even easier—to believe in gods. Indeed, many recent studies have shown that the more difficulty people have with thinking about others' minds, the less likely they are to be religious (Norenzayan, Gervais, & Trzesniewski 2012; Reddish, Tok, & Kundt

2016; Willard & Norenzayan 2013). This suggests that the cognitive systems responsible for mentalizing are an essential component of religious thought. This makes some sense in at least two ways.

First, people appear to focus on gods' minds in religious discourse (Boyer 2001). Central to religious systems around the world are beliefs about gods, ghosts, and other spirits. Also important are the contents of these supernatural agents' minds—their knowledge, desires, likes, and dislikes. Throughout the world people claim that their gods desire the particular rituals they perform and abhor the foods from which they abstain. People pray to gods and burn incense because they think the gods can hear them and maybe even smell the incense. In sum, people frequently mentalize when they engage with their gods.

Second, cognitive systems for detecting other minds may be linked to cognitive systems for regulating our social behavior, and religion undoubtedly affects our social behavior. The cognitive link between detecting agency and social regulation should seem quite intuitive. People may have evolved the ability to mentalize because doing so made navigating social environments easier. Anticipating others' behavior probably gave our ancestors a distinct advantage over those who had to rely more on responding to behaviors after they had happened (Baron-Cohen 1995). That said, there may be deep cognitive links between mentalizing systems and what might be called "moral cognition," or mental systems that regulate our social behavior. One may trigger the other. If we can anticipate someone's perceptions of something nasty we might do, and we expect that their response would be to retaliate, we might reconsider, partly by virtue of our moral cognition springing into action. These two systems—detecting agency and social regulation—may have coevolved. Indeed, research suggests that this link is present among humans (Gray, Gray, & Wegner 2007; Gray, Young, & Waytz 2012).

Yet it is one thing to say that your mother wants you to share with your brothers and another to say that a god is watching your behavior and cares about what you do. Mothers are often concerned with making sure we are kind to others—nothing surprising there. But we can generally point to our mothers. Gods are much different; believing that some entity without a clearly defined body is paying attention to us is unique to our species. That a non-obviously-existing entity knows what you are up to and cares about your actions is remarkable. Even in the case of a government "watching you," we can at least point to some individuals and/or machines doing the work of monitoring us. Pointing to the presence of a god is not so straightforward, and when people do "point" to gods, they use different criteria to argue for their existence than they would arguing for the existence of their mothers or governments. Yet all around the world, people claim that their gods care about what they do. What actions, then, do gods around the world care about?

In normal human conversation, people express the belief that gods are concerned about human morality, ritual, environmental preservation, and etiquette (Barrett 2008; Boyer 2001; Purzycki & McNamara 2016; Purzycki & Sosis 2011). Why gods' interests are generally limited to these areas remains to be well understood. One general approach toward understanding this assesses what functions religions might serve (Shariff, Purzycki, & Sosis 2014). Many researchers consider religion to be something that helps us make sense of the world, brings us comfort, and gives us meaning in life (Barber 2011; Inzlicht, Tullett, & Good 2011). It may. But evolutionary researchers also seek to assess whether or not—and if so, how—religion serves functions related to human fitness; specifically, they want to determine whether religious practices increase the chances that individuals survive and reproduce over long periods of time (Bulbulia et al. 2008). According to this theory, religions operate as behavioral frameworks for minimizing social and environmental challenges.

One important challenge that people face everywhere is building and maintaining stable cooperative relationships. In small communities, the context in which most of our evolutionary history has occurred, people are remarkably interdependent, and they rely on reciprocal relationships to help them when in need. In such communities, if you are a chronic rule breaker and fail to engage in cooperative behavior, you might be ostracized or suffer other punishments as a consequence. So some researchers have suggested that natural selection may have favored strong cognitive connections between gods and social regulation, because these connections would have contributed to cooperation that aided survivorship and reproduction. According to this theory, gods function as ways to help us avoid very real punishment; religion reduces the costs involved in secular punishment precisely because gods get us to behave. This prediction is part of what has become known as the supernatural punishment or supernatural monitoring hypothesis (Atkinson & Bourrat 2011; Johnson 2005; Norenzayan 2013; Purzycki et al. 2016; Schloss & Murray 2011). To test this idea, our study was aimed at assessing the cognitive connection between gods and social regulation. We wanted to know how intuitive it is for people to associate gods and godlike beings with knowledge of moral information.

Hypotheses

Is there a cognitive link between the moral information and thinking about other minds? If so, it should be evident in how quickly and easily we respond to questions about the moral knowledge that others possess. If our reasoning about gods' minds also taps into moral cognition, we should also find it easier to cognitively process information that explicitly links these two. In other words, people should be better prepared to answer *Does God know that Benjamin hurts people?* than *Does God know that Richard likes curry?* even though those people might believe that God knows the answers to both of these questions.

We designed our study to determine whether or not people could rapidly process certain classes of information about gods' and other agents' knowledge. Even though people might think gods know everything, if they strongly associate gods with moral behavior, they should respond more quickly to questions about gods' knowledge of moral information than trivial, nonsocial information. Moreover, we suspected that negative social information would be especially accessible. In other words, negative social information would have a particularly close relationship with what gods know, particularly in cultures where people assume that the gods punish the violation of social norms.

27

We also predicted that if our minds process gods' knowledge this way, we are likely to similarly process an omniscient government's knowledge. For instance, while putting up cameras everywhere or monitoring phone calls might mean collecting a lot of mundane data, such practices are designed and rationalized to catch and prevent criminality. Whether such devices work is an important question, but not a question addressed by our study. Rather, we examined how rapidly our minds process the relationship between moral information and omniscient beings. So gods and nosy governments might be designed to trigger our moral cognition, but what about an omniscient agent that does not interact with people or care about their behavior? We predicted that there should be no real differences in processing such an agent's knowledge across moral and nonmoral information. In other words, an omniscient but apathetic being should not intuitively have better access to moral information.

Methodology

We conducted four different experiments among four different samples of student participants. Participants sat at computers and answered a host of questions. The experimental questions asked about three types of information concerning people: nonmoral information, information about immoral behavior, and information about good or moral behaviors. We also included distractor questions[1] to ensure that participants were following instructions. To make sure they were the same length (i.e., shorter questions might have quicker responses), target questions all had ten syllables, and there were ten questions for each category.

Examples of "nonmoral" questions are *Does _____ know how fast Joey's heart beats?* or *Does _____ know how many freckles Sharon has?* Questions involving "immoral behavior" were questions like *Does _____ know that Jane has stolen a car?* and *Does _____ know that Jen lied to her mother?* Examples of "good or moral behavior" questions are *Does _____ know that Ann gives to the homeless?* or *Does _____ know that Sam always helps his friends?*

Purzycki recorded himself asking these questions and trimmed each sound file to ensure that they were of similar length. To be more certain that recording lengths were not likely to affect response time, we statistically analyzed all recording lengths to make sure they were the same length on average, and they were. We then uploaded these files onto a program that randomly played questions and awaited a response. We encouraged participants to answer each question as quickly as they could, and they did so by pressing one button for "yes" and another for "no." As participants answered questions, the computer recorded in milliseconds how long it took them to respond.

Participants in the experiments answered questions about either God, Santa Claus, a fictitious surveillance government called "NewLand" (a bit like George Orwell's surveillance government), or a fictitious (as far as we know) omniscient alien species we called "The Ark."[2] God and Santa Claus are similar insofar as they are supernatural beings. NewLand is an omniscient government system without any special powers beyond punishing the bad and rewarding the good. NewLand has cameras everywhere and records what its citizens do. The Ark are an alien species (i.e., not really "supernatural" per se) that observe everything on Earth "down to the tiniest of details." However, we described them as completely noninterfering. In other words, while they may know everything that transpires on our planet, they never do anything about what happens here. NewLand and the Ark are "natural" insofar as they are not spiritual or spirit-like beings with supernatural powers.

Results and Analysis

Our analyses consisted of a variety of statistical tests to see whether or not response times were in fact different across category types. We were not really interested in the absolute response times to questions; it didn't matter that it took someone on average 1,000 milliseconds longer to answer some questions than others. Rather, we were interested in the magnitude of differences. One standard way to transform data to capture this is to take the natural logarithm[3] of a given value. So, we log-transformed the response times.[4]

Figure 3.1 shows an image of these log-transformed average response times by experiment and question type, with 95 percent confidence intervals[5] of those average speeds. In each experiment, participants responded significantly more quickly to moral questions than they did to nonmoral questions. We provide a discussion of what a "p-value" is and how we used it to determine significant differences as a note.[6]

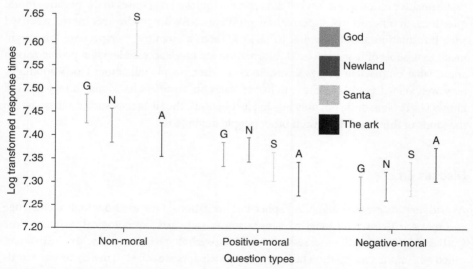

Figure 3.1 95 percent confidence intervals of the mean log-transformed response time by question type across experiments. Notice the general trend of faster responses toward the negative moral questions.

What is striking about these results is that response times for the God (G) and NewLand (N) experiments were quite close to each other; people were quickest to respond to the questions about immoral behavior, followed by the positive moral behavior questions. They responded more slowly to nonmoral questions about people. In other words, participants appear to process omniscient gods and governments in very much the same way. Responses to Santa's knowledge were also curious. We might say that Santa has better access to moral information than the average person, but just how omniscient participants think him to be is not quite clear. We found that participants answered 60 percent of the questions about Santa's knowledge of nonmoral information with a "no." However, there were no significant differences[7] in response times between those who answered "yes" or "no" for these questions. This suggests that individuals' responses had little to no impact on their response times. Moreover, the response times to the "naughty" and "nice" questions were unsurprisingly similar, but both were in stark contrast to the relative lethargy in answering the nonmoral questions (the "S" interval near the top of Figure 3.1). Finally, even in the case of omniscient but noninterfering aliens, participants took more time to answer nonmoral than moral questions[8].

We ran further analyses to indicate whether or not the familiarity of the agent (God, Santa, etc.) had any effect on overall response times. In other words, maybe participants were slower to answer questions about the Ark and NewLand because they had never heard of them before. We did not find this. We then assessed which features of these agents accounted for the results: supernaturalness and/or ability to punish. We found that when agents are both supernatural and able to punish, this predicted slower responses to nonmoral questions. Overall, these features did not appear to alter the speed of responding to the positive moral questions but did appear to quicken responses to the negative moral questions. In other words, supernatural, punitive agents are predictably more associated with information about *immoral* behaviors. From a cognitive perspective, this might mean that pools of negative social information are more accessible when people reason about what omniscient beings know. So even when people talk about God's goodness, how well versed God is in the number of hairs on a camel's back, and how well God knows God's plan, quite possibly lurking just beneath the surface of such discussions are the kinds of things we don't want other people doing to us.

Discussion

As with any study, ours had blind spots and limitations. One methodological challenge was that our items were long by comparison to standard psychological response-time studies. Many researchers assessing implicit psychological biases use an instrument called an "implicit association task," where participants are asked to match certain words (Greenwald, McGhee, & Schwartz 1998). In our study, participants answered relatively longer questions. Even though we found time differences in responses, we are unsure as to whether or not we were measuring the time people took to reason about these agents' knowledge or whether or not there were close conceptual relationships between moral things and such deities.

One major limitation with the study sample was that it was drawn exclusively from university students in the United States. Of course, American university students are not a representative sample of the rest of the world, let alone of Western countries (Henrich, Heine, & Norenzayan 2010; Sears 1986). Importantly, not all deities around the world are assumed to be concerned with moral behavior (i.e., how we treat each other). Many are thought to be primarily interested in ritual, environmental preservation, or taboos (Purzycki & McNamara 2016; Purzycki & Sosis 2011). Would we find similar results among people whose deities are concerned with these other matters?

Some research suggests this might be the case. Purzycki followed up on this study at his field site in the Tyva (pronounced TOO-vuh) Republic, in southern Siberia. He found that when Tyvans were asked to list things that local spirits cared about, they predominantly claimed the spirts cared more about ritual and resource management than morality (Purzycki 2016). However, when he directly asked them whether or not these spirits knew and cared about various things, they were more likely to respond affirmatively to questions about morality than nonmoral things (Purzycki 2013). While he did not measure response times, the results do suggest that humans subtly associate supernatural agents with moral information even when these agents are not generally expected to care about moral behavior.

This again raises the question of the source of this bias. Is it simply because gods and spirits have agency that people are quick to associate them with moral information? In other words, because we think gods have minds, do we just default to associating gods with moral concern even when there is not a cultural expectation to do so? As we mentioned earlier, people attribute agency to all sorts of things. But do we subtly associate moral domains when we anthropomorphize cars, the weather, and other things? Or do gods' alleged interests in our lives trigger moral cognition? Experimental research is useful for teasing apart these complicated and often overlapping processes.

Another way to address the source of this bias would be to assess how it develops throughout the course of an individual's life and the factors involved in its development. Quite likely, the consistent association with God and moral conduct that people hear builds a close conceptual relationship between moral and religious cognition. However, as mentioned above, it may be a much deeper relationship; if our ability to reason about other minds coevolved with moral cognition, we may be prepared to create the association between morality and other minds quite early, even in cases where people do not talk about their gods as concerned with moral behavior.

Moreover, if gods subtly trigger moral cognition—even when people don't explicitly think of them as caring about morality—why aren't they all simply concerned with how we treat each other? Decades of research suggest a link between morally concerned deities and various factors of our social and natural environments. These studies suggest that some beliefs and practices function in ways that resolve social problems that develop as a result of our interaction with the natural world. Gods that care about morality appear to pop up predominantly in high-population societies (Johnson 2005; Stark 2001; Wallace

1966), societies suffering from water scarcity (Snarey 1996), and herding societies where people vie for land (Roes & Raymond 2003). While important, all of these studies rely upon cross-cultural or cross-national data that were not necessarily collected to answer such questions. Perhaps now more than ever is a good time to investigate such questions ethnographically by asking living people about what they think. Observing their behavior in natural settings will inevitably shed light on these and other important questions about why gods matter so much in people's lives.

CHAPTER 4
DO CHILDREN ATTRIBUTE BELIEFS TO HUMANS AND GOD DIFFERENTLY?
K. Mitch Hodge and Paulo Sousa

Introduction

In "Children's Attributions of Beliefs to Humans and God: Cross-Cultural Evidence" (Knight et al. 2004), the authors sought to investigate cross-culturally how and when people acquire concepts of different agents, in particular the concepts of a human agent and of God. Normal adults understand human agents as having limited capabilities, while, at least in many religious traditions that have a conception of God, they understand God as much less limited: God is omnipotent, omnipresent, and omniscient. When and how do children acquire these different understandings?

The article addresses this question, focusing on an aspect of the understanding of agency that is fundamental to folk psychology (aka theory of mind): the attribution of beliefs, that is, of mental representations about the world that play a fundamental role in guiding intentional behavior. Normal adults accept that human agents can have false beliefs (e.g., a person may believe that she left her keys in the living room, when in fact she left them in the kitchen), while also understanding God as being omniscient (i.e., as knowing everything and hence always having true beliefs). When and how do children begin to attribute beliefs differently to humans and God?

There are two broad theoretical perspectives on the acquisition of the concepts of human agency and God's agency. One view hypothesizes that during childhood, people acquire the concept of human agency first and then use this concept to build the concept of God by analogy—that is, over cognitive development, people differentiate and extrapolate a God concept from the human agent concept. According to this view, the concept of God is initially quite similar to the concept of human agency, so this perspective is called the similarity perspective. Many authors, most notably Piaget (1960, 1969), have defended this perspective. It posits that intuitions about God's beliefs come from intuitions about attributions of beliefs to human agents. This leaves open two possibilities in terms of how children acquire the God concept. In one, the initial human agency concept is based on an infallible parent. In this case, God is intuited to know everything in the same way that the young child believes their parents know everything. In the other, the initial human agency concept is of a normal, limited agent. Hence, the God concept is initially modelled in terms of this normal agent, who can have false beliefs, and only later, children learn via cultural transmission that God is omniscient.

The alternative perspective hypothesizes that during childhood humans acquire, from the outset, a separate God concept independent from the human agent concept. Since in this perspective the concept of God is initially distinct from the concept of human agency, this perspective is called the nonsimilarity perspective. This perspective has been defended by the authors of the original article (see also Barrett & Richert, 2003; Barrett, Richert, & Driesenga, 2001), which entails that, very early in cognitive development, humans have intuitions that God is omniscient and that these intuitions are unrelated to human concepts.

Methodology

To assess which, if any, of the aforementioned perspectives are correct, the authors of the original article needed to find an experimental task that would provide evidence on whether the acquisition of the God concept is dependent on the human agent concept as far as attributions of beliefs are concerned. As Dennett (1978) pointed out, it can only be claimed that a subject is attributing a belief to an agent if there is evidence that the subject understands what it would be for that agent to entertain a false belief. From this point, psychologists developed the now famous false-belief task to determine whether and when humans and other animals attribute a belief to another agent.

Numerous versions of false-belief task have been developed in the last thirty years. In one of them (the "surprising contents task"), the experimenter shows children a closed container (usually a cracker box with a conspicuous picture of its contents on the outside) and asks what they believe is in the container. The experimenter then opens the box to reveal that the crackers have been removed and that small rocks (or a similarly unexpected item) have been put in their place. After reclosing the container, the experimenter checks that the children are still clear on what the box contains. The experimenter then introduces a doll (used to represent a human being) who has not seen the inside of the box and asks the children what the doll would think is in the container. The point of the experiment is to establish whether children are capable of attributing false belief to other agents. If the children say the doll would think that there are crackers in the container (a false belief), the experimenter could be certain that the child is capable of attributing mental representations, specifically beliefs different than their own, to other agents. At the time of the publication of the original article, the bulk of the data available suggested that this ability starts around the age of four and becomes stable around the age of seven (Perner, Leekam, & Wimmer 1987; Wellman & Bartsch 1988; Wellman & Woolley 1990; Wimmer & Perner 1983).

An original aspect of the research carried out by Barrett and collaborators is that, in addition to probing children's attributions of beliefs to humans, this research probed children's attributions of beliefs to God. For example, in the context of the false-belief task described above, the experimenter would ask children what both the doll and God would think is inside the container. Moreover, putting the similarity and nonsimilarity perspectives in the context of the false-belief task, one can envisage a variety of positions on how children would attribute beliefs to humans and God. Figure 4.1 offers a tree diagram showing how these positions are related to each other.

In all graphs, the top line represents attribution of beliefs to a human, and the bottom line represents attribution of beliefs to God. On the Y axis, performance is mapped; the higher the line, the more likely it is that a child would attribute false beliefs to the agent in question—to say that a human or God would think that the box contains crackers, for example. The X axis shows the developmental time frame. As indicated by the dotted lines, the age range of four to seven is the most relevant to our discussion, since it is then that children, according to the current literature, come to attribute false beliefs to human agents.

At the highest level of the tree, the opposition is between similarity and nonsimilarity perspectives. From a nonsimilarity perspective, children would start to differentiate humans and God (attributing more false beliefs to humans than to God) from the very beginning of the developmental stage of our concern. From a similarity perspective, children would attribute either true beliefs or false beliefs to both humans and God *in equal measure, initially, and for at least some part* of this developmental time frame.

The strong similarity stance (graphs 1 and 2 in Figure 4.1) corresponds to two possible interpretations of Piaget's work (1960). In graph 1, the child uses an infallible

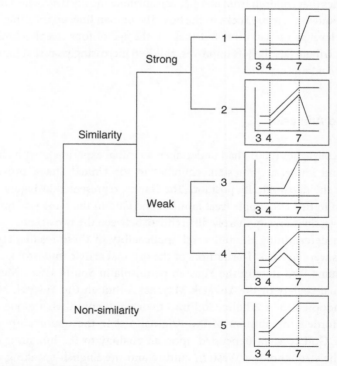

Figure 4.1 Predictions of false-belief task performance.

parent (who is capable of knowing what is inside the box without having to see it) as the basis to understand God until quite late in development. At some point, children start to recognize that parents can entertain false beliefs, but they do not transfer this characteristic to God, since at this same point they start to learn that God has special qualities such as omniscience. For example, children would initially say that both agents believe that rocks are inside the box, then, only by age seven, they would start to say that humans believe that crackers are inside the box, and God believes that rocks are inside. Conversely, in graph 2, the child uses an average human being as the basis to understand God until quite late in development. At that point, children start to learn that God possesses certain special characteristics that set God aside from common humans.

The weak similarity stance postulates that children initially use humans as a basis to understand God's beliefs but start to differentiate them earlier in development than Piaget claimed, before reaching the age of seven. In graph 3, the child uses an infallible human as a basis to understand God. In graph 4, the child instead uses a normal fallible human as the basis. This explains why both the human and the God line stay flat for some time in the first instance and initially climb in the second.

Finally, a nonsimilarity perspective (graph 5) would predict that children being tested on the false-belief task would start differentiating between humans and God very early in development. In graph 5, the God line, one the one hand, remains close to floor level, which signifies that children from an early age attribute mostly true beliefs to God—that is, that God knows there are rocks in the box. The human line, on the other hand, starts at the same level as the God line but then by the age of four steeply climbs—as their capacity to attribute false beliefs improves, children increasingly say that humans believe that the box contains crackers.

Results and Analysis

Barrett and colleagues (2001) had undertaken an initial experiment with children from Reformed and Lutheran Protestant churches in the United States, providing initial evidence for the nonsimilarity position. The results, represented in Figure 4.2, showed that children in this US sample treat humans and God in the same way up to age four, but by age five, they already sharply differentiate between the two agents.

To aid in determining the universal applicability of these results, cross-cultural experiments were needed. The authors of the original article undertook experiments in the Quintana Roo state in the Yucatán peninsula in Southeastern Mexico among the traditional society of the Yukatek Mayans. Although the Yukatek Mayans have long since adopted the Catholic God into their pantheon, their unique culture and language afforded the authors of the original article the opportunity to examine whether the God concept depended upon an analogy to the human agent concept outside of the stronghold of Western culture and the English-speaking world. Such

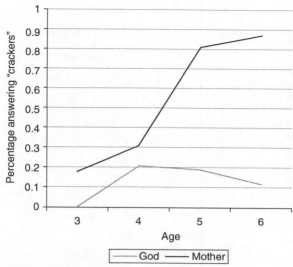

Figure 4.2 False-belief task—US children.

cross-cultural research is crucial when attempting to make universally applicable claims about human psychology. This is even more the case when examining something as culturally diverse as religious beliefs. By placing their study outside of the Western European tradition and within a different linguistic and religious culture, the authors of the original article sought to offer such insight and support for one of the opposing perspectives.

The authors recruited 48 Yukatek Mayan children across the developmental age range, from four-year-olds to seven-year-olds (11 four-year-olds, 12 five-year-olds, 12 six-year-olds, and 13 seven-year-olds, distributed across 26 males and 22 females). The surprising contents task used a container called *ho'ma*, replacing its normal content (i.e., tortillas) with a completely unusual one (i.e., shorts). The research was carried out in the children's primary native language, Yukatek. The attributions of beliefs concerned a doll (as a proxy for a human being) and God. The results were in the direction of the nonsimilarity perspective, as shown in Figure 4.3.

The five- and seven-year-olds both demonstrated a significant difference in false-belief attributions to the human agent over God. The children reported that the human agent was significantly more likely than God to believe that there were tortillas in the *ho'ma* rather than the novel contents (i.e., shorts). Although the Yukatek Mayan children start to attribute false beliefs to humans reliably only after the age of five, and the difference between the human agent and God did not reach significance with six-year-olds, the overall trend still remained much closer to the nonsimilarity pattern. Therefore, the authors of the original article concluded, it seems unlikely that the attribute of omniscience, embedded in the God concept, is analogically dependent upon the human agent concept.

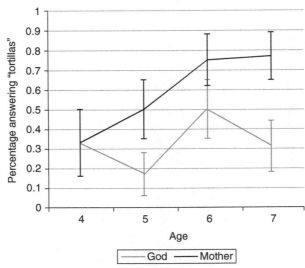

Figure 4.3 False-belief task—Maya children. Error bars show ±1 standard error.

Discussion

There is always a need for further research, especially cross-cultural research. Indeed, new research has questioned the above results that support the nonsimilarity perspective. Lane, Wellman, and Evans (2010) replicated the above research, albeit with some differences in the design of study. In addition to normal human agents and God, the researchers queried children's attributions of beliefs to an animal (a cat) and a human agent possessing superhuman knowledge (Mr. Smart), as well as a human agent possessing superhuman perception (Heroman with x-ray vision). They used a surprising-contents task with a crayon box in which they replaced crayons with a red plastic frog. (The box had a small hole in its side, which, when illuminated, revealed the surprising content.) The children were then presented with brief images and descriptions of the agents, such as the cat's ability to see in the dark, Mr. Smart's incredible knowledge, and so on. Their study included fifty-seven American children (thirty-two males) with an age range of just over three years old to six years old. Experimenters showed each child the novel content of the crayon box by illuminating the inside of the box and inviting them to peer through the small hole, but all agreed that when the light was off, they could not see the contents.

By more carefully discriminating the age groups, they found that children between the ages of 4.375 and 4.875 years of age were significantly more likely to attribute a false belief to all characters, including God. Even Mr. Smart, who served as a control for God and about whom the children were explicitly told that he "knows everything," was reported by the children at this age to have a false belief about the crayon box's contents, in line with the other human agents and God. In fact, going by the reports of children at this age, God was statistically closer to normal human agents than was Mr. Smart. Moreover, even though all the agents started off at approximately the same level at the youngest age group, only the oldest group reported a true belief for Mr. Smart and God. According to Lane et al. (2010, 2012), this finer methodological manipulation of discriminating the ages showed strong support for the analogical dependency of the God concept upon the human agent concept, albeit they did not observe the distinctions between the types of similarity perspectives as described above.

Although this more recent research goes in the direction of the similarity perspective, some intriguing questions remain. For instance, to what extent might children understand God's omniscience? Some studies (Purzycki 2013; Purzycki et al. 2012) have found evidence to suggest that children more readily attribute knowledge of socially strategic information, especially morally relevant information, to God over mundane knowledge. And, *if* children are analogically relying on the human agent concept to reason about other agents, what does it mean that they so easily are able to amend it with superhuman capabilities without question? To fully understand the conceptual genesis of God concepts, these and many more questions will need to be addressed with further research.

CHAPTER 5
WHICH GOD IS WATCHING?
Rita Anne McNamara

Introduction

Take a moment to look around you. More likely than not, you're living in a city (United Nations 2014). Life in dense, globally mobile, cosmopolitan cities makes the world look a certain way: humanity's dominion over and separation from nature seem obvious; the nuances of place and history seem unimportant. But now take a moment to think back: Where did you come from? Where did your parents come from? Where did their parents come from? How often do you think about your ancestors? About the ground beneath your feet? About how you and the land intertwine?

Life in the city can make it easy to overlook these connections among ancestry, tradition, and place—connections that were the lifeblood of human experience for most of our history. But in the small places of the world—where people still look to tradition for answers, where living on, in, and with the land is still a necessity for survival—these traditional, ancestral, local connections often form the core of one's worldview. How does such a worldview shift our priorities? How do we decide whom to trust? Whom to share our hard-earned resources with? And how, historically, did we as a species ever manage to expand beyond our local borders to build the massively interconnected web of humanity we live in today?

Theory

One theory about how we as a species began to expand our social horizons is that we developed a cultural solution—beliefs about particular kinds of supernatural agent minds spread socially as elders passed on this knowledge to subsequent generations and took these beliefs with them as they moved into new communities (Norenzayan et al. 2015). According to this line of reasoning, the secret cooperation-boosting ingredients to such beliefs are the following:

1. People believe that supernatural agents are watching over them, even when both they and other people can't see the supernatural agent (aka supernatural monitoring: Bering 2002; Johnson 2009; Johnson & Bering 2006).

2. Supernatural agents care about whether people behave toward each other in a morally upright manner (aka morally concerned, however "morally" might be locally defined: Boyer 2001; Purzycki et al. 2016; Roes & Raymond 2003; but see also Watts, Greenhill, & Lieberman 2015).

3. Supernatural agents can punish those who fall out of line with the morally correct path (aka supernatural punishment: Schloss & Murray 2011).

The cultural spread of belief in all-seeing, all-powerful, morally concerned gods historically coincides with regions of scarcity (Botero et al. 2014; Peoples & Marlowe 2012). Scarcity, or material resource insecurity, also shows up across many different species as an impetus to increase cooperation (Rubenstein & Wrangham 1986). For example, when fresh water is hard to come by, people might have to work together more to collect water, build wells, and protect the wells they have. In humans, scarcity often leads to greater reliance on local social structures, especially family, in creating informal networks of cooperation partners to help ensure survival (De Weerdt & Dercon 2006; Fincher & Thornhill 2012; Gelfand, Nishii, & Raver 2006; Hruschka et al. 2014). So on the one hand, it appears that this history of scarcity may have helped spur the spread of beliefs in a moralizing god. But on the other hand, people are generally less inclined to reach out to strangers when times are tight. So, while scarcity might make people work together more with their local family and friends, it might also make it harder to reach out to strangers.

The crux of the theory that moralizing, powerful gods can support expanding social circles lies in the idea that the god can act as the unseen arbiter of human affairs. Such a god can support people in trusting unknown others by punishing deal-breakers both here and now and in the great beyond (Atkinson & Bourrat 2011; Tan & Vogel 2008). The link between the beliefs and trust in other people comes by communicating belief and/ or commitment—often through ritual (Gervais, Shariff, & Norenzayan 2011; Purzycki & Arakchaa 2013; Sosis 2005).

But, as any student of religious studies might tell you, the all-seeing, all-powerful God of Abraham (in the Jewish, Christian, and Islamic traditions) is not the only supernatural agent in town. Across history and around the world, societies have revered supernatural agents that vary in omniscience, omnipotence, and the degree to which they care about how morally upstanding their devotees are (Boyer 2001; Purzycki 2013; Purzycki & Sosis 2011; Purzycki et al. 2012; Willard & McNamara 2016). Many of these smaller, lesser-known entities care only about the people or lands in their immediate vicinity and in the local customs and norms of their community of followers (Purzycki & McNamara 2016). So would these smaller gods have the same effects on believers as the God of Abraham?

Looking across this research on cooperation from supernatural punishment beliefs and cross-cultural variation in what people believe supernatural agents care about, we may suppose that supernatural punishment beliefs should also depend on what people think the supernatural agent cares about. For example, we would expect that people who believe their god cares about theft would also associate a harsh supernatural punishment for robbers. Similarly, if they don't think their god cares about laziness, we would expect them not to assign any supernatural punishment to someone who doesn't do their share of the work. In other words, the content of the belief is as important as whether the belief is present or not.

If we add in the tendency for people to rely more on local friends and family when resources are insecure, we reach a series of hypotheses. If punishing supernatural agents support maintaining particular social networks, as people become more worried about the security of their material resources, their beliefs about supernatural punishers should also change. Specifically, the beliefs about what supernatural agents will punish you for should be influenced by how worried about resources people are; supernatural agents might support keeping things local to combat the insecurity of resources, or they might support expanding to new social networks even though it could be more of a risk in an insecure environment. If this is the case, then it is important to know not just that people believe in a supernatural punisher but also about what the contents of those beliefs are— and we need to know whether people are feeling secure or insecure about their local resource availability. In order to explore and test these relationships, we will discuss two studies conducted in small, traditional, rural communities in Yasawa, Fiji.

Ethnographic background: Yasawa, Fiji

Yasawa is the northernmost island in the Yasawa Island chain, located off the western coast of Fiji's main island, Viti Levu (Figure 5.1).

The island is small even by Fijian standards: six villages of around 100–250 residents are spread across the long, narrow island (approx. 2 km/1 mile wide by 20 km/12.5 miles long). Yasawa is still relatively remote—the closest major urban center, Lautoka, is a six- to thirteen-hour boat ride away, across oft rough seas. Yasawa's small size and distance from major urban centers means that people living there have limited access to the money-based exchange common in markets. It is far more common for people to rely on what they can produce themselves and distribute among family members. Some Yasawans earn income by working in local tourist resorts, though the majority earn money by selling local produce—fish, cassava, woven mats, and so forth—to nearby resorts or in the markets on the mainland (Viti Levu). This means two things: (1) The majority of economic interaction on Yasawa is not money-based and (2) Yasawans depend on what they can produce from the land and sea around them.

However, Yasawa's climate and ecology make it difficult to predict how much one can produce in a given year. November to April is cyclone season in the South Pacific; these *cagilaba* ("murderous winds") hit Yasawa on a regular basis, with storms strong enough to cause major damage happening about once every ten years. One storm in particular devastated most of the villages that participated in the research described here: in December 2012, a category 4 storm, Cyclone Evan, destroyed many houses and most of the 2013 *tavioka* (cassava)[1] crop. In the dry winter seasons, fires often destroy crops as well.

The people of Yasawa are indigenous iTaukei[2] Fijians who rely on traditional gardening and fishing techniques for their daily subsistence. Yasawans live in small villages established around a highly structured, hierarchical kinship system that organizes food collection, production, and other essential activities (McNamara & Henrich 2016). People in Yasawa primarily interact with members of the same clan for

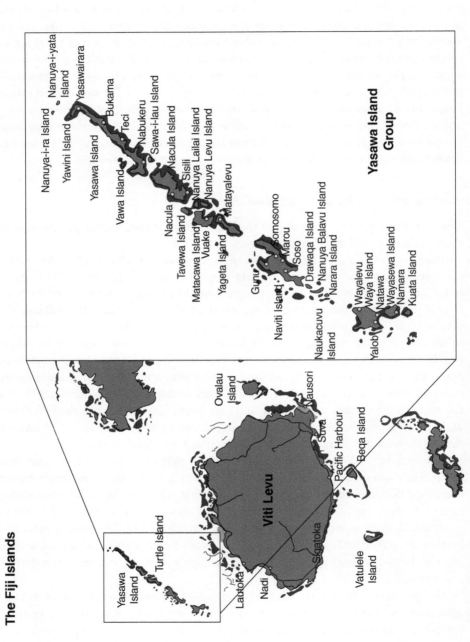

Figure 5.1 Yasawa Island in relation to the Fijian archipelago.

day-to-day affairs, while men from across the clans work together on communal projects like village maintenance, planting the chief's crops, and performing public works for the village school. Women work together on domestic tasks like cooking, childcare, as well as fishing and mat weaving, primarily within their husbands' extended families.[3] Monthly *soli* ("offerings") feature communal meals and rituals. Though Yasawan villages are distinct entities, kinship ties and intermarrying also promote cooperation across village lines.

The Yasawan kinship system includes several units that incorporate increasingly large groups beyond the immediate family. The biggest unit, the *yavusa*[4], is a cluster of *mataqoli* (clans) linked by a common male deified ancestor or *Kalou-vu* (see the "Religion in Yasawa" section below). The prototypical *yavusa* is subdivided into five *mataqoli*, linked via common descent from one of the five brothers who founded the village (though in practice today, not all villages still have five *mataqoli* present). In Yasawa, those who trace ancestry back to the eldest brother are the chiefly clan. The *yavusa* and *mataqoli* are also the primary units of traditional political organization; people seek and give aid in all aspects of daily life based upon these kinship networks (France 1969; Nayacakalou 1955, 1957). Beyond the *yavusa*, people are linked within the *vanua* concept, which inextricably binds people and land together and was the primary organizing principle in Fiji before colonization and missionization (Ryle 2010). More recently, *vanua* has become a primary unit of ancestral identity (Jolly 1992) and a major symbol in Fijian politics (Srebrnik 2002; Williksen-Bakker 1990).

Religion in Yasawa: Christian "Bible God" and Kalou-vu

Yasawans, like many iTaukei Fijians, are both devoutly Christian and keenly aware of local spirit activity. Their system typically includes "Bible God" (*Kalou ni vola*, "God of the book")[5] and *Kalou-vu* ("root/ancestor god/s"), locally concerned, less powerful, deified ancestors (Katz 1999; Ryle 2010; Tomlinson 2009). Both belief systems are cited to justify and maintain traditional village life. Importantly, these supernatural agents also promote different social expectations within and beyond the kin group. Many Yasawans follow Wesleyan Methodism, a denomination often cited as a foundational unit of iTaukei Fijian culture; others follow the increasingly popular Pentecostal evangelical movements with membership in the Assemblies of God (AG) church. Both groups cite the Bible God as concerned about universal issues that affect Christians everywhere; both believe the Bible God wants them to be honest and cooperate with each other.

As mentioned above, *Kalou-vu* are the mythical founding fathers of local *yavusas*; they are the spiritual and genealogical roots that connect iTaukei around Fiji to the lands their *mataqoli* inhabit (Abramson 2000). As the progenitors of the local communities, *Kalou-vu* are believed to be most concerned about local customs[6]—affairs that the Bible God often overlooks. *Kalou-vu* help maintain traditional values, are mainly credited with punishment, and are cited as responsible for spirit possessions, bad luck, illness, and death. Sorcery is another common explanation for illness and misfortune, though a sorcerer's power comes from invoking the *Kalou-vu*. The targets of *Kalou-vu* anger are those who disobey the unwritten, traditional values at the core of the *bula vakavanua/ bula vakatruakga*, or the traditional/chiefly way of life (Gervais 2013; Katz 1999). One particularly important traditional value that *Kalou-vu* might punish people for violating is for more well-off community members to give to the needy (Gervais 2013). Within this core value, when villagers have more secure material resources, they are expected to give to others according to their kin relationships (Farrelly & Vudiniabola 2013; Schlossberg 1998).

When an angry *Kalou-vu* is suspected of causing misfortune, Yasawans often pray to the Bible God for help and forgiveness. Further, iTaukei often cite being a good, church-going Christian as a primary trait of a good Fijian (Purzycki et al. 2016; Purzycki et al. 2017). This informal syncretism between traditional beliefs and Christian values is reflected in the three pillars of iTaukei Fijian society: *vanua* ("land and people/ community"), *lotu* ("church," especially Wesleyan Methodism), and *matanitu* ("state"; Ryle 2010). Many pre-Christian practices carried over into Methodist practice, though the *lotu* and traditional beliefs are still not in perfect harmony. Pentecostal movements have been especially antagonistic to traditional beliefs, often rebranding any spirit as a *tevoro* ("demon") and any spirit-related activity as sorcery (Brison 2007; Newland 2004). Elsewhere in Fiji, tensions arising from Methodists embracing tradition and the Pentecostals rejecting it have led to violence (Newland 2004). In the Yasawan communities that participated in the present research, Methodists and AG parishioners typically interact more based on family ties than church membership, so the research did not uncover differences between them.

Methodology

For this research, we asked participating Yasawans to play an economic game known as the Random Allocation Game (RAG; see Hruschka et al. 2014; McNamara & Henrich 2017; McNamara, Norenzayan, & Henrich 2016; Purzycki et al. 2016). The goal of the RAG, like most economic games, is to examine how participants decide to distribute money to different people. In this case, the participants were given thirty coins and asked to distribute these coins to two different individuals, though the identity of those recipients varied. In both study conditions, one recipient was a DISTANT other—a person from another island—while the other was someone closer to home—either another villager (LOCAL condition) or the participant themselves (SELF condition). Participants would place the coins for each recipient in cups, marked with Standard Fijian writing and simple line drawings to show who would get the coins in each cup (see Figure 5.2).

We kept everything anonymous so that participants never knew exactly who received the money. We asked participants to decide whom to give each coin to based on the results of rolling a two-colored, six-sided die. Before each die-roll, we asked the participants to decide which recipient would receive the coin for either color—and to do this silently. For example, for the first coin, the participant might decide that red meant the coin was

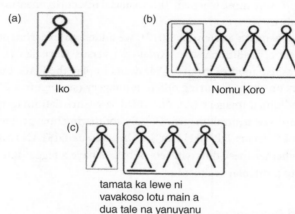

Figure 5.2 Cups to hold coins in the Random Allocation Game. (a) You (the participant), (b) Someone from your village, (c) Someone from another island.

for the DISTANT other. They might roll the die and get red, then decide that, in fact, red should be the color that told them to put that coin in their own cup.

The die introduced an element of chance, so we could predict that if participants were following the rules, they should give a coin to either recipient about as often as would be expected based upon the *binomial distribution* (the distribution you get when there are two *binomial* possible outcomes—like flipping a coin). So over the course of all participants choosing how to give out all thirty of those coins, we could see if participants showed *favoritism*—or the tendency to give a little (or a lot) more money to one recipient than would be expected by chance. This *favoritism* measure is our primary *dependent variable*—or the variable that we expect to be changed by the *independent variables*.

For Study 1 (McNamara et al. 2016), we focused on three *independent variables*. Our first independent variable was the recipient (either SELF or LOCAL vs. DISTANT).

But that still left out how religious belief played into all of this. To figure that out, we also asked participants to answer a series of questions about how negative (punishing, harsh, vengeful, etc.) or positive (loving, forgiving, peaceful, etc.) they believe the Bible God and *Kalou-vu* are. We combined their scores so that when people have a higher final number, that means they think that the entity is more negative/punishing. We used this measure of beliefs about supernatural agents' tendency to punish or reward as our second independent variable. As we discussed above, beliefs don't occur in isolation. Instead, they operate in people's minds within a wider context of other factors in the social and ecological context (the socioecological context). One factor that might be particularly important is material insecurity—how much people worry about not being able to meet their and their family's needs. To measure this degree of uncertainty about future resource access, we asked a series of yes/no questions about whether participants were worried about having enough food or money in the next one month, six months, one year, and five years. We combined the answers so that higher scores meant people were more worried. This material insecurity measure was our third independent variable.

For Study 2 (McNamara & Henrich 2017), we added an experimental measure to pinpoint the effects of traditional (i.e., *Kalou-vu*) versus Christian (i.e., Bible God) beliefs. We again asked another group of Yasawans to play the RAG, but this time we asked them to play on cloths featuring different imagery (see Figure 5.3). One-third of the group saw traditional imagery (A), one-third saw Christian imagery (B), and the remaining one-third saw neutral imagery (C). By comparing how people distribute the coins to either SELF versus DISTANT or LOCAL versus DISTANT, we could more closely pinpoint whether these different sets of beliefs have a bigger impact on choices to give resources to particular recipients.

Hypotheses and Predictions

Drawing from economic rationality theory, which suggests that all people want to get the most gain possible for themselves, we predicted that, in general, people want to give more money to themselves in the SELF condition and more to fellow villagers in the LOCAL condition.

Prediction 1: Participants should show favoritism toward LOCAL and SELF.

However, if belief in powerful supernatural punishers leads people to follow rules more and show less bias toward particular others, then we would expect more equal amounts of money to be given to everyone—in other words, less favoritism toward LOCAL/SELF, leading to larger amounts of money given to the DISTANT others.

Prediction 2: Participants who believe that supernatural agents are more punishing than forgiving should show less LOCAL and SELF favoritism.

Figure 5.3 Imagery primes for traditional (a), Christian (b), and neutral (c) conditions in Study 2's Random Allocation Game.

Our material insecurity should heighten focus on the local in-group. When people are worried about making ends meet, the local community—and especially family—is typically the best, last hope people have for survival.

Prediction 3: Participants who are more worried about material resources should show more LOCAL and SELF favoritism.

Finally, because beliefs operate in a wider socioecological context, we expect supernatural beliefs and perceptions about resource security to have effects that depend on each other. *Kalou-vu* are believed to be more concerned about the local community, and more worry about material resources should also lead to more reliance on the local community.

Prediction 4: Participants who are more worried about material resources and who believe Kalou-vu *are more punitive should show more LOCAL favoritism.*

For Study 2, we expected that images on the cloth playing surface showing Christian imagery should remind participants of Christian values and therefore increase coins given to DISTANT others. However, since *Kalou-vu* and other traditional beliefs are typically more focused on the local group, we expected the traditional prime to show the opposite.

> *Prediction 5: If Bible God beliefs encourage focus on treating all believers inside and outside the community well, then Christian imagery primes should lead to less favoritism. If traditional beliefs encourage support of local communities, then imagery primes of traditional items should show more LOCAL favoritism.*

Results and Analysis

The RAG can only show the probability of favoritism, but because there were many chances for each participant to select which recipient to give a coin to, we could find patterns across the choices and see whether the patterns differ based on the belief and material insecurity measures as predicted above.[7]

> *Prediction 1: Was there favoritism? Yes—for both SELF and LOCAL recipients.*

We looked for favoritism by comparing how many coins participants gave to the LOCAL recipient or the SELF compared to what we would expect by chance (shown in Figure 5.4). We used the binomial distribution as our expectation of chance, because the dice that participants rolled had two color options, so there were two possibilities for where each coin could go.

In both studies, we found evidence that people were giving more to themselves and to local recipients than would be expected purely by chance; this indicates that there indeed was some favoritism happening.

> *Predictions 2, 3, and 4: Do beliefs and material insecurity predict favoritism?*
> *Yes, but only when we consider how they depend on or interact with each other.*

As shown in Figure 5.5, when participants reported few worries about having enough money and food in the future (low material insecurity), they showed the predicted effect for supernatural punishment beliefs for both the Bible God and *Kalou-vu*. These participants with low material insecurity were less likely to show favoritism for the SELF or LOCAL recipient—in other words, more likely to give roughly the same number of coins to the DISTANT other—when they believed that these supernatural agents were more punitive. This replicates other work in Western societies showing that more punitive supernatural agent beliefs also predict more cooperative behaviors (Shariff & Norenzayan 2011).

Results that we do not find in other studies with more materially secure populations show up when we look at how people who said they were more worried played the game.

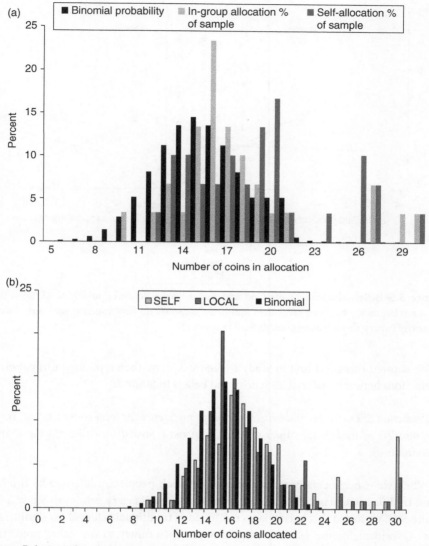

Figure 5.4 Coin distributions to recipients for (a) Study 1 and (b) Study 2. Both studies show more coins given to LOCAL and SELF than would be expected by binomial chance, indicating that some participants showed favoritism for self and the local in-group.

We see for these highly materially insecure participants that the beliefs about the Bible God's forgiveness (more negative numbers) or punishment (more positive numbers) make no difference in predicting how much favoritism they will show. However, when they believe that the local ancestor *Kalou-vu* gods will punish them, the odds of their showing favoritism to either themselves or their fellow villagers (the LOCAL in-group) rise.

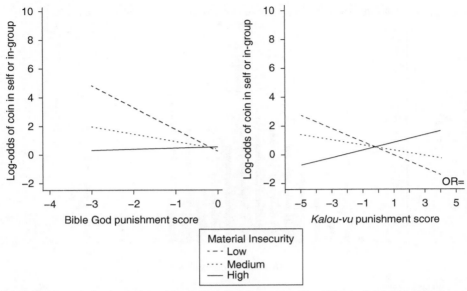

Figure 5.5 Beliefs about the Bible God and *Kalou-vu* predict SELF and LOCAL favoritism, but the relationship between favoritism and belief depends on how much people feel material insecurity (worry about having enough food or money).

We showed this effect first in Study 1 (Figure 5.5); we then replicated this pattern of interactions between material insecurity and beliefs in Study 2.

Prediction 5: Do traditional beliefs encourage preference for local communities? Yes, reminders of traditional values specifically increase favoritism to benefit the local community.

When we experimentally manipulated how much people are likely to be thinking about traditional, Christian, or neutral values with our imagery primes in Study 2 (see Figure 5.6), we found that participants reminded of traditional values show significantly more favoritism for the LOCAL village recipient. Contrary to our other prediction, the Christian imagery prime did not significantly change favoritism compared to neutral distribution. These results suggest that the traditional values in iTaukei Fijian communities may be specifically targeted at supporting local social ties that people rely upon for day-to-day life.

Discussion

The results of these two studies show that it takes more than mere presence of belief to affect behavior; the *contents* and *context* of belief are also important. Without taking these

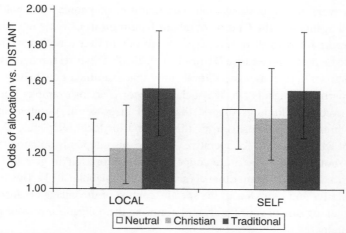

Figure 5.6 Results of imagery primes on LOCAL and SELF conditions of the Random Allocation Game in Study 2. Error bars show 95 percent confidence intervals. For situations when we do not know the true value of the *population mean*, we calculate the *95 percent confidence interval* on the *sample mean*. The 95 percent confidence interval tell us that, if we took a large number of *repeated random samples* from the population (in this case, Yasawans) and calculated the confidence intervals for each sample, we would expect the true population mean to fall into this interval 95 percent of the time. In other words, we say that this interval has a 0.95 probability of containing the true population mean. The traditional imagery prime was the only condition to show a significantly larger amount of favoritism than the neutral condition, and this increase in favoritism was for the LOCAL community recipient.

different elements into account, the results shown here would not have been visible. These studies also underscore the importance of including diverse religious belief systems from traditional and rural communities in research on the effects of religious beliefs. Studies conducted in Western or urbanized populations that only follow Abrahamic traditions would not have been able to show these relationships.

Implications and extensions

These results also hint at the potential for different sets of religious beliefs to co-reside with each other—even within the minds of the same individuals—and serve different social functions depending on the context. On the one hand, Christianity and other Abrahamic faiths have been remarkably successful at traveling around the globe, an effect that may be due in part to their ability to link people into wider social networks (Norenzayan et al. 2015). On the other hand, Abrahamic traditions have not always totally overcome the local beliefs and traditions, such that syncretism is seen in many places around the world. These differing social effects of varying sets of beliefs may in part explain why syncretic traditions persist: perhaps the old beliefs have survived because they are still used in daily life.

Previous work has also shown that communities of people who hold beliefs in supernatural agents like the God of Abraham (common in Christianity, Judaism, and Islam) are more likely to distribute resources to others in a way that we in the West determine to be more cooperative (Henrich et al. 2010). Other researchers expanded on the results shown here in a cross-cultural study that examined how beliefs in different kinds of supernatural agents affected social behavior (see, for example, Purzycki et al. 2016). Cross-cultural findings suggest that belief in powerful, punitive supernatural agents also predicts less favoritism for the self and for local recipients. However, the definition of what counts as "cooperative" or "fair" also depends on context—in some places like Yasawa, it may be more cooperative and more fair to give to local others who are in need than to distant others (Farrelly & Vudiniabola 2013). This may be both more cooperative and more fair in the specific context of the village because village life depends on taking care of your family and honoring the obligations of your place in the family hierarchy.

Criticisms and limitations

One of the biggest limitations to our method is that we cannot tell whether or not any specific choice to give a coin to either recipient was in line with the die roll. We are relying on the chance distribution to determine whether participants gave a bit more or a bit less than we would expect; different methods that can more precisely pinpoint these choices can help clarify what is going on. This research also does not specifically show how resource insecurity might impact supernatural punishment beliefs; it is possible that people who experience more long-term worries about having enough food or money come to believe that they are being punished, or that the deity whom they believe watches over them is more punitive than deities of others who have more reliable access to resources.

Conclusion

Day in and day out, people around the world look to many supernatural causes as explanations for what happens to them and justifications for why they might act (or not act) in a certain way. One of the most influential traditions the world over comes from the God of Abraham and the belief communities that follow these ideals. But countless other spirits and local gods are believed to influence people's lives. In many cases, these spirits and deities link people back to their history and their land to evoke deep ancestral ties that bind believers into tight-knit communities. These beliefs can sit side by side with other traditions or compete for space in the brains of believers. In order to understand these religious belief dynamics and the social dynamics they influence, it is important to include all of these religious and community perspectives in our wider research program.

CHAPTER 6
DO PEOPLE THINK THE SOUL IS SEPARATE FROM THE BODY AND THE MIND?
Rebekah Richert and Kirsten Lesage

Introduction

Some of the most exciting ideas develop through an off-hand question that you realize does not seem to have an obvious answer.

After completing graduate school, I (Rebekah Richert) had the opportunity to continue my education through a National Science Foundation (NSF)-funded postdoctoral research experience that allowed me to spend one year studying with Dr. Harvey Whitehouse (an anthropologist) and a second year studying with Dr. Paul Harris (a developmental psychologist). As I began my second year of this training with Dr. Harris, we began by reading a book that had been recently published by Paul Bloom (2004), *Descartes' Baby*. In this text, Bloom (2004) argued that human minds operate in accordance with a common-sense dualism in which, from infancy, humans distinguish agents as having "bodies" and "souls." The support for this supposition comes from a wealth of studies into the development of social cognition and understanding the mental states of others. While reading this book, Dr. Harris and I began to discuss what might be underlying cognitive processes that support the development of a soul concept. Having grown up in a religious home and having spent a lot of time around other religious people, my intuition was that people who believe in the soul believe it goes beyond psychological traits and characteristics; they would not "reduce" a person's soul to that person's preferences, beliefs, desires, memories, and so on.

At this point, my advisor posed a rather straightforward question that did not have an obvious answer: If people do not believe the soul is about the mind and mental processes, then what do people think the soul is about?

The soul: Mentalistic or essential?

Around this same time, Susan Gelman (2003) released a book summarizing a body of studies outlining essentializing (e.g., the idea that entities have an underlying, nonobvious, "true" nature) and how the tendency toward essentializing plays an important role in early cognitive development. Toddlers and young children tend to assume that members of a category share an internal essence that makes them a member of that category and the same as other members of that category (Gelman 2003). At that time, despite a relatively large and growing body of research documenting essentialism in early childhood, I could not find any psychological research documenting whether children or adults attributed an individual and personal essence to a person. As Bloom (2004) had outlined in *Descartes' Baby*, much of the existing research on dualism was based in attributions of psychological versus biological properties.

Thus, our first study began with a very simple question: Do children view there to be a part of a person that is not accounted for by biological or psychological processes? We began our study of this question with children for two primary reasons (Richert & Harris 2006). First, my advisor and I are developmental psychologists primarily driven by research questions about how cognitions develop, because the study of concept development can reveal the cognitive foundations of cognitive processes. Additionally, one way to examine these questions is to figure out what (if any) aspects of a person children believe continue after a person dies. Studies at that time had suggested that children come to believe biological processes (e.g., eating) stop at death but that psychological processes (e.g., remembering) continue after death (Astuti & Harris 2008; Bering & Bjorklund 2004). This pattern of responding in children indicated that children separate the functions of the mind from the body when thinking about what happens after death. We expanded these studies to examine if children additionally separated the functions of the soul from the functions of the mind.

We tested four- to twelve-year-old children who had been raised in religious homes and exposed to the concept of the soul (some Lutheran, some Catholic). We were especially interested in what processes children attributed to the soul that they may not have attributed to the brain or the mind. For the first study, we tested children's beliefs about what aspects of a person were influenced by a religious ritual. We hypothesized that if children believe an aspect of a person exists that is not the body or the mind, that is the aspect that would be influenced by spiritual activities. Indeed, we found children were more likely to say the soul was changed after a baptism, rather than the mind or the brain. In the second study, we found that children attributed different kinds of processes to the soul than to the mind or the brain. In particular, children tended to say that the soul (but not the mind or the brain) has spiritual functions and remains constant over time.

Thus, the answer to the question, "If it's not the mind, then what is it?" appeared to be that children believed the soul was a stable part of a person, distinct from the mind and the body, serving that person's spiritual functions (e.g., communicating with God, going to heaven after death). We followed up on these findings (Richert & Harris 2008) to examine (a) if these distinctions persist into adulthood and (b) the influence of these concepts of the soul on ethical decision making.

Testing the theory

Our goal (Richert & Harris 2008) was not only to examine what characteristics people judge as the defining features of either the soul or the mind but also to test two competing hypotheses that other researchers had put forth. The first hypothesis claimed that the notion of a soul as a separate entity from one's body is intuitive (Bering 2006; Bloom 2004). That is, starting as early as infancy, humans will readily attribute psychological abilities (e.g., ability to feel emotions or have goals) to other humans and animals, and they may even claim that some of these abilities continue to exist after a person dies. After all, it is difficult trying to imagine not being able to imagine (Bering 2006).

The other hypothesis takes this a step further by claiming that there is a difference not only between soul and body but also between mind and soul (Astuti & Harris 2008; Richert & Harris 2006). This position separates cognitive functions associated with the mind (e.g., thinking) and spiritual functions associated with the soul (e.g., immortality). This hypothesis is influenced by evidence showing that some cultures endorse the belief that when an individual dies, they continue living as an ancestor and are still able to interact with family members but, yet, are limited in some capacities (e.g., seeing people).

In order to test these competing hypotheses, we created a study derived from our previous studies with children by testing a different population: young adults. We specifically chose this age group because we hypothesized that young adults' concept of a soul results from long-term exposure to their own religious upbringing and cultural traditions. We examined whether the differences evident in childhood persisted and perhaps became even further delineated into adulthood. Additionally, we examined whether participants' beliefs about the soul were more predictive of their responses to ethical questions than their beliefs about the mind. We tested our questions with a group of undergraduate students who were diverse both religiously (e.g., Christian, Buddhist, nonaffiliated) and ethnically (e.g., Asian, Latino/Hispanic, White, African American).

Methodology

We created an online survey that included questions about the *existence* of both the mind and the soul, including (a) belief in existence, (b) when (if ever) each begins, (c) if each remains constant over time or can develop and change, and (d) what happens to each at death. We also asked about the *function* of the mind and the soul by asking participants to imagine losing their mind or soul and to report what would happen to several cognitive (e.g., one's ability to remember) and spiritual (e.g., one's ability to continue on after death) abilities. Because the soul is often associated with some type of spiritual essence in religious communities, we also created combined variables that indicated how "spiritual" participants' concepts of the mind or soul were. For example, a person with a very spiritual concept of the soul would believe the soul "(a) exists before birth, (b) does not change, (c) survives death, (d) contributes to a person's life force, (e) contributes to a person's ability to live on after they die, (f) contributes to a person's ability to connect to a higher power and (g) contributes to a person's spiritual essence" (Richert & Harris 2008: 108).

Lastly, we asked participants about their views of the mind and the soul for three ethical issues: stem cell research, life support, and human cloning. We asked participants whether they believed embryos, a person on life support, and a human clone have a mind or a soul. Then we asked participants if they believed that scientists should be allowed to use embryonic stem cells, if a person in a persistent vegetative state should be disconnected from life support, and if scientists should create human clones.

Results and Analysis

Overall, participants did treat the *existence* of the mind and the soul differently. Specifically, participants were more certain of the existence of the mind than the soul (though almost all claimed they both existed). Most thought that the mind begins at conception, during pregnancy, or at birth; that the mind is able to change and develop over time; and that the mind stops existing at death. However, most participants claimed that the soul begins prior to conception, at conception, or at birth (indicating that the soul begins before the mind); that the soul is able to change and develop across time (although less than the mind); and that the soul continues existing after death in some form.

We also found that participants treated the *functions* of the soul and the mind differently. Specifically, participants tended to claim that they would lose more cognitive functions if they lost their mind, but they would lose more spiritual functions if they lost their soul. That is, if you imagine losing your mind, you are more likely to claim that you'll also lose the ability to remember, solve problems, or tell right from wrong. But if you imagine losing your soul, you are more likely to think about the implications of the afterlife or connection to a higher power. Participants were relatively evenly split in if they thought a person could no longer feel emotions after losing the mind or soul, yet participants did not differ in their judgments between losing the mind or soul.

In terms of soul spirituality versus mind spirituality, we found that similar to children (Richert & Harris 2006), adult participants also viewed the soul as more spiritual than the mind. When we added up the seven variables described above that were used to measure spirituality for both mind and soul, we discovered that participants attributed more of these spiritual attributes to the soul than to the mind. In fact, most of the participants assigned at least one of these seven characteristics to the soul, whereas hardly any participants attributed these same characteristics to the mind.

Finally, we found that participants treated the mind and the soul differently for each ethical issue. Specifically, participants for the most part did not support, or were not sure about, using embryos for stem cell research, and they were more likely to claim that embryos have a soul than a mind. However, participants were quite evenly split in their decision of whether or not an individual in a vegetative state should be disconnected from life support, and participants overwhelmingly thought that individuals in vegetative states were more likely to have a soul than a mind. Lastly, participants were more likely to claim that human clones have a mind than a soul, and over half of the participants did not think scientists should make human clones.

As with the research with children, these findings suggested that adults also distinguish the soul from the mind. In addition, concepts of the soul are related to individuals' ethical decision making, but concepts of the mind are not.

Extending the theory

I conducted a study to follow up on these findings with a graduate student (Richert & Smith 2012). Dr. Erin Smith and I specifically wanted to examine what aspects of the soul concept are related to ethical decision making when people are thinking about beginning-of-life (abortion, embryonic stem cell research) or end-of-life (euthanasia, disconnecting people from life support, suicide) ethical dilemmas. With a diverse sample of undergraduates, we first demonstrated that Christians, Agnostics, and Buddhists had similar conceptions of the soul to those documented in Richert and Harris (2008), although Buddhists were somewhat more likely to assign cognitive functions to the soul than Christians or Agnostics. Regarding ethical dilemmas, we found that participants' beliefs about the nature of the soul (what the soul is), but not about the functions of the soul (what the soul does), predicted their responses to the ethical dilemmas. Specifically, participants were less likely to endorse abortion, embryonic stem cell research, and suicide if they believed the soul starts before birth and remains constant over a person's life.

This theory has been further examined by a current graduate student studying with me (Kirsten [McConnel] Lesage), who has coauthored this chapter. Here, she describes how this approach informed her senior thesis while she was an undergraduate at Northwestern College (McConnel & Edman 2013a, 2013b).

Although uncommon, there are individuals who do believe that the soul is about the mind and mental processes, and that the body and soul are joined together as one physical entity. This view is called monism and is different from the more commonly held, dualistic view of the soul that claims the body and soul are distinct, separate entities. For my honors thesis as an undergraduate, I was interested in the idea that people can use different types of cognitive processing when thinking about a concept: slow, reflective processing in which people can think about the concept as long as they wish, and fast, intuitive processing in which people have to answer with the first thing that comes to mind (Kahneman 2011, McCauley 2011). Previous research examining the soul claimed that a dualistic notion of the soul is intuitive and a monistic view of the soul is counterintuitive (Bloom 2007). If these claims are true, then individuals should use fast, intuitive processing (i.e., online processing) when thinking about the soul in dualistic terms but slow, reflective processing (i.e., offline processing) when thinking about the soul in monistic terms. This might even lead monistic individuals to supporting dualistic notions of the soul when they are asked to respond as fast as possible because the "intuitive dualism" could override their reflective beliefs.

"I tested these claims by giving undergraduate students an online processing task containing twenty-eight statements supporting either monism or dualism. Participants had only five seconds to read each statement and indicate if they agreed with the statement or not. Contrary to the claims of previous research, my results indicated that the monist participants agreed with the statements supporting monism and disagreed with the statements supporting dualism—showing that they did not resort to dualistic beliefs even when they did not have time to think about their response. Dualist participants showed the same pattern for dualistic statements. However, both groups of participants took more time to respond to the monistic statements, indicating that there might still be some support to the claim that dualism is intuitive and monism is not."

Discussion

Debates about the cognitive foundations of the soul concept continue. Here, we provide examples from fields related to cognitive science of religion, of new research that revolves around two themes: debates about intuitive mind–body dualism and the influence of cultural context on the developing soul concept.

Questioning intuitive dualism

Similar to the research described above (McConnel & Edman 2013a, 2013b), one primary line of new research has continued to examine how people view the relation between the body, the mind, and the soul. Lindeman, Riekki, and Svedholm-Hakkinen (2015) identified three different types of views that tend to characterize how an individual sees the relation between the body, the mind, and the soul: monists (who attribute biological, psychobiological, and psychological processes only to the brain), emergentists (who attribute biological, psychobiological, and psychological processes to both the mind and the brain), and spiritualists (who attribute biological, psychobiological, and psychological processes to the soul, the mind, and the brain). Unlike Richert and Harris's (2008) study, Lindeman et al. (2015) did not ask participants about the spiritual functions of a person, although we would hypothesize that the spiritualists would be more likely to associate spiritual functions to the soul than the monists or emergentists.

Roazzi, Nyhof, and Johnson (2013) further distinguished the concept of the soul from concepts of spirit. Roazzi et al. (2013) hypothesized that while the soul may develop from cognitive foundations rooted in essentializing, a separate concept of spirit may derive from intuitive beliefs in a vital (life-sustaining) force. Roazzi et al. (2013) found that adults in Brazil were less likely to differentiate the functions of the soul from those of the mind and the brain than participants in Indonesia or the United States. Roazzi et al. (2013) also found that all participants tended to associate a person's passion with their spirit rather than their soul.

Based on this kind of psychological evidence, and further drawing on anthropological and historical evidence, Hodge (2008) has argued that the concept of the soul being distinct from the mind suggests that a mind–body dualism is not an intuitive cognitive stance. Hodge and colleagues have followed up on this theoretical approach in several compelling pieces tying concepts of the soul to the socially embodied nature of reasoning about others (Hodge 2011).

Culture and concept development

Within the field of developmental psychology, recent research has continued to examine how the concept of the soul develops and has extended that research to examine differences in soul concepts in varying cultural contexts (Emmons & Kelemen 2014, 2015; Watson-Jones et al. 2016).

In a recent study, Watson-Jones et al. (2016) examined beliefs in both Vanuatu and the United States about what bodily functions continue after death. Similar to prior studies, they found that children and adults in the United States viewed psychological functions, but not biological functions, as continuing after death. However, children and adults in Vanuatu claimed that both psychological and biological functions continue after death. These findings are important as they show that individuals' views of the soul are shaped by the culture in which they are raised. As such, these findings speak to the importance of gathering cross-cultural evidence before drawing conclusions about the extent to which certain intuitive cognitive processes are *universally* intuitive, as well as for understanding the developmental mechanisms through which certain cognitive processes become intuitive.

In a complementary line of research, Emmons and Kelemen (2014, 2015) have examined prelife conceptions. Although they did not ask children specifically about the soul, the researchers asked urban-raised children and rural indigenous children in Ecuador if six different bodily functions (biological, psychobiological, perceptual, epistemic, emotional, and desire) existed at three different time-points in an individual's life: prelife, in utero, and infancy. Consistent with the finding that children and adults are more likely to view the soul than the mind as existing before a person is born (Richert & Harris 2006, 2008), children in both settings claimed that emotions and desires existed prelife and during the fetal period, but epistemic functions (e.g., to think) did not (Emmons & Kelemen 2014). Additionally, children believed that emotional states and desires were not necessarily the product of physical maturation, unlike epistemic states (Emmons & Kelemen 2015). Together with findings suggesting children and adults largely support the view that most psychological functions continue to exist after death (Bering 2002; Richert & Harris 2006, 2008), one developmental possibility is that infants and children broadly essentialize by assuming that humans (as well as animals and objects) have some kind of undefined, nonobvious element that imparts identity or category membership. When specifically applied to humans, a person's essence then can be further differentiated (through cultural learning) into mind and soul.

Essential missteps

One of my favorite aspects of studying religious thinking is the cross-disciplinary conversations and debates that it fosters. However, for students interested in cognitive science of religion, I would like to share some wisdom gained through trial, error, and linguistic missteps in my first forays into cross-disciplinary discussions. My early presentations of the findings described in this chapter occurred in the context of conferences and academic audiences with whom I was familiar, primarily developmental psychologists and cognitive scientists. For these audiences, the term "essentialism," once defined in a psychological framework, was readily and unproblematically accepted. Within the fields of developmental psychology and cognitive science, the human tendency toward essentialism is generally viewed as a productive cognitive adaptation that facilitates learning in early childhood (Gelman 2003).

I had a very different experience the first time I was invited to present this research at an interdisciplinary meeting. As soon as I used the term "essentialism," I could feel the room turn against me. In fields within the humanities, such as religious studies, cultural studies, and history, essentialism and essentializing are primarily discussed in the context of their negative outcomes. In the same way that psychological essentialism promotes assignment to and inductions about category membership that can support early learning, these cognitive intuitions have varieties of negative and harmful outcomes when used to remove an individual's identity and only assign to that person the "essences" that we associate with membership in a particular social category. In this way, essentialism can lead to racism, sexism, and homophobia. It can be used to support and promote discrimination and to denigrate members of social groups we consider to be "less" than ourselves. It can also carry with it the connotation that people cannot change and cannot therefore be agents of social change.

Through this experience, and through continued engagement in cross-disciplinary conversations, I have learned the profound importance of not relying on jargon to communicate what I want to communicate, to listen closely to those who critique my research methods, and to be open to constructive debate and dialogue about the interpretation and meaning of my findings. These practices do not always come easily (or intuitively), but they are critical for any scholar who aims to engage in a productive, innovative, and impactful program of research in cognitive science of religion.

Conclusion

In Richert and Harris (2008), we set out to unpack the hypothesis that humans are intuitive mind–body dualists, viewing other persons as consisting of two distinct elements. We found that our concepts of others are more complex than dividing the functions of a person into those performed by the body and those performed by the mind. Our data suggested that an early emerging intuition toward essentializing plays a critical role in how we view the nature of ourselves and other people. In particular, beyond cognitive and biological functions, people seem to associate an individual essence to the self—the soul—that has unique functions (spiritual, emotional) and remains relatively constant, from before birth over the course of a person's life, and into the afterlife.

CHAPTER 7
WERE EARLY CHINESE THINKERS FOLK DUALISTS?
Edward Slingerland

Introduction

One of the most basic hypotheses in cognitive science of religion (CSR) is that religious beliefs are somehow related to human beings' "theory of mind" or "mentalizing" ability. Our tendency to project intentionality and agency onto other humans, the reasoning goes, might overfire, causing us to see storms as caused by angry gods, misfortunes by hungry ancestors, and—most diffusely—meaning in our lives. Our ability to switch between mentalizing (analyzing the world in terms of intentions or goals) and physical reasoning (seeing it as a chain of mechanistic, billiard ball–like causality) is also thought to give rise to "folk dualism," or the tendency to think of ourselves and others as composed of distinctive physical bodies and immaterial minds.

I learned about these ideas when I began, about ten years ago, to become interested in the nascent field of CSR. Having been trained as a specialist in early Chinese thought, however, I also began to encounter colleagues in CSR who, when I mentioned that I worked on early China, said, "Oh, we heard the Chinese were different. They don't have mind–body dualism, do they?" I tried to assure them that this was just a myth, part of the Orientalist picture of China as the Place Where Everything Is Different, but I had to acknowledge that there were people in my field who did continue to make claims like this. I had long thought that there was simply overwhelming qualitative archeological and textual evidence against the strong mind–body holist claim—that is, the claim that the early Chinese, or "the East" more generally, completely lacked any sense of distinction between mind and body and saw what we might be tempted to call mental functions as completely on par with other bodily functions. Having begun to hang out with scientists, I now began to wonder if the debate between mind–body holists and their critics might be put on a more solid quantitative footing. The goal was to try to get beyond the cherry-picking and bald assertion that characterizes much humanistic debate, on this and other topics.

Our ability to get beyond selectively sampling particular bits of textual evidence to support our interpretations has been greatly enhanced in recent decades with the advent of fully digitized, searchable corpora. In the case of early China, all of our received texts, as well as many of the more recently discovered archeological texts, are available in this format. Together with colleagues with expertise in digital technologies and statistics, as well as some of my advanced PhD students, I decided to explore alternative ways of "reading" texts that might produce generalizations that would hold up to rigorous, statistical inquiry.

Theory

If there is a word in classical Chinese that would correspond to the English *mind*, everyone would agree it is *xin* 心. Referring originally to the physical organ, the heart, *xin* served in the early Chinese view as the locus of what we would think of as higher cognition as well as certain emotions. The strong mind–body holist position holds that *xin* is simply one organ in the body among others, not in any way qualitatively different from the other organs, and having no special relationship with the physical body. It also claims that the Chinese did not distinguish between reason and emotion.

To evaluate this claim, we began with the assumption that, if the strong holist position were correct, *xin* should have no sort of unusual relationship to the other organs or the physical body, the latter generally denoted with three main terms with slightly different semantic ranges: *xing* 形 (physical body, form), *shen* 身 (physical body, self), and *ti* 體 (physical body, substance). Moreover, *xin* should be equally related to functions that we dualistic Westerners would be tempted to class into reason and emotion.

Methodology

Phase 1 of the project took the form of a large-scale, team-based qualitative coding exercise. Together with my collaborator, Maciej Chudek, we extracted passages containing *xin* from an online database of the entire received pre-Qin corpus[1] as well as the Guodian archeological texts.[2] To get a sense of changes over time, these texts were classified into three rough periods: pre–Warring States (c. 1500 to c. 475 BCE), early Warring States (late fifth to mid-fourth century BCE), and late Warring States (mid-fourth century BCE to 221 BCE).

The result of our keyword search for *xin* 心 in this corpus was 1,321 passages, automatically chunked into traditionally established textual units by the search engine. The coders we recruited were graduate students of mine, who were blind to the hypothesis that I wanted to explore. We then randomly sampled 60 passages and inductively developed a set of 29 codes to classify the usage of *xin* 心 (see Figure 7.1).

Next, the three coders applied these codes to 620 randomly sampled passages, presented in a randomized order. First, each passage was independently coded by two of the three coders. Passages for which both coders' decisions agreed on all 29 codes were considered finalized at this point (310 passages, or about half). For the remaining passages, a third coder (i.e., the one not in the pair who initially coded that passage) independently coded these passages, and where their 29 decisions corresponded exactly to one of the first two coders, these passages were again considered finalized (159 passages, or approximately half of the remaining passages). The remaining disagreements were arbitrated and finalized by myself, with full access to the original coders' decisions and notes. Considering the rather high standards set for agreement—perfect matching on 29 separate decisions—intercoder reliability was quite good, with an initial 0.50 correlation in Round 1 and 0.76 correlation having been achieved by the end of Round 2. In order

Coding Criteria

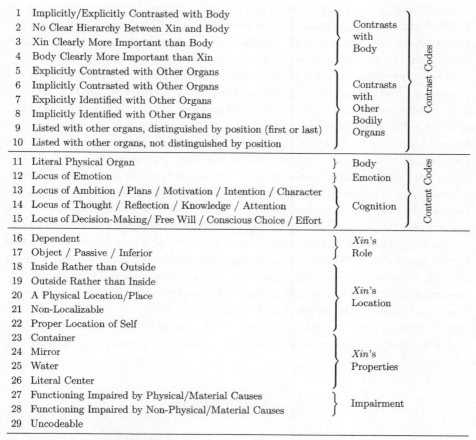

1	Implicitly/Explicitly Contrasted with Body	
2	No Clear Hierarchy Between Xin and Body	Contrasts with Body
3	Xin Clearly More Important than Body	
4	Body Clearly More Important than Xin	
5	Explicitly Contrasted with Other Organs	
6	Implicitly Contrasted with Other Organs	Contrasts with Other Bodily Organs
7	Explicitly Identified with Other Organs	
8	Implicitly Identified with Other Organs	
9	Listed with other organs, distinguished by position (first or last)	
10	Listed with other organs, not distinguished by position	
11	Literal Physical Organ	} Body
12	Locus of Emotion	} Emotion
13	Locus of Ambition / Plans / Motivation / Intention / Character	
14	Locus of Thought / Reflection / Knowledge / Attention	Cognition
15	Locus of Decision-Making/ Free Will / Conscious Choice / Effort	
16	Dependent	Xin's Role
17	Object / Passive / Inferior	
18	Inside Rather than Outside	
19	Outside Rather than Inside	
20	A Physical Location/Place	Xin's Location
21	Non-Localizable	
22	Proper Location of Self	
23	Container	
24	Mirror	Xin's Properties
25	Water	
26	Literal Center	
27	Functioning Impaired by Physical/Material Causes	Impairment
28	Functioning Impaired by Non-Physical/Material Causes	
29	Uncodeable	

(Contrast Codes / Content Codes)

Figure 7.1 Codes applied to textual passages (from Slingerland & Chudek 2011b).

to assure that my own coding in Round 3 did not distort the results, we also did a check and assured that all of the trends discussed below were still significant after Round 2, before I made any coding decisions: all effects retained their statistical significance and directions, and their magnitudes remained close to those reported below.

Results and Analysis

Of the codes applied to the passages, two main categories bear directly on the issue of mind–body dualism versus holism: (a) whether or not *xin* is contrasted with the body and (b) whether it is used to refer to a bodily organ, locus of feelings and emotions, or a locus of cognition in the deliberate, reflective sense usually connoted by *mind*. To begin with, we found that passages involving an implicit or explicit contrast between the *xin* and the body[3] were quite common, constituting 4 percent (7/179) of pre–Warring States passages, growing to 8.5 percent (3/35) of early Warring States and over 10 percent (42/406) of late Warring States passages (see Figure 7.2). This increase in frequency of contrasts over time was statistically significant, suggesting that mind–body disjunction was becoming a more prominent concern or theme.

One question that came up when I presented our preliminary results to groups of psychologists was how this frequency of *xin*–body contrasts compared to contrasts between other organs and the body. My initial response was that there *were* no examples of other organs being contrasted with the body. My intuition was that, although *xin*–body contrasts slip under the interpretative radar because they accord with our innate folk dualism, any mention of a liver–body or ear–body contrast would have stood out. In the spirit of quantitative demonstration, however, we put this to the test: to provide a baseline for comparison, we did a quick follow-up study looking for any contrasts between the body and four other commonly mentioned organs in Warring States texts, two external (*mu* 目 "eye" and *er* 耳 "ear") and two internal (*gan* 肝 "liver" and *fu* 腹 "stomach"). Of the 864 passages containing occurrences of these terms in our pre-Qin textual database, only 337 also contained one of the predominant "body" terms (*xing* 形, *shen* 身, *ti* 體) and thus were likely candidates for a contrast. These 337 were coded by two coders working independently on mutually exclusive subsets. Only one contrast—a single passage where the mouth is contrasted with the body[4]—was found. This means that the odds of *xin* being contrasted with the body were about 77 times greater than that of the other organs we examined. In other words, *xin* is essentially unique in being

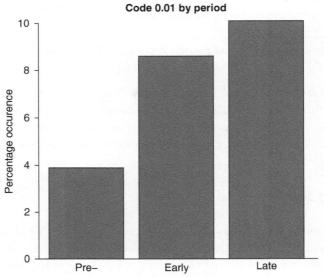

Figure 7.2 Code 0.01 (*xin* implicitly/explicitly contrasted with body) as a percentage of overall occurrences of *xin* over the three time periods (from Slingerland & Chudek 2011b).

contrasted with the body. This finding alone seems to render completely untenable the claim that the *xin* is in no way qualitatively different from the other organs.

A second trend in which we were interested was the extent to which *xin* was portrayed as primarily a physical organ, a locus of emotion, or a locus of "higher" cognition,[5] and whether or not there were any patterns in such references that changed over time. What we found is that the frequency with which *xin* referred to a bodily organ did not differ significantly between the three periods, but the rates of reference to *xin* as locus of cognition and emotion did. Throughout all three periods, *xin* referred to a physical body organ at a consistently low rate (about 3 percent). This suggests that, although the actual physical organ in the body is part of the semantic range of *xin*, this is actually a quite rare use of the term. *Xin* as locus of cognition was much more frequent in the early and late Warring States periods compared to the pre–Warring States period, although there was no statistically significant difference in frequency between the early and late Warring States periods. In contrast, *xin* as locus of emotion showed the reverse pattern: it was referred to significantly less in the early and late Warring States periods than the pre–Warring States period, while also not significantly differing between the early and late periods. The general pattern of our findings is illustrated in Figure 7.3.

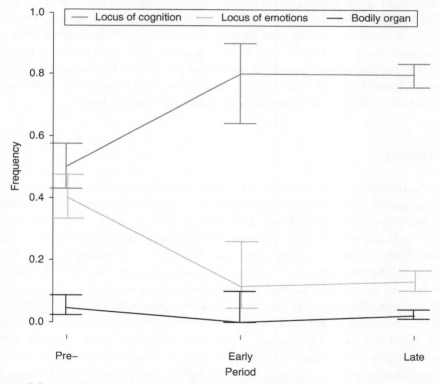

Figure 7.3 Temporal trends in the rate at which *xin* refers to a physical organ, a locus of emotion, or a locus of cognition, in the pre-, early, and late Warring States periods, with 95 percent confidence intervals—the margin of possible statistical error (from Slingerland & Chudek 2011b).

During the pre–Warring States period, *xin* referred about equally often to a locus of emotion or cognition. By the early Warring States period it was being used to refer to the locus of cognition far more frequently (about 80 percent of the time) than emotions (about 10 percent of the time), and this pattern persisted into the late Warring States period. This change also corresponded to a rise in the frequency of explicit contrasts of *xin* with the physical body (see Figure 7.2).

To summarize the results of this study, although *xin* is often portrayed as the locus of emotion as well as other cognitive abilities in the pre–Warring States period (roughly 1500 BCE to 450 BCE), by the end of the Warring States period there is a clear trend whereby the *xin* is less and less associated with emotions and becomes increasingly portrayed as the unique locus of "higher" cognitive abilities, such as planning, goal maintenance, rational thought, categorization and language use, decision making, and voluntary acts of will. This neatly maps onto a parallel trend in the translation of early Chinese texts: in pre–Warring States texts, *xin* is almost exclusively translated as "heart," whereas translations begin to switch to "heart-mind" (or simply vary among themselves between "heart" or "mind") by the early Warring States period and then render *xin* almost exclusively as "mind" by the time we reach such late Warring States texts as the *Zhuangzi* or *Xunzi*. This trend, when noticed at all, has often been attributed to linguistic sloppiness on the part of the translators. This study suggested that, in fact, the situation is quite the opposite, in that *xin* seems to gradually shed its associations with emotions—especially strong, "irrational" emotions—and comes to be seen as a faculty whose abilities map on fairly closely to the folk notion conveyed by the English *mind*. Most importantly, in terms of the basic concept of mind–body dualism, the *xin* alone of all the organs is singled out to be contrasted with the various terms used to refer to the physical body.

Discussion

What is so interesting about this early Chinese case is that linguistic resources seem to militate against mind–body dualism: the term that came to refer to the seat of cognition was represented by a graph denoting the physical heart, a concrete organ embedded in the body and also the locus of desires and emotions. Nonetheless, over a several-hundred-year period, texts employing classical Chinese still managed to develop a quite strong form of mind–body dualism that strikingly mirrors modern Western folk conceptions, and that also fits well with basic assumptions of folk dualism that inform CSR research. Moreover, this remained the default picture for the rest of its history. While identification of potential causation is necessarily speculative, my coauthor and I concluded that the best explanation for the trend is that it represents a semantic shift that was driven by a need for increased conceptual precision that accompanied the vast expansion of literacy as we move into the late Warring States period, and that was guided by intuitive folk dualism. In other words, as more and more human beings began using classical Chinese as a means of communication, the semantic range of words like *xin* converged on a cognitive anchor point provided by intuitive folk dualism.

Although the methods employed in this study are standard for scientific qualitative coding exercises, to anyone trained in interpreting texts for a living, several potential limitations immediately leap out.[6] The formulation of the initial coding categories has an obvious role in shaping the results, and coding decisions were no doubt at least somewhat biased by individual coders' cultural models and individual assumptions about the texts. Moreover, the very idea of "hypothesis-blind" coding seems undermined by the signals sent by the chosen keyword and coding categories, as well as the high degree of personal knowledge on the part of the coders of my own pre-assumptions. Most generally, pre-Qin texts are notoriously difficult to understand: classical Chinese is an uninflected language, and the inevitable ambiguities present in the original texts are often resolved in a very particular—but perhaps inaccurate— direction by the traditional commentaries and English translations that my coders were allowed to consult.

There is, on top of all of this, the problem of proper rhetorical framing mentioned above. The single most common issue that ended up having to be adjudicated by me in Round 3 concerned the rather abstract codes having to do with *xin* being implicitly or explicitly contrasted or identified with the body and other organs. Even specialists in the field would seriously disagree about which codes to apply to passages such as *Mencius* 6:A:7, where it is argued that the *xin* has a taste for morality (*yi* 義) in the same way that the eye has a taste for beauty, or the mouth for delicious food. A colleague of mine in early Chinese studies, Jane Geaney, would have coded it as "0.3 Xin Conceptually (Explicitly) *Identified* with Other Organs" (Geaney 2002), whereas I would argue that one needs to *add* the code, "0.2 Xin Grammatically/Rhetorically (Implicitly) *Contrasted* with Other Organs," to pick up the proper rhetorical framework: the explicit identification makes no sense without a background, implicit assumption of contrast. This is difficult—and debatable—stuff. Finally, I think it is fair to say that humanities scholars in general are suspicious of attempts to handle the complexity of textual interpretation by means of a process that results in graphs and charts and statistical margins of errors. The statistical cleanliness could potentially mask a host of potential systemic complications. I have found that many of my colleagues see this 2011 study as an instance of the sciency-sounding smoke and mirrors being used to obscure the messiness of interpretation— an attempt to borrow the prestige of the "ethnoscience of the West" to push my own interpretative agenda.

I obviously disagree. Despite the many reasons for being cautious in both applying and interpreting the results of such methods, I think that they can serve as a useful example of how techniques from the natural sciences—large-scale, team-based analysis, random sampling, statistical analysis—can be put to good use in the humanities. Humanists have always been empirically minded, in the sense that scholarly claims are not taken seriously unless supported by textual or archeological evidence. This sort of evidence has, however, typically been gathered and presented in a highly biased and unsystematic manner. Scholars arguing for mind–body holism in early China, for instance, will cherry-pick a dozen or so passages from among hundreds or thousands on the topic to defend their claim. François Jullien, to take a habitually egregious example, cites only a single substantive passage in support of his argument that the early Chinese concept of a holistic mind–body is quite alien to "our" dualism (Jullien 2007: ch. 4), and this passage is from a late Warring States text portraying the *xin* as a physical organ—a category that makes up 2 percent of the passages we coded from this period. Even careful scholars such as Geaney, who makes much more of an effort to substantiate her claims with copious textual evidence, are constrained by the standard of our genre to limit themselves to a subset of available passages that have been chosen in anything but a disinterested manner. Of course, each partisan in any given debate works under the assumption that his or her chosen passages are somehow more representative or revealing that that of his or her opponents, but there has been a surprising lack of interest among humanists in adopting techniques to compensate for personal bias that have long been pillars of the scientific method.[7]

The sort of large-scale corpus sampling method employed in this study is expensive and, frankly, irritating to implement. As I quickly discovered upon embarking on this project, large-scale corpus coding projects share many of the liabilities of scientific inquiry in general. They are enormously time-consuming, expensive, full of administrative difficulties, and *boring*. For a scholar used to working solo in the pristine silence of his or her office, managing a team of coders, with all of their personal dramas and idiosyncratic takes on the coding process, is surprisingly difficult. Certain rules of thumb—coding sheets should be *simple*, coding schedules generous—can help to reduce the burden, but simple funding limitations (coders need to get paid, software needs to be purchased) will no doubt slow the adoption of these techniques. Despite these limitations, the ability of large-scale corpus analyses to give us relatively objective overviews of huge quantities of historical materials should not be dismissed by scholars of religion.

As we note in our reply to Klein and Klein (2011), who see the problems inherent in interpreting early Chinese texts as potentially fatal to our project, our approach is not intended to sidestep the problems of textual interpretation but rather to use the power of sheer quantity to help put qualitative disagreements into perspective:

> [L]arge-scale coding and statistical analysis allow the noise of randomly distributed interpretative differences to be distinguished from the signal of genuine historical patterns by exploiting large samples and statistical inference. These methods also quantify qualitative disagreements, providing measures of inter-coder reliability that specify just how much difference in interpretation exists. They provide a path out of endless cycles of disagreement by specifying precisely documented techniques for resolving disagreements, which can be replicated, systematically altered and statistically analyzed. (Slingerland & Chudek 2011a: 185)

Such techniques can also provide counterintuitive results that help us to better situate our qualitative intuitions and can reveal unexpected patterns. For instance, I was very much surprised by the sharp reduction in *xin* as locus of emotion in the late Warring States period. My intuition, I think shared by most in my field, was that *xin* maintained a strong emotional component throughout the Warring States period. Our study results suggest that this intuition is wrong. Large-scale corpus analyses therefore can, and should, play an important role in supporting, supplementing, and—when necessary—correcting traditional approaches.

At the same time, as humanists become more familiar with the manner in which qualitative analysis is undertaken in the sciences, their deep familiarity with the problems inherent to cross-cultural comparison, and hermeneutics more generally, can and should begin to have an impact. It is significant that, in the initial version of their piece in *Cognitive Science*, Klein and Klein strongly contrasted the more objective, "unproblematic" coding issues faced in most psychological experiments with the interpretative challenges inherent to studying early Chinese texts. In fact, interpretation is very much front and center in most areas of the sciences. This is a point that has been made loudly and clearly in the "science studies" literature, and that has resulted in retractions of some controversial interpretations of, for instance, primate behavior.[8] This means that injecting a bit of humanistic hermeneutic *Angst* into the sciences would be extremely helpful, provided that it is done in a constructive manner. My experience with work in cognitive and social psychology suggests that most scientific researchers are much less concerned than they ought to be about potential complications that are screamingly obvious to anyone coming out of the humanities. Problems of translation, differing cultural models, pervasive conceptual bias on the part of investigators, and similar issues tend to glide under the radar when studies are designed and results published. This means that the quality of this sort of work would be vastly improved by input from humanities scholars, not merely as data providers (glorified research assistants) but as theoretical and methodological advisors involved in the most preliminary steps of study design.

Follow-up studies

The limitations of human-based coding suggest that it would be promising to explore semiautomated and fully automated methods of textual analysis, which have the great advantages of being relatively cheap and fast to run, as well as having the capacity to handle corpora of any size. A further advantage of these techniques is that they remove many of the ordinary sources of interpretative bias. In a series of studies reported in Slingerland et al. (2017), we drew upon a large (almost six-million-character) corpus, the Chinese Text Project (CTP; www.ctext.org) database, which has several advantages over the much smaller corpus used in Slingerland and Chudek (2011b). Its breadth encompasses genres such as medical, military, mathematical, and historical texts, answering worries that our text sample might be biased in favor of poetry or philosophy (Klein & Klein 2011). The vast historical sweep of the CTP means that we include texts from the pre–Warring States period (prior to fifth century BCE) through the Warring States period and the Han Dynasty (206 BCE to 220 CE), as well as a small number of post-Han texts dating up to the Song Dynasty (960–1279 CE). The fact that our information retrieval and analysis were fully automated allowed us not only to handle such a massive corpus but also to respond to concerns about potential biases in human coders.

We used a variety of both supervised (highly prestructured) and unsupervised (relatively unstructured) methods to analyze this massive corpus. These included word collocation, or the measurement of how frequently individual terms of interest occur with regard to one another in a textual corpus within a given textual window; hierarchical cluster analysis, an unsupervised method whereby an algorithm runs through the corpus and create a dendrogram, or "tree," showing the physical distances between individual terms; and topic modeling, where an algorithm identifies statistically unusual clusters of terms.

The guiding hypothesis for all of the studies using these techniques was that, if the authors of the CTP texts *tacitly* endorsed strong mind–body holism, we should find *xin* behaving just like any other term for a bodily organ in proximity to our three common "body" terms (*shen* 身, *xing* 形, and *ti* 體). In other words, whatever early Chinese thinkers might explicitly *say* about *xin*–body relations, if they genuinely embraced a holistic view of body and mind, the patterns of collocation between *xin* and the body terms should look no different than those for other organs. Our basic assumption was that large-scale patterns of language use can tell us something about implicit cognition. So, even if Mencius claims (as in 6:A:7) that the *xin* is the same as the other organs, if we find him, and other early Chinese writers, habitually mentioning *xin*, and only *xin*, in close proximity to the body terms, this suggests that *xin* occupies a distinct cognitive space in the early Chinese mindset, whatever the explicit claims of the author(s) in question might be.

All three methods returned similar results: *xin* is a wild outlier in early Chinese texts. It appears in close proximity to the body terms much more often than any other organ and clusters tightly with the body terms (and well away from the other organ terms) in dendrograms of the corpus (see Figure 7.4). It is the only organ that appears in any of the topics produced by our topic modeling study, appearing together with words for planning, higher cognition, and decision making and never with words for strong

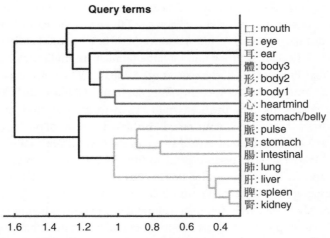

Figure 7.4 Dendrogram of *xin* with body terms and other organ terms (from Slingerland et al. 2017).

emotions or passions. These three methods not only corroborate one another, but they also fit very well with the qualitative coding results obtained in the original Slingerland and Chudek (2011a) study.

Directions for further research along these lines include working with even larger corpora with a more-than-two-thousand-year temporal span, which would allow us to better analyze changes in patterns over time; expanding to consider other keywords possibly related to mentalizing or dualism; and comparing the early Chinese results with results obtained from analyzing digital corpora from other world cultures, such as ancient Greece, India, or Japan.

CHAPTER 8
HOW DO PEOPLE ESTABLISH PERSONAL IDENTITY IN REINCARNATION?
Claire White

Introduction

Every day we make assumptions that the people around us are who they appear to be based on how they look. For the most part, we do this automatically, without conscious reflection. For instance, this morning as I arrived at my local coffee shop, I smiled at the barista and told her that I was having my regular. I didn't actually have to tell her what specific type of coffee I wanted; I assumed she already knew. And she did. Within a few minutes, she served my soy latte, and I was on my way. I didn't have to think about whether the person behind the counter was Amanda. Even from the end of the coffee line, I could see her distinctive shimmering blonde hair and dip-dyed pink ends, and my brain automatically calculated that this morning's barista was Amanda.

Judgments about who's who enable us to effortlessly maneuver the social world in a way that extends beyond the convenience of seamlessly ordering a cup of coffee. To illustrate the extent to which we depend upon the automaticity of identifying people by their physical features, consider the neurologist Oliver Sacks, author of *The Man Who Mistook His Wife for a Hat and Other Clinical Tales* (1970). Sacks wrote about patients with neurological and neuropsychiatric conditions, but he also personally suffered from one. Sacks had prosopagnosia, often referred to as "face blindness": impairment in recognizing faces. Even though he suffered from a moderate form of the disorder, it impacted his life, often causing him embarrassment. For instance, he once failed to recognize his personal assistant of six years in a hotel lobby, even though he had gone there to meet her.

As Sacks's example shows us, from the moment we are born, we start to configure our social world based on cues such as sight, touch, and even smell. While we focus on mastering motor-based skills such as crawling and walking, our brains are busy configuring constellations of networks for specific people that we frequently encounter. When we as toddlers see the blurry, tall, brown-haired woman at the far end of the room— or when they hear her voice—a distinct neural network lights up the brain, a network that is specific to Mom, including her preferences and our unique interactions with her. One reason why we instinctively use physical appearance as the basis to track people is because it is reasonably accurate. People do not typically change their appearance from one moment to the next, and it makes sense that we tend to rely on more stable markers of identity to configure and reconfigure who people are. For example, most people have had the experience of an acquaintance greeting us, and we momentarily hesitate as we search our mental rotary to identify this person. My guess is that if this happens to you, you are likely to scan the person's face and not their shoes, because facial features tend to be more stable over time (near-expired passport photos aside). Physical features are also used as a proxy (i.e., a convenient cue) for identity in circumstances where there are multiple contenders and a high price. Consider a routine suspect lineup, where a witness is asked to identify the perpetrator of a crime among similar-looking volunteers. In these circumstances, the witness is especially likely to identify the criminal based on distinctive features that many other people are unlikely to share. Such features could be a uniquely shaped nose or a tribal tattoo, for instance. This strategy is an empirical one, because it is based on the statistical improbability of two people having the same distinctive features. Thus, in addition to using physical appearances to identify people, we are also empiricists, weighing up the likelihood that two people will share the same feature.

The idea that some people—such as those who suffer from prosopagnosia—are not able to rely on the automaticity of physical cues as markers of identity seems foreign to the rest of us as we go about our daily lives, identifying people with relative ease. Yet consider a world where the people around you are not who they appear to be, where after death, they are reborn in a different human body. Biological birth does not mark the beginning of a life but a return to it in a new form. How would you recognize your cherished grandfather? Or the local kid who died in a tragic accident? Would you be able to override the tendency that we all have to identify a person by their physical features? Or would you devise some method to test for other similarities between them and the person you were looking for? This is not a hypothetical situation but rather applies to around 30 percent of cultures in places such as Melanesia, South Asia, North America, and West Africa, where many people adopt reincarnation ideologies and practices (see Obeyesekere 2002). In these places, people seek out beloved family members among villagers and even across countries. These seeking practices are not undertaken half-heartedly, because they have huge social consequences; they determine the distribution of names, titles, property inheritance, wealth distribution, child-rearing, and, in Tibet, even religious governance (see White, Sousa, & Berniunas 2014).

One important question concerns how people reason about the identity of others whom they think have been reincarnated. Do people fall back on the default of relying on physical cues? Or do they override this tendency and focus on other, psychologically based aspects of the person? Investigating these questions in reincarnationist cultures is especially important because people subscribe to a view that the person is reborn in another body. To be technically accurate—or when based on a dogma, to be "theologically correct"—we would expect people to reason as though physical similarities between the living and the deceased have no bearing on decisions about who has been reborn as whom. Yet there is reason to suspect that this is not how people actually reason. Detailed accounts (ethnographies) from anthropologists—who often spend extended periods of time understanding the worldview of the people they study—showcase the reality that people use physical similarities as evidence to identify a living person as the reincarnation of a deceased relative or friend. Of course, there is the possibility that these accounts do not represent general trends.

To investigate the possibility that the accounts do not represent general trends or that people do use physical characteristics to identify their reincarnated loved ones, I recruited a team of research assistants, and we consulted a database containing detailed records of reincarnation beliefs from ethnographies for 122 North American and Inuit cultures (Matlock & Mills 1994; White 2016a). These records included details on the methods commonly used to establish the identity of children who were thought to have been reincarnated. We found that people used solely physical features to establish the identity of children in 34 percent of cultures, and people in 41 percent of the cultures used physical features in conjunction with other features (e.g., memory test, behavior) to establish identity. (We will return to the finding about memory later.) Based on this evidence, it seems fair to conclude that people often use physical features to establish identity in reincarnation (see Table 8.1).

The next question that naturally follows these findings is, Why? Why do people rely upon physical similarity to determine identity in reincarnation, when reincarnation involves a bodily change? Researchers in cognitive science of religion have demonstrated that there is often a discrepancy between the religious dogma that people ascribe to, or their explicitly stated beliefs, and how they reason off the cuff, without reflection (often referred to as implicit, unreflective, or maturationally natural reasoning; see Pyysiäinen 2004). These phenomena are often labeled "theological incorrectness" and have been reported in people's reasoning about other supernatural agent concepts, such as gods (see Barrett 1998, 1999; Barrett & Keil 1996; Slone 2007).

Researchers explain such discrepancies by the fact that humans are cognitive misers and in certain contexts will revert to intuitive representations for agents. As discussed, our use of physical similarities as an indicator that a person is the same person over time begins the moment we are born and is the primary strategy employed daily by people of sight everywhere. It is a habitual, convenient, and typically reliable method (see Bloom 2004; Gobbini et al. 2004). One possibility is that people may implicitly revert to default strategies for representing an agent as continuing (being the same person) in everyday

Table 8.1 Frequency of features used (individually and total times) to determine identity in North American and Inuit cultures in North America (cultures $n = 122$).

	Individually		Total Times	
	Frequency	Percentage	Frequency	Percentage
Physical	15	34	38	41
Memory	13	30	32	34
Behavior	16	36	23	25
Total	44	100	93	100

contexts, even when this contradicts their explicit supernatural ideas about the people who are continuing (i.e., they occupy a new body). Just like the suspect lineup, people may well be reasoning as empiricists, weighing up the likelihood of having two people with the same physical features.

For these questions about how people reason, we need to go beyond the ethnographic records to conduct controlled studies. Before we get to the studies, however, we need to go back to the finding in the ethnographic literature about the use of memory tests to establish identity in reincarnation. To explain this finding, let's look at the topic of personal identity.

Personal identity

Philosophers have pointed out that the kinds of decisions that we have been discussing, about the continuity of people, are not the same as decisions about personal identity—what we think constitutes a person. To illustrate with an example, let's return to my coffee this morning and my barista in particular. Amanda may well dye her hair brown, and I may momentarily have difficulty recognizing her, but I will ultimately represent her as Amanda, because I don't represent her identity as tied to her hair. Yet there is an overlap between the two judgments, because if something always continues over dramatic changes we assume that it is a contender for identity. For instance, Amanda could cut and dye her hair, gain or lose a significant amount of weight, and have surgery to reshape her nose, but I might still recognize her as Amanda because of the color of her eyes, the sound of her voice, and similar markers. In some circumstances, the association of aspects of identity with personal identity becomes more obvious.

The Notebook is a modern romantic drama that depicts an elderly man, Noah, telling a nursing home resident the story of a young couple that falls in love. Of course, the twist in the movie (and I apologize for the spoiler) is that the resident is his wife, and the story is theirs. His wife has dementia, and Noah retells their love story to help her remember. In the periodic moments where his wife remembers him, Noah lights up with delight, because he feels as though he is temporarily reunited with her and the love they shared. Why does Noah privilege his wife's episodic memory (i.e., memory of events that happened to her) and not another type of feature that may define her, such as her appearance or personal preferences, or even her memory of facts she learned in school or of how to play the piano? We can easily follow the story and empathize with Noah's plight, because we implicitly represent people as at least partly constituted by their memories.

In The Notebook, the couple's life story—the events the wife experienced, including those shared with her husband—provides her with a unique and continuous identity so that we can say that she is the "same person," even though we know on some level that she has changed in many aspects. These intuitions help to explain the ambiguity over the identity of loved ones of those suffering from memory impairments, including Alzheimer's disease. Some family members will attest that the person both is and is not the same person, others will proclaim that the person they knew is already dead, while still others will continue engaging in daily rituals—such as bringing the person coffee in the morning—in an attempt to reengage them (see Ronch 1996). For centuries, philosophers have suggested that we regard episodic memories (i.e., memories of events that happened to oneself, such as having dinner the previous night) as more linked to a person's identity than other psychological features (see Klein & Nichols 2012). Like behaviors, memories indicate knowledge about one's personality (e.g., "I am usually stubborn"), but they also infer properties and relations between the person at the time of encoding and the later time of retrieval, including a self-referential quality (i.e., a sense of "mineness") that may be the best proxy of underlying psychological stability that people have access to.

In fact, we use episodic memory in much the same way to establish our own personal identity. You take the fact that you remember graduating from college, blowing out candles on your eighteenth birthday party, or even falling off your bike as a young child as evidence that it really was you, and that you existed at that time. This is something that many philosophers have also argued: "My thoughts, my actions, and feelings change every moment—they have no continued, but a successive existence; but that self or I to which I belong is permanent, and has the same relation to all the succession thoughts, actions and feelings, which I call mine . . . How do you know—what evidence have you—that there is such a permanent self which you can call yours? . . . To this I answer, that the proper evidence I have of all of this is remembrance" (Reid [1785] 1969: 318). In fact, research that I (along with colleagues) conducted with US spiritual seekers demonstrated that people who think they have lived before believe that their episodic memory continues across lives (White, Kelly, & Nichols 2015). We intuitively regard memory as the most reliable anchor that holds otherwise disenfranchised events together to form a coherent picture of who we—and others—are. These strategies may operate even though the person in question is a supernatural agent, having survived biological death. Research in cognitive science of religion, for example, has shown that children and adults find it difficult to represent some psychological states, especially remembering, as ceasing to exist after death (Bering 2002).

If memory is regarded universally as retaining identity, then we would expect people who are deciding whether a person has returned to the human world to look for evidence that the person remembers someone or something from their past. As alluded to earlier (in Table 8.1), this is what happens in many cultures. In addition, people privilege memory as a cue to continued identity even when it seems to contradict their explicitly stated beliefs and corresponding dogma on the process of reincarnation. In many Buddhist traditions, for example, people profess that the concept of *anattā* maintains that there is no permanent, unchanging self, yet they seek out similarities in memory to establish the identity of reincarnated Lamas (see Haraldsson & Samararatne 1999). Yet we have to be careful about how we interpret these findings. On the one hand, people could use memory tests as the key to unlocking an individual's true identity, but on the other hand, they could be reasoning about memory in much the same way as they reason about physical features. In other words, people may be simply extending their reasoning as empiricists to memory continuity. After all, people tend to judge the reliability of a memory by how distinctive it is, especially when this is subject to external verification (e.g., that a person remembers the layout of a historical building). The important question here is, To what extent does the distinctiveness matter? If, like physical features, people rely on episodic memories only to the extent that those memories are distinctive, then they are using memories in the same way as they use physical features. If, however, the distinctiveness affects (i.e., weighs the likelihood of a decision) but does not determine (i.e., provide unequivocal evidence for) their decisions, then we can conclude that—as many scholars have argued—there is something special about the relationship between episodic memory and personal identity.

Studies with Western participants

Ideas about how to determine who has been reborn as whom are situated in a particular sociohistorical context. Such ideas are therefore influenced by cultural context. There is, however, a possibility that these ideas are not only mediated by belief in reincarnation or cultural context but also dictated by them. That is to say, perhaps ideas are not rooted in default intuitions about persons at all but are, rather, simply constructed by culture or are a product of believing that reincarnation exists. This is a chicken-and-egg problem that cannot be solved by psychological studies. It is, however, possible to understand something about the relative influence of cultural discourse (and related belief in reincarnation) by investigating similarities and differences between people who live in reincarnationist cultures and accept reincarnation as fact, and those who do not live in reincarnationist cultures and may or may not believe in reincarnation. A related issue with the research described thus far is that it assumes that reincarnation is a bodily change. This assumption is founded on cross-cultural researchers who have reported that reincarnation is endorsed as a bodily change, but what if they are wrong?

To test for these possibilities in our study, US adults (some of whom believed in reincarnation and some of whom did not) first described what they thought the term "reincarnation" meant, and we coded these descriptions to see whether or not they regarded reincarnation as a bodily change (White 2015). Participants also completed imaginative perspective-taking studies in the role of a village leader who believed that reincarnation occurred. The leader (really the participant) had to decide how likely it was that any individual from a number of people (candidates) was the reincarnation of a deceased relative (using a scale, ranging from 1—Very Unlikely to 5—Very Likely) and under constrained conditions (only one candidate could be ranked 5—Very Likely, 4—Likely, etc.). Participants based their decisions on information about the deceased person's features and the candidates' features. (Each candidate had one similar physical, memory, or categorical feature to the deceased.) This task mimics the conditions in which many people who live in reincarnationist traditions actually find themselves. As expected, based on the ethnographic reports and the theories outlined so far, participants judged candidates with a similar episodic memory (i.e., memory of an event) or physical mark (i.e., a scar) to the deceased as more likely to be the reincarnation over candidates with other similar features, including categorical features (e.g., personality traits, behaviors), types of memories (e.g., procedural), and physical similarities (e.g., physique).

The results of these studies suggest that the feature's distinctiveness also drove participants' decisions. Importantly, this was especially true for physical marks. In one study, for example, participants ranked the likelihood of candidates who shared similar generic versus highly distinctive physical marks and similar generic versus highly distinctive episodic memories with the deceased. The distinctive features were similar to the generic examples but with additional information that would make them more distinguishing (e.g., exact size of the physical mark). In this study, participants could rank more than one candidate in the same position (i.e., more than one candidate could be ranked as 5— *Very Likely*), and thus participants were not as restricted in their choices. We found that the candidate with a similar distinctive physical mark to the deceased was rated highest overall, higher than the candidate with the distinctive episodic memory. Further, the mean scores of the highly distinctive features were significantly higher than their generic counterparts. Furthermore, these patterns held across all studies, largely irrespective of whether or not participants believed in reincarnation and even though the vast majority explicitly described reincarnation as involving a bodily change, which suggests that these assumptions are not simply a product of belief or explicit concepts of reincarnation.

In sum, investigating how people identify reincarnated people in cultures where reincarnation is accepted contributes to existing research in two important ways. First, it enables a more refined understanding of how people reason about continued identity when cultural discourse about the process of reincarnation contradicts intuitions about how to identify a person. Second, it provides a naturalistic case study of how people reason about personal identity, something that philosophers have debated for decades. These were the questions that drove the decision to ask people to reason about how they would identify someone who had been reincarnated.

First, as we've seen, we conducted a series of perspective-taking studies in the United States, where reincarnation is not the dominant cultural belief about the fate of people after death, and with participants who did and did not believe that reincarnation was possible. The findings were consistent with the ethnographic records on identification practices and also with theories about the use of physical features and episodic memories to identify people. Next, we conducted a version of the studies with people who lived in the reality of reincarnation. (See White 2016b for the full report of these studies.)

Methodology

Sample

Research with US adults suggests that people are guided in their decisions about how to establish continued identity in reincarnation by both the category to which the feature belongs and, especially for physical marks, by the feature's distinctiveness and thus the reliability of evidence. We know little about whether, and how, these intuitions operate under different cultural input, however. Thus, one important task is to establish, under controlled conditions, whether these ideas are similar or different in another tradition, especially beyond Western cultures, because they tend to be overrepresented in experimental research. We investigated these possibilities by presenting Jain adults in South India with a modified version of the perspective-taking task.

The Jain tradition is reincarnationist, and karma determines rebirth. Jainism endorses the existence of a permanent and enduring self, but what precisely the self entails remains vague (Dundas 2002). This presents an opportunity to probe folk interpretation of ideas about reincarnation. Further, Jains think that with the right prompting, people and other agents can remember their past life, but this is an exception rather than the norm. Furthermore, Jainism lacks cultural practices designed to establish the identity of special people who have been reincarnated, and although they accept as fact that every living person has been and will be reborn, Jains are not concerned with establishing the past-life identity of the living. Thus participants are not able to simply draw upon cultural information about how to establish identity in reincarnation, so they are more likely to depend upon other input. In addition, since information about how to identify reincarnated agents is lacking from Jain scriptures, this allows for the possibility that participants will also draw upon intuitive expectations about the stability of personal identity over time and how to establish it.

Three questions of interest led these new studies. First, will Jain participants also distinguish between different types of physical and psychological features in terms of their likelihood to indicate continued identity in reincarnation? Second, will they judge physical marks and episodic memories over other features as indicating reincarnation? Third, to what extent will increasing the distinctiveness of a physical mark and episodic memory affect people's reasoning about how likely these features are to indicate a person's return to the human world?

Several distinct possibilities follow from what we know about Jains. First, regarding physical features, in Jainism the body is regarded as a vehicle for the *jiva* (i.e., consciousness), but it leaves the body during the process of rebirth. Thus, one possibility is that participants will reason according to the doctrine concerning reincarnation and will not regard physical features—including similar physical marks—between the deceased and living as evidence of continued identity in reincarnation. On the other hand, if participants' decisions are not governed exclusively by doctrine, then participants will regard candidates with similar physical features, including distinctive physical marks, as more likely than other candidates to be the deceased's reincarnation. Second, regarding psychological features, one possibility is that participants will not judge candidates with similar memories to the deceased as more likely to be the reincarnation than candidates with other similar psychological features, because Jainism does not endorse the view that ordinary people can remember their past lives. Another possibility is that Jain participants will judge episodic memories, and especially distinctive episodic memories, as evidence for continued identity.

Participants, materials, and procedure

Participants were sixty-three student volunteers who attended the University of Madras in Chennai, the capital of the Indian state of Tamil Nadu and the fourth-largest city in

India. Jains make up approximately 13 percent of Tamil Nadu, but the university attracts many Jain students due to the Jainology department. The students completed the study on paper, individually, and we instructed them to answer the questions as quickly as possible, without giving them too much thought. The same participants completed Studies 1 and 2 in the same questionnaire, and we conducted Study 3 after the first two studies with a new set of participants.

To get a sense of how the studies were conducted, consider Study 1. First, we presented participants with the following information:

Imagine that you are the leader of a Jain village where they believe that everyone who dies is reborn. As the leader, you must decide how likely five people are to be the reincarnation of the deceased, based on information about the deceased, when he was alive, and these individuals. You must rank them in terms of the likelihood that they are the reincarnation of the deceased. You will now read a description of the deceased person, when he was alive, and decide how likely it is that each of individuals presented is the reincarnation. There is no right or wrong answer. There are no tricks. You have to make an informed judgment based on the information you have.

Participants then completed a perspective-taking task, where they read information about the deceased person when he was alive and information about five living people who were potentially his reincarnation. The deceased was described as having five features. The main question of interest was whether any of the five candidates would be ranked consistently higher or lower than the others, especially candidates with a similar physical mark and an episodic memory to the deceased. We included the other features because they appear in the ethnographic records as guiding people's decisions in real-world contexts. These features were a characteristic behavior and personality trait. We included a fifth property, name, to provide an example of a similarity that was not dependent upon physical or psychological properties. For example, in Task 1, participants read that

The deceased was called Akash [NAME]. He had a mole on his left arm [PHYSICAL MARK]. He widened his eyes a lot when he spoke [BEHAVIOR]. He remembered the day he found a ball [EPISODIC MEMORY]. He was shy when he met new people [PERSONALITY].

In Task 2, participants read that

The deceased was called Salil [NAME]. He had a scar on his right leg [PHYSICAL MARK]. He used his hands a lot when he spoke [BEHAVIOR]. He remembered the day he found a pair of shoes [EPISODIC MEMORY]. He was outgoing and liked to meet new people [PERSONALITY].

Participants then read about five candidates, each of whom had one matching feature to the deceased. For example, in Task 2, candidates were described as the following:

Candidate 1: Was called Salil.
Candidate 2: Had a scar on his right leg.
Candidate 3: Used his hands a lot when he spoke.
Candidate 4: Remembered the day he found a pair of shoes.
Candidate 5: Was outgoing and liked to meet new people.

Participants then ranked each of the five candidates depending on how likely they were, in relation to the other candidates, to be the reincarnation of the deceased.

Results and Analysis

Study 1

In Task 1, participants ranked the likelihood of each candidate to be the reincarnation of the deceased using a forced-choice 5-point scale, ranging from *1—Very Unlikely* to *5—Very Likely*, and based on five matching features between the deceased and each of the five candidates. They did this twice. In Task 2, we provided a new example of the five features as a check that it was the type of feature, not the particular example, that was driving participants' decisions.

The results of Study 1 show that participants judged episodic memory and physical mark categories as cues to continued identity in reincarnation across both tasks. Candidates with a similar episodic memory were placed in the highest possible rank category 73 percent ($n = 92$) of the time. Candidates with a similar physical mark to the deceased were placed as *4—Likely* in 61.9 percent ($n = 78$) of all decisions. Overall, at least 84 percent of all judgments for candidates with a similar episodic memory or physical mark ranked them in the highest possible two categories. This demonstrates a consistent privileging of these categories as indicators of continued identity.

Across the two tasks, participants ranked episodic memory significantly higher than all other candidates, including physical mark, and physical mark ranked significantly higher than all other candidates except episodic memory. The mode (i.e., number that appears most often) for each feature was recorded for Tasks 1 and 2, and Figure 8.1 displays the average of these two modes. Furthermore, a statistical test compared how the items tended to be ranked. It showed that the differences between each of the categories (except between name and behavior) were unlikely to be by chance. In other words, people were consistently judging both an episodic memory and a physical mark as indicative of continued identity, and an episodic memory as the most indicative overall.

Like their US counterparts, Jain participants consistently ranked episodic memory and physical marks as the most reliable cues to continued personal identity. Two findings are of particular interest. First, participants ranked physical marks as indicating continued identity, even though the body changes following rebirth in Jain theology. Perhaps

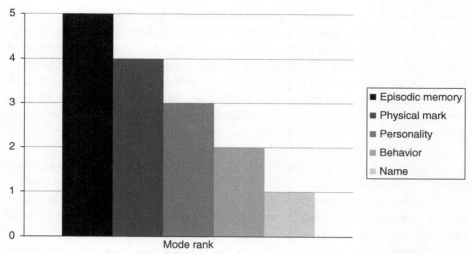

Figure 8.1 Mode rank for features in Tasks 1 and 2 combined.

individuals do not represent reincarnation as entailing a bodily change. We explored this possibility in Study 2 by asking participants their ideas about reincarnation. Another interpretation of this finding is that Jain participants are also influenced in their decisions about reincarnation by unconscious processes of person recognition used to identify people on a daily basis everywhere. A further question of interest is whether Jain participants, like their US counterparts, would distinguish between the likelihood of different types of physical features to indicate continued identity in reincarnation. We investigated this question in Study 2 by asking participants to rank candidates with different types of physical features, including basic facial similarities or bodily marks, as the deceased's reincarnation.

The second finding of interest is that the candidate with the similar episodic memory had a significantly higher mean rank score than all other candidates, including the candidate with the similar physical mark. Why do Jain participants regard memory as such a robust indicator of continued identity after reincarnation? One possibility, as discussed in the introduction, is that participants regard memory as something that provides evidence of continued identity because of the unique psychological relationship it conveys between the encoder and the retriever. Although participants may be reasoning that memory provides evidence of *jiva*, Jain doctrine does not discriminate between different types of memory. For example, a memory of a fact (i.e., semantic) should provide equally robust evidence of consciousness as a memory of an event. One way to investigate this is to assess whether participants will, like US participants, privilege episodic memories as identity markers over other memory types. We also explored these possibilities in Study 2.

Study 2

In Study 2, participants completed another two perspective-taking tasks. In Task 1, participants had to rank five candidates in terms of how likely they were to be the reincarnation of the deceased. Again, only one candidate could be placed in each rank. To determine whether participants privileged physical marks over other physical features, each candidate had a different corresponding physical feature to the deceased, namely, a physical mark, a facial feature, physique, a physical abnormality, and hair type. In Task 2, participants ranked five candidates with different types of memories in terms of their likelihood to be the reincarnation of the deceased. We included three subtypes of long-term memory (i.e., declarative, procedural, semantic) and one memory ability (i.e., aptitude) to investigate whether episodic memories were perceived as more robust cues to continued identity than other kinds of memory.

To determine whether participants held a concept of reincarnation as entailing bodily change, they completed another task at the end of Study 2. We asked participants to select the statement that they thought most accurately characterized reincarnation from a list of four options, including the option "Following reincarnation the body ceases to exist and the person continues to exist in a new body."

Candidates with a similar physical mark and episodic memory to the deceased had a higher mean rank than other candidates in their respective categories, and both were ranked most often as 5—Very Likely. For physical mark, 60.3 percent of participants ranked the candidate as 5—Very Likely and 25.4 percent as 4—Likely. The frequencies for episodic memory likewise suggest that participants also ranked the candidate consistently highly: 74.6 percent selected 5—Very Likely and 14.3 percent selected 4—Likely. Therefore, for both categories, at least 85 percent of all participants placed these features in the highest two ranks (4–5).

Statistical analyses: Comparing mean rank scores for physical features

We conducted statistical tests comparing how the items tended to be ranked to determine whether there was a difference in the mean rank scores for each of the five candidates in the physical feature category. Results revealed a significant increase in most mean rankings, except for hair and physique. Of particular interest was the finding that the candidate with the similar physical mark to the deceased was ranked significantly higher than all other candidates.

Statistical analyses: Comparing mean rank scores for memory features

We conducted another series of tests to determine whether any of the mean rankings for the five candidates in the memory category differed significantly. They demonstrated a significant increase in two mean rankings: from procedural to semantic and semantic to episodic. Of most importance, the candidate with the similar episodic memory to the deceased was ranked significantly higher than all other candidates.

Participants' concept of reincarnation

The vast majority (84 percent) of participants characterized reincarnation as "the body ceases to exist and the person continues to exist in a new body."

The results of Study 2 reinforce the results of Study 1 by showing that Jain participants regard particular types of physical and mnemonic (i.e., memory) cues to establish continued identity in reincarnation, especially physical marks and episodic memories. In addition, Study 2 also demonstrated that Jain participants privileged physical marks and episodic memories over other physical and mnemonic features. Again, these findings parallel findings from the US version of this task, with participants who held mixed views about the fate of the body after death, and cross-cultural reports, which suggest that these two types of features are frequently used to determine the identity of reincarnated agents.

These results beg the question of why episodic memories and physical marks are privileged over other, similar physical and mnemonic features. The consistent use of episodic memory by Jain participants requires explanation. The one proposed here is that they implicitly represent episodic memory as a robust indicator of continued identity because of the basic psychological relationship it conveys between the encoder and the retriever. Another finding that necessitates further attention is the use of physical marks to establish identity in reincarnation. This is of particular interest because Jain dogma presents the physical body as changed in reincarnation. This study also confirmed that the vast majority of participants endorsed a concept of rebirth that aligned with Jain doctrine, ruling out the possibility that we were superimposing a Western concept of reincarnation, which entailed bodily change, upon them. Thus, on the one hand, participants claimed that the body changed in the process of rebirth, but on the other, they reasoned as though physical cues, and especially physical marks, were robust indices to continued personal identity in these contexts. This is commensurate with the theory proposed in the introduction: explicit beliefs about personal identity do not inhibit mundane processes of person recognition where physical similarities provide reliable evidence of continued identity.

It is of further interest, however, because other physical features (e.g., a peculiarly shaped nose) likewise depend upon convenient recognition cues. If participants do reason in terms of the mundane processes of personal recognition, then why do they privilege physical marks in particular? There are likely to be many factors not dependent on the type of feature alone that influence participants' decisions in the tasks. For instance, participants may be acutely aware of any features that indicate an unusual occurrence, how unusual they are for a "normal" person to exhibit, whether the features are present from birth, and even the probability of surface features being alike (e.g., a similar name). Yet in most of the tasks, these individual factors do not appear to sway participants' judgments on their own; rather, participants consistently privilege certain types of features even though different examples of the features are given. It may be the case that some features are regarded as stronger cues to continued identity when accompanied by some of these additional factors.

One factor hypothesized to elicit this effect is the distinctiveness of the features. As discussed, US participants were influenced in this task according to how distinguishing the feature was. Thus, in situations requiring the identification of persons, participants may unconsciously revert to habitual strategies they use to establish identity every day by seeking out physical similarities between people. One possibility is that in the current task, Jain participants were reasoning about these features in terms of their distinctiveness, in other words, how unique or uncommon they would be in the general population. Perhaps, for instance, people regard bodily marks as highly distinctive. Likewise, in addition to the assumption that episodic memory entails personal ownership over the memory, perhaps participants also implicitly represent episodic memories as containing more detailed and specific information than other memories, and they also are reasoning according to the distinctiveness of the memory.

Furthermore, one limitation of the previous studies was that participants could rank each candidate in a different position, so that only one could be 5—*Very Likely*, 4—*Likely*, and so on, because this limited the freedom of participants to rank several candidates as equally likely or unlikely. Therefore, in the final study, like in the US version, participants could rank multiple candidates in the same rank order, which gives a more reliable indication of the reliability assigned to different candidates, independent of others. Study 3 explored these possibilities.

Study 3

The aim of the third and final study with a new set of thirty-four participants was to investigate the extent to which the distinctiveness of a feature (i.e., how distinguishing or unique it was) and/or the category to which it belonged (i.e., physical mark or episodic memory) was driving participants' decisions. We investigated this by manipulating the distinctiveness of the physical mark and episodic memory in the task so that the task contained one generic and one distinctive physical mark, and one generic and one distinctive episodic memory. Participants had to rank four candidates in terms of the likelihood that they were the deceased's reincarnation, but this time, to remove the previous constraints in Studies 1 and 2, they could rank more than one candidate in the same position (i.e., more than one candidate could be ranked as 5—*Very Likely*, 4—*Likely*, etc.). The examples of the physical mark and episodic memory in the task were similar, but one of them contained additional information that would make them more distinctive (i.e., unique or unusual and thus statistically improbable for other people to have). For example, a 2.5-cm birthmark on a person's right arm is a highly distinctive physical mark, whereas a mole on a person's left arm is less distinctive and thus generic. More people have moles on their arms than 2.5-cm birthmarks.

Statistical analyses: Comparing mean rank scores

A statistical (Friedman) test showed that the mean rank score for the generic episodic memory was not significantly higher than the generic physical mark. There was, however, a significant increase in the mean ranking within categories and by distinctiveness from physical mark to distinctive physical mark, and from episodic memory to distinctive episodic memory. Further, there was no significant increase in the mean rank scores for distinctive candidates across categories, from the distinctive physical mark to the distinctive episodic memory.

The results of Study 3 fit the theory that mundane processes of identification, especially considerations about the statistical probability of a person sharing a particular feature with another person, affect reasoning about personal continuity in reincarnation. The results also showcase the cross-cultural similarities in reasoning about reincarnation between Jain participants in South Asia and US participants. Three findings are of particular interest.

First, the data suggest that Jain participants regard physical marks and episodic memories as more or less equally robust cues to establish continued identity in reincarnation, because they did not rank candidates differently according to the category to which the features belonged (generic physical mark or episodic memory). This finding reinforces the findings of Studies 1 and 2. Even though Study 1 suggests that the candidate with a similar physical mark was ranked significantly higher than the candidate with a similar episodic memory, the more general pattern of findings, and especially the frequencies across all studies, show that both features are regarded as robust cues to continued identity. Thus, the findings should not be interpreted as indicating that these categories are not important; on the contrary, there is a ceiling effect reported in the frequencies across Studies 1–3 (i.e., most participants ranked all candidates as 5—*Very Likely* or 4—*Likely*), which indicates that both physical marks and episodic memories are consistently categorically privileged as cues to continued identity. These findings also parallel those with US participants, who also regarded both generic examples of these features as similar in terms of their likelihood to indicate continued identity.

The second finding of interest is the significant increase in the mean rank score from generic to distinctive physical mark and generic to distinctive episodic memory. This suggests that in addition to the high baseline by virtue of candidates possessing a similar physical mark or episodic memory to the deceased, the distinctiveness of these features increased the strength of participants' judgments that they indicate continued identity in reincarnation. This result provides a clear confirmation that distinctiveness of features influence participants' judgments, even when this contradicts explicit ideas about reincarnation as involving a bodily change. This finding can be contrasted to the US version of the study, where the increase from rank scores between generic and distinctive features was significant for the physical mark only. It is important not to overestimate the extent of these differences, however. Both US and Jain participants' rankings increased for both features as a product of distinctiveness; the difference lies in the extent to which they increased for episodic memory.

The third and final finding of interest is the similarity in mean rank score for both the distinctive physical mark and the distinctive episodic memory, and the corresponding nonsignificance in magnitude between them. This suggests but does not offer conclusive evidence for the possibility that Jain participants, like their US counterparts, regard both feature combinations (i.e., physical marks plus distinctiveness and episodic memory plus distinctiveness) as more or less equally robust cues to continued identity in reincarnation.

Limitations

The studies have provided evidence of some relevant cognitive constraints to explain similarities in reasoning about physical marks as evidence of reincarnation, especially heuristics (i.e., convenient ways of thinking) concerning person recognition and the statistical probability that a feature occurs in two people and thus serves as an index of the feature's reliability. Proposed, but not tested, is the possibility that decisions concerning episodic memory may also be underpinned by universal assumptions about what indicates underlying personal stability. Determining which properties of episodic memories led people to use them to establish personal identity in reincarnation is worthy of further investigation.

This research has investigated cognitive processes, but of course ideas about reincarnation do not occur without culture. A more complete explanation of reincarnation should also reference the sociohistorical processes that also give rise to and facilitate these beliefs. Future programs of research should consider how cognition interacts with culture to produce the similarities and differences among reincarnation concepts and associated behaviors cross-culturally. The current research project has taken the first step toward identifying what some of the basic cognitive features in this ultimate explanatory story would be.

Discussion

The aim of this research was threefold: first, to determine whether people in the reincarnationist tradition of Jainism differentiate between types of physical and psychological features as cues to continued identity; second, to establish whether they also show a preference for episodic memories and physical marks; and third, to understand the extent to which feature distinctiveness influences their decisions. The findings suggest that in all three questions, they do. Jain participants, who explicitly endorsed a concept of reincarnation where the physical body changes but where consciousness continues, consistently privileged physical marks and episodic memories, especially those that were highly distinctive, over other personal characteristics.

The results of this research are significant in several ways. First, they complement the ethnographic literature by demonstrating, under controlled conditions, the relative invariance of reasoning about how to identify reincarnated agents. Jain adults from South Asia and US adults who held mixed beliefs about the fate of the person after death reasoned similarly in the tasks. Namely, they reasoned as though similar physical marks and episodic memories between the deceased and the living indicated that they were one and the same person through the process of reincarnation. These similarities held even when they contradicted theological doctrine, such as the divergence between explicit beliefs about reincarnation as involving a bodily change and participants' reliance on physical marks as a robust indicator of identity. Thus, Jains, like people everywhere who use physical marks to establish identity, reason about reincarnation in theologically incorrect ways.

Second, this research is the first to offer a psychological explanation for the trends in reincarnation practices documented around the world and especially in Eastern traditions. More broadly, the research reported here serves as a case study for why scholars in the scientific study of religion need to meaningfully engage with research on how humans think if they are to explain the recurrence of religious ideas across cultures. Practices designed to establish who has returned to the human world are underpinned by similar psychological assumptions about what constitutes evidence of this fact. Intuitive expectations for agents everywhere govern ideas about supernatural agents, and in the face of explicit doctrine they do not simply "shut off" but rather facilitate and constrain so-called religious practices in predictable ways. In line with other research in cognitive science of religion, this demonstrates that there are thus cognitive, or natural, foundations to religious concepts.

CHAPTER 9
IS MEMORY CRUCIAL FOR TRANSMISSION OF RELIGIOUS IDEAS?

Michaela Porubanova

Introduction

Ideas that spread like viruses

In the age of social media, what makes something "go viral"? While the answer to this question is complex, the key element of a viral artifact is that it relates to both the deeper culture in which it takes place as well as the artifact's content. In this light, viral internet content functions as a system of cultural aggregation, maintenance, and perpetuation of ideas through which individuals learn and transmit information. A popular tool for the creation of internet content are so-called memes. Memes repetitiously employ particular images (images shown to have wide-ranging, "viral" appeal) paired with a user-imposed text to illustrate a point about shared social experiences. Facebook and other social media platforms make the transmission of memes quite effortless.

The name "meme" derives from the concept of "cultural memes" put forth by the famous evolutionary biologist Richard Dawkins. In his book *The Selfish Gene* (1976), Dawkins describes memes as vessels for transmitting cultural ideas (fashion styles, tunes, songs, phrases, ways of making things) that spread akin to viruses (i.e., virally) and through this quality easily pass from one person to another. With the rise of technology and social media in particular, the viral potential of information can play an essential role in attracting customers, spreading an important message, reaching an appropriate and/or global audience, raising awareness about a lesser known issue, and, most importantly, changing people's beliefs. But what drove the dispersion of ideas in the time before internet technology?

Some cultural material and ideas clearly possess qualities that make them not only worthy of our attention, but also perhaps worthy of distribution to other people around us. The fate of any information in the process of its transmission—its likelihood of becoming widespread—is contingent, *inter alia*,[1] on its inherent features and qualities. Some ideas have a greater psychological appeal than others and therefore are more easily transferred from one person to the next. Many cultural artifacts—such as narratives, folk tales, artistic expressions, ritualized behaviors, or religious beliefs—historically disseminated throughout cultures are still prevalent, widespread, and quite resistant to potential extinction. An example of an abundant concept is the idea of gods (all-knowing, magically powerful, protective agents that expose sanctions on us), who clearly must have access to our private lives as they are readily available and at our disposal when we need them. But similarly featured concepts can be found in children's stories. As a child, I was fascinated by and obsessively watched an Italian fairy tale series called *Fantaghiro*. The series features a strong heroine with superhuman powers and her ever-present helpers: a stone that could give her advice, a talking wise duck, and a horse savior—three powerful and loyal companions. Similar to many religious concepts, the main protagonists in this fairy tale possess powers and abilities that are beyond their physical, biological, and psychological limits, violating our expectations about them. These kinds of violations are attractive to our cognitive system—we are more likely to remember them, which makes them perfect candidates for cultural transmission. We are more likely to discuss ideas that come easily to our mind, those that are out of the ordinary and those that will be of interest to others as well.

The first systematic examination of the factors that impact cultural transmission began in the 1990s, which, unsurprisingly, coincided with the establishment of cognitive science of religion, an interdisciplinary endeavor to study religion as a naturalistic[2] phenomenon and a by-product of our ordinary mental processes. This systematic study has resulted in our ability to understand why some religious, cultural, and social artifacts and phenomena (ideas, concepts, books, fairy tales) have prevailed and have been preserved over others, and why they have resisted potential cultural erosion and other evolutionary pressures.

Much evidence from religious, anthropological, and psychological research shows that religious beliefs, rituals, and behaviors are by-products of our cognitive and mental functions that had not necessarily evolved for religious purposes (Boyer 1994, 2001; Norenzayan & Atran 2004). Some examples of those functions are theory of mind, detection of agency, and understanding of causality. Theory of mind (TOM) refers to our ability to infer the mental and psychological states of others. TOM makes it much easier to believe in supernatural agents who might have access to our thoughts and secret activities (and therefore can impose sanctions on us). In addition to TOM, our profound and effortless ability to detect agency—understand which entities in the environment possess the ability to perform self-propelled motion, or intentionally decide on a course of action—is evident. Analogously, seeing agents in ambiguous stimuli gives us a tremendous survival "better safe than sorry" advantage. It is clear how those abilities helped prevent potential compromises of our survival throughout evolutionary history.

Expectation violation and memory: Minimal counterintuitiveness

How do those abilities relate to proliferation of religious or cultural ideas? Researchers have suggested that religious beliefs are probably only an expansion of predictions made by the human cognitive system. The pioneering, seminal work of what underlies cultural transmission can be credited to cognitive scientist Dan Sperber and anthropologist and psychologist Pascal Boyer. Both postulate that one of the most crucial determinants of cultural transmission is the idea's memorability (Boyer 1994, 2001; Sperber 1996). In other words, the extent to which an idea "exploits" our cognitive system is contingent on its ability to attract our attention and subsequently be memorized. According to

Sperber and Boyer, the reason why many concepts in religion, fairy tales, or folktales are widespread is that they violate a small number of our innate expectations about the world—or, in other words, possess minimal counterintuitiveness (MCI), which makes them attractive (think of Fantaghiro's companions).

Take, for instance, a levitating dog. Children early on in their ontogenesis[3] understand that despite dogs having agency (the ability to act on their own), they cannot fly. Therefore, the concept of a levitating dog violates their understanding of naïve biology (dogs do not have wings) and naïve physics (if one does not have wings, levitation would be against the laws of gravity). When there is a minimal violation to our innate (ontological) inferences about the world, our cognitive system will be drawn to this violated information, resulting in greater attention and, subsequently, memory for that information. Therefore, as Boyer (1994, 2001) suggested, the culprit of high incidence of certain cultural and religious ideas is this higher level of memorability. MCI theory has gained popularity and become a staple in the field of cognitive science of religion as many experimental, ethnographic, and historical/text analysis studies corroborated its central tenets.

Another important phenomenon accounted for in the overabundance of religious ideas has been proposed by Justin Barrett (2004). Barrett posits the existence of a human agency detection device (HADD). HADD serves a tendency to overattribute agents and their actions in situations of ambiguity. This is an extension of pareidolia, a perceptual propensity to attribute meaningfulness to otherwise nonmeaningful situations (e.g., seeing animals or objects in the clouds). The clear evolutionary benefit of HADD in particular is self-evident, as the failure to miss an agent might pose a survival threat.

The motivation behind the study

The objectives of the study discussed in this chapter were both theoretical and methodological. The main contribution was based on the following key points that needed to be addressed and were neglected by previous studies on the memory for MCI information:

1. Examining memory advantage not only for violations to our ontological (innate) expectations but also for expectations acquired in life through exposure to cultural information (such as that a teacher must be literate or somebody who drives cannot be blind).

2. Taking into account the effect of agency (presence or absence of agents on the MCI effect).

3. Contrasting various types of expectation violation.

4. Reconciling some methodological deficits neglected by previous research studies by controlling for potential confounds.

The key questions that Porubanova et al. (2014) attempted to answer were as follows:

1. Is information featuring expectation violations truly more memorable than information not featuring violations?

2. Are breaches in ontological (innate) inferences embedded in our understanding of folk sciences[4] more memorable than violations to inferences acquired through cultural learning?

3. How does agency play a role in memory for those violations?

4. If this enhanced recall is observed immediately, does it resist long-term memory decay pressure[5] (as that's the most important factor for cultural transmission)?

The author of this chapter hypothesized, in line with the MCI theory, that violations to our intuitive ontologies (how the physical, biological, and social/mental worlds function) will be particularly memorable. However, based on the ample evidence from psychological research showing a profound impact of any type of expectation violation on memorability,[6] expectation violation in general, regardless of its type, should yield greater memorability. However, as pointed out by Pascal Boyer (2001, 2004), violations to our ontological expectations pertaining to folk physics, folk biology, and folk psychology (as explained in note 4) are particularly worthy of one's attention and potent for cultural transmission due to their higher memorability. Previous studies, however, overlooked core-knowledge violations that are based on cultural learning, or learning of conceptual knowledge comprising what can be expected. Thus, a violation to our conceptual knowledge does not necessarily result in violations to ontological expectations. One example could be a judge who is immoral and engages in unethical behavior. We expect judges to abide by jurisprudence and ethics, and this type of expectation is not innate but very much learned through our life experience or education. Our study therefore also included violations to cultural ideas based on our conceptual knowledge (such as an illiterate teacher) in contrast with violations of our ontologies (such as a jumping maple). Additionally, information containing agents (due to their salience) should be recalled more than information devoid of any agents.

Previous studies have observed this memory advantage for MCI, and the results were mixed. However, our research team identified some particular methodological problems that our study aimed to rectify. For instance, it is well known in psychological literature that many factors affect memory. Some of these factors include word frequency (the prevalence of individual words in daily language), word length (determined by the number of individual letters included in the words), and precise exposure time. Our study accounted for all these potential confounds.

Methodology

We developed three types of concepts with respect to expectation violation: one without any violation and two comprising expectation violation—MCI concepts (those that violate our innate, intuitive assumptions) and cultural violation concepts (those violating our core knowledge). In addition to the expectation violation category, each concept could be represented by one ontological category: person, animal, plant, or object. This was to examine whether agency (humans and animals are agents, while plants and objects are not) affects recall for concept categories differently. Each concept contained a noun and a modifying adjective (e.g., "blind driver" contains a human agent and a cultural expectation violation, "levitating rabbit" contains an animal agent and an ontological violation, "drying orchid" contains a nonagent plant and no violation).

There were a total of forty-eight concepts (sixteen per concept category, four per ontological category in each concept category). Since one of the objectives of the research study was to reconcile some methodological deficiencies of previous studies, all concepts were controlled for word length as well as word frequency (determined by the frequency indicator from a database called SUBTLEx) across all concept categories.

The study involved a simple learning procedure. Researchers seated participants at the computer and instructed them to memorize each concept. This was an intentional memory task; the participants were aware that at the end of the experimental session, they would be asked to recall the presented concepts. Each concept was presented in a fully randomized order for five seconds, which gave the participants sufficient time to encode and memorize the material (and perhaps use intentional mnemonic strategies). After a two-minute break, the researchers asked the participants to type all memorized concepts. Two independent coders coded individual responses.

In order to examine the purported long-term survival of MCI concepts, we employed a surprise recognition test. We contacted the participants two weeks after their initial experimental session and asked them to complete a survey that included old concepts but also an equal number of fabricated concepts. Participants' task was to indicate whether each concept was presented in the first, original research session.

Results and Analyses

As already mentioned, we were interested in understanding the memory advantage of different types of concept violations (ontological and cultural) vis-à-vis intuitive, everyday concepts. Additionally, we examined how agency (the presence or absence of agents included in the concepts) affects this memorability.

Immediate memory recall

In terms of recall, as illustrated in Figure 9.1, participants remembered concepts that included cultural violations (CUL) the most, followed by everyday intuitive concepts (INT), and MCI concepts (ONT) the least. Perhaps the most interesting finding emerged when comparing concepts that included agents with those in which agents were absent. More specifically, participants recalled any expectation-violating concepts that included an agent (a human or an animal) significantly more than those devoid of agents. However, this distinction did not matter for intuitive concepts, as participants remembered both nonagents and agents equally.

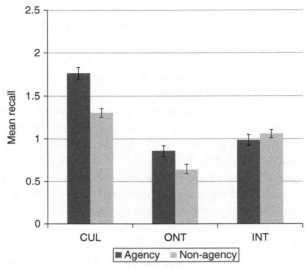

Figure 9.1 Mean recall in terms of concept category and presence of agents.

Delayed recognition

In terms of delayed recognition (two weeks after the original experiment when participants were asked to indicate whether a concept was presented in the original experiment), displayed in Figure 9.2, we found that participants remembered both expectation-violating concepts more than intuitive information. Similar to the results of the immediate recall test, memory for agents was superior for expectation-violating concepts, but the difference between agents and nonagents was not significant for intuitive concepts.

Participants recalled significantly more agents involving concepts with ontological violations and cultural expectation violation; however, this was not true for intuitive concepts (without breaches). Figure 9.2 represents data for the surprise recognition test.

Discussion

The general conclusion that we can take away from the reported study is that expectation violation is a pervasive psychological mechanism that attracts attention and consequently enhances memory, particularly when the violation concerns agents. Furthermore, violating inferences learned through ontogeny (i.e., association between frequently encountered phenomena; e.g., a teacher should be literate) yields more powerful memory effects than violating our innate (ontological) inferences (e.g., a flying coconut). Perhaps violating inferences and predictions we have learned throughout our lives represent an important event; it has a greater predictive value than events that we expect and that meet our predictions. Researchers have conducted much work on probabilities and expected values of an event in the area of statistical learning in terms

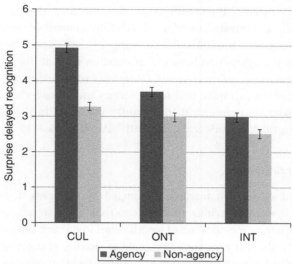

Figure 9.2 Surprise delayed recognition performance in terms of concept category and agent presence.

of Bayesian statistics.[7] Even though most research in Bayesian decision making has been dedicated to the visual domain predictions, it concerns learning in general. Reactions to any stimuli are very much affected by their conditional probability of occurrence (Summerfield & de Lange 2014).

The research by Porubanova et al. (2014) provides further evidence that expectation violation might have played a powerful role in the dissemination and perpetuation of cultural material that contains this expectation violation. Based on the findings from the surprise recognition test (two weeks after the study, when participants were not motivated any longer to memorize the concepts), memory for both types of violation was enhanced, particularly when pertaining to agents.

As there are objections with any study, the study could be criticized for using two different dependent measures in the immediate and delayed memory tasks. In general, recognition (measured in the delayed memory study) is much less cognitively taxing than actual recall (tested in the initial study). Additionally, we might need recall for cultural transmission, as recognition alone might be insufficient. In order to relay information or a story in its original format, we have to readily recall it.

Another objection that needs to be addressed is the study's "organicity." When it comes to learning new information in a cultural environment, remembering is much more incidental—the individuals do not have the intention to remember the information. Therefore, the information that survives the limitations of our cognitive system might possess especially salient and cognitively attractive qualities without utilizing any mnemonic strategies. Our study, however, specifically required the participants to remember the presented material.

Lastly, we can make a theoretical point that memory alone cannot guarantee that a person will be motivated to relay information to another person. Gervais and Henrich (2010) suggested that the epidemiology of belief[8] cannot be explained solely by content biases, the interaction between information content (for instance, violation of expectation) and our cognitive systems. Other cues such as the transmitter's success, prestige, and other demographic and social factors might underlie the likelihood of information transmission and, most importantly, the belief in that information (see Boyd & Richerson 1985; Gervais & Henrich 2010; Porubanova 2015).

Significance of findings

These results and subsequent research conducted by the team helped rectify some methodological flaws of previous studies (controlling for a series of confounding factors highly impacting memory: word length, word frequency, control of latency *inter alia*). Additionally, the study incorporated the presentation of ontological violations in competition with violations to conceptual knowledge. Furthermore, the study is the first to explore the role of agents in mediating the effect of expectation violation on memory, a subject that previous research has largely omitted. The findings have brought important insights to the study of the role of memory in cultural transmission but are also of broader significance to the social sciences, having wider implications for psychological and anthropological theories of cultural transmission.

The study has shown that if information contains expectation violation, it has a potential to attract attention and be more memorable. Through a simple concept-learning paradigm, we showed that individuals remembered expectation violation, particularly violations to cultural expectations. However, the study has further corroborated the postulation that concepts that include expectation violation gain memory advantage over time, which is crucial for cultural transmission (Barrett & Nyhof 2001; Norenzayan et al. 2006). The study has provided challenges to the MCI theory while controlling for important confounds. Purzycki and Willard (2015) in their recent article contested that MCI theory alone accounts for the explanation of ubiquity (adundance) and high survival of religious beliefs. Additionally, others suggested that MCI-ness coupled with other factors of representational content, or the type of concept (agency, emotional evocativeness, or cultural familiarity), might be needed to better explain cultural transmission (Atran 2002; Porubanova 2015; Porubanova & Shaver 2017). For instance, there is a preferential existence of gods possessing predominantly agentlike (human or animal) character, and many supernatural concepts activate emotional responses, as they allow for extenuation of death and anxiety (Atran 2002). In conclusion, the study helped elucidate the validity of MCI theory and the role of memory in potential cultural transmission.

CHAPTER 10
WHAT TYPES OF CONCEPTS MAKE FOR GREAT RELIGIOUS STORIES?
Ryan D. Tweney

Introduction

Almost twenty years ago, a young faculty member from the nearby Findlay University came to my office in the Psychology Department of Bowling Green State University and asked if he could sit in on my graduate course in cognitive psychology. He had a fresh PhD in religious studies, but he had become convinced that we could learn a lot about religion by using approaches from psychology to understand the way in which ordinary people think about religious ideas. His name was Jason Slone, and he is the coeditor of the book you are holding.

As we talked, it became clear that there was a series of interesting research studies that we could collaborate on. We drew in some others as well: Afzal Upal, a computer science faculty member at the University of Toledo; Lauren Gonce, a graduate student in our program; and Kristin Edwards, an undergraduate. We formed the "I-75 Culture and Cognition Group," so named because the three universities—Findlay, Toledo, and Bowling Green—were all along Interstate 75, with Bowling Green roughly in the middle. To avoid the need for Jason and Afzal to get formal parking permits on each visit, we held meetings at Grounds for Thought, a lively bookstore and coffee shop—arguably the intellectual heart of the town of Bowling Green!

Over the next two or three years, our group held discussions, developed research plans, studied the data collected on our campuses, and, in the end, produced four published papers and one PhD dissertation. One of the papers is reprinted below, slightly abridged, and another (by Slone et al.) appears earlier in this book.

Our focus was on what we called the minimally counterintuitive (MCI) hypothesis, the claim that minimally counterintuitive concepts are easier to remember and communicate. According to this view, concepts that violate a limited number of people's expectations are easy to remember compared to concepts that violate no such expectations or too many such expectations. Thus, a minimally counterintuitive concept, a "talking tree," say, is easier to remember than an intuitive concept such as a "green tree" or one that is maximally counterintuitive, such as a "talking tree that flies." Before we started our research, there had been published findings (e.g., Boyer & Ramble 2001) that confirmed the MCI hypothesis—in most cases but not all. Our goal across the four papers and one dissertation was to find out what circumstances contributed to this effect and what circumstances led to a different outcome. The chapter below describes our attempt to extend the idea beyond simply memory and communication.

Memory for culture: The MCI hypothesis

Recent research on the role of minimal counterintuitiveness (MCI) on memory is an extension of the classic work by Bartlett (1932). Using a variety of methods and kinds of material, Bartlett showed that when people recall complex material, they not only lose much of the content, but they also substantially distort what they remember. Arguing for a constructive theory of memory in which an organized representation of a subject's interests and attitudes, called a "schema," together with specific outstanding detail, was used to reconstruct a coherent whole, Bartlett found that people tended to omit culturally unfamiliar concepts or change them into familiar concepts—a finding that seems, at first sight, to contradict the claim that minimally counterintuitive concepts are easier to remember and transmit. Thus, in using a Native American story, "The War of the Ghosts," with British university students, Bartlett observed that the culturally unfamiliar aspects of the ghosts—indeed, any mention of ghosts at all—were often removed in successive rememberings and retellings. By contrast, Barrett & Nyhoff (2001), who presented Native American folktales to American university students, found that students better remembered minimally counterintuitive items in the stories than intuitive items.

For some years now, cognitive attempts to understand the pervasiveness and universality of religious belief have relied heavily upon MCI as an explanation for why certain concepts are easy to remember and transmit. The idea has been applied to the understanding of religious belief; in virtually all of the world's religions, supernatural beings are humanlike in most respects but violate only some of the essential (or "ontological") aspects associated with living, conscious agents (Atran 2002; Boyer & Ramble 2001; Lawson & McCauley 1990; McCauley & Whitehouse 2005). Gods may have emotions (anger, love, etc.) like humans but be invisible, be humanoid in form but lack physical bodies, and so on. Even within religious systems that posit highly abstract and maximally counterintuitive beings, for example, an omnipotent and omniscient nonmaterial god, there is a tendency in popular discourse to reduce them to less counterintuitive form, such as "an old man with a beard in the sky" (Slone 2004). The "naturalness" of religion has been related to similar processes, in contrast to the "unnaturalness" of science (McCauley 2000).

The success of any such explanation of religious concepts faces a considerable challenge in bridging the gap between a purely cognitive account based on memory processes and a full account based upon an examination of actual religion. In the present chapter, we address one aspect of the implied cognitive processes: Can people use counterintuitive concepts in creative ways? Can they invent contexts that make sense of such concepts? To address this issue, we asked creative writing students to compose stories using items on a list of supplied concept terms. Analysis of the resulting stories sheds light on the way in which contexts can be generated to locate counterintuitive concepts in a meaningful context. This could suggest how the creation of new religious movements happens and the way existing religions maintain beliefs.

Research on the effects of counterintuitiveness on memory has generally supported the claim that MCI items are better recalled than intuitive (INT) items (e.g., Barrett & Nyhoff 2001; Boyer & Ramble 2001). Norenzayan and Atran (2004), however, found that study participants better recalled INT items like "closing door" than MCI items like "blinking newspaper" from extended lists of both kinds of items. In a subsequent experiment using MCI, INT, and maximally counterintuitive items (MXCI, i.e., items like "cheering limping turtle" that violated more than one essential expectation), Norenzayan and Atran (2004) again found that participants better recalled INT items than MCI items, which in turn they better recalled than MXCI items.

Gonce et al. (2006) presented INT, MCI, and MXCI items both as mixed lists of items and as lists accompanied by justificatory or contradictory context. In lists, participants best recalled INT items and least recalled MXCI items, as in Norenzayan and Atran's study. But when relevant supportive context was present, they better recalled MCI items than INT items, as Barrett and Nyhoff had found. Further, the presence of contradictory context could change an INT item into the functional equivalent of an MCI item (thus enhancing its recallability), while contradictory context accompanying an MCI item, thus changing it to an INT equivalent, lowered recallability. The experiments were taken to show that context was essential to understanding the role of counterintuitiveness on recall, implying that no "item-centric" explanation could work.

Upal et al. (2007) developed a model of recall in which the interaction between the prior context of a counterintuitive item and the posterior context (i.e., the context following the use of a counterintuitive item) together determined the recallability of the item. Thus, consider the following text in which the relevant MCI concept is a "flying cow":

> "I had just woken up and gone to the kitchen to make some coffee," said the farmer. "That's when I saw the _flying cow_. The twister had lifted the 500-pound creature well over 50 feet above the ground."

In this instance, the flying cow has low _predictability_ based on the prior context but high _postdictability_ based on the context that follows the MCI concept in the story. Once readers know the posterior context, they can combine this with the prior context and the MCI concept to provide a justification for the counterintuitiveness of the concept. Upal et al. manipulated the predictability and postdictability of various concepts and showed that predictability and postdictability ratings and recall of the concepts varied as predicted.

Clearly, what counts as counterintuitive depends upon a dynamic context and hence implies an active rememberer. However, most research on the MCI hypothesis has provided limited opportunity to observe such active processes. Instead, the task demands in every case have required subjects either to remember material or to transmit it to another person. Thus, the present study sought to engage subjects in a more intensive creative exercise to maximize the opportunity for researchers to observe such processes. By using students in an elective creative writing class, and by using a story creation task that possessed "ecological validity" (in the sense of appearing relevant and interesting to the subjects), we hoped to observe productive uses of counterintuitiveness that would shed light on its active processing. Our study was *not* a true experiment. That is, we did not try to manipulate what the students did. Instead, it was an exploratory study; we were hoping to discover something interesting. Our only hypothesis was pretty vague. We expected only that there might be differences in how MCI, INT, and MXCI items were used creatively, but we did not have specific hypotheses about what the differences might be.

Methodology

Subjects

Subjects were seventeen advanced undergraduate students at a small private midwestern college enrolled in an upper-level creative writing class. One student chose not to participate, leaving sixteen subjects (six males and ten females) for analysis.

Materials

We gave each student the same list of twenty-four items—eight INT items, eight MCI items, and eight MXCI items chosen from an earlier study (Gonce et al. 2006). The items were listed in three columns in random counterbalanced order (Table 10.1). Note that MXCI items were longer than either INT or MCI items. In previous research, Gonce et al. (2006) found no difference in recall due to item length (two vs. three words), and we felt that this would not make a difference in the present task.

Table 10.1 Items by item types (number of subjects who used each item in the story task in parentheses).

INT items	MCI items	MXCI items
Meowing Cat (7)	Swimming Cow (6)	Speaking Flying Horse (3)
Hunting Coyote (6)	Admiring Frog (6)	Running Dying Stone (3)
Floating Ice (6)	Giggling Seaweed (6)	Accelerating Turning Plant (2)
Wandering Deer (6)	Chattering Turtle (5)	Singing Dancing Telephone (1)
Sitting Duck (6)	Sobbing Oak (5)	Squeaking Flowering Marble (1)
Crumbling Marble (5)	Melting Lady (3)	Shopping Sleeping Train (1)
Crystallizing Glass (2)	Arguing Car (3)	Chanting Grazing TV (1)
Gossiping Child (2)	Limping Newspaper (3)	Walking Solidifying Pens (0)

Procedure

We administered the task during regular class time. Each student had twenty minutes to construct a story using at least three of the provided items. They were told to write an interesting story with a true narrative structure—that is, one with a beginning, middle, and end—and were asked to not erase but instead to use strikethroughs for deleted material.

Results and Analysis

To analyze the stories, we used two kinds of approaches; one was quantitative—that is, we measured various aspects of each story and computed the average (the "mean," indicated by M below) across the entire group. We also computed the "standard deviation" (SD below); this is a measure of how much (on average) each story varied from the mean. In what follows, you will also find the results of our "statistical significance tests." These are procedures used to determine whether or not two different means are different enough to serve as evidence that they are actually different. This sounds like a paradox; if two means are not identical, why not simply say they are different? The answer has to do with the SD; when it's large, we can't be sure we're looking at a "real" difference, as opposed to one that merely reflects what one or two students did, or simply the fact that there are so many differences among students that the average difference in means is not interesting, or not able to serve as evidence. In the following, you can spot the statistical tests by looking for a "p-value"; for example, $p = .01$. By convention, the p-value has to be .05 or less for the comparison to be "statistically significant."

We also carried out qualitative analyses, a fancy term for saying that we read the stories and tried to see what was different among them. By comparing those that differed in how they used the various kinds of items, we hoped to discover the active role of, especially, MCI items in a creative task.

We gave the sixteen analyzed stories titles and transcribed them for analysis, preserving misspellings, grammatical errors, and strikethroughs. Stories ranged from 109 words to 436 words in length (M = 275.4 words, SD = 92.19 words), the distribution being roughly bell-shaped. Most stories had at least a rudimentary beginning, middle, and end, although a few were less like narratives than scene sketches. We found no differences due to the order of list items.

To initiate analysis, two of the authors independently coded each story on a 1-to-5 scale for overall creativity (without this term being specifically defined). There was relatively little exact agreement between the two sets of ratings, with $r = +0.375$ (r is a "correlation coefficient" that measures the similarity of the ratings from the two raters; it can vary from -1.0 to $+1.0$), although twelve of the sixteen pairs of ratings were either identical (five cases) or within one scale point (seven cases). The remaining ratings differed more widely. Given the unreliability of these ratings, however, there was little or no relationship to any of the other variables assessed, and we will say little more about the ratings. (In a sense, this result is unsurprising. Most studies of creativity emphasize the difficulty of defining the term, and most emphasize that its assessment cannot be based upon the work alone but must include the context of the work. That is, we consider Picasso's paintings to be "creative" not by simply judging the paintings themselves but by judging the role of the paintings among the products of other artists of his time; by their relation to the wider social, cultural, and intellectual context; and so on.)

All of the stories used at least three of the provided items, as instructed, but there were wide differences in the number and kind of items used. Across all stories, students used INT items most often (M = 2.5 items per story, SD = 1.55 items), MCI items almost as often (M = 2.4 items per story, SD = 1.71 items), and MXCI items least often (M = 0.6 items per story, SD = 1.41 items); a significance test indicated that this was a large enough difference (due almost entirely to the very low value for MXCI items), with $p = .0019$. The observed ordering of usage corresponds to the order of recall that Gonce et al. (2006) observed, even to the relatively small difference between INT and MCI items and the larger difference with MXCI items:

$$INT \approx MCI > MXCI$$

where the $\approx$ symbol indicates "approximate equality." All but two subjects used at least one MCI item, and of these two, one used an MXCI item. Thus, with one exception, all subjects took advantage of counterintuitiveness in constructing their story.

Close reading of the sixteen stories suggested that subjects in the task used at least two broad strategies. For some subjects, the strangeness of the provided items appeared to be something to overcome. That is, these subjects appeared to *assimilate* a strange concept into a context such that it was no longer counterintuitive. For example, in the story "Sobbing Oak," the tree for which the story was named was given a metaphorical interpretation, a symbol of impending disaster, thus changing the counterintuitive strangeness of a tree literally crying to a common, everyday meaning. Other subjects *accommodated* (rather than assimilated) counterintuitiveness by constructing a story in which the strangeness of the concept was preserved by constructing a scenario in which "strange things could happen." Thus, in "Strange Forest," a "Speaking Flying Horse" was a character that accompanied the narrator on a journey through an unusual forest that contained a literal "Sobbing Oak."

In an initial classification, six of the sixteen stories appeared to be accommodative in this sense, and the remainder were assimilative. To assess the reliability of the codings, three additional raters, who were blind to the purposes of the analysis, repeated the initial classification. Note that, while it is possible for a single story to use some concepts assimilatively and to accommodate others, in practice there were only a few cases where a rater even suggested a "mixed" coding. For all stories, a global coding into one or another category seemed appropriate to most raters. All four raters (including the initial rater, the first author of this chapter) agreed on the classification of nine stories, and three out of the four raters agreed on the remaining seven stories, for an overall weighted agreement of 89.1 percent. There was 100 percent agreement on four of the accommodative stories and 75 percent agreement on two additional accommodative stories.

Large differences in quality of writing were apparent. Among the stories, one seemed especially imaginative, "Lost on a Dinghy," shown in the Appendix. The story was classified as accommodative, based on its use of a scenario that embodies the chattering turtle and giggling seaweeds, both MCI concepts. Note also that the subject used the sitting duck, categorized as an INT concept, as the equivalent of an MCI concept, since the duck is given a major speaking part! This novel use of an intuitive concept was found only in this one story. By contrast, the integration present in "Lost on a Dinghy" was absent in the story called "Robbers" (see Appendix). This quite mundane account of being awakened by a noise builds a certain amount of drama but uses only INT items, in one case ("Sitting Duck") merely as a figure of speech. We classified this story as assimilative. Interestingly, this is the only story that used *only* INT items. "Spring Day" (see Appendix) is a more typical instance of an assimilative story. The story is scenelike, having only a weak narrative structure. Note that the admiring frog (an MCI item) in this story contributes to the mood but is incidental to the narrative, having been fully assimilated to the structure of the story.

Across subjects, there was a correlation of +0.728 for the number of MCI and MXCI items used, although only four subjects used any MXCI item. All four wrote accommodative stories. Across all stories, there was no statistically significant difference in the number of INT items as a function of kind of story: M = 2.8 Accommodative versus M = 2.3 Assimilative (p = .52). However, there was an almost significant difference in the use of MCI items, almost twice as many of these being used in accommodative stories: M = 3.3 Accommodative versus M = 1.8 Assimilative (p = .08). For this last result, R^2 = 0.202 (R^2 is similar to r, a measure of how strong the relationship is), much higher than the R^2 values for the other comparisons (0.080 for creativity ratings and 0.030 for INT use). Finally, there was a significant difference in the use of MXCI items: M = 1.7 Accommodative versus M = 0.0 Assimilative (p = .0054).

The beginning of "Strange Forest" provides an example of how an accommodative process worked in the story generation:

Once upon a time in the forest of the Sobbing Oak where we will be going on a journey through the forest with Heratio the Speaking Flying Horse looking at the mystery of the forest . . .

The Sobbing Oak is ambiguous in its initial usage—we do not at first know if the term is meant symbolically or literally, but a literal interpretation is suggested once the Speaking Flying Horse is introduced. That the horse has a name suggests that the meaning is literal, setting a context for the rest of the story and allowing counterintuitive concepts as literal entities. In the further development of the story, the writer introduced other such concepts, a total of four MCI and three MXCI, each of which was taken as literal.

By contrast, the opening of a typical assimilative story, "Spring Day," sets an ordinary context, one of walking beside a pond in the woods. The third sentence introduces an

MCI term, admiring frog, but the subsequent context assimilates this item to the rest of the scene:

[I] saw an *admiring frog* hopping around on the grass, looking around at all the beauty of the spring weather and glad to be out of hibernation. I also saw something amazing; a *wandering deer.*

Here, it is the wandering deer that is "amazing," not the admiring frog, because the nominally MCI frog has been assimilated to a context and is no longer unusual.

In addition to analyzing the differences among subjects, we also classified the data by looking at differences among the items used. Table 10.1 summarizes these results. Note that each of the INT items was used by at least two subjects, and each of the MCI items was used by at least three subjects. MXCI items were used much less frequently, four by only one subject each and one item by no subjects. Note that the bottom three MXCI items represented technological artifacts: a train, a TV, and a pen. All of the other concepts provided to subjects were in the domain of folk physics (four items), folk zoology (eight items), folk botany (three items), or folk psychology (two items), and subjects used all of these categories more frequently than the technological categories. The mean number of uses for the technological categories was $M = 1.6$, compared to $M = 5.6$ for all other categories combined ($p = .0005$).

Discussion

Overall, the results confirmed expectations derived from earlier studies of the relation between counterintuitiveness and recall; MCI items were heavily used in this productive task, just as in recall tasks they seem to "stand out." Further, the relative ease of use of an item was seriously reduced when more than one ontological expectation was violated (the MXCI items), confirming Atran's (2002) argument that ontological expectations, as such, matter in defining the degree of counterintuitiveness. The results also support the expectation that similar principles are at work in both recall and story production, as is implied by the claims of Bartlett (1932) and others that remembering is a constructive process.

Are there processes in the story production task that are *not* mirrored in the recall tasks? The most striking such difference in the present results concerns the division into accommodative stories in which sobbing oaks really cried, versus assimilative stories in which the oaks didn't really cry but instead evoked, say, a mood of sadness. Both kinds of stories suggest that the constraints implied by using a counterintuitive item engendered a need to construct a story around the item in such a way that the counterintuitiveness was made explicable, consistent with the argument of Upal et al. (2007) about how the context affects interpretation of a counterintuitive item. However, the present study suggests that there may be different strategies for constructing such context.

Is accommodation more difficult than assimilation? This might be suggested by the fact that fewer subjects generated accommodative stories (although the difference is small and statistically unreliable). Ward (1994), Perkins (1981), and others have suggested that it is easier to generate novel or creative materials when there are constraints on the task that limit the range of possible variations. Presumably, such constraints reduce the cognitive "load" on the imaginative system.

Murphy and Medin (1985) argued that most concepts are in fact part of a larger network of explanatory frameworks and rely upon extensive knowledge of the function, origin, and settings of objects within the category. Knowing that a knife is a handheld device used to cut things, for example, explains why the blade is sharp and why the handle is not. Further, the importance of expectation violation and its subsequent justification (Bruner 1990) is understandable in the context of such accounts—the resolution of expectation violation requires placing the violating concept in an explanatory context, and that is exactly what our subjects did.

Our results suggest the possibility that the role of counterintuitiveness in belief depends upon an equilibrium between preserving counterintuitiveness and explaining it away, between novelty and the expected, between the "taming" of the strange (assimilation) and its acknowledgment (accommodation). Piaget (1958) argued that cognitive development, like all development, manifested both assimilative and accommodative processes, and these had to attain an equilibrium for successful adaptation: "Without assimilation, the organism or subject would be like soft wax, . . . ceaselessly modified by chance encounters or changes in the environment. Without accommodation, the organism or subject would be withdrawn within itself and beyond the reach of any external action" (p. 837). It is not necessary to adopt all of Piaget's theory to see that, in his terms, our subjects displayed a process that could move in either of two directions: toward incorporation into preexisting schemata, or away from preexisting schemata in the direction of the creation of new schemata. Such dynamic processes in imaginative tasks are consistent with the constructive processes discussed by Bartlett.

Our findings also support the claim that the constructive processes by which ordinary memory operates are similar to imaginative processes that produce novel content, as Ward (1994) has argued. Ward's Structured Imagination tasks asked subjects to create new objects by drawing imaginary alien creatures. Most of the invented creatures preserved certain basic aspects of the ontological expectations of earth creatures (bilateral symmetry, two eyes, and four limbs). Thus, his subjects "invented" but not wildly, staying within an MCI context. In an interesting extension of Ward's results, Durmysheva and Kozbelt (2004) asked experimental group subjects to draw alien creatures and were told that their creatures could *not* have two eyes, four limbs, or bilateral symmetry. Control group subjects given Ward's original instructions produced creatures like those Ward saw, but experimental group subjects, who mostly avoided two-eyed and four-limbed creatures but not bilateral ones, produced very different creatures, more like our MXCI concepts. In this study, instructions to avoid basic ontological expectations were partially successful; subjects could move away from earthlike creatures, albeit only up to a point. Apparently, too much novelty exceeded a cognitive optimum, and the subjects thereby simply ignored one aspect of the instructions. In a more extensive study, Ward, Patterson, and Sifonis (2004) instructionally manipulated an alien drawing task across three experiments. They found that instructions that were more abstract (versus those that were specific) led to greater novelty, that is, creatures that were less earthlike. When asked to construct aliens living on specified planetary environments (e.g., a cold, dark, snowy one), subjects were more likely to produce aliens with unearthly adaptations, especially in sensory systems and appendages. In our terminology, Ward et al.'s subjects were able to accommodate their imaginative processes to unusual situations, in contrast to the usual tendency to assimilate to earthlike contexts.

McCauley (2000) argued that one of the overwhelming differences between scientific belief and religious belief has to do with the scope of each as a cultural phenomenon. Religious belief of one sort or another is universal—no human culture so far studied has lacked it, whereas very few cultures have produced what might be regarded as science. Does counterintuitiveness provide any clues as to why this might be?

Like religion, science includes counterintuitive propositions. Wave–particle duality is no less counterintuitive than an all-powerful supernatural being. Even on the level of the day-to-day activity of scientists in research laboratories, the counterintuitive plays a role. For example, Dunbar and Fugelsang (2005), in an "in vivo" study of scientific laboratories, found a high proportion of discussion centered on unexpected results, with a good part of the work done by scientists devoted to understanding such "counterintuitive" results. Similarly, in an analysis of the historical development of induction coils, Cavicchi (2003) noted that utter confusions played an important role in the search for order underlying the complex behavior of various configurations of coil, magnet, materials, and so on. Tweney, Mears, and Spitzmüller (2005) found similar productive confusions in the notebooks of the nineteenth-century scientist Michael Faraday.

By contrast with religion, however, counterintuitive results in science invariably evoke attempts to remove the counterintuitive parts. A result that does not meet expectations must be explained. A theory that makes a wrong prediction must be revised. At this level, science resembles an assimilative process, dependent upon critical, even disconfirmatory, processes (Tweney, Doherty, & Mynatt 1981). Furthermore, these processes are continuing; within the context of a scientific community, there is an ongoing shift from assimilation to new anomalies to further assimilation, and so on. By contrast, religion demands accommodation from its believers; doubt must be resolved in the right way, or heresy is the result. In established religions, although many aspects of dynamic change are preserved, the community of believers is asked to accommodate to a fixed, unchanging, even eternal order. In this sense, the counterintuitiveness of religious concepts is maintained over time and across believers. Such differences in the cognitive and collective dynamics of science and religion are worthy of further investigation.

The paper discussed above has left many questions open. As the other chapters in this volume make clear, there is no one explanation for the prevalence of religious belief; while the MCI hypothesis has been confirmed in a variety of studies, it is clear that much else needs to be understood for a full explanation. This is not surprising—religion and religious thinking are complex and dynamic processes that unfold over time (both historical time and developmental time within an individual). There is nothing "simple" about them. The same is true of studies of creativity. Our study showed that MCI concepts can be used creatively, but that hardly amounts to a general account, not even for story-writing. For one thing, the study has not been replicated, that is, it has not been shown (by ourselves or others) that similar effects can be found with other materials, other subjects, or other tasks. Much remains to be done, and perhaps some of the readers of this book will pick up the issue!

Appendix: Example Stories

(List items are underlined; strikethroughs, spelling, and grammar are uncorrected.)

Story 1.3: "Lost on a Dinghy"

"Its been ~~nine~~ seven days. ~~Nine~~ Seven days out at sea in this weak, yellow dingy that has a hole the size of a pin. Second by second, air is released and I come closer to dying. Oh, cruel world! Why must I die like this!?"

"Oh, come ~~now~~ neh. Iss nah that bahd," said the <u>sitting duck</u> with a ~~British Irish~~ Scottish accent. He has sat on the dingy's edge for four days, telling me "iss nah tha end uf tha world." I've tried to tell the sitting duck to leave, but he continues to sit there, staring at me, watching me dissolve into nothing. The <u>chattering turtle</u> mocks me. Tells me to shut my face and die already. But I refuse to give up. The duck does not like the turtle, and the turtle hates the duck. But most of all, I hate the <u>giggling seaweeds</u> who laugh at my fate. They cling to the dingy, over powering my weak hand as I try to pick them off. ~~Nine~~ Seven days without food and water has left me weak as a sick kitten. On the fifth day, I tried to eat the sitting duck but he bit my hand. The chattering turtle told me to eat the duck, and the giggling seaweeds laughed in unison, impressed by my eagerness to eat the duck. The sitting duck said, "Wahtch oot, mate. Ah'll bite yore hand oof before Ah let yoo ate meh." The chattering turtle said, "Eat him. Eat him! EAT HIM!" The giggling seaweeds surrounded the Dingy and latched on, mocking me.

The sun was blistering. My skin was turning into red sandpaper. Out in the horizon, NO sign of life emerged. This is it, I thought. I'm dead.

"Yore nah dead. Come naw, come get ah bit," the sitting duck said, lifting it's heavy rump in the air. I lunged for the duck, but the bastard bit my hand again. "Nice trah." The chattering turtle swore at the duck. The giggling seaweeds laughed louder. The dingy lost air. I was dying.

Story 1.9: "Robbers"

It was the middle of the night and I heard a quite peculiar noise come from outside. Clammering, Banging. IT sounded as if there were robbers outside. If I went outside, I'd be a <u>sitting duck</u>.

Maybe it isn't a robber. I walked out the back door and heard the noise again.

Something caught my eye. I strained to see it. Just my old, continually <u>meowing cat</u>. That couldn't be making the noise.

It wasn't. I quickly retrieved my gun and walked toward the shadows. And then it came at me. It was harmless, so I let it go. It was just a <u>wandering deer</u>. No robbers at all.

Story 1.2: "Spring Day"

It was a clear march day and I was walking beside a pond in a ~~field~~ woods. Since the whether had started to warm up, there were chunks of <u>floating ice</u> in the pond, as it was no longer frozen solid and the sun had come out. I was sitting on the bench at the picnic table beside the pond, looking around, when I saw an <u>admiring frog</u> hopping around on the grass, looking around at all the beauty of the ~~weather~~ spring weather and glad to be out of hibernation. I also saw something amazing; a <u>wandering deer;</u> a whitetail doe, came out of the woods and went right up to me. I had never seen a deer up close like this before. The deer stared at me for a while, then turned and walked slowly back into the woods. I then went home, awed by the beauty of animals and the coming springtime.

CHAPTER 11
HOW DO RELIGIOUS ENVIRONMENTS AFFECT OUR BEHAVIOR?
Dimitris Xygalatas

Introduction

The relationship between religion and morality is one of the most researched topics in cognitive science of religion, as well as one of the most debated ones. The doctrines of the world's major religions are largely preoccupied with regulating people's moral behavior, which leads many to expect that religious people behave more morally (Chaves 2010; Orbell et al. 1992; Saroglou, Pichon, & Trompette 2005; Tan & Vogel 2008) and that atheists lack morals (Gervais, Shariff, & Norenzayan 2011; Gervais et al. 2017). This assumption that religious people have the moral high ground, which is often perpetuated by religious leaders, politicians, and religious scholars, has been called the "religious congruence fallacy" (Chaves 2010).

Of course, morality is a very broad concept, so there is a lot of ambivalence and disagreement on how to define it and measure it (Xygalatas & Lang 2016). In cognitive science of religion, we take a *fractionating* approach, breaking such concepts down to their simpler manifestations (e.g., cheating, helping, cooperative behavior, etc.) and studying those one at a time. And the bulk of the empirical evidence shows that in reality the relationship between religion and morality is much more complicated than the religious congruence fallacy would have it.

Surveys show that religious people consistently report acting more morally with respect to numerous domains such as empathy, forgiveness, charitable giving, helpfulness, cooperation, and more (Friedrichs 1960; Furrow, King, & White 2004; Grønbjerg & Never 2004; Koenig et al. 2007; Saroglou, Delpierre, & Dernelle 2004). However, almost all existing studies that have looked at real behavior show that this is not actually the case (Batson, Oleson, & Weeks 1989; Darley & Batson 1973; Eckel & Grossman 2004; Galen 2012; Goldfried & Miner 2002; Grossman & Parrett 2011). Similar inconsistencies emerge when we look at attitudes. For example, religious people are more likely to promote compassion and forgiveness, but at the same time more likely to support bigotry and intolerance (Stegmueller et al. 2012).

Large-scale data are no less ambivalent. Pew Research Center measures of religiosity by US state (Pew Research Center 2016) correlate with measures of charity collected by some surveys (Chronicle of Philanthropy 2014) but not others (CAF America 2017). But even if religious states do have higher rates of charity, they also have higher rates of murder (US Department of Justice 2017).[1] So, which of the two is the most relevant relationship? The answer is, probably neither one. If you have taken any introductory course in psychology, chances are that you have heard the phrase *correlation does not imply causation*. This means that just because two things occur together, this does not necessarily show that one caused the other to happen. For example, ice cream consumption may correlate with deaths by drowning, but we should not readily assume that eating ice cream causes people to drown. A more plausible explanation might be that when temperatures are higher, people are more likely to eat ice cream and they are also more likely to go swimming, which increases the risk of drowning. This, of course, also does not mean that correlational data are not useful. On the contrary, they can help us investigate naturally occurring variables in situations that cannot easily be studied experimentally (e.g., using historical/archival data), and they often motivate further research by providing preliminary evidence and revealing interesting patterns.

All this confusion led researchers to realize that the relationship between religion and morality is not as straightforward as we thought. Perhaps, then, we have been asking the wrong question. Instead of asking whether religion promotes morality, it might be more useful to ask when, or under what conditions, religion can promote specific moral behaviors. Two online studies asked this question and yielded fascinating findings. The first examined the relationship between religiosity and the consumption of pornographic material (Edelman 2009), and the second looked at the relationship between religiosity and charitable giving (Malhotra 2010). Both studies found that there was no statistical difference between religious and nonreligious participants. However, both found the same pattern: on days when they attended religious services, religious people watched less porn and made more contributions to charity, although they made up for this on every other day of the week. This behavioral pattern is now known as the "Sunday effect" (Malhotra 2010; Pazhoohi, Pinho, & Arantes 2017).

What this body of research suggests is that while religious individuals do not seem to be more moral than nonreligious ones, being reminded of religion does have an impact on moral behavior. For example, when people are exposed to religious concepts, they are less likely to cheat (Mazar, Amir, & Ariely 2008; Randolph-Seng & Nielsen 2007; Shariff & Norenzayan 2007) and more likely to be generous, altruistic, or helpful (Ahmed & Salas 2008; Pichon, Boccato, & Saroglou 2007; Shariff & Norenzayan 2007). In other words, the effects of religion on moral behavior have less to do with the religious *disposition* and more with religious *situation* (Norenzayan & Shariff 2008).

Several studies had confirmed these findings by using a technique known as *priming*. Priming consists in exposing subjects to a stimulus without any instruction or guidance, in order to study the unconscious effects of this exposure. One of the most commonly used methods has been the "scrambled sentence task," where participants are given lists of words that they must use to make sentences. Some participants receive lists containing religious words like "spirit," "divine," or "God," while others only receive neutral words, like "jury" or "contract." After completing this task, subjects engage in a second task that is meant to assess their behavior (e.g., by providing an opportunity to cheat to win a monetary reward). Those who have been exposed to the religious stimuli are typically found to cheat less in the task (Shariff & Norenzayan 2007).

However, those studies were conducted in laboratory settings, and as a result the situations they used as reminders of religiosity often bore little resemblance to something one might encounter in real life. To address this limitation, I designed a field experiment which used real-life stimuli as naturally occurring primes (Xygalatas 2012). This way, rather than taking people out of context and moving them into a lab, this allowed me to bring the lab into context by moving it into the field (Xygalatas 2013).

The goal of this study was to examine whether people would behave in more prosocial ways when situated in religious environments compared to secular ones. I used an economic experiment to measure one key aspect of prosocial behavior: cooperation. My prediction was that religious disposition (how religious individuals were) would not make a major difference in people's behavior, but those located in a religious environment would be more cooperative.

Setting

The study took place in Mauritius, where I was conducting ethnographic fieldwork at the time. Mauritius is a tropical island located in the Indian Ocean. Due to its tremendous ethnic, religious, and linguistic diversity, it is a fascinating place to study social behavior (Xygalatas et al. 2017). A great variety of religious traditions are practiced in Mauritius, including all major denominations of Hinduism, Christianity, and Islam, as well as Taoism, Buddhism, and various forms of spirit worship.

Because conflict between the numerous ethnic and religious groups is limited, Mauritius is often discussed by social scientists as an example of successful multiethnic coexistence (Christopher 1992). But when one digs deeper, it becomes apparent that there is generalized distrust and suspicion in Mauritian society, both between and within the various groups (Eriksen 1988; Ware & Dethmer 2009). Despite this overall distrust, however, intergroup violence is rare on the island and the local communities successfully interact and cooperate in everyday affairs. One domain of public life where this interaction is most evident is the religious sphere.

During my ethnographic fieldwork, I observed how personal rivalries and antagonisms between local people were often put aside when visiting the local temple or participating in religious events. Moreover, people frequently participated in religious events of other communities. One could see statues of Jesus in Hindu temples, Christians participating in Hindu ceremonies, or Muslims engaging in spirit worship. This syncretism (the blending of different religious beliefs and practices) was further facilitated by state policies, such as having public holidays for the main festivals of each of the island's main religious groups, so that everyone could participate.

Methodology

To examine the effects of religious environments on prosocial behavior, I designed a field experiment that would allow me to overcome some of the limitations faced by previous studies. First, I needed to find a way to expose people to either a religious or a secular stimulus (prime) without providing any explicit guidance, in order to see whether that exposure would have any impact on their behavior. As we have seen, previous studies had done this in the laboratory, but at the time no one had used real-world stimuli in an experimental design.

In the Mauritian context, religious temples provided one of the main loci of socialization. Especially in rural areas such as the coastal village of Pointe aux Piments where I was living at the time, temples were among the few places where people of different families, genders, ages, and castes spent so much time together, along with the local restaurant. These two venues were also fairly similar in terms of their dimensions and spatial partitioning; each consisted of a front porch and a building divided into two main parts: a public room with seating arrangements at the front and a more secluded area at the back (the sanctuary and the kitchen, respectively). I thus decided to use those two settings (the temple and the restaurant) as my stimuli.

This might sound straightforward, but running a field experiment requires a lot of careful planning and involves complicated logistics of the kind one would never have to worry about in a lab setting. Before even beginning to plan the study, I had to discuss the idea with the temple committee and get their approval to use the premises, and I had to do this without revealing the study design to anyone, in case this might influence the behavior of potential participants. In addition, I had to convince the restaurant owner to allow me to use his space for my study and negotiate an acceptable compensation. I also obtained his permission to remove or cover religious symbols displayed on the walls of the restaurant, to avoid priming those participants with religious concepts (since that was supposed to be the secular prime). Obviously, I was asking for a lot of favors, which would have been impossible if I hadn't been living in the village for several months and developed personal relationships with these people. A very important part of ethnographic research is spending enough time with the local community and building networks and connections. And even then, it is never guaranteed that people will go out of their way to help you. I am certainly aware of and grateful for the fact that I have been particularly lucky in receiving so much support from my friends and acquaintances in the field.

Finally, I had to make sure that the two venues were empty and that the experiment did not get in the way of any other activities taking place there. This meant that I only had a window of about three hours per day, during which the restaurant was closed (after lunch and before dinner time) and the temple was not being used.

Besides the locations, I also needed a *dependent variable*, that is, some measure of prosocial behavior that could change as a function of my manipulation (the nature of the stimulus). One of the most common methods for assessing prosocial behavior comes from game theory, which examines people's strategic decisions vis-à-vis those of other individuals. To study these decisions, game theorists often use economic games, where participants' decisions determine their monetary rewards. The advantage of this approach is that it focuses on actual behavior rather than self-reports, which are often unreliable (Brenner 2011). In these experiments, participants must literally put their money where their mouth is. It's cheap to say that if you found twenty dollars on the street you would split it with whoever was sitting next to you. But if an experimenter actually handed you the money, then splitting it has an actual cost of ten dollars. Would you still do it? This is the kind of scenario that economic games create to study people's decisions.

Specifically for this study, I used a task called a common-pool resource game (Ostrom, Gardner, & Walker 1994). A "common pool resource" is a resource that can benefit an entire community but is sensitive to overexploitation by individuals. Human societies deal with the problem of managing such resources all the time. For example, most natural resources, such as water, fishing grounds, forests, minerals, fossil fuels, and so forth, can provide various benefits if managed responsibly, but their overexploitation can cause problems for everyone.

This type of game had already been used in previous studies (Sosis & Ruffle 2003) and resonated with the local context, because bargaining over collective resources was a common part of everyday life in the village, and the widespread suspicion that usually entered into these interactions required people to engage in constant attempts to second-guess other people's intentions. Indeed, when I tested this task before actually running the study (a process called "piloting"), I found that the local people readily understood the rules and outcomes of the game and were able to apply their negotiating skills to the decision-making process.

The rules of the game were as follows: Two participants played the game simultaneously but in separate locations, without knowing who the other player was. They were shown a box containing 500 rupees (a substantial amount, at the time equivalent to a few days' salary for an unskilled worker). This box was a "common pool"—participants could withdraw money from it as they pleased, but their return would also depend on the actions of the other players, and overexploiting the common pool could cause everyone to lose money. Specifically, after each player decided how much they wished to withdraw from the common pool, any money still left in the pool would be increased by 50 percent and divided equally between the two players. However, if the total amount withdrawn by both players exceeded the money in the pool (500 rupees), then both players would lose, and no one would receive any money.

Consider the following example: Players A and B withdraw 100 rupees each. This leaves 300 in the common pool, which is then increased by 50 percent and divided between the two players, so each player receives the 100 rupees they requested plus 225 (50 percent of 450 rupees), so their total reward is 325 each. Now consider this example: Player A withdraws 250 rupees, and player B withdraws 300. Because the combined amount is higher than the money in the common pool (550 > 500), the pool is depleted and neither player receives any money.

As you can see, there is a tension between what is best for the individual and what is best for the group here. Therefore, players of this game need to balance between the selfish impulse to claim as much money as possible for themselves and the consideration for the common good, which is to claim as little money as possible. The amount of money that each player claims from the common pool is taken to be a measure of cooperative behavior—the less the claim, the more cooperative they are considered to be.

In a laboratory study, one typically manipulates the stimuli, for example, by randomly assigning either a religious or a secular prime to each subject. But in this setting, the opposite needed to be done. That is, the stimuli (the two buildings) remained stable, and the participants were the ones who would be randomly assigned and taken to either of these locations. With the help of my local research assistants, I recruited sixty-two participants (thirty-three male and twenty-nine female, mean age = 34.45, SD = 14.71). All of them were from the village and members of the Hindu majority. Two different assistants located in different parts of the village would recruit one person each. Then, one of them would take their participant to the temple, and the other to the restaurant. The order was decided with the help of a coin toss. Participants were not told who or where the other player was.

Once everyone had taken their places, the research assistant explained the rules of the game, providing some examples, and allowed participants to make their decision. They also asked them why they had decided to withdraw that particular amount and how much they thought the other player would withdraw. When the first player had made their decision, the assistant called the other venue on a mobile phone and confirmed a decision had been made, without revealing the decision. Then, when the second player had also made his/her decision, the assistant called back, and both revealed their decisions. During this process, there was never any direct communication between participants. At that point, players were told what the other party had decided and were asked to calculate their own earnings. This allowed us to make sure that they had understood the rules of the game, which everyone did.

Before leaving, participants filled in a short questionnaire and received their earnings. The questionnaire included some demographic information as well as measures of religiosity. The term "religion" means different things to different people, and it is often said that there are as many definitions of religion as there as scholars of religion. This of course makes religiosity very hard to measure, and no measure of religion is perfect, so we can only try to do the best we can by using the measures that make the most sense to our participants themselves. For the purpose of this study, I operationalized religiosity based on two questions: how religious people considered themselves to be and how frequently they participated in religious rituals.

Results and Analysis

My prediction for this experiment was that religious situation (the primes), not religious disposition (religiosity), would affect levels of cooperation in the economic game. Indeed, neither religious belief nor religious attendance had any significant impact on people's decisions. Of all the variables that I collected, only the location had a statistically significant impact on people's behavior in the game. That meant that the priming had worked as predicted. Those who played in the temple claimed on average 170.32 rupees, compared to 231.45 rupees for those who played in the restaurant ($t(60) = 3.90$, $p < .001$).

To make sure that people's decisions had not been motivated by risk aversion (an attempt to lower uncertainty by avoiding risk), I examined how much they expected the other player to withdraw. Comparing the two locations showed that people's expectations were very similar: on average, those who played in the temple said that they expected others to claim 234.51 rupees, and those in the restaurant said 229.84 rupees—a difference that was not significant. Moreover, there was no correlation between those expectations and the amount people claimed.

In addition to quantitative data (consisting in numbers), qualitative data (consisting in words) can also be quantified. This is what I did with participants' answers to the question of why they had chosen to claim the specific amount that they did. When I looked at those answers, I saw that they tended to fall under one of two broader categories: Most people (58 percent) justified their decision in terms of strategy, or logic. In other words, they did what they had to do in order to maximize their profits. But many others (34 percent) justified them on the basis of morality, meaning that they took into consideration what they thought was fair to the other player. The remaining 8 percent gave a variety of other reasons, such as having used their lucky number or relied on chance.

When I compared these answers between the two locations, I found that there was a significant difference. Those who played in the temple had mentioned fairness as part of their justification much more frequently (48 percent) than those who played in the restaurant (19 percent). On the contrary, those in the restaurant were much more likely to mention strategic calculations (68 percent) compared to those in the temple (48 percent). A chi-square test revealed that those differences were significant: $\chi^2(2) = 6.66$, $p < .05$ (Fisher's Exact < .01).

Discussion

A number of studies had provided support for the idea that religious primes can have positive effects on prosocial behavior. Most of those studies were conducted in laboratory settings (Ahmed & Salas 2008; Mazar, Amir, & Ariely 2008; Pichon, Boccato, & Saroglou 2007; Randolph-Seng & Nielsen 2007; Shariff & Norenzayan 2007). The advantage of those studies is that they provide high levels of control, because everything is designed by the experimenter. The downside of those studies, however, is that they take place in artificial environments, which makes it difficult to assess their *ecological validity*. This means that it is hard to know whether what is observed in the lab might also occur in the real world. This becomes an even bigger problem when we study things like religion, which are highly sensitive to their specific cultural contexts (does a lab feel as sacred to a believer as a temple does?).

Similar evidence had come from correlational field studies (Ahmed 2009; Sosis & Ruffle 2003). Those studies have greater relevance, because they take place in real-life settings. However, they cannot support any causal claims, because the researcher has no control over what happens and no way of determining what factors are responsible for the observed effects.

By conducting a true experiment in the field, this study was able to combine a high level of control with ecological validity. A "true experiment" must include a manipulation (e.g., alternating locations), a control group (e.g., a group playing in a secular location), and random assignment (e.g., participants are not found in the locations they have chosen to attend but are assigned to a location by a coin toss). Needless to say, however, there is no such thing as a thing as a perfect study. A natural environment will always be messier than a laboratory, and we still cannot be sure that these effects are not specific to the population that was tested. And even within this natural setting, the measure of prosociality (behavior in the economic game) was not a naturally occurring one (Gurven & Winking 2008). However, more field experiments conducted independently have confirmed these findings (Ahmed & Salas 2013; Aveyard 2014; Duhaime 2015).

One remaining question is how this phenomenon works, that is, what mechanisms underlie the effects of religious primes? It is possible, for example, that people were more prosocial in the temple because the temple is a gathering place for the community, and not because it is associated with religion (Randolph-Seng & Nielsen 2008). This is a plausible hypothesis, but this was the reason that I used the restaurant as the control group—it was a gathering place that was not religious. So this is an unlikely explanation in this case.

Psychologists of religion (Shariff & Norenzayan 2007) have proposed two more mechanisms, which might very well operate simultaneously. First, it is possible that being in a religious setting activates semantic associations with morality because religions and gods are concerned with moral behavior (Bargh, Chen, & Burrows 1996; McKay et al. 2011). In other words, upon entering a temple, people are reminded that it is good to behave nicely. Second, it is possible that religious environments provide a sense of being watched. As most places of worship contain representations of supernatural agents (all those statues, icons, and frescoes looking down on visitors), people might feel that they are under surveillance. Studies show that merely painting a pair of eyes on a wall or computer screen can make people act more prosocially (Bateson, Nettle, & Roberts 2006; Haley & Fessler 2005), and it has been suggested that this happens because of our inborn propensity to pay excessive attention signals of agency in our environment (Guthrie 1995). Images of religious agents in particular may bring about notions of supernatural monitoring and punishment, which are known to motivate prosocial behavior (Johnson & Bering 2006; Purzycki et al. 2016; Roes & Raymond 2003).

As mentioned, these two possibilities are not mutually exclusive. Indeed, in subsequent work, my colleagues and I found support for both by exploring each separately in two further field experiments. In the first study, which was conducted in a library in the Czech Republic, we found that agency cues that were unrelated to religion were also effective in promoting prosocial behavior (Krátký et al. 2016). And in the second study, conducted again in Mauritius, we found that religious agency primes were more effective than secular agency primes (Xygalatas et al. 2016). And in fact, the latter study also showed that the effects of those primes interact with religiosity, that is, they work more for more religious people (Miyazaki 2017). In other studies, we also found that other aspects of religion, such as ritual participation (Xygalatas et al. 2013) or religious music (Lang et al. 2016), can often nudge social behavior.

Research on religious priming has been one of the most prolific areas of inquiry for cognitive science of religion. There are now hundreds of studies published on the topic that have used numerous types of primes and measures of prosociality. Taken together, this body of research suggests that the effects of religious primes on prosocial behavior are robust, albeit not universal (Shariff et al. 2015; Xygalatas et al. 2017).

Good research generates more questions than answers. There are still many things that we want to know about religious prosociality, both from a theoretical and a methodological standpoint. For example, what is the effect of religious primes on nonbelievers or outsiders? And conversely, what is their impact on people's views of out-groups? More generally, what is the dark side of religious priming? And how can we design better studies in the future? For instance, how can we conduct more naturalistic studies without losing experimental control? How can we make reliable cross-cultural comparisons while maintaining contextual sensitivity? And what are some naturally occurring measures of prosociality?

Studying human behavior is never straightforward, especially when dealing with complex cultural domains such as religion. For this reason, it is imperative that we base our inferences on cumulative evidence rather than any single study and that we keep working toward better models, that is, better approximations of reality. Research on religious prosociality is taking these problems seriously and is making real progress toward answering some of our most pressing questions about religion.

CHAPTER 12
CAN WE MODEL RELIGIOUS BEHAVIOR USING COMPUTER SIMULATION?
Justin E. Lane and F. LeRon Shults

Introduction

Many of the studies discussed in this volume illustrate the fruitfulness of cognitive science as an approach to explaining recurrent patterns of religious belief and behavior. What sets cognitive science apart from other sciences, and cognitive psychology apart from other branches of psychology, is its focus on the way in which humans represent, process, and transform information. Given this strong emphasis on information processing within cognitive science, it might come as a surprise that so few scholars in cognitive science of religion (CSR) have employed computational models to study the processing of "religious" information. The good news is that the use of such models is rapidly growing in popularity.

The study we discuss here is an example of a scientific attempt to study the mechanisms of religious belief and behavior *in silico*, that is, within artificial minds and societies programmed into computer software. Many scholars work with the assumption—either implicitly or explicitly—that human information processing utilizes a kind of software (a set of evolved cognitive mechanisms) that is generally shared across the species as a result of natural selection. By way of analogy, we can think of the "brain" as the hardware of a computer and the "mind" as the software that runs on (or through) it. Cognitive scientists are preoccupied with the algorithms of this "mind" software. Algorithms are simple sets of rules and directions that can be followed to achieve some purpose, such as a calculation. Algorithms are used in many ways in computer science; for example, to send and receive emails, to track posts on social media, and to analyze "big data" for analytic or predictive purposes (Siegel 2013). So, if algorithms can be programmed in computer software, and our minds can be said to work by processing information with psychological algorithms, why not use computer software to study *religious* aspects of the human mind? This is exactly what we did in the study discussed in this chapter.

Although in recent decades computer modeling and simulation has become seen as a "third pillar" of science, alongside theory and experimentation (Yilmaz 2015), it has only recently taken root within CSR (Braxton, Upal, & Nielbo 2012; Lane 2013). People all too often shy away from computational methods because of the learning curve involved in becoming a good programmer. However, a computer model is simply a formalization of a theory (or integration of theories) in computer code. The theories involved do not have to be reinvented. The "architecture" within a computational model can take a theory that is presented in a narrative (such as a book on religion) or graphical form (such as a flow chart describing the relationship between different things) and put it into a coded form.

Naturally, using a tool such as a computer puts specific demands on the researcher. For example, all aspects of the theory must be carefully specified. This allows one not only to clearly demarcate the interrelationships between variables but also to clarify what the theory covers and what it does not. Computer modeling also provides a way of combining theories and testing the extent to which they are compatible with one another. In the research described below, we developed a computational architecture that integrated insights from empirical findings based on multiple theories relevant for understanding and explaining the relationship between religiosity and threats to an individual's own life.

Theoretical Background

The construction of the computer model and design of the simulation experiments in the current study was guided by terror management theory (TMT). One of the most empirically verified theories in psychology, TMT has grown in importance as concerns about death threats, and their possible connection to religion, have increasingly gripped our attention in recent years (Pyszczynski, Greenberg, & Solomon 2003). TMT looks at what is called *mortality salience*, or an awareness of one's own death. The basic hypothesis of TMT is that when mortality salience is stimulated (e.g., through the perception of threats), humans somewhat automatically process that information using a set of cognitive defaults, such as scanning for hidden agents and implicitly defending one's worldview. For example, after a major earthquake in New Zealand, which presented people there with the very real possibility of their own death, church attendance increased significantly (Sibley & Bulbulia 2012).

How is this relevant for religion? Many empirical studies have shown that perceiving gods and practicing rituals can alleviate some of the fear and anxiety associated with the experience of hazards in the natural or social environment. In other words, mortality salience amplifies people's tendency to believe in—and look for—familiar supernatural agents as well as to participate in—and long for—familiar religious rituals (e.g., Norenzayan et al. 2009; Vail, Arndt, & Abdollahi 2012). One of the most common findings in this sort of literature is that individuals with higher initial religiosity (or fundamentalism) will also have higher susceptibility to these tendencies. As we will see below, the computational architecture of the model in the study under discussion takes this into account.

The study design also tried to account for several other theories about related cognitive mechanisms. For example, some information processing systems evolved to help us navigate threats such as predators or disease. Other more general systems evolved to support our capacity for socializing within groups. In the deep evolutionary past, our ancestors would have needed to be wary of many potential threats, including those that fall into the general categories of predation, social others, contagion, and natural disasters. While our modern world is less "risky" for the average human, we are still vulnerable and our evolved minds respond to all of these threats. For example, outdoor excursions in many parts of the world could potentially result in people coming across the path of a predatory animal. Similarly, contagion poses a serious threat in many contexts. Although not a natural "predator," the animal which kills the most humans—hundreds of thousands every year—is the mosquito, which carries diseases such as malaria. Additionally, natural disasters such as tornadoes, floods, blizzards, tsunamis, and volcanos, which affect the lives of millions of individuals each year, often have high death tolls. Lastly, threats from social others can challenge our sense of existential security. In the ancestral past, being excommunicated from a group could be akin to a death sentence, since solitary living would have been extremely difficult in many regions.

Scholars generally agree that certain ways of reacting to these sorts of threats were naturally selected in ancestral environments. For example, the tendency to engage in ritual behaviors, which helped to reduce anxiety when confronted with such hazards, could have been selected both for its health-producing and society-strengthening benefits. For the purposes of this chapter, the main point is that a variety of theories from disciplines such as evolutionary biology and cultural anthropology shed light on the mechanisms that shape the mutual impact of mortality salience and religion. But what, exactly, is religion? As scholars such as J. Z. Smith (2004) have pointed out, "religion" is not a single thing in the concrete world but an academic abstraction. In other words, it is not a "natural kind" (such as "flowering plants," which are distinct from "nonflowering plants" in nature) and cannot be studied as a physical object. Rather, "religion" is a constructed category (such as "weeds," a term used in some cultures to identify unwanted plants), and "religion" is a highly contested constructed category.

In the current study, it was important to develop a definition that would allow us to measure—if only indirectly—the types of beliefs and behaviors that are typically referred to as "religious" in the real world. For the purposes of this study, we used the term *religion* to designate "socially shared cognitive and ritual engagement with supernatural agents postulated within one's in-group." This usage was intended to capture the variables that are relevant for the most common findings in the TMT literature described above. We conceptualized religiosity as the combination of two reciprocally reinforcing, evolved dispositions: the tendency to infer humanlike supernatural causes and the tendency to prefer coalition-favoring supernatural norms, both of which are activated when people are confronted with ambiguous or frightening phenomena. Following Shults (2014), the study referred to these sets of mechanisms as "anthropomorphic promiscuity" (AP) and "sociographic prudery" (SP).

Methodology

As mentioned above, this research study utilized computer modeling and simulation methodologies. It developed two models and designed several simulation experiments to analyze and explore the relationship between terror management and religion. The first was a system dynamics model (SDM), which attempted to capture the basic interactions among the key variables mentioned above as they impact an *individual's* processing of information related to death threats and religion. The second was an agent-based model (ABM), which attempted to capture these and other group-related variables in order to analyze and explore the *social* interaction among agents in an artificial environment. The details and source code for both models are available online at https://github.com/ SimRel/20160417_NAHUM.

An SDM formalizes the interactions between variables using flows, stocks, dynamic variables, and static variables (or parameters). SDMs also assume that there is a "currency" that flows through the model (like water flows through pipes, or electricity through wires). In this case, the currency is information related to death and religion. "Flows" move the currency from one place to another. "Stocks" store the currency as it waits to be moved to another place (another stock). "Dynamic variables," such as the strength of one's religiosity after a particular experience, can change during a simulation. "Static variables" (or parameters), such as the rate at which a particular experience loses its power in our minds, don't change throughout a simulation. The SDM shown below (Figure 12.1) depicts the postulated interactions among the relevant religiosity and hazard variables in our study.[1]

Notice that the architecture depicts all four of the hazard types discussed above, as well as their impact on AP and SP. In other words, the model captures the interaction of both personal and environmental variables. Without going into all the technical details, it is important to point out that the model also includes two "decay" rates. *Religiosity_ Decay* is the rate at which an individual's heightened levels of religiosity (AP and SP) decrease over time. *Habituation_Rate* measures the rate at which an individual's threat-related anxiety decreases over time as they perform rituals with other in-group members. An example of this can be found in the way that many people find comfort when their group holds prayer circles or candle-light vigils after traumatic public events like acts of terrorism.

As we described in the theory section, there are clear overlaps between terror management theory and hazard precaution theory (including the security motivation system). Computer modeling helped us not only formalize each theory but also specify how we understand the theories fitting together within a more complex picture of human cognition. However, the SDM is only able to portray the information processing of a single individual's way of managing terror. It does not allow exploration of the social interactions of heterogeneous individuals from distinct groups as they respond to environmental threats. For that, we needed to develop an ABM, which involves many individual programs (agents) that can interact with each other and their environment. As they interact during a simulation, the agents and the environment are altered. In the model below, agents were assigned to one of two groups so that we could account for differences between in-group and out-group interactions.

This second model took the form of a multiagent artificial intelligence model (Lane 2013). In this case, the rules each agent follows (or their "cognitive architectures") were inspired by psychological mechanisms tested in the empirical literature. The agents are

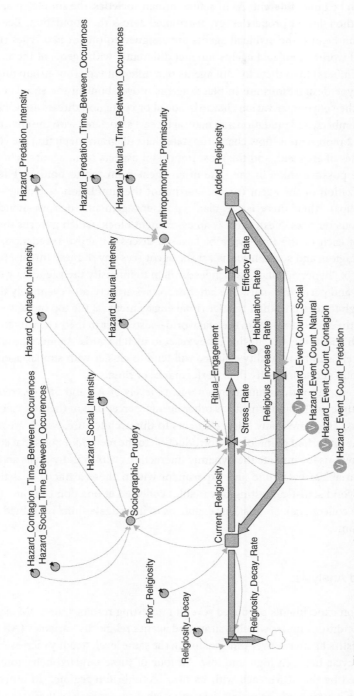

Figure 12.1 Depiction of the variables in the system dynamics model and their interactions.

heterogeneous, which means that their internal variables, such as the tendency to react to threats, can be quite different. As in actual human societies, the simulated agents are unique, and the relevant properties are distributed across the population. Before each simulation run begins, the artificial agents are assigned to one of two types (groups). As in the real world, simulated agents interact differently with agents of the same type (in-group members) than they do with agents of a different type (out-group members). Once these type designations are in place, agents move about in the simulated world and react as they encounter various hazards: social or contagion threats associated with out-group members, and predation and natural threats associated with the environment.

Figure 12.2 represents a "flow chart" (or state chart diagram) depicting the rules that affect the states of an agent, and the most important aspects of an agent's actions. One can trace the possible shifts in the state of an agent from top to bottom. First, there is the initialization of the agent (or the starting of the simulation, when agents were put into groups). Then there is "regular" ritual engagement, such as attendance at weekly religious services. Next, there is an assessment block, which governs the agent's perception of each of the four types of hazards discussed above (predation, natural hazards, contagion, and social hazards). If the agent sees any of these threats, the agent enters a state of "hypervigilance," which leads them to intensify their tendency to create ritual groups and perform rituals. The latter decreases anxiety, and eventually the agent is calm enough to return to their regular ritual engagement (at the top of Figure 12.2).

Agents in the simulation—as in the real world—also differ in their capacity to tolerate threats, which affects the way in which they react to such hazards. Agents whose stress is strongly exacerbated by mortality salience will tend to cluster with similar agents from their own group and to intensify their performance of rituals.

In any given run of the simulation, an agent's levels of AP and SP (i.e., religiosity) change over time, which in turn affects other agents' perception of them as viable ritual coparticipants. There are many other elements to this architecture, which are available online, but the important point for this introduction to the methodology is that computer modeling allows us to simulate the dynamic interactions within individuals and groups (and their variables) over time and experiment within these artificial societies. This moves far beyond statistical testing of variables collected at one point in time (or even over multiple collections). Simulations enable us to investigate shifts in individuals and groups over time.

Results and Analysis

Our simulation experiments produced several interesting results. Our SDM allowed us to find the conditions under which a simulated agent's religiosity variables (AP and SP) follow four distinct patterns over time: maintain the same level, steadily increase, steadily decrease, or cycle between high and low. All four of these targeted behavioral trends were produced by the SDM, each with its own "equilibrium regime." In other words, the simulation experiments helped us determine what causes each of these trends in the

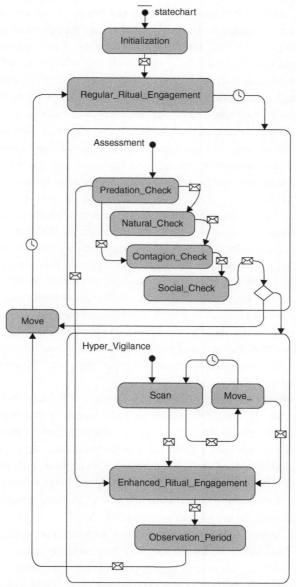

Figure 12.2 Key parts of the state chart diagram for the agent-based model.

model and the most likely conditions (compared to all potential settings) that would optimize the chances of the emergence of each trend. These simulation experiments replicated the findings of other types of experiments in TMT literature (Norenzayan et al. 2009; Poulter et al. 2016; Vail et al. 2010), which lends plausibility to the causal architecture of the model.

Let's take the "cyclical" behavioral regime as an example. Keep in mind that the SDM only deals with a single individual. Our experiments showed that simulated individuals tended to cycle between low and high levels of religiosity when the habituation rate was relatively high and the religiosity decay rate much higher than any of the other target outcomes (maintain, increase, or decrease). The "optimal" cyclical condition emerged when an individual in the simulation encountered highly salient threats with moderately high frequency. Individual religiosity is normally preserved at a base level but increases in the presence of environmental threats. Individuals can then alleviate their stress by intensifying their scanning for supernatural agents and their participation in in-group religious rituals. This has been found in other cross-cultural studies as well that have found a relationship between environmental threats and religious ritual behavior (Gelfand et al. 2011).

The SDM validation experiments resulted in some patterns that we had not anticipated. Extreme changes in religiosity occurred as the distance between AP and SP values increased. In other words, the more that a person's tendency to detect supernatural agents differed from their tendency to protect the norms of their group, the more likely they would be to experience an *extreme* change (increase or decrease) in religiosity. By revealing this sort of surprising relationship between variables, computer modeling can raise new research hypotheses, which can then be tested using laboratory experiments or other methods. If an individual's religiosity variables (AP and SP) could be manipulated so that they differed strongly, would this lead to extreme changes in their religiosity? What sort of theoretical implications would follow from such an empirical finding?

The ABM simulations also produced interesting results. One set of experiments was able to replicate the common finding in TMT literature that fundamentalists are more affected under threat, that is, that their religiosity spikes more strongly than nonfundamentalists when they experience mortality salience. As expected, simulated agents who were initialized with high religiosity had the highest levels of culminating AP and SP, while individuals with low prior AP or SP never achieved the same high levels of religiosity as they responded to threats and engaged in simulated ritual interactions. This finding helped validate the causal architecture of the ABM.

Perhaps more interesting were the results from the second set of experiments, which focused on the relationships between majority and minority groups, and the way in which mortality salience was related to group ritual size. We found that the religiosity (AP and SP) of individuals in minority groups was more likely to increase than that of individuals in majority groups. This was especially the case for SP. If the tendency to protect the norms of one's in-group is easily activated by encounters with threats from social "others," it is not surprising that agents in the minority group, who would be more likely to be confronted by a member of the majority group, would have higher religiosity. This is an example of the way in which computational models can "generate" the phenomena being investigated. We did not program the macro-level or group phenomena into the model; instead, it emerged—or was generated—from the micro-level behaviors and interactions of the simulated agents.

What emerged in the simulations was in fact similar to what emerges in the real world. For example, members of the African American minority group in the United States are far more likely to be religious than white majority group members. A similar argument can be made in relation to another finding of this simulation experiment, namely, that the largest ritual clusters in the artificial society were more likely to be formed by homogenous populations with low levels of tolerance. In the United States, churches with clearly delineated shared beliefs and relatively little tolerance for deviance have historically declined less rapidly than other churches and in some cases experience significant growth (Kelley 1986). The study had several other interesting findings, but these examples should give the reader a sense of how computer simulation can help us explore and analyze the relationship between death threats and religion.

Discussion

This study is significant for both material and methodological reasons. First, the simulation experiments shed light on the variety of ways in which mortality salience can affect the religiosity of individuals as they interact across groups in response to real or imagined threats. The phenomena associated with "religion" are quite complex, as are the relationships between environmental stimuli and religious beliefs and behaviors. The research described in this chapter helps to clarify the ways in which different kinds of "hazards" can alter different aspects of religiosity. SP (protecting supernatural norms) is impacted more strongly by social and contagion hazards, while AP (detecting supernatural agents) is impacted more strongly by natural disasters and predatory hazards. This makes sense: threats related to disease and challenges to in-group norms are socially mediated, while predation and environmental threats are typically perceived as beyond human control.

The computational methodology utilized in this study enabled scholars to explore the cognitive mechanisms that guide human responses to mortal threats in a far more systematic way than ever before. By formalizing and integrating the relevant theories within a single computational architecture, the models described here provide a tool for other scholars in CSR and other fields to use in their own explorations of the relationship between terror management and religion. The use of "computer modeling" might seem out of reach to many scholars, but there are a variety of relatively easy-to-use tools that are freely available, such as the software platform NetLogo (Wilensky 1999) and BehaviourComposer (Kahn & Noble 2010). There are also introductory books to aid newcomers, such as Railsback and Grimm's *Agent-based and Individual-based Modeling* (2011).

Criticisms/weaknesses

One of the main weaknesses of the two models in this study was that agents' religiosity never goes below the state at which it is initialized. This is probably why the simulation experiments did not also replicate the curvilinear relationship between religiosity and mortality salience that is found in other TMT research (Poulter et al. 2016). A model that could simulate that sort of relationship would require agents that could have extremely low or no religiosity. Such a model could also shed light on the differences between the ways in which religious and secular worldviews can impact terror management.

Suggestions for further studies

Several recent studies have begun to delve further into the way in which cultural and environmental differences can affect the activation and operation of the hazard precaution system. For example, a study by Mort, Fux, and Lawson (2015) found that people in the United Kingdom and South Africa had significantly different interpretations of the salience of various hazards (e.g., predation was of far less concern in the former than in the latter country). That same study found that participants of different genders and ethnicities also showed significant differences in their assessment of hazards. The computational models described above could be extended to incorporate these kinds of demographic variables and further validated using the data collected by Mort et al.

The popularity of computer modeling in CSR continues to grow. This relatively new tool enables us to formalize complex theories about social and "religious" phenomena with far greater specificity than has been possible with narrative formulations of theories, such as those typically used in religious studies. It also provides a way of designing experiments on these phenomena *in silico*, which overcomes some of the feasibility problems and ethical limitations of experiments in the laboratory or *in situ*, such as those typically done by psychologists or anthropologists. Scientific research often involves a reduction of the phenomena associated with religion into component parts in order to study small sets of causal variables. Computer modeling and simulation complements such methodologies by "reproducing" the phenomena that they have "reduced," incorporating and integrating their insights into computational architectures which, in turn, generate new hypotheses for further testing.

CHAPTER 13
DOES GOD MAKE YOU GOOD?
Azim Shariff and Ara Norenzayan

Introduction

It has been twenty-five centuries since Critias—author, tyrant, uncle of Plato—raised the question of whether believing in the gods makes humans more ethical. Despite ample discussion over the ensuing millennia, no satisfying last word on this question has emerged (and you're unlikely to get one here). However, by taking advantage of rigorous research methods from psychology and experimental economics, our article from more than a decade ago (Shariff & Norenzayan 2007) potentially served as the first word in a new approach to trying to test Critias's question.

The theoretical question: Why might God make us good?

Prosocial behavior, defined simply as behavior that benefits others at an immediate cost to the self, is a critical component to the large-scale cooperation that has made our species so successful. Mechanisms that allow small-scale cooperation are innate, evolved fixtures of human psychology—and to some degree that of thousands of other species. When a mother bird regurgitates a worm into the greedy mouths of her chicks, that is a prosocial act—the mother is expending her energy searching for (and half-digesting) food for the benefit of her children. This type of family-based prosociality is explained by the evolutionary math of "kin selection"; the genes of generous, prosocial parents are more likely to thrive than are those of selfish parents who let their helpless offspring starve (Hamilton 1963). Similarly, genetic evolution can explain why people are willing to engage in reciprocal, I-scratch-your-back-you-scratch-mine arrangements; doing someone a favor now in exchange for them doing you a favor later leaves both parties (and their genes) better off (Trivers 1971). But these genetic mechanisms can't explain how large groups of anonymous, unrelated strangers can live together in relative harmony. And indeed, this type of hypersociality is a relatively recent phenomenon. Prior to about twelve thousand years ago, and for the vast history of our species, humans only lived with people whom they knew well, with group sizes hovering around 50 and never exceeding about 150—the theoretic maximum for how many people you can know well (Dunbar 1993). With no relevant genetic change that can explain what changed from 10000 BCE (when group sizes were small) to, say, 6500 BCE (when Çatalhöyük, Turkey, boasted 7,500 residents), we turn to cultural, rather than genetic, explanations.

God beliefs are a natural candidate for the type of cultural innovation that could have helped scale up cooperation. Today, most of the world believes in gods that share a set of common features: they tend to be moralizing (caring about humans' moral transgressions), omniscient (able to monitor humans' immoral behaviors—and sometimes thoughts), and punitive (able to dole out punishments and rewards for those immoral behaviors—and sometimes thoughts) (Norenzayan 2013). These features make the belief in gods appear to be an ideal solution to the problem of anonymity-driven freeriding. The omniscient eyes of God robbed people of the anonymous corners in which people could previously transgress with impunity. A god that could see everything and punish anyone served as a divine police force—one unrestricted by the physical limitations of its earthly counterpart.

But gods were not always thus. Archeological evidence and observation of modern hunter-gatherer tribes (who serve as loose analogues to how our ancestors lived prior to the agricultural revolution and settling into large sedentary communities) suggest that these moralizing, omniscient, punitive "big" gods are (relatively) recent innovations. The old gods were small, weak, fallible, and unconcerned with human morality (Boehm 2008; Swanson 1960). Big gods were not the default; they were cultural innovations. They came about for a reason. As societies became larger, the gods became bigger. And while there are multiple explanations as to why, we and others have argued that these big gods emerged precisely because of how effective they were at deterring large groups of anonymous strangers from morally transgressing and freeriding on each other (Norenzayan 2013; Norenzayan & Shariff 2008; Norenzayan et al. 2016; Shariff, Norenzayan, & Henrich 2009). This occurred, we suggest, through a process of cultural evolution: those societies that stumbled on the idea of big punitive gods were able to stabilize more cooperation and thus grow larger and in turn compete more favorably against other smaller and less cohesive societies. Over time, these societies—and the beliefs they carried—displaced others and inherited the earth.

There is circumstantial evidence supporting this hypothesis. For one, these types of big gods tend to be more likely to emerge in places in which such cooperation is especially necessary, such as in larger societies (Roes & Raymond 2003) and those with deep market integration (Henrich et al. 2010) and acute water shortages (Snarey 1996)—both of which require a high level of trust and cooperation. However, the theory requires it to be true that the thoughts about gods—about these divine deterrents—actually compels people to act in less selfish, more cooperative ways toward anonymous strangers. In other words, it requires an affirmative answer to Critias's question.

The methodological question: How can we test the hypothesis?

Earlier research had attempted to test Critias's question by comparing whether people who reported being more religious also reported engaging in more prosocial behavior. The results generally showed that indeed the religious were more prosocial. For example, in his analysis of the Social Capital Community Benchmark Survey, Brooks (2003) found that 91 percent of religious people (operationalized as those who reported attending religious services once or more per week) donated to at least one charity, whereas the comparable figure for secular people (those who explicitly indicated that they had no religion, or attended services fewer than a few times per annum) was 66 percent. The pattern was the same for volunteering: 67 percent of religious people reported volunteering, compared to 44 percent of secular people, and this pattern held when controlling for gender, age, political identification, education level, marital status, and income. Other research corroborated these findings even when removing church donations from the calculus or when using informal metrics of donation such as blood donation or giving food to the homeless (Brooks 2006). Based on this body of work, Brooks drew the conclusion that "religious people are, inarguably, more charitable in *every measurable way*" (Brooks 2006: 40, emphasis in original).

But this method of research has potentially serious limitations. First, self-reports of prosocial behavior are notoriously unreliable, given that people are motivated not just to present a positive picture of themselves to others (something called *impression management*), but also because people are motivated to hold exaggeratedly positive views *of themselves* (something called *self-deceptive enhancement*) (Paulhus 1984). Moreover, this social desirability issue casts suspicion not only over reports of prosocial behavior but also over people's reports of their religiosity. Because piety tends to be socially valued, and religious doubt socially frowned upon (Gervais et al. 2017), people tend to overreport their religious participation (Brenner 2011; Cox, Jones, & Navarro-Rivera 2014) and belief (Gervais and Najle 2017). Thus, self-report measures of both prosociality and religiosity are compromised by these biases. Worse still, since there is a common factor—socially desirable responding—underlying the degree to which people are likely to misrepresent their both prosociality and religiosity, the correlation between the two reports may simply be revealing the difference between who exaggerates more and who exaggerates less. In other words, finding that people who report being more religious also report being more prosocial may simply be finding that people who are more willing to inflate their reports of how religious they are, also happen to be the same people who are willing to inflate their reports of how prosocial they are—which doesn't tell you much at all.

Finally, even if we could be confident that the self-reports of religiosity and prosociality were producing accurate and honest measures, the correlational data can't tell you whether religion is *causing* people to be prosocial. It is possible that being prosocial makes people more religious (a reverse-causation explanation) or that some common factor such as a personality trait or upbringing might cause people to be both more religious and more prosocial (a third-variable explanation). Though researchers do try to statistically control for possible alternative explanations (such as political identification or income), they cannot discount all alternatives.

Thus, we sought to address these problems by taking a new approach. Instead of relying on correlational designs, we would conduct a true experiment, where we randomly assigned people to different conditions so that we could be sure that any difference between the two groups would be due directly to the variable we manipulated. Instead of trusting self-reports of prosocial behavior, we would measure prosocial behavior directly. To accomplish this new approach, we rifled through the toolbox of social scientific research methods that had been left for us by previous scientists.

Methodology

Religious priming

Though we couldn't manipulate people's religious *disposition* (that is, we couldn't randomly assign some people to "be religious" and others not to), we could manipulate the religious *situation*; we could set up the experiment such that some people were in a religious frame of mind, while others were left relatively undisturbed. Since our question concerned whether thinking about God stimulated people to act more prosocially, we simply needed to arouse thoughts of God. In order to do so in a subtle way that wouldn't obviously alert our participants to the purpose of the experiment, we used a scrambled sentence task (modified from Srull & Wyer 1979) that implicitly brought thoughts of God to mind (see Box 13.1). The task involved ten word scrambles, each comprised of five words. For each, participants needed to drop one word and unscramble the remaining words to make a four-word sentence. In the religious priming condition, five of the sentences contained religious keywords (*spirit*, *divine*, *God*, *sacred*, and *prophet*) that together formed the idea of God in the back of people's heads—something called implicit priming. In the control condition, participants either did not complete a scrambled sentence task (in our first study) or completed a neutral version of the task in which there were no meaningfully coherent keywords (in our second study). Thus, whether people received the religious prime, or whether they received no prime or a neutral prime, was the independent variable.

Box 13.1 Three scrambles included in the implicit religious priming task.

1. felt she eradicate **spirit** the _____
2. dessert **divine** was fork the _____
3. appreciated presence was imagine her _____

Religious keywords (shown here in bold) were included in five of the ten sentences.

The Dictator Game

In order to measure whether people in the religious priming condition acted more prosocially, we borrowed a tightly controlled task from experimental economics known as the Dictator Game (DG). The DG is an economic task that tests how generous people are in situations where issues of reputation and reciprocity are minimized. The game works by bringing two people into the lab separately, so they don't meet each other, and putting them into separate rooms (they are later dismissed separately, so they don't meet each other on the way out). One of the people is randomly assigned to be the Dictator and is given an allotment of money—in our case, ten dollars. The other participant is assigned to be the Receiver and is allotted no money. Crucially, the Dictator is given the opportunity to split her money in any proportion with the Receiver. She could divide the money equitably—a fair thing to do given that she was only randomly chosen to be the one to receive the money—and allocate five of her ten dollars to the Receiver. Or she could be more selfish and allocate just one dollar to the Receiver while keeping nine for herself. Or she could do what most people tend to do: keep all ten dollars for herself and give nothing to the Receiver (Hoffman, McCabe, & Smith 1996). The reason people are willing to act so selfishly is because when they are assured anonymity from the Receiver and confidentiality regarding their decision, there is little remaining reason to give, aside from the prosocial motivation of being fair to a stranger (who will never be able to thank you or reciprocate your generosity) at your own expense. That's why this is used as a measure of prosociality—it removes all the other things that people's decision could hinge on and just isolates the thing that economists and psychologists are interested in testing.

We expected that our participants—like most DG participants—would be generally quite selfish in the game and would allocate little money, if any, to the Receiver. What we wanted to know is whether that amount would increase for those who had been previously primed with God.

Results and Analysis

Given the simple study design, we conducted a simple t-test to compare the behavior of participants in two groups. As we had predicted, there was a significant difference between the two. The mean amount given to the Receiver in the control condition, in which participants had not received the religious prime, was $1.84 (SD = $1.80). The modal amount given (that is, the most common donated amount) was nothing at all—an option chosen by 36 percent or participants. The mean amount given by those who *had* received the religious prime was $4.22 (SD = $2.65), significantly more than what was given in the control condition, $t(48) = 3.69$, $p < .001$ (Figure 13.1). And the modal donated amount was five dollars—the equitable 50/50 split—chosen by 52 percent of participants (only 12 percent in the control condition chose the 50/50 split).

Additional study: A secular path

We conducted a second study that served as both a replication of the first study as well as an extension. This additional study had three differences from our initial study. First, instead of drawing our study sample from our convenient but hardly representative local population of psychology students, we recruited this new study's sample from the wider community, resulting in a more variable and representative reflection of the general population. This is important because psychological research has been rightfully criticized for relying on college students as study participants and then

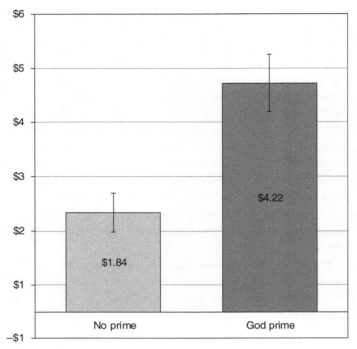

Figure 13.1 Dictator Game results from Study 1.

using these quite peculiar people (younger, wealthier, more educated, less religious than the average human) to draw inferences about people in general. The second difference was that, instead of no prime, the control condition participants in this second study completed a neutral prime, meaning they went through the same task, only without the religious keywords to activate thoughts of God. Third—and perhaps most importantly—we added a third condition in which we primed, not thoughts of God, but thoughts of secular institutions of law and order. The keywords here were *court*, *contract*, *jury*, *police*, and *civic*. The motivation to include this study was to test whether an alternative manipulation could produce similar effects. After all, there are a lot of things that could make people act more prosocially. And secular institutions of justice, in particular, have been often positioned as alternatives to religious cultures. In fact, if you look across countries, you find that the more people have confidence in the institutions underscoring the rule of law, the less importance people attach to religion (Figure 13.2).

Other than those three changes, the experiment was identical to the first. We ended up replicating our initial finding. Though the community participants in our neutral prime condition left an average of $2.56 out of $10 in the DG, making them slightly more generous than the unprimed student participants from Study 1, we nonetheless saw a comparable bump in prosociality when people were primed with the God concepts. God-primed participants left $4.56 in the DG (the modal response was, again, an equitable

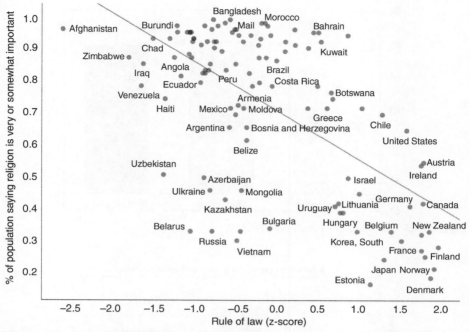

Figure 13.2 A scatterplot depicting the relationship between the religiosity of a country and its relative confidence in the institutions underlying the rule of law, $r^2 = 0.37$.

$5). Importantly, the amount participants in the secular prime condition left for the other player—$4.44—was also significantly higher than in the neutral prime condition and was statistically indistinguishable from the amount left in the God-primed condition.

While this finding was not, to us, as theoretically interesting as the religious priming effects—after all, we already know that those secular institutions have been explicitly designed to foster cooperation between strangers within a society—it was an important addition, if only to clearly demonstrate two different paths to cooperation. Religion is not a necessary condition for cooperation, within economic games or within societies. This may seem an obvious point, especially when many of the world's least religious countries are among the most harmonious. Nevertheless, when half the United States believes that belief in God is a necessary precondition for being a moral person (Pew Research Center 2017), we felt the point worth making.

Potentially more interesting is the interaction between the primes and whether the participant was a theist or atheist. We didn't actually report this result in the original manuscript, but reanalyzing the dataset shows an interesting pattern (Figure 13.4). The God prime only appears to have evoked more generous behavior among theists—a finding that we have since replicated (White et al. 2017) and detected in our meta-analysis on religious priming (Shariff et al. 2016; see discussion below). This indicates that God primes do not universally lead to prosociality but require existing beliefs to "activate." In contrast, the secular prime raised contributions for both theists and atheists. This too

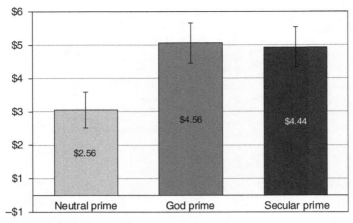

Figure 13.3 Dictator Game results from Study 2.

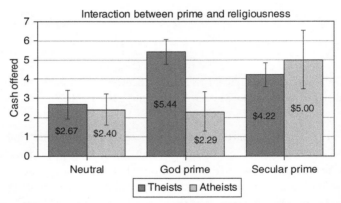

Figure 13.4 Interaction between the experimental primes and the participants' theism, in Study 2.

makes sense since there is no disagreement about whether policemen or courts exist. Everyone subscribes to secular institutions.

Discussion

The goal for the original article was to use the modern methodological innovations in the social sciences to find a new way to tackle an age-old question. I still find this to be a promising strategy. Psychological methods are powerful (though not all-powerful). And when they are unleashed on questions from outside disciplines—be it philosophy or politics or cultural studies or whatever—they can offer novel insight. Thus, it serves students well to build a toolkit of methodologies from within psychology, but to make sure they don't limit themselves to those boundaries in their reading. There are important discussions in these other fields, and psychologists can often make considerable contributions.

The original article was based on the research for my master's thesis and was published while I was a third-year graduate student (the simple design and statistics of the studies were useful to having it broadly understood, but they were actually the product of my limited knowledge). Much has changed since then—not just within the study of the relationship between religion and prosociality but also within the field itself. It's worth reflecting on the study in the context of these changes.

Things I might now have done differently

With ten years of hindsight, there are several things I would have changed about how we had conducted the study. Chief among these would be to quadruple the sample size. One of the big innovations the field has seen in recent years is a tightening up of research practices in order to increase confidence in psychological findings. Psychology attempts to make accurate inferences about the world, but like any system, it makes errors. In doing so, psychology needs to balance a trade-off between making false positive errors (also called "false alarms")—which report an effect about the world that in reality doesn't exist—and false negative errors (also called "misses")—in which the findings report a null effect for something that really does exist out in the world (Figure 13.5).

The landmark paper that has stimulated changing norms across the field is "False-Positive Psychology" by Simmons, Nelson, and Simonsohn (2011), which revealed a number of common research practices that make false positive findings more likely, flooding the literature with many claims that fail to replicate and thus potentially reflect erroneous claims about the world. One of the key recommendations the authors proposed for reducing both false positives and false negatives was to increase sample sizes in studies.

		Status in real world	
		Effect exists in real world	Effect doesn't exist in real world
Inference from research	Research reports positive effect	Correct inference ("Hit")	False Positive ("False Alarm")
	Research reports null effect	False Negative ("Miss")	Correct inference ("Hit")

Figure 13.5 The potential errors in inferences that psychological studies make about the world.

Suppose you flipped a coin ten times. If it came up "heads" eight times, you might suspect that the coin might be weighted to bias "heads," but there is a high likelihood that it was simply a fluke that your ten coin flips deviated from an even split of "heads" and "tails." But if you flip a coin a *thousand* times, and it comes up "heads" eight *hundred* times—now you can be more certain the coin is screwy. Similarly, the greater the number of people you sample from a population, the more confident you can be about conclusions that you draw regarding that population. Though the sample size of 25 per cell in our studies exceeds Simmons et al.'s (2011) recommendation of "at least 20 observations per cell" (p. 1363), today that recommendation seems almost laughably small.

Fortunately, in the years since our article, several other studies have tested the impact of religious primes on prosocial behavior. Though not all have found significant differences between the religiously primed and control conditions (e.g., Gomes & McCullough 2015), a meta-analysis we ran of twenty-five studies with a total of 4,825 participants found a robust overall effect (Shariff et al. 2016).

A second aspect I might reconsider, were I designing the studies today, is the use of the implicit "scrambled sentence" primes. The logic for using these implicit primes was to disguise the purpose of the study—and specifically of the God prime manipulations— so as to avoid demand effects. If participants knew what the study was attempting to test, they may have modulated their behavior to bias the study in the direction of their preferred outcome. For example, if pro-religion participants knew we were testing whether religious thoughts compelled people to act more generously, these participants might be inclined to actively and consciously adjust their behavior in order to support the hypothesis. But while avoiding this possibility was important, the scrambled sentence primes have proved unreliable (Kahneman 2012; though see Weingarten et al. 2016). Since it is not important from a theoretical standpoint that God primes be implicit, tying the study to an unreliable and indeed embattled method has been a bit of a distraction. Many studies have since used the implicit God primes we created to test any number of hypotheses (see Shariff et al. 2016 for a review). However, a failure to show that implicit God primes affect X might indicate that your hypothesis was wrong—that thoughts of God don't increase X—but such a null result might simply reflect a failure of the scrambled sentences to adequately rouse thoughts of God.

For this reason, in more recent work, we have placed less reliance on the scrambled sentence methodology and turned to more overt primes that are less vulnerable to these reliability issues. For instance, in a paper examining the effects of both reminders of God and of Karma on prosociality (White et al. 2017), we used the much more explicit and face-valid manipulation of simply asking our participants to "think about God" or "think about Karma."

Conclusion and further reading

The article discussed above provided the first empirical support for a larger project investigating the relationship between religion and prosociality. Since its publication, continuing work has extended and added nuance to the results. In addition to affecting generosity as measured by the DG, religious priming has been found to increase charitability (Pichon, Boccato, & Saraglou 2007), willingness to volunteer (Sasaki et al. 2013), honesty (Randolph-Seng & Nielsen 2007), and cooperation in the Public Goods Game (Ahmed & Salas 2011) and Prisoner's Dilemma Game (Rand et al. 2013). Though, notably, religious priming has also been found to increase racism (Johnson, Rowatt, & LaBouff 2010; LaBouff et al. 2012), conformity (Saroglou, Corneille, & Van Cappellen 2009), and submissiveness to authority (Van Cappellen et al. 2011), while decreasing tolerance for ambiguity (Sagioglou & Forstmann 2013) and altruistic punishment (Laurin et al. 2012).

Building off correlational research suggesting that it is especially God's punishing nature that deters people from unethical behavior (Purzycki et al. 2016; Shariff & Norenzayan 2011; Shariff & Rhemtulla 2012), Yilmaz and Bahçekapili (2016) found that priming God's punitive aspects significantly increased prosocial intentions, whereas priming nonpunitive elements of God made no statistical difference compared to control conditions.

We published a brief review of our theoretical approach to religious prosociality shortly after this article was published (Norenzayan & Shariff 2008), but we recently expanded on it considerably (Norenzayan et al. 2016). In this latter article, we summarized the research on religion and prosociality up to that point and embedded it within a larger theory about the cultural evolution of religion. The paper remains our most comprehensive treatment of Critias's question—addressing not just whether religious belief makes people act more ethically but delving deep into explanations of how it accomplishes this feat and, perhaps most importantly, why.

CHAPTER 14
DO WE OUTSOURCE POLICE WORK TO GOD?
Azim Shariff and Kristin Laurin

Introduction

You're at a bar. There are only a few other people there. Across the room, a man you don't know and have never seen shoves his wife violently. You immediately stand up from your table. The blood flows to your fists and you are prompted, almost without thinking, to engage in what could be a very costly altercation.

Why would you do this? Why would you risk the costs of a physical fight to avenge a wrong between people you don't even know? There are many ways this could turn out very poorly for you: the man is bigger than you; he could have a knife; he may have friends who could back him up. And yet there is the motivation to brave those risks and mete out punishment, despite no tangible gain to yourself.

This is what economists call third-party punishment (also called costly or altruistic punishment): punishing someone who hasn't wronged you directly (Fehr & Gächter 2002). From an evolutionary perspective, third-party punishment is a bit of a puzzle: natural selection should favor those whose behaviors narrowly help themselves and their kin and should cull those who, like third-party punishers, imperil themselves for no gain. From a societal perspective, though, the presence of people willing to sacrifice personally to safeguard moral norms can be vital. The more people fear reprisal—even from mere onlookers—for engaging in immoral behavior, the more they will be deterred from doing so (Johnson & Krüger 2004). Such deterrence helped spread the large-scale cooperation necessary for large societies of anonymous strangers to survive. In lab-based experiments, even just having the threat of punishment makes people cooperate more with each other (Fehr & Gächter 2000)—a point that will become critical in a moment.

So, fists balled and face contorted in rage, you stride over to where the wife-beater is sitting. But halfway to his table, a thought occurs: Is this your job? Is it your duty to punish this man? Is there not some other entity who should shoulder the burden of punishment?

In modern society, we outsource many elements of third-party punishment to the formal institutions of law and order. We pay the costs—in the form of taxes—to support the police and judicial systems. And these costs are hardly insignificant; in the United States,

$185 billion, or 1.8 percent of the country's entire GDP, was spent on law and order in 2003 (Hughes 2006). Though the system of law and order in the United States is far from perfect, it is a feat of modern civilization—one that has been honed over hundreds of years. The more the state has been able to leverage its central authority, its trust, and its tax coffers, the more effective the mechanisms of law and order (police, courts, contract enforcement, etc.) have become (Pinker 2011).

But these secular institutions have not been the only forces of deterrence throughout the history of human civilization. Many researchers have argued that religions have filled a similar function—with watchful and punishing deities serving as a form of supernatural police force (Norenzayan et al. 2016). Evidence for this supernatural punishment hypothesis has accumulated over the last ten years. Researchers have shown that reminders of these agents make people give more money to anonymous strangers (Shariff & Norenzayan 2007; White et al. 2017), cooperate more with others (Ahmed & Salas 2011), and cheat less (Randolph-Seng & Nielsen 2007). Another recent study showed that the specific belief that gods are knowledgeable and punishing is linked with greater generosity (Purzycki et al. 2016). Moreover, these types of powerful gods have tended to be more likely to emerge in places where it was particularly important to foster cooperation and deter defection—for example, places with scarce resources and/ or where people's livelihood relies on herds of animals that can be stolen (Botero et al. 2014; Snarey 1996).

These theories suggest that the very reason that people believe in gods with omniscient and punitive characteristics is because such beliefs proved so effective at getting people to cooperate. In fact, it seems likely that these beliefs were culturally selected for in a process akin to Darwinian evolution (Boyd & Richerson 2005): societies that didn't take on these god beliefs were less able to cooperate with one another, which limited their prosperity and ultimately led them to lose out to cultures that had adopted the adaptive beliefs.

If people believe God punishes the immoral, then not only should belief in the threat of supernatural punishment deter wrongdoing, it should also free people from the need to engage in punishment themselves. This should be most apparent in cases where punishment is costly and less personally relevant—that is, in cases of third-party punishment. Norm violators must be punished, but if I believe God will take care of that, then I can save my resources—not to mention my tax dollars—for other causes. This was the hypothesis that our studies tested: Does the belief in a punishing God serve to downregulate one's drive to enact third-party punishment? More specifically, we tested whether beliefs in a *powerful* God—one who has the capacity to punish wrongdoers— could reduce people's willingness to spend resources punishing a stranger who has violated an important social norm.

A picture of a bearded and scowling God—a God that monitors, a God that punishes—flashes through your mind. You shoot the wife-beater a final glare, spin around, and return to your drink. He'll get his, in this life or the next . . .

Methodology

To test our ideas, we paired two different methodologies. As our independent variable—that is, the phenomenon we manipulated in a study to see if it affects something else—we used a salience technique to manipulate the momentary awareness (or *salience*) of a powerful god. And for the dependent variable—that is, the outcome measure that might be affected by the independent variable—we used the *third-party punishment game*, to measure participants' willingness to incur costs to enforce a prosocial norm.

Salience manipulation

The first thing we needed to do was create a group of participants who we knew would be thinking about a powerful god who might plausibly shoulder the responsibility for punishment, and some comparison groups of participants who would be thinking about no such thing. Our manipulation to this end was based on two principles. First of all, there are individual differences in terms of how much people believe in a powerful god: some people are firm believers in a god who intervenes in people's everyday lives, while others believe in a different, more removed kind of god (one not actively involved in the moral matters of humans), while still others believe in no god at all (e.g., Norenzayan 2016). And second of all, no matter what people believe in general, humans' cognitive capacities are limited, and only a subset of their beliefs will be at the forefront of their conscious minds at any given moment (Higgins 1996; Molden 2014). Such beliefs are much more likely to influence judgments and behavior than those which are not currently at the top of someone's mind. For example, if you are not currently thinking about your goal to get into medical school, you might choose to attend a friend's wild birthday party rather than study the night before a big biology exam. Similarly, someone who is not currently thinking about their belief in a powerful god who can punish wrongdoers might not think to outsource that role, so they might be just as likely to take it on as someone who believes in no such god.

What we sought to do, then, was to identify participants who believed strongly in a powerful god, and at the same time manipulate whether that belief was *salient* to them: whether it was something they were consciously aware of at the time of the experiment and which might influence their judgments and behavior. We therefore separated participants into two groups. Half our participants, those in the *salient* condition, completed a measure of their belief in a powerful god at the beginning of the experiment. For these participants, whatever their belief in a powerful god, we reasoned that that belief would be on their minds for the duration of the experiment. In other words, for people who believed God was powerful, this belief was now on top of their minds, and for those who believed something else (e.g., that there is no god or that God is more like the proverbial Switzerland, reluctant to intervene in human affairs), that belief was made salient.

The other half of participants, those in the *nonsalient* condition, completed the same measure but only at the end of the experiment. We certainly acknowledged that some of these participants might just happen to be thinking about their powerful God beliefs earlier in the experiment, but we suspected this would be relatively rare. On average, we reasoned that these participants would be less likely than those in the salient condition to be thinking about their belief in powerful gods during the experiment.

This method allowed us to compare the behavior of participants (a) who believed strongly versus did not believe in powerful gods, specifically (b) when those beliefs were made salient and therefore could influence their judgments and behavior or were not made salient and therefore should not be influencing their judgments and behavior. Thus, this is an example of testing an interaction with one manipulated variable (whether participants answered the belief question before or after the dependent measure) and one subject variable (variation in people's existing beliefs). We expected when both (a) the participant believed in a powerful god involved in human affairs *and* (b) this belief was made salient, we would see less willingness to incur the costs of altruistic punishment than in the other conditions, since these participants would tend to offload that responsibility to the powerful god (see Table 14.1).

Third-party punishment game

To measure people's willingness to engage in third-party punishment, we used an established economic game aptly called the third-party punishment game, or 3PPG. Participants learn that the game involves three players. Player 1 receives an initial endowment of $20 and can split this endowment any way they choose with Player 2, in increments of $1. Player 2 receives no initial endowment and is purely at the mercy of Player 1. Player 3 receives an initial endowment of $10 and has the option of spending that money to punish Player 1. Specifically, for every $1 that Player 3 chooses to spend in this way, Player 1 loses $3. This behavior on the part of Player 3 meets the conditions for third-party punishment: Player 1 and Player 2 are anonymous strangers; Player 1's

Table 14.1 The 2×2 mixed (between and within subjects) study design.

		Manipulated variable	
		Beliefs made salient (by asking belief question before the dependent measure)	*Beliefs not made salient (by asking belief question after the dependent measure)*
Subject variable	Believes in powerful god involved in human affairs	THIRD-PARTY PUNISHMENT SHOULD BE LOWER	
	Doesn't believe in powerful god		

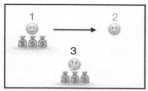 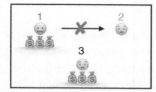 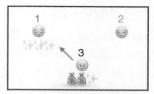

Players 1 and 3 are given a monetary allotment. Player 2 is given nothing, but Player 1 has the option to split hers with Player 2.

Player 1 decides not to share anything with Player 2.

Player 3 can punish Player 1 by spending some of her allotment to take away 3 times as much from Player 1.

Figure 14.1 An example of a third-party punishment game, in three acts.

behavior has no bearing on Player 3's own outcomes, and Player 3 can choose to punish Player 1 if Player 1 is selfish with the initial endowment, but that punishment will cost Player 3 money that they otherwise could have kept at the end of the experiment. (See Figure 14.1 for an example of the game.)

In our version of this game, participants believed they were in a group along with two other participants. They learned about the game, then drew a slip of paper from a bowl containing three slips. Ostensibly this served to "randomly" assign them to a role in the game, but in reality, no matter which slip they drew, it assigned them to the role of Player 3. Participants then learned that while they waited for the other participants to be assigned their roles and for Player 1 to make a decision, they could make their own decisions. Specifically, participants considered every possible decision Player 1 could make, from keeping all $20 for him- or herself to giving it all to Player 2, and for each possible decision, participants indicated how much of their own money they would spend to take money away from Player 1.

From these numbers, we then needed to calculate an index of third-party punishment: How much would each participant tend to be willing to punish Player 1 for being selfish and violating fairness norms? We reasoned that, at least in North America where we ran this study, prosocial norms dictate that fair behavior in this game—where Player 1 simply receives a $20 windfall for no reason other than chance—means sharing that money evenly with Player 2 (Henrich et al. 2010; Krupka & Weber 2013). Therefore, we considered that Player 1 keeping any amount over $10 represented some degree of selfishness—of violating a cooperative norm. We thus began by summing up the total amount of money participants said they would spend on punishing decisions if Player 1 kept more than $10.

We were concerned, though, that this amount was not a pure measure of people's willingness to incur the costs of third-party punishment, because it was necessarily contaminated by a generalized desire to punish others—mean-spiritedness, essentially. To remove that contaminant, we also summed up the total amount of money participants said they would spend on punishing *nonselfish* decisions—decisions wherein Player 1 kept $10 or less. In our analyses, we statistically controlled for this measure of mean-spirited punitiveness, which means that our findings reflect participants' willingness to incur costs to punish *specifically* selfish, norm-violating behavior.

Procedure

Now that we have described the key building blocks of our studies, explaining how they unfolded is simple. In one prototypical study, participants came into the lab and completed a demographics form, which either did (salient condition) or did not (nonsalient condition) include the measure of their belief in a powerful god. They then completed the 3PPG as described, and if they were in the nonsalient condition, they ended the experiment by completing the measure of belief in a powerful god.

Two other studies were slight variations on this theme: In one, which was conducted entirely online, we only included the salient condition and therefore only compared responses of participants whose belief in a powerful god was salient during the 3PPG to those of participants whose lack of belief in a powerful god was salient. In the other, rather than use the 3PPG to assess altruistic punishment, we described an instance of white-collar crime and asked participants how many of their tax dollars they would like to see go toward catching and punishing the perpetrators of such crimes.

Results and Analysis

Primary results

In all cases, we analyzed our data using multiple regression—a type of statistical analysis that allows us to look at the relationship of multiple factors (as well as the interactions between these factors) with our dependent variable. In our prototypical study, we found an interaction between salience condition and participants' belief in powerful gods, $\beta = -.55$, $t(49) = 2.08$, $p = .04$ (in inferential statistics, the p-value, which stands for *probability value*, gives an indication of the likelihood of obtaining this result if this interaction did not really exist in the population. This indicates that there is a 4 percent chance of finding this result if no interaction actually existed. Traditionally, a p-value lower .05 is deemed to indicate a *statistically significant* inference). This interaction means that participants' belief in powerful gods predicted their altruistic punishment differently, depending on whether that belief was salient or not. Indeed, when participants' beliefs in powerful gods were salient, those who believed more strongly in such gods punished less than those who did not believe as strongly, $\beta = -.90$, $t(49) = 3.11$, $p = .01$. When these beliefs were not salient, participants punished similarly regardless of their belief, $\beta = -.12$, $t(49) = 1$, $p = .61$ (see Figure 14.2).

In the study that only included the salient condition, we found similar results: Participants punished less to the extent that they had (salient) beliefs in powerful gods, $\beta = -.58$, $t(17) = 2.22$, $p = .04$. And in the study where we used the measure of support for state-sponsored punishment in lieu of the 3PPG, we found similar results, as well: another interaction between salience condition and belief in powerful gods, $\beta = -.82$, $t(66) = 2.95$, $p = .01$. Once again, when participants' beliefs were salient, those who believed more punished less, $\beta = .57$, $t(66) = 2.21$, $p = .03$, whereas when beliefs were not salient this was not true; if anything, the effect was reversed such that participants

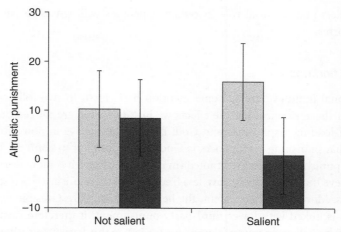

Figure 14.2 Punishment among strong (dark bars) and weak (light bars) believers in powerful gods, as a function of salience condition (altruistic punishment).

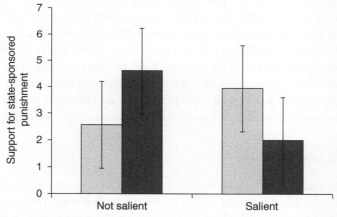

Figure 14.3 Punishment among strong (dark bars) and weak (light bars) believers in powerful gods, as a function of salience condition (support for state-sponsored punishment).

punished *more* the more they believed in a powerful god, $\beta = 0.60$, $t(66) = 2.00$, $p = .05$ (see Figure 14.3).

In other words, the results supported our hypothesis: When participants' beliefs were salient and therefore could influence their behavior, those who believed more strongly in a powerful god were less willing to incur the costs of third-party punishment. However, when participants' beliefs were *not* salient and therefore should *not* be influencing their behavior, the same effect did not occur. This suggests that the relationship between believing in a powerful god and being unwilling to mete out third-party punishment is not some spurious association, whereby the kinds of people who believe in powerful gods just happen to be the same kinds of people who will not punish. Rather, it appears that the beliefs play a causal role in reducing people's willingness to pay to enforce prosocial norms.

Additional findings

Two additional findings deserve some mention here. First, in two follow-up studies, we found further evidence that the effects we just described are indeed due to strong believers off-loading responsibility to God. People who believe in powerful gods tend to believe that punishing wrongdoers is God's responsibility; in contrast, they do not believe that punishment is less warranted (in fact, they believe it is more warranted), nor do they believe that wrongdoers have less free will and therefore are less responsible for their actions. Moreover, when salient, the belief that God is responsible for punishing wrongdoers is linked with lower third-party punishment. It therefore seems plausible that people who believe in powerful gods engage less in third-party punishment *because* they view that punishment as God's responsibility.

Second, in all our studies we contrasted belief in a powerful god with general religiosity. More often than not, religiosity showed the *reverse* pattern, compared with belief in a powerful god: when religiosity was salient, the more religious participants were *more* likely to incur the costs of third-party punishment. This contrast points to an important puzzle for future research: What is it about being religious, absent the belief in a powerful god, that makes people more willing to spend their own resources enforcing cooperative norms? Speculatively, we suspect that it may have something to do with other elements of religion that encourage people to value prosociality and therefore to perhaps be more outraged by people acting selfishly, but no work has yet tested this hypothesis.

A final methodological note

We would be remiss to conclude without making note of an important development in research methodology more broadly. For the last several years, there have been vast advances and dissemination in the science of what constitutes good research practices to guard against the possibility of false negatives in our work—findings that appear to be significant but turn out to reflect the vagaries of chance rather than an underlying truth about psychology (Simmons, Nelson, & Simonsohn 2011). One specific recommendation has been that researchers use far larger sample sizes than most, including us, had been using in the past. The research we describe in this chapter is based on a solid theoretical foundation, but it would be useful to replicate it using sample sizes more in line with current best practices.

Discussion

These findings show that people are willing to outsource to God—or *Godsource*—the responsibilities of third-party punishment. This supports the theories described in the introduction arguing that societies have come to feature beliefs in powerful and punishing gods because such beliefs have had social value (Norenzayan et al. 2016; Wilson 2002). Other work shows that these God beliefs yield benefits in terms of increasing cooperation and deterring defection (e.g., Purzycki et al. 2016; Shariff & Rhemtulla 2012; Yilmaz & Bahçekapili 2016); our work shows that they offer the additional benefit of deferring some of the costs of earthly punishment otherwise borne by individuals or the collective.

At the same time, the findings raise a number of questions. First, this was a lab-based demonstration—a conceptual test of the theory that beliefs about God affect people's punishment behavior. It remains unclear how this psychological phenomenon operates in the real world, at the level of societies. That said, there is good evidence that the 3PPG we used is indicative of real-world behaviors in a range of societies (e.g., Henrich et al. 2010). Moreover, by examining people's preexisting beliefs in powerful gods and merely manipulating their salience, we get one step closer to seeing how these beliefs operate in nature.

Another important question is, How are such beliefs in powerful gods maintained when there is no (scientifically verifiable) evidence of any god actually engaging in third-party punishment? Here we see how religious belief builds off fundamental features of human psychology. Consider four interacting psychological phenomena. First, people have a strong drive to see the world as ordered, especially as morally ordered (Heine, Proulx, & Vohs 2006; Lerner 1980). Second, people are highly vulnerable to the confirmation bias, under which they favor information that conforms to their existing beliefs and expectations, and discount information that violates these beliefs (Wason 1960). Third, people have a tendency to infer "teleology"—or goal-directed purpose—in what are actually random events (Kelemen 2004). Fourth, when it comes to events that involve harm or benefit, people impose a "moral template" under which they intuitively perceive there to always be a moral actor (who caused the moral event) and a moral recipient (or moral "patient"—on whom the moral event is performed; Gray & Wegner 2010). In other words, when there is not an obvious doer (moral actor) or feeler (moral recipient), people's minds will automatically try to find someone, such as a powerful god, to complete this moral "dyad."

The combination of these four features of our mind—the drive for moral order, the vulnerability to confirmation bias, the overperception of teleology, and the innate moral dyadic template—leads people not only to readily infer the moral hand of God behind events but also to specifically see that moral hand operating in ways consistent with expectations of punishment. That is, when a believer does something immoral or sees someone else do so, the believer will subsequently interpret negative events that befall the transgressor not as random events but as divine punishment. God is seen to act through unfortunate IRS audits, slippery banana peels, backstabbing friends, and errant bird poop. Moreover, the confirmation bias ensures that disconfirming evidence to this karmic template—that is, good things that happen to bad people—is explained away. The wife-beater from the bar gets laid off from work? That's divine action. He finds a dollar on the ground? That's just luck. This type of psychological flexibility can sustain the convincing appearance of divine justice even in a world without any.

CHAPTER 15
DO RELIGIONS PROMOTE COOPERATION? TESTING SIGNALING THEORIES OF RELIGION
Richard Sosis

Introduction

The first year of college is tough. If you are mature enough to know that you need a gap year before entering college, you probably don't need one. I was not mature enough, but I figured it out after drifting aimlessly through my first year of university life, so I decided to take a year off before returning to sophomore studies. I spent the year working and living in several collectivist communities in Israel, known as kibbutzim.

My kibbutz experiences planted in me a dual interest, or one might even say obsession, with humans' obstinate desire to create so-called utopian social structures and our equally tenacious yearning to attain and maintain cooperative social relationships. Upon my return to university, I enrolled in an anthropology course—much more exotic than the engineering curriculum of my first year—and while reflecting on a year of kibbutz life, I became fascinated by the study of cultural variation.

This fascination carried me to graduate school in anthropology and back to a kibbutz for four months of reconnaissance fieldwork in order to set up my dissertation research. My initial project did not work out, an all-too-common experience for anthropology graduate students, and I decided to pursue my interests in cooperation on Ifaluk, a small, remote atoll in the Federated States of Micronesia. But in the back of my mind I hoped that someday I would return to conduct research on an Israeli kibbutz.

Signaling theory

Toward the end of graduate school, I had a conversation with one of my advisors about why research in human behavioral ecology, my area of specialty, had focused almost exclusively on foraging and mating decisions. (My dissertation focused on cooperative aspects of the former.) Why had behavioral ecologists ignored other important social behaviors, such as religion? It turned out that he had just returned from a conference in which a behavioral ecologist, Bill Irons, had delivered a paper on religion. I was able to get a copy of the paper, and although I was captivated by Irons's argument, I utterly disagreed with his thesis.

Irons (1996, 2001) argued that natural selection favored the evolution of religion because of the benefits it offered adherents. Specifically, religious behaviors served as hard-to-fake signals of group commitments, enabling groups that shared a religion to overcome the inherent free-rider problems—why work hard, or at all, if you can receive the same benefits regardless of your effort?—that plague human cooperation. I was excited by such an evolutionary interpretation of religion, but I was resistant to Irons's thesis because of my own experiences on Israeli kibbutzim.

One implication of Irons's argument is that religious groups should be better at overcoming problems of cooperation than secular groups. However, my own experiences suggested otherwise. The kibbutzim where I had lived were all ardently secular, yet it seemed to me that they had achieved a level of cooperation that was exceptional. I was convinced that Irons was wrong, and with my freshly minted PhD I set out to disprove his theory.

Testing the theory

I turned my attention to communal societies. I knew that Israeli kibbutzim were not the first secular experiments in collective living, and I reckoned that understanding how secular communes succeeded would provide ammunition for challenging Irons's theory of religion. During my background literature search I fortuitously stumbled across a book on US communes written by Yaacov Oved, an Israeli historian who, incidentally, lived on a kibbutz. In the appendix of this book, *Two Hundred Years of American Communes*, Oved (1988) offered descriptive data on 277 communes. Critically, the appendix included the motivational ideology of each commune— whether it was secular or religious—and the years that the communes existed cooperatively. I analyzed data from 200 of these communes, limiting myself to the nineteenth century, which was a notably prolific era in the development of utopian societies within the United States. I found that religious communes were much more likely to survive in every year of their existence than secular communes (Sosis 2000). In other words, religious communes were evidently better than secular communes at solving the cooperation and free-rider problems inherent in communal life. Score one for Irons, zero for Sosis.

These results were intriguing, but I wondered if the greater longevity of religious communes was a consequence of the obligations demanded of members. Did religious communes demand more of their members than secular communes? Were these obligations hard-to-fake signals of commitment that facilitated cooperation by weeding out free-riders, as Irons had argued? I decided to explore these questions with an exceptional University of Connecticut undergraduate student, Eric Bressler, who is now a professor of psychology at Westfield State University.

We developed a long questionnaire aimed at determining the constraints and obligations that communal societies imposed on their members. We recruited undergraduates to search through thirty-seven historical texts on nineteenth-century US communes and complete the questionnaires based on their findings. The questionnaires revealed twenty-two costly requirements. (These of course excluded requirements that were exclusively religious, such as prayer.) The historical texts provided sufficient data for analyses on 83 of the 200 communes included in my initial study.

As in the original sample, religious communes had much higher survivorship rates than secular communes. Based on Irons's theory, we predicted that both religious and secular communes that imposed costly requirements would have higher survivorship that those that lacked such costly requirements, but to our surprise this prediction was only supported for religious communes. Indeed, we found a strong positive relationship between the number of costly requirements and religious commune longevity (score two for Irons), but costly requirements were completely unrelated to secular commune longevity (Sosis & Bressler 2003). We were puzzled by this result because it seemed to us that there were plenty of secular groups—such as militaries, athletic teams, and collegiate Greek fraternities—that made costly demands on their members in order to increase solidarity and ensure group commitments. (Yes, by this point my data were convincing me that Irons was on to something; see Sosis 2003.) Motivated by our results, some of my graduate students (now, graduated graduate students) and I examined the costly obligations and rituals of Greek fraternities. We conducted extensive interviews and ran trust games with Greek fraternities and, for comparison, other social clubs and organizations at the University of Connecticut. Our results were consistent with the commune study: fraternities exhibited higher levels of within-group trust and cooperation than other collegiate organizations, but the costs of fraternity obligations were unrelated to their level of trust and cooperation (Shaver et al. 2018). Needless to say, more research needs to be done to unravel this puzzle.

The kibbutz revisited

Playing with historical data is fun, but I was trained as an anthropologist, so my ultimate goal was to work with extant, not extinct, communal societies. I realized that the kibbutzim that I had lived on after my first year of college and abandoned for my dissertation research would provide an ideal place to further test Irons's theory. So, while I was conducting the research on nineteenth-century US communes, I also initiated a project on Israeli kibbutzim.

Like the overwhelming majority of the more than 250 Israeli kibbutzim, those that I had lived on were zealously secular. However, beginning in the 1930s, a small group of religious socialists decided to establish communities based on the kibbutz economic model, in which the outputs of labor would be collectively shared. Ultimately, more than a dozen religious kibbutzim were established. These religious kibbutzim are particularly interesting because they reveal a pattern that is similar to what Bressler and I had observed among nineteenth-century communes. While there are many economically successful secular kibbutzim, data show that on average, religious kibbutzim have been economically more successful than secular kibbutzim in every decade of their existence (Fishman 1994; Fishman & Goldschmidt 1990). In the late 1980s, media reports revealed that the kibbutz movement was collectively over four billion dollars in debt and largely surviving on government subsidies and diaspora philanthropy. When news of their extraordinary debt surfaced, what went largely unnoticed in the academic and media projections about the inevitable collapse of the kibbutz movement was that the religious kibbutzim had achieved economic stability. In the words of the Religious Kibbutz Movement Federation, "the economic position of the religious kibbutzim is sound, and they remain uninvolved in the economic crisis" that has affected so many of the kibbutzim.

The economic success of the religious kibbutzim is especially remarkable given that many of their religious practices inhibit economic productivity. For example, Jewish law does not permit Jews to milk cows on the Sabbath. Although rabbinic rulings have permitted these religious kibbutzniks to milk their cows to prevent the cows from suffering, in the early years of the religious kibbutzim none of this milk was used commercially. Jewish law also imposes significant constraints on agricultural productivity. Fruits may not be eaten during the first several years of the tree's life, agricultural fields must lie fallow every seven years, and the corners of fields can never be harvested but must be left for society's poor. Although these constraints appear detrimental to the productivity of the religious kibbutzim, costly signaling theory suggests that they may actually be a key to their economic success.

There are undoubtedly many factors that have contributed to the economic success of the religious kibbutzim, but I was particularly intrigued by the possibility that religious practices fostered solidarity and trust within their communities, which enabled these kibbutzniks to better overcome the inherent, collective challenges of communal living than their secular counterparts.

Another feature of religious kibbutzim that made them particularly intriguing to study was their normative gender differences in religious activity. Members of religious kibbutzim overwhelmingly adhere to a form of Judaism known as Modern Orthodoxy. These Jews are halachically observant; that is, they strictly follow Jewish laws and traditions, but they are also fully engaged in the contemporary world. Of significant interest to our study is that Modern Orthodoxy is not sexually egalitarian with regards to ritual obligations. Notably, males are expected to pray thrice daily in a collective quorum of at least ten men, whereas women do not assemble in groups for prayer, with the exception of on the Sabbath and holidays. Anthropologists, including Irons, had long suggested that collective ritual performance can enhance group solidarity and cooperation. Thus, the difference in ritual obligations between the sexes on religious kibbutzim offered an opportunity to explore the effects of ritual performance on cooperation.

Methodology

While in graduate school, in addition to my load of biology and anthropology courses, I enrolled in several classes in economics. The study of cooperation, at least in part, is an economic problem. During my studies I learned about the experimental games that behavioral economists employed to understand human decision making. As I began to consider a research project on Israeli kibbutzim, I realized that such games offered me methods that my anthropological toolkit had been missing: systematic measures of trust and cooperation. I had never conducted economic experiments before, but I was fortunate to find a talented collaborator, a Canadian economist working in Israel, Bradley Ruffle.

We were motivated by several questions. Was it the case that religious kibbutzniks were more cooperative than secular kibbutzniks? If so, was this a consequence of their religious practices, as Irons would predict? To answer these questions, we decided to develop an economic game that measured kibbutzniks' willingness to cooperate. Specifically, we developed a game that aimed to mimic the types of cooperation problems kibbutzniks regularly faced. Some cooperative challenges on the kibbutz take the form of common-pool resource dilemmas. Common-pool resources are publicly available goods that, once consumed by an individual, are no longer available for others' consumption. Food, cars, and electricity are all common-pool resources on kibbutzim. The economic experiment we developed is a type of common-pool resource game.

In the experiment, two players, who remain anonymous to each other, are told that they collectively have access to an envelope containing 100 shekels (about 25 US dollars at the time of the experiment). Independently, they can each take out as much of the money from the envelope as they wish. If the amount they take out collectively exceeds 100 shekels, they each receive no money and the experiment is over. If they collectively take out fewer than 100 shekels, the amount of money left in the envelope is increased by 50 percent (i.e., multiplied by 1.5) and divided equally between the players. The more a player shows self-restraint and cooperates by not consuming the public resource, the more money will be available for both players.

With our experiment we sought to test three predictions. First, we predicted that religious kibbutzniks would take out less money from the envelope than their secular counterparts. Second, because of their communal prayer practices, we expected male religious kibbutzniks to take less out from the envelope than female kibbutz members. Third, we anticipated that male synagogue attendance would be negatively correlated with the amount taken out of the envelope; that is, the more a player attended daily prayer services, the more he would cooperate and exhibit self-restraint.

In order to test these predictions, several options lay before us. The most obvious option at the time was to invite kibbutzniks to Ruffle's behavioral economics lab at Ben Gurion University (BGU) in Israel. We debated the logistics and ecological validity of such a plan, and we ultimately decided that rather than bring the kibbutz to us, we would bring the lab to the kibbutzim. This was a fairly novel idea at the time, although economic field experiments are now a regular practice for both anthropologists and behavioral economists. We realized that running dyadic experiments on a kibbutz would take time, but if the experiments stretched over too much time, kibbutz members were likely to discuss their experiences with each other, thus potentially influencing the decisions of those who had not yet participated. We needed to conduct the experiments relatively quickly, ideally simultaneously, to avoid our sample from becoming contaminated. Our solution: We trained twenty BGU economics graduate and undergraduate students to help conduct the experiments.

For this particular study—we developed a series of kibbutz studies—our sample consisted of seven religious kibbutzim and eleven secular kibbutzim that were closely matched in terms of their economic success, levels of privatization, population size, and year of establishment. Once we attained the appropriate permissions from the leaders of each kibbutz, we contacted members in order to schedule times to visit their homes and conduct the experiments and interviews. We practiced our data collection methods at BGU and three secular kibbutzim that were not in our sample. For the students, this was their first "fieldwork" experience, and during the training we cautioned that research in the field never runs as smoothly as it does in the laboratory. Indeed. During our first pilot study, the electricity went out on the kibbutz, and we were forced to conduct the experiments and interviews by candlelight.

Results and Analysis

Did the data we collected support our predictions? Generally, yes. Our experiments were aimed at measuring cooperative behavior in order to determine if there were differences across kibbutzim in members' levels of cooperation with other members of their own kibbutz. Controlling for effects such as the age and size of the kibbutz, level of privatization, and numerous other variables, we found that members of religious kibbutzim exhibited higher levels of intragroup cooperation than members of secular kibbutzim.

Furthermore, a closer examination of the data supported our second prediction. Religious males were significantly more cooperative than religious females, whereas among secular kibbutzniks we found no sex difference at all. This result is understandable if we appreciate the types of rituals and demands imposed on religious Jews. Although a variety of requirements are equally imposed on males and females, such as keeping kosher and not working on the Sabbath, male ritual requirements are largely publicly oriented, whereas female requirements are generally pursued privately or in the home. Indeed, the three major requirements imposed on women—the laws of family purity (e.g., attending a *mikveh*, or ritual bath), separating a portion of dough when baking bread, and lighting Sabbath candles—are done privately. These are not rituals that signal commitment to a wider group; they appear to signal commitment within the family.

Males, on the other hand, engage in highly visible ritual requirements, most notably public prayer, which occurs three times daily; hence our third prediction. Among male religious kibbutzniks, we found synagogue attendance to be positively correlated with our measures of cooperative behavior. There was no similar correlation among females, which is not surprising; as we've seen, attending services is not a requirement for women and thus does not serve as a signal of commitment to the group. Thus, the costly signaling theory of religion is able to offer a unique explanation for our results.

Discussion

The phone call

After our article (Sosis & Ruffle 2003) was published, I received a phone call—I was living in Israel at the time—from a religious woman who had read a media account of our results. She resided in a religious community, and she invited me to give a lecture about my research to the members. This sounded promising, but then she added that while she looked forward to me talking with everyone in her community, she especially wanted me to engage with the rabbi of her community. As she understood our results, women living in religious kibbutzim were less cooperative than their male counterparts because they did not engage in collective rituals like men did. Therefore, and quite logically, she suggested that women should be encouraged to gather collectively for prayer or engage in other collective rituals, so that they could also create the sense of cohesiveness that our study revealed for males.

This made me nervous for a variety of reasons. Our results were statistically significant and thus we could suggest, as we did, that our findings supported our hypotheses. However, in published academic research, some statistically significant results are stronger than others, and our results were not particularly strong. Indeed, the differences we explored between categories of people—religious and secular, male and female—revealed average differences of only a few shekels in the amount they respectively removed from the envelope. And these differences were only evident when we controlled for various factors such as age, fraction of life spent on the kibbutz, education, and marital status. Moreover, as I explained to this woman, experimental results need to be replicated before findings can be trusted, and at that time the experimental study of the prosocial effects of ritual practice was in its infancy. More disconcerting, however, was that I had no idea what the impact of such a change would have on her community. While it was possible that daily collective prayer would increase solidarity among these women, it was also possible that such a change could have unintended consequences, including the diminishment of cohesiveness within the community. Ritual performance does not exist within a social vacuum, and we simply do not know how changes in ritual activity affect other aspects of religion and broader social structures. Although I personally sympathized with the changes she sought, I was uncomfortable using our results as justification for such social changes, and I declined her invitation.

Her phone call highlighted a growing concern I harbored about trends in the scientific study of religion in general, and the evolutionary and cognitive sciences of religion specifically. Religions are organic systems (Alcorta & Sosis 2005; Purzycki & Sosis 2009, 2013; Sosis 2016), and if those of us who study religion continue to ignore this fact, we do so at our own peril. There are countless examples of well-intentioned scholars, policy makers, and religious leaders who have sought to alter some aspect of religion, for the benefit of either the religion itself or society, only to have the alterations create other problems, often worse than the problems that motivated the changes. (For one of my favorite examples, see Berman's [2009] account of the Israeli government's attempt to influence Israeli Ultra-Orthodox communities.)

Subsequent kibbutz studies

As mentioned above, Ruffle and I conducted a whole series of studies on the cooperative behavior of kibbutzniks. In one subsequent study, we were able to further support our claim that male synagogue attendance fostered cooperation. Specifically, we developed a graphical and mathematical model demonstrating how ritual performance, such as collective prayer, could function as a signal promoting cooperation. We also reanalyzed our original data using more rigorous statistical techniques (Ruffle & Sosis 2007) than we had used in our initial study. This research upheld and more strongly supported our original findings—that religious kibbutzniks were more cooperative than secular kibbutz members and that these differences were a consequence of males regularly attending synagogue.

We were also curious just how cooperative kibbutz members were in general. Were they, for example, more cooperative than Israeli city residents? We evaluated this question on a new sample of secular kibbutzim and residents of Beer Sheva; we employed the same economic game and methods we had previously used. Our results showed that kibbutz members are more cooperative toward each other than city residents are toward each other; however, kibbutzniks are not universal cooperators. Kibbutz members, it turns out, are no more cooperative toward city residents than city residents are toward each other (Ruffle & Sosis 2006; Sosis & Ruffle 2004).

Conclusion

One of the reasons I respectfully declined the religious woman's lecture invitation was that research results need to be replicated—again and again—before we can be confident that the results accurately describe some real phenomenon in the world. When we published our results we had no way of knowing that the next decade would see numerous publications providing evidence of extensive religious cooperation and trust (e.g., Ahmed & Salas 2011; Malhotra 2010; Ruffle & Sosis 2010; Tan & Vogel 2008). These include studies that further support signaling explanations of religion (e.g., Bulbulia & Mahoney 2008; Hall et al. 2015; McCullough et al. 2016; Power 2017; Soler 2012; Sosis, Kress, & Boster 2007) but also studies supporting alternative theories of religious cooperation, such as big gods theory (Norenzayan 2013; Purzycki et al. 2016, 2018), supernatural punishment theory (Johnson 2016), and moral community theory (Graham & Haidt 2010). None of these theories are mutually exclusive, and none of them claim to fully explain religious cooperation. Indeed, researchers widely recognize that there are undoubtedly multiple causal factors involved in religious cooperation and that at least several theoretical perspectives are likely to be in play for any adequate accounting of such a complex phenomenon (Norenzayan et al. 2016). Since our original publication, the academic understanding of religious prosociality has advanced beyond our wildest imagination, and with what appears to be increased interest in the evolutionary and cognitive study of religion (as the publication of this volume attests), the years ahead look even more promising.

CHAPTER 16
DO RITUALS PROMOTE SOCIAL COHESION?
Dimitris Xygalatas

Introduction

Rituals are strange—if not to those who enact them, certainly to outsiders. They involve large expenditures of time, effort, and resources but offer no obvious benefits and often have no apparent purpose. (Think of all the extravagant rituals of the British monarchy that seem utterly comical to any foreigner.) But there is strange, and then there is dangerous: some rituals can involve high levels of stress, effort, and pain, and can pose serious risks for their practitioners. Examples of such extreme rituals include being stung by a swarm of venomous bullet ants, getting nailed on a cross, and walking on fire. Given such high costs, the prevalence of those practices around the world and throughout history constitutes an evolutionary puzzle (Xygalatas 2012).

Based on ethnographic observations (the human activities and relationships anthropologists observe in the field), various scholars have argued that the answer to this puzzle lies in the social functions of these rituals. Specifically, the reason such behaviors survive despite the risks they involve is that they contribute to social cohesion, that is, they strengthen the bonds between community members by producing emotional alignment (shared emotions), fostering collective identities, and promoting solidarity (Atran & Henrich 2010; Sosis 2003). For example, sociologist Emile Durkheim (1915) described a phenomenon he called "collective effervescence": an ecstatic feeling of togetherness, which is experienced by participants of high-arousal rituals and makes them feel one with the group. My colleagues and I investigated this phenomenon by measuring heart-rate activity among performers and spectators of a fire-walking ritual in a Spanish village (Konvalinka et al. 2011). Our measurements revealed the physiological markers of collective effervescence, showing that people's heart rates were synchronized during the ritual, irrespective of their physical activity, and that this extended not only to active performers but even to local spectators. My ethnographic research in the village suggested that this physiological alignment was also felt at the level of subjective experience: participants reported that during the ritual they felt that they became one with the crowd, and this event changed their relationship with other participants, bringing them closer together.

Nonetheless, there is still a gap between these *phenomenological* reports (related to participants' own lived experience) and our physiological measurements. If ritual intensity really contributes to social cohesion, then we should be able to see the effects of participation at the behavioral level. But how can we measure a vague concept like social cohesion? The answer to this question depends on what is theoretically interesting as well as feasible in a real-life setting. Anthropologists can convey a sense of this cohesion by looking at everyday interactions between participants, but such anecdotal evidence is highly subjective and is hard to systematize and quantify. Taking a more quantitative perspective, one could use surveys, for example, asking participants to rate how close they feel to their peers or to the group as a whole. The problem with this approach is that self-reports are often poor indicators of actual behavior, as they are plagued by various biases and serious limitations in individuals' awareness and introspective abilities (Xygalatas & Martin 2016). In addition, self-reports are particularly problematic when they relate to traits and behaviors that are regarded as positive or desirable, because people are more likely to exaggerate these desirable traits (which is why this problem is known as "social desirability bias"; Fisher 1993). Alternatively, one could try to measure specific aspects of those interactions, such as how often people touch one another or how frequently they visit their peers after performing the ritual together. However, in the context of a collective ritual that can involve hundreds or thousands of participants, the logistics of such an undertaking would probably be unmanageable.

And then there is the issue of ritual intensity: since we are interested in examining the effects of extreme rituals, we need a measure of this extremity, which is our *independent variable* (the thing that we expect to be the cause of something else). In an ideal world, we would be able to manipulate this variable by randomly assigning people to varying degrees of ritual intensity. This is what Elliott Aronson and Judson Mills (1959) did in a study where they asked college women to take a test in order to be admitted to a reading group. In the *severe* condition, the test required participants to read out a series of sex-related, obscene words, which were aimed to provoke embarrassment. In the *mild* condition, participants read a series of words that were not obscene, and in the *control* condition, there was no test. After they joined the group, researchers asked the women how interesting they found the group's discussion sessions (which were the same for all conditions). Those participants who went through the embarrassing initiation reported liking the group more.

At the time, Aronson and Mills's study made a seminal contribution to social psychology. However, it lacked what we call *ecological validity*, that is, the ability to make reasonable generalizations about real-life situations based on what was observed in the laboratory. The experiment was conducted among college students, who went through an artificial task that was neither framed nor perceived as a ritual, in order to join a group of little or no personal importance to them. Moreover, the embarrassment task did not even come close to the kinds of costs involved in real-world, high-intensity rituals.

In fact, such rituals could never be studied in a laboratory setting, for a variety of ethical as well as practical reasons. For example, an institutional review board (a university committee that oversees the ethical treatment of participants in research) would never allow an experimenter to subject people to some of the excruciating ordeals found in some hazing or initiation rites. But even if they did, and even if researchers managed to convince people to participate in such a study, these activities would be meaningless outside of their natural context. An important factor underlying the prosocial effects of ritual is the fact that all participants regard the actions involved as sacred. Indeed, in our study of the Spanish fire-walking ritual, we found that the emotional alignment brought about by the ceremony extended only to locals (including both performers and spectators of the ritual), who shared the same cultural background as the fire-walkers. The outsiders who came to watch the ritual as curious tourists did not experience this emotional alignment (Xygalatas et al. 2011).

These limitations, however, do not mean that we have to give up. In fact, there are many scientific areas where true experiments (involving a manipulation and random assignment) are often practically impossible (think of astronomy) or ethically unacceptable (think of epidemiology), but those areas apply rigorous scientific methods nonetheless (Diamond & Robinson 2012). The scientific process consists in systematic observation that leads to the formulation and examination of testable hypotheses about cause-and-effect relationships between variables. This can be done both in the laboratory and in a more natural setting. But while in the laboratory the experimenters manipulate the variables of interest, in a naturalistic experiment (also known as a *quasi-experiment*) these variables occur "in the wild." Thus, instead of taking the phenomena or people we wish to study out of their natural context and moving them into a lab, we take the lab into context by moving it into the field (Xygalatas 2013).

Setting

In order to test the effects of ritual intensity on prosociality, I needed to find some really extreme rituals. There are many such rituals in the world, but few are as intense and at the same time as widespread as the Thaipusam Kavadi. This ritual is performed by millions of Tamil Hindus in India and around the globe in honor of Lord Murugan, the Hindu god of war, also known as Kartikeya. The Thaipusam festival involves a ten-day period of fasting and prayer that culminates with the kavadi ceremony, which involves piercing the body with sharp metallic objects. Although women do not engage in the extreme forms of this ritual (they either have a single piercing or just a scarf around their mouth), men can have hundreds of piercings throughout their body, ranging from needles and hooks from which they hang lime fruit to skewers and rods the size of broomsticks pierced through their cheeks. These rods are often so long and heavy that the bearer has to support them with both hands to prevent tearing of the face. Once these piercings are in place, devotees embark on a several-hour-long procession to the temple of Murugan, each carrying a *kavadi attam*. The kavadi is a large structure made of bamboo, wood, or metal and decorated with flowers and peacock feathers. It can weigh over 40 kilograms (almost 90 pounds) and is carried on the pilgrims' shoulders throughout the entire procession (the word *kavadi* in Tamil literally means "burden"). Some devotees walk on shoes made of nails; the rest walk barefoot, which can be terribly painful because this ritual is typically performed in tropical places, where the sun makes the asphalt scorching hot. In addition to all this, some practitioners drag enormous chariots the size of minivans, using chains that are attached to their skin by hooks. To make matters worse, temples of Murugan are traditionally built on hilltops, which means that pilgrims have to carry their kavadi all the way to the top of the hill, where they can finally have their piercings removed. During the entire procession, they are not allowed to drink, eat, or speak, and they never put their burden down. Clearly, this is a very intense ritual, and in order to study it, I decided to go to Mauritius.

Mauritius is a tiny island nation in the middle of the Indian Ocean. Although it was one of the last places in the world to be inhabited by humans, it is one of the most diverse societies in the world and home to a great variety of religious traditions (Xygalatas et al. 2016). Participation in the kavadi is massive in Mauritius, not just by Tamils but by all Hindus and even by members of other religious groups. The ceremony is organized by hundreds of temples all over the island, some of which draw thousands of participants. This was exactly the kind of context I was looking for.

Methodology

Before conducting a field experiment, one must become familiar with the local culture and establish a social network of connections with participants, local assistants, and gatekeepers (key local contacts who are in position to provide or facilitate access to informants). And the only way to do this is by conducting ethnographic fieldwork, that is, by living with the local community, participating in people's everyday lives, and observing their customs and behaviors. This is a very time-consuming, demanding, often frustrating, but ultimately extremely rewarding process. In this case, it took me almost two years of fieldwork and preparation before I was able to run this experiment. Moreover, field experiments such as this one involve the combination of various methods and skills, as well as a lot of labor, which means that a single researcher cannot easily conduct this kind of study. For this specific study, I brought together an interdisciplinary team consisting of experts in religious studies, anthropology, psychology, statistics, and computer coding, as well as a group of local research assistants.

We designed a field experiment (Xygalatas et al. 2013) with the goal of testing two hypotheses. First, based on previous empirical and theoretical work on the communal effects of rituals (Konvalinka et al. 2011; Norenzayan & Shariff 2008; Sosis & Ruffle 2003), we hypothesized that ritual intensity would increase prosocial behavior for the entire community. And second, based on psychological studies of social identification (Festinger 1962; Tajfel, Billig, & Bundy 2005) and evolutionary theories of parochial altruism (directed preferentially toward members of one's group) (Choi & Bowles 2007; Ginges, Hansen, & Norenzayan 2009), we hypothesized that ritual intensity would increase participants' affiliation with their religious subgroup at the expense of more inclusive superordinate (larger, more inclusive) identities.

In a field setting, we cannot always manipulate our key variables, so we need to find situations where these variables occur naturally (which is why this is also called a *naturalistic* study). The kavadi ritual in the town of Quatre Bornes provided ideal situations for this study. Within the span of a few days (i.e., during the Thaipusam festival), the same people perform two dramatically different types of rituals at the same place, in the context of the same festival: a low-intensity collective prayer that involves three hours of chanting and singing, and the high-intensity kavadi ordeal that involves all the painful activities described above. Moreover, there are many devotees who take part in the high-intensity ritual without engaging in any of the painful activities: they do not have any piercings, they do not carry a burden, and they do not walk barefooted or on nails—they simply accompany the procession as pilgrims. Thus, this setting provided three naturally occurring conditions: a low-ordeal group, a group of high-ordeal performers, and a group of high-ordeal observers (see Figures 16.1 and 16.2).

During the festival, we recruited eighty-six men (that is because, as you will remember, only men engage in the extreme forms of the ritual). Specifically, we tested thirty-five participants after the "low-ordeal" collective prayer and fifty-one participants after the "high-ordeal" kavadi ritual, including people who had performed the painful ordeal and others who had merely observed it. All of our participants were members of the same Hindu community, lived in the same neighborhood, worshipped the same gods, and attended the same temple. Importantly, the people in our sample took part in both rituals, and even the observers had participated as performers in the past. This allowed us to make a reasonable assumption that any behavioral differences observed between these groups as they went through each ritual would be due to the nature of the ritual actions involved and not due to *self-selection bias*, that is, due to preexisting differences in participants' personalities.

Figure 16.1 A "high-ordeal performer" accompanied by "high-ordeal observers" during the ritual.

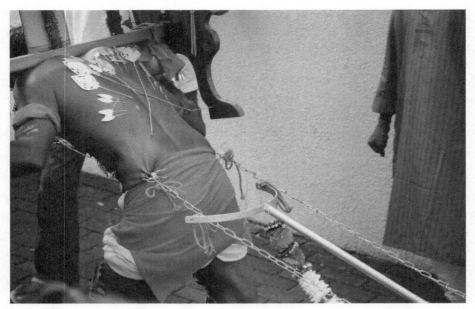

Figure 16.2 In addition to carrying the kavadi, many participants also drag chariots by chains attached to their skin by hooks.

Immediately after each ritual, our local assistants approached participants and invited them to enter a room near the temple, where they were presented with a short questionnaire (written in the local Creole language) that we used to collect demographic information, ratings of the perceived painfulness of the ritual experience, and reports on social identity. Our design involved a comparison between people's identification with a more exclusive, parochial religious group (Mauritian Hindus) and a more inclusive, superordinate national identity (Mauritians). Although my ethnographic work suggested that these two identities were not binary (people felt both Hindu and Mauritian, not one or the other), we were interested in seeing how the intensity of religious rituals, which are meaningful reminders of the more parochial affiliation, might affect the dynamic overlap between these two social identities. For this reason, our questionnaires used continuous sliding scales on a screen, which were anchored by one of these identities at each end. In other words, imagine a straight line ranging from "Hindu" to "Mauritian," where participants can choose which exact point on the line best represents how they feel. This allowed us to see under what circumstances people viewed themselves as being more Hindu or more Mauritian. Using the same type of question, participants also reported on their views of the other main ethnoreligious groups on the island so that we could see how ritual participation would affect attitudes toward religious out-groups such as Christians and Muslims.

Pain is a subjective sensation, so self-reported measures are the best way to assess it. The same goes for social identity, which is an intangible and subjective concept.

However, as we mentioned, self-reports of prosociality are not reliable, so it is best to look at people's real behaviors. But what kinds of behaviors? In other words, we needed to *operationalize* prosocial behavior, that is, to define this phenomenon in terms of a specific manifestation that could be measured precisely. Although there are numerous ways of assessing nonverbal behavior (Manusov 2005), one of the most common paradigms in the study of prosociality focuses on economic interactions, because they involve actual monetary costs that are salient to the participants, forcing them, quite literally, to put their money where their mouth is. However, one problem with economic experiments is that they often feel alien to participants because they do not resemble real-life economic exchanges. To deal with this problem, we looked at how much money people chose to donate to a charity, a task that was familiar and felt natural to our participants. And to avoid *demand characteristics* (participants changing their behavior when they know that they are taking part in an experiment), we presented the task outside of the context of the experiment.

After they answered our questionnaire, we paid participants 200 Mauritian rupees (a substantial amount) as compensation for taking part in the study and thanked them for their participation. However, as they exited the room, a confederate (an actor who is actually part of the experiment) informed them of a local charity and asked them if they would like to make a contribution from their earnings. If they agreed, they were shown a private booth where they could make their contribution. This was done to ensure anonymity, because people behave differently when they know that their behavior is publicly accessible. To facilitate a variety of choices in the amount people would donate, we had made their payments in ten coins of 20 rupees each, which provided them with a behavioral scale of 1–10 right in their pocket.

The need to observe anonymous behavior raised both ethical and practical problems. How could we record people's choices without compromising their anonymity, which was crucial to our design? To solve this problem, we used a system of marked envelopes that the confederate handed to each participant for their donation. The envelopes contained a hidden serial number, which could be linked to participants' answers to the questionnaire without revealing their name. In fact, we never recorded their names, so we could not trace their personal data even if we wanted to.

This design allowed us to compare a high-arousal ritual with a low-arousal one. But to get a more complete understanding of the relationship between ritual intensity and prosociality, we would also need a control group. For this reason, we returned to the same location several months later and collected data from a different group of fifty locals outside of the context of the ritual. This allowed us to get a baseline measurement of prosociality within that community.

Results and Analysis

Our first prediction was that the painful ritual would incite more prosocial behaviors among all attendants, irrespective of their role. Our results confirmed this prediction.

After taking part in the "low-ordeal" collective prayer, participants donated an average of 81 rupees. On the other hand, after attending the "high-ordeal" kavadi ritual, people on average donated 151 rupees—a difference that was highly significant. But when we compared performers to observers of that ritual, there was no significant difference between the groups. In other words, everyone who took part in the high-intensity ritual was more generous. As for the control group, they donated an average of 52 rupees, which was significantly lower than even the low-intensity ritual performers (see Figure 16.3). To examine the effects of ritual intensity more closely, we looked at the relationship between pain and donations. We found that there was a positive correlation between the two variables, meaning that the more participants suffered during the ritual, the more money they donated to the charity. Taken together, these findings suggest that (a) collective rituals can have positive effects on generosity, (b) those effects are amplified by ritual intensity, and (c) they can extend to the entire community.

Our second prediction was that the painful ritual would have an effect on social identification, resulting in stronger identification with the religious in-group at the expense of more inclusive social identities. However, the results suggested a more interesting story. Specifically, we found that higher pain drove people to identify more with the inclusive Mauritian identity. Similarly, we found that those who took part in the

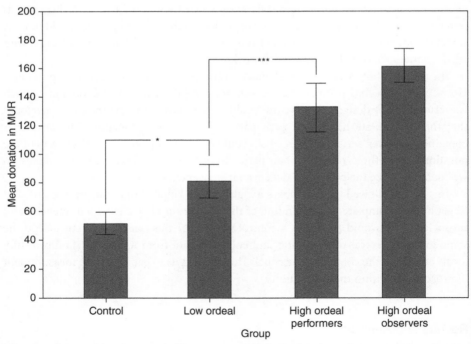

Figure 16.3 Both performers and spectators of the high-ordeal ritual were significantly more generous compared to participants in the low-ordeal ritual, who in turn were more generous than the people who took part in no ritual (the control group).

painful ritual saw not only themselves but also other religious groups, that is, Christians and Muslims, as being more Mauritian. These results suggest that participation in the high-intensity ritual led to an expansion of the prosocial circle for this community.

Discussion

The results of our field experiment provide support for long-standing theories on the role and function of extreme rituals. Specifically, we found that ritual intensity increased prosocial behaviors and attitudes, an effect that applied to the entire community, that is, not only for those who underwent the painful ordeal but also for spectators of the event. In contrast, people's self-reported religiosity had no bearing on generosity. This confirms research in cognitive science of religion suggesting that religious prosociality is a matter of situational factors (circumstances) rather than dispositional ones (personality) (Shariff & Norenzayan 2007; Xygalatas & Martin 2016).

In addition, we saw that ritual intensity led participants to identify with a more inclusive social identity and to see other social groups as being closer to that overarching identity as well. In a different context, the ritual practices of a group might increase in-group cohesion at the expense of the out-group, that is, might serve to mark this group as distinct from and superior to others. However, in the Mauritian context, the Thaipusam Kavadi is celebrated on a national scale and is frequently attended by members of other ethnoreligious groups, who coexist in a relatively nonconfrontational way (Xygalatas et al. 2017). In this context, this ritual serves as a celebration of Mauritian-ness, affirming the inclusive nature of the superordinate Mauritian national identity (Clingingsmith, Khwaja, & Kremer 2009; Gaertner et al. 1999; Hornsey & Hogg 2000). Once again, we are reminded that human cognition and behavior are always situated (embedded) within specific sociocultural contexts, and we must take these contexts into account when designing, conducting, and interpreting our studies (Henrich, Heine, & Norenzayan 2010).

However, each individual study only adds a single piece to the puzzle. Science is a cumulative process, which means that in order to solve the puzzle of extreme rituals we need to look at multiple lines of evidence. For example, although our study was the first to quantify the prosocial effects of ritual intensity in a real-life ritual, it did not address the question of how these effects come about, that is, the specific mechanisms that drive the effects. To answer this question, we can turn to other relevant findings from the disciplines of psychology and anthropology.

One obvious feature of extreme rituals is that they involve a lot of effort and pain. Numerous studies have demonstrated that the higher the cost of an activity, the more meaningful and important it feels to its practitioners (Bem 1967; Festinger 1962; Norton, Ariely, & Mochon 2012). And when this activity is performed in a collective context, then this meaningfulness is extended to the entire group, leading to increased liking for fellow participants (Aronson & Mills 1959; Gerard & Mathewson 1966). Similarly, research on pain also shows that suffering can increase prosocial behavior (Olivola & Shafir 2011) and sharing dysphoric (unpleasant) experiences can lead to increased cooperation (Bastian, Jetten, & Ferris 2014). This can happen via the alignment of empathic responses among ritual participants (Konvalinka et al. 2011; Xygalatas et al. 2011), the formation of shared memories and narratives about their common experience (Schjoedt et al. 2013; Whitehouse 1992; Xygalatas & Schjoedt 2013), and the activation of powerful collective identities produced by this shared experience (Whitehouse & Lanman 2014).

At the same time, performing a strenuous ordeal can signal commitment to the community's norms and values (Henrich 2009), because only those who are really serious about their group membership would pay such a high cost to partake in the community's traditions. This is known as the *costly signaling theory* (Sosis 2000), and it has received empirical support from anthropological studies. For example, those who pay higher ritual costs enjoy reputational and cooperative benefits (Power 2017a, 2017b; Sosis & Ruffle 2003) within their communities, and religious groups that have costlier ritual requirements have better survival rates, that is, are less likely to dissolve (Sosis & Bressler 2003).

Finally, extreme rituals might produce beneficial effects at the individual level. Such rituals are often believed to have healing powers, and there might well be some health-related benefits to participation, whether these function merely as placebos or are the products of such things as physical activity and socialization (Snodgrass, Most, & Upadhyay 2017; Tewari et al. 2012). In addition, research suggests that despite the suffering involved, the neurochemical effects of prolonged pain and exertion may bring about feelings of bliss and euphoria (Fischer et al. 2014).

Extreme rituals have always puzzled scholars of religion, leading to fascinating descriptions and speculations about their functions. These scholars proposed insightful theories to explain the existence and persistence of those rituals, arguing that they play an important role in boosting social cohesion and maintaining social order. However, they lacked the proper scientific tools to put them to the test. Recent developments in research areas like cognitive science of religion are now providing these tools by using new interdisciplinary methods to shed fresh light on these age-old questions.

CHAPTER 17
ARE MUSLIM COSTLY SIGNALS CHRISTIAN CAUTION SIGNALS?
Deborah Hall, Erik Porter, and Richard Grove

Introduction

Imagine that you wake up one day in an alternate reality where, despite the familiar faces, you don't know whom you can trust. You cautiously navigate each and every interaction—with friends, coworkers, and even family members—uncertain of the extent to which you can rely on anyone. What behaviors might others perform that would make them seem more or less trustworthy to you? For example, how might observing a stranger return a lost wallet to its owner, seeing a neighbor throw trash on the ground, or learning that a coworker maintains a strict kosher diet influence how trustworthy you perceive each of these people to be? Now, consider the behaviors that you might perform, intentionally or unintentionally, that might signal to others the extent to which *they* can trust you. It should come as no surprise that people rate trust as one of the most valued characteristics in a relationship. Fortunately, most people live in a reality where their most important relationships are with people they trust. What we hope to emphasize, however, is that trust is also a vital part of even our more fleeting social interactions with the wide range of people we encounter in our daily lives.

Trust may be especially important in interactions involving people from different cultures and backgrounds. Yet behaviors that promote trust in one culture might seem untrustworthy in others. For instance, the social meaning of eye contact varies across regions of the world. In some cultures, making eye contact conveys warmth, interest, and honesty; in others, it can be alarming or even insulting. Despite the benefits of building trust across cultural lines, there has been little psychological research on cultural variables that affect trust, and even less is known about religion and trust. In the present studies, we investigated two aspects of religion that might affect levels of trust: whether a person belongs to one's own religious group or a different religious group, and whether or not the person performs behaviors that signal their commitment to that religious group.

Religion and group identity

Take a moment to think about what makes you who you are. Your identity is made up of many parts, with some aspects reflecting the qualities and traits that make you unique and others stemming from your membership in various social groups. Your sense of self may, for instance, be based partly on your membership in a specific political party, whether you cheer for the Yankees or the Red Sox, or your status as an American citizen or a citizen of another country. For many people, religion serves as a powerful source of group identity; they identify with a particular religious affiliation or group based on shared religious values and beliefs, and their membership in the group is an important part of who they are.

Research in social psychology has shown that group membership has a profound impact on how we think about and interact with others. We have warmer and more favorable feelings toward members of our *in-groups* (i.e., groups to which we belong) than we do toward members of *out-groups* (i.e., groups to which we do not belong). As a result, we frequently act in ways that favor our in-groups and are biased against out-groups (Tajfel & Turner 1979). When it comes to religious groups, people tend to trust members of their own religious group more than they trust members of other religious groups (Daniels & von der Ruhr 2010; Johansson-Stenman, Mahmud, & Martinsson 2009).

Religious costly signaling

Another aspect of religion that might influence trust involves behaviors that communicate one's commitment to a specific religious group. *Religious costly signaling* refers to religious behaviors that are costly to perform—that require a considerable amount of effort and self-discipline—and signal a genuine commitment to one's religious group precisely *because* they carry a cost to the self (Sosis 2005). Examples of religious costly signaling include elaborate religious rituals, donating to a religious charity, and adhering to religion-based dietary restrictions. For instance, because a strict kosher diet requires effort and self-discipline to maintain, Jewish people who choose to adhere to a kosher diet are often seen as more devoted to the Jewish faith than those who do not. Importantly, researchers also have linked religious costly signals to greater cooperation and trust among members of religious groups (Sosis & Alcorta 2003).

Theory

To summarize, people trust members of their own religious group more than they trust members of other religious groups. Across religions, people sometimes choose to perform religious behaviors that require considerable effort or self-discipline. These "costly" behaviors serve as signals of commitment to the religious group and can increase perceptions of trust within that group. A critical question that remains is how behaviors that signal a strong commitment to a different religious group—a group that might be perceived as promoting very different values and beliefs from one's own—influence levels of trust. On the one hand, complex rituals that demonstrate trustworthiness to members of one's own religious group might appear strange or threatening to those who practice a different religion. On the other, members of other religious groups who engage in costly signaling might be seen as having strong character and being more generally trustworthy. We designed a series of experiments to examine this question.

Methodology

Participants in our studies were college students who identified themselves as Christian. In the first two studies, we showed participants what appeared to be the social media profile of a stranger and asked them how trustworthy the person in the profile seemed. We varied key aspects of the profile so that the stranger—or "target person"—ostensibly belonged to participants' own religious group (i.e., was a fellow Christian) or a different religious group (i.e., was a Muslim), and the person either did or did not engage in religious costly signaling (by mentioning in the social media profile that they donated 10 percent of their annual income to religious charity).

So, try to envision that you are a participant in one of our studies. You are a college student, and on a preliminary questionnaire, you have indicated that you are a Christian. We, the researchers, have told you that the experiment involves viewing a stranger's social media profile and then sharing your initial impressions of that person. Unbeknownst to you, you have been randomly assigned to view one of four different social media profiles that we created (see Table 17.1).

Note: Participants were randomly assigned to view one of the four social media profiles (i.e., Profile A, B, C, or D).

You are randomly assigned to Profile A, so you view the profile of a person who likes pizza, rock climbing, and going to the movies; is a Christian; and mentions donating a portion of their income to a Christian charity each year. Next, we ask you to rate this person on a range of dimensions, based solely on your first impressions. Take a minute to think about how outgoing, conscientious, intelligent, and trustworthy you would guess that this person is. In fact, how likely would you be to lend this person money and expect to get it back, or tell this person a sensitive secret? Now, think about how you might answer these questions if you had viewed a social media profile that was identical to Profile A except that the target person is a Muslim who donates to a Muslim charity each year—or if you had viewed the profile of a Christian or Muslim person who mentioned that they do *not* donate to religious charity.

Table 17.1 Experimental conditions for Studies 1 and 2.

		Target person's religious group	
		Religious in-group member (Christian)	*Religious out-group member (Muslim)*
Religious costly signaling status	Costly signals	Profile A Christian who donates 10% of income to religious charity	Profile B Muslim who donates 10% of income to religious charity
	Does *not* costly signal	Profile C Christian who does *not* donate to religious charity	Profile D Muslim who does *not* donate to religious charity

Results and Analysis

When we asked our participants to rate the target person based on the social media profile they had viewed, a remarkably consistent pattern emerged. Participants saw targets who engaged in religious costly signaling by donating to religious charity as more trustworthy than those who did not. This finding held regardless of whether the target person was a fellow Christian—and was thus a member of participants' religious in-group—or was a Muslim and was thus a member of a religious out-group (see Figures 17.1 and 17.2). That is, we found that behavior that signals devotion to a religious group increased perceptions of trust among Christian participants, regardless of whether the commitment was to one's own religious group (i.e., Christians) or to a different religious group (i.e., Muslims).

At this point, you may be questioning whether donating to a religious charity is really an example of costly signaling. Perhaps donating to any charity, religious or secular, builds trust because it signals generosity and compassion for others. If so, our findings might have less to do with behavior that conveys religious commitment and more to do with behavior that communicates a desire to help others. We were wondering the same thing. So, we designed more experiments to find out.

In a third study, we had participants read a brief vignette about a person who was either a Christian or a Muslim, and who either did or did not adhere to religious

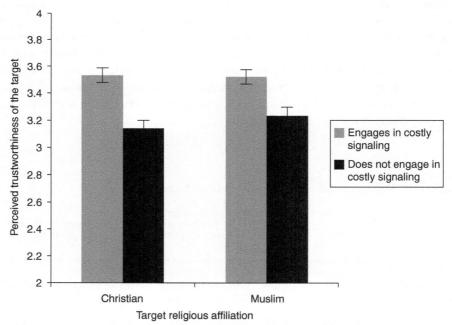

Figure 17.1 Effect of costly signaling on perceived trustworthiness of Christian and Muslim targets in Study 1.

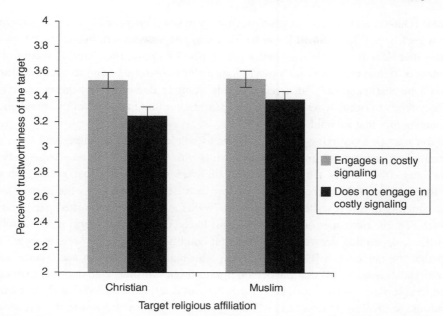

Figure 17.2 Effect of costly signaling on perceived trustworthiness of Christian and Muslim targets in Study 2.

dietary laws. Specifically, participants read about a Catholic target (named John)—who either did or did not adhere to religious dietary restrictions during Lent—or a Muslim target (named Samir)—who either did or did not adhere to Halal dietary laws surrounding the way in which certain foods are prepared. We chose this type of religious costly signaling because, in contrast to donating to religious charity, maintaining a strict, religion-based diet provides no direct benefit to others. Again, we found that Christian participants trusted a target person who engaged in religious costly signaling—this time, by adhering to religious dietary laws—more than a person who did not, regardless of whether the diet signaled a commitment to one's own or a different religious group.

In a final study, we used a different method for investigating the association between trustworthiness and religious costly signaling. We adapted an experimental paradigm that draws on a classic error in thinking known as the *conjunction fallacy* (Tversky & Kahneman 1983).

The conjunction fallacy occurs when people mistake the combined probability of two independent outcomes or events occurring as greater than the probability of just one of the outcomes or events occurring. Statistically, the combined probability of two independent outcomes will always be equal to or lower than the probability of either of the outcomes alone—never higher.

To illustrate, imagine meeting a student named Kelly, who has bright purple hair and several facial piercings. Which do you think is more likely—that Kelly is a psychology major (Outcome 1) or that Kelly is a psychology major (Outcome 1) who also plays in a punk rock band (Outcome 2)? If you are like many people, your intuition is that it is more likely that Kelly is a psychology major who is also in a punk rock band (Outcome 1 + Outcome 2) than that she is just a psychology major (Outcome 1 only). Yet your instincts would be mathematically incorrect. As this example demonstrates, the conjunction fallacy tends to occur when we are given information that fits with our existing beliefs or stereotypes that we hold.

You may be wondering how this relates to religious costly signaling and trust. In our final experiment, we presented participants with information about a target person who was either highly trustworthy (e.g., the person returned a lost wallet with all of its contents to the correct owner) or low in trustworthiness (e.g., the person kept the contents of a lost wallet and threw the wallet away). We then asked participants which of three outcomes or events was most likely: (1) that the person is a [Catholic/Muslim], depending on which experimental condition participants were assigned to, (2) that the person is a [Catholic/Muslim] who maintains a diet in accordance with [Lent/Halal] rules, or (3) that the person is a [Catholic/Muslim] who does *not* maintain diet in accordance with [Lent/Halal] rules. Statistically, the likelihood that the person is Catholic or Muslim (Outcome 1) will always be greater than or equal to the likelihood that the person is a Catholic or Muslim who either does or does not adhere to religious dietary laws, because each of these latter options represents the combined probability of two outcomes—that the person is a Catholic or Muslim (Outcome 1) *and* that the person does or does not costly signal (Outcome 2).

Although complex, this study design allowed us to measure perceptions of trust in a more subtle way than we were able to with the self-report measure of trust used in the previous studies. We expected evidence of a cognitive association between perceived trust and costly signaling to emerge in the type of conjunction fallacy that participants would make. In other words, we predicted that participants who read about a highly trustworthy target would mistakenly believe that it was most likely that the person was a Catholic or Muslim who engaged in religious costly signaling, whereas participants who read about an untrustworthy target would mistakenly believe that it was most likely that the person was a Catholic or Muslim who did *not* costly signal. Furthermore, we expected this pattern to hold regardless of whether the target person was Catholic or Muslim.

Not all participants fell victim to the conjunction fallacy. Across experimental conditions, some participants correctly identified the first answer choice—that the target person was merely Catholic or Muslim—as the most likely. Yet many of them did fall prey to the conjunction fallacy, and their errors in thinking were consistent with the perception that religious costly signaling and trustworthiness go together (see Table 17.2). That is, participants who read about a highly trustworthy Catholic or Muslim target person were more likely to guess that the person also adhered to religious dietary restrictions, and participants who read about an untrustworthy Catholic or Muslim were more likely to guess that the person did not adhere to religious dietary restrictions.

Table 17.2 Counts (and percentages) of the outcome rated most likely in Study 4.

	Catholic target (n = 290)		Muslim target (n = 255)	
	Low trust condition (n = 143)	High trust condition (n = 147)	Low trust condition (n = 119)	High trust condition (n = 137)
Is Catholic/Muslim	17 (11.9%)	87 (59.2%)	37 (31.1%)	62 (45.3%)
Is Catholic/Muslim who costly signals	3 (2.1%)	55 (37.4%)	5 (4.2%)	68 (49.6%)
Is Catholic/Muslim who does *not* costly signal	123 (86.0%)	5 (3.4%)	77 (64.7%)	7 (5.1%)

Note: n indicates the number of participants in each of the experimental conditions.

Discussion

Returning to the idea that we opened this chapter with, how would your life be different if you one day awoke and could no longer remember whom you could trust? How might your interactions with others—from the barista at the coffee shop to fellow drivers on the road and even your closest family members and friends—be different in the absence of trust? What information would shape the degree to which you relied on others? Which behaviors would be most helpful for building trust, particularly when you interacted with people whose beliefs and values were noticeably different from your own?

In the present research, we investigated two aspects of religion—religious group identity and behaviors that are performed to signal a commitment to one's religion—that we believed might influence trust. The results of four experiments, which drew on multiple research designs, converged in the perhaps theoretically surprising finding that religious costly signaling increases trust both within and across religious group lines. Simply put, the knowledge that a stranger donates a portion of their income to religious charity or adheres to religion-based dietary laws increased the perceived trustworthiness of the person, regardless of whether they belonged to one's own or a different religious group.

Across the studies, we examined Muslims as a religious out-group of the Christian students in our samples, in large part because of the increased prevalence of anti-Muslim prejudice in the United States and Europe (Raiya et al. 2008; Strabac & Listhaug 2008) relative to many other religious groups. Our research thus contains a potentially hopeful message for religiously diverse and pluralistic societies. To be trusted by Christians, Muslims do not have to abandon their religious practices. In fact, these practices can promote trust by members of the majority religious group.

It is essential to note, however, that our studies were limited in ways that highlight important directions for future research. For example, it is possible that people are more inclined to trust an individual member of a religious out-group than to trust the religious out-group as a whole. Our findings may thus have positive implications for one-on-one interactions between Christians and Muslims that do not necessarily apply to interactions on a broader, group level. Additionally, three of our four studies relied on participants' self-reported perceptions of trust. Although we adopted an indirect measure of trust in our last study, none of our studies measured true behavioral indicators of trust. An intriguing way to extend the current findings would be to examine differences in the likelihood that the Christian college students in our samples would leave a valuable personal item unattended in a room with a religious out-group member who either does or does not costly signal. Finally, one of the most significant limitations is that our samples consisted entirely of college students and self-identified Christians. Given differences between millennials and older adults and between college students and the general US population on issues pertaining to pluralism and tolerance, as well as in degree of religiosity (Pew Research Center 2010), future research should clarify whether these results can be replicated with more diverse samples of participants, and when evaluating perceptions of trust across a wider range of religious groups.

CHAPTER 18
IS RITUAL BEHAVIOR A RESPONSE TO ANXIETY?

Martin Lang, Jan Krátký, John Shaver, Danijela Jerotijević, and Dimitris Xygalatas

Introduction

Imagine the following scenario: You are a student sitting in front of a committee during finals, waiting for the professors to come up with a question that will take the next hour or so to answer. There are several factors playing in your favor: you know the professors, their interests, and their favorite questions; the list of usual exam topics was circulated well in advance; and you have prepared for weeks. Everything should go smoothly. You hope. Now imagine a slightly different scenario. At the Department for the Scientific Study of Religions in Brno, Czech Republic (where our group works), the faculty decided to introduce a new, supposedly unbiased mechanism governing the topic-selection process, namely a thirty-two-sided die. The rationale for the use of the die is simple: because topics are chosen at random, no one can complain about fickle and eccentric professors giving tricky questions. But the die substantially changes the game for the students. They cannot reasonably anticipate the question based on professors' interests or previous exams; the only thing they know for sure is that they will face an uncontrollable, random process that will select the questions for them.

So, although you prepared really well for the exam, you couldn't read all the materials. And surely there is a question about Heideggerian metaphysics waiting for you. No one in their right mind knows about such things! If only there was a way to influence the die and make it choose anything but Heidegger. Note that we have nothing against Heideggerian philosophy; it just seems complicated to students at times. Perhaps doing something will help. Anything! You can't just do nothing! And so, before rolling the die, you reach into your pocket to touch your lucky rabbit's foot, or perhaps you quickly recite a short prayer—"Please, God, no Heidegger." Perhaps this may help a bit, you think. It's certainly better than doing nothing, right? Indeed, many of us would behave in a similar way. Few of us would be so blindly optimistic as to just take the die and roll it without doing *something*.

Stressful situations are common in our lives: public performances at schools or in sports are frequent, serious family situations befall us all too commonly, and natural disasters, unfortunately, occur. People cannot have full control over every possible situation. Think about the last time you experienced stress. Your heart probably raced and your body tensed. This physiological state is a useful mechanism, since it motivates people to react immediately and, in most everyday situations, to adopt rational and instrumental actions to avert undesirable but likely outcomes (e.g., avoiding entering dark forests in favor of well-lit streets). However, as a response to events that cannot be prevented, stress and anxiety can be detrimental for our coping abilities and, in the long term, for our health. Attempting to influence the odds by doing any kind of action can prevent us from feeling utterly powerless and help us manage our anxiety, despite the fact that such actions usually have unknown or only dubious causal connections to the desired outcome (such as rubbing a rabbit's foot prior to an exam). Often recognized as ritual behaviors due to their opaque causal relationship with desired goals, such actions are of interest to anthropologists, psychologists, and cognitive science of religion.

Perhaps the most widely recognized theory of ritual and anxiety comes from Bronislaw Malinowski (1948/1992), one of the first anthropologists conducting fieldwork. Malinowski spent two years living in the Trobriand Islands with the locals, studying their language, their customs, and their culture in general. While observing Trobrianders' rituals, Malinowski uncovered a startling pattern: the rituals usually occurred before events that were beyond an individual's control. For example, Trobrianders would perform their magic before going to fish on the open sea, which was risky, uncontrollable, and uncertain. In contrast, they would not perform rituals before fishing in the local lagoon, which was easy to navigate and guaranteed a safe catch—so much so that even kids engaged in lagoon fishing. On the basis of these and other similar observations, Malinowski concluded,

[A Trobriander] knows that a plant cannot grow by magic alone, or a canoe sail or float without being properly constructed and managed, or a fight be won without skill and daring. He never relies on magic alone, while, on the contrary, he sometimes dispenses with it completely, as in fire-making and in a number of crafts and pursuits. But he clings to it, whenever he has to recognize the impotence of his knowledge and of his rational technique. (1948/1992: 32)

Malinowski is here describing a situation similar to our test-taking: everyone knows that having a rabbit's foot, while completely ignoring exam materials, will not yield an A+. But when you've done as much as you could and there is still some lingering uncertainty surrounding the exam, you might as well try to do something extra (*like a ritual*) to bring good fortune. From these and similar examples, we can derive a general prediction: when people find themselves in uncertain situations that do not allow direct control of future events through clearly linked actions, they will engage in ritualized behavior in an effort to influence the outcomes.

We have just made a step from ethnographic observations[1] to a general scientific prediction. But how can we go about testing the prediction? One way would be to carry out more systematic fieldwork, such as in the study conducted by Giora Keinan (1994) in Israel during the Gulf War. Keinan surveyed 174 Israeli citizens living in two cities: Tel Aviv and Jerusalem. An important difference between these two cities is their proximity to Iraqi borders: while Jerusalem was safe from Iraqi missiles, participants in Tel Aviv lived in constant fear of unpredictable and uncontrollable missile attacks. As a result of these threats, Keinan predicted that people from Tel Aviv would perform more magical rituals. Through a series of questionnaires on magical thinking and behavior (e.g., "It is best to step into the sealed room right foot first"), Keinan showed that the uncertain and uncontrollable conditions of living in Tel Aviv were associated with a greater frequency of ritual behavior. Other researchers have investigated the relationship between anxiety and ritualized behavior in various contexts, such as among athletes, gamblers, or students during test-taking, and they all arrived at the same conclusion: anxiety-inducing situations tend to be associated with an increased frequency of ritual behavior (Felson & Gmelch 1979; Schippers & Van Lange 2006; Sosis & Handwerker 2011).

While these studies make very valuable contributions, they are limited in their explanatory power because they investigate correlations (statistical association) among variables but do not help to understand causal patterns. In other words, the previous studies (e.g., Keinan's) cannot tell us whether it is really the anxiety-inducing situation in Tel Aviv that leads people to perform more rituals, or whether people performing rituals tend to live in Tel Aviv for some other reasons. In order to disentangle the causal relationships, it is necessary to introduce an experimental manipulation, which will allow us to examine the phenomenon in question in the assumed logical sequence. Furthermore, while introducing an experimental manipulation, we need to make sure that no other variable is influencing (or confounding) the predicted relationship; that is, researchers need to control for other external variables that could be driving the effect. Laboratory experiments address these problems through a strenuous control of the lab environment, well-designed procedures, and by manipulating one thing at a time. In the next section, we turn to experimental methods and explain how we used a laboratory experiment to investigate the relationship between ritual behavior and anxiety (Lang et al. 2015).

Methodology

Laboratory experiments are an extremely useful tool for scientists, yet they also present a significant challenge: in order to control for the numerous variables that naturally occur in concert with the variables under investigation, researchers must reduce the phenomenon of interest into a simplified model of the real world and perform their tests on this model. However, this step comes at a steep cost—our models are mere simulations (approximations) of reality and not reality itself. Thus, researchers have to make sure that the way they operationalize their questions (i.e., how they create their models of reality) sufficiently captures all of the important aspects of the phenomenon of interest. For example, if we operationalized anxiety as the amount of sweat participants produce (recall sweaty hands when stressed), we would need to make sure that this measure sufficiently captures the levels of anxiety that people experience in uncertain situations (aside from controlling for more basic confounds like varying temperature in the lab).

This problem grows in proportion to the complexity of the studied phenomenon, especially when such a phenomenon is deeply embedded in its cultural context. While increased sweating is a reliable indicator of physiological response to anxiety (due to the inner workings of the sympathetic nervous system), operationalizing and measuring ritual behavior is much more challenging. First of all, what is ritual? How can we distill ritual's essential aspects from its cultural context without missing its crucial components? And if ritual is culturally specific, what if some participants do not belong to that specific culture/religion? Will the desired effect occur? These are difficult questions with no clear answers.

In our research, we turned to a methodological paradigm from clinical psychology, where researchers identify the main aspects of a particular behavior by examining its exaggerated version as it manifests in some psychiatric disorder. Specifically, we turned to obsessive-compulsive disorder (OCD), in which patients exhibit pathological ritualization. For example, OCD patients repeatedly check whether they have locked the doors or turned off a stove, or they may perform elaborate routines before starting to prepare a meal. People suffering from OCD need to follow such routines down to the last painstaking detail in order to assuage anxiety. Interestingly, the behaviors that are distinctive in OCD resemble some of the rituals described by anthropologists, exposing the important aspects of the ritual form, which is characterized by an invariable sequence of actions (Dulaney & Fiske 1994). Synthesizing the literature on OCD with anthropological insights, Pascal Boyer and Pierre Liénard identified core aspects that are shared by both cultural and OCD rituals, namely, their rigidity, repetitiveness, and redundancy (Boyer & Liénard 2006; Liénard & Boyer 2006). For example, ritual participants put emphasis on the correct, prescribed way of performing ritual actions (the ritual script cannot be changed, much like in OCD food preparation); the sub-actions of rituals are often repeated several times (as in OCD door lock–checking); and, finally, it is not clear how the particular sub-actions involved in rituals are connected to the desired outcome (why is locking the door ten times more effective than just once?). Consider, for instance, the Muslim prayer (*salat*). Ritual participants follow an unchangeable and purportedly ancient form of praying: first they join hands while standing, then they bow, kneel, and touch the floor with their foreheads, and finally kneel with their backs upright. This sequence is repeated many times during each prayer session, yet it is not clear why this specific form (and not any other) leads to the successful worship of Allah.

Apart from human psychopathology, we also sought insights from animal models of anxiety. By exposing various animals, such as mice or voles, to an image of a predator, ethologists (scholars studying animal behavior) have elicited behaviors that include a high degree of ritualization (Eilam, Izhar, & Mort 2011; Eilam et al. 2006). Assuming that an analogy in responses to anxiety between humans and nonhuman animals is appropriate, these ethological studies motivated us to focus on observable behavior rather than self-reports, which can be subject to all sorts of biases (cf. Lang et al. 2017; Xygalatas & Lang 2017). In other words, we were interested in the behavioral responses to anxiety that may be shared across various cultures and therefore likely have deep evolutionary roots. Of course, such an approach is not appropriate when cultural variation is the subject of a study! One can be interested in why two different religious traditions have various ritual forms and the historical pathways leading to those forms. In our research, we do not claim that ritual content is unimportant; quite the contrary, it can sometimes entirely change the nature of the ritual (e.g., by introducing anxiety itself!). However, we decided to put cultural variation aside for the moment and to focus on the behavioral forms that we predicted to be the main reaction to anxiety. Thus, our basic prediction was that when people experience anxiety, they will display behaviors characterized by rigidity, repetitiveness, and redundancy.

However, this prediction still leaves many questions open: How can we manipulate anxiety, and how can we make sure that this manipulation works, that is, that participants are really anxious? And how can we measure ritual behavior? As you can imagine, these questions could be answered in various ways. This stage of reducing real-world phenomena to laboratory models is often the most difficult step in research. Researchers need to make sure that their materials will simulate the real world as accurately as possible, while still controlling for any variation that is not of interest.

At this point, a survey of previously used methodologies (often in different disciplines) can be most helpful. Experimenters can get an idea of what worked before and how it could be usefully adapted in their own research. We chose to employ the public speaking paradigm, a common psychological method used to induce anxiety in research participants. We divided our subjects into two groups and asked one group to prepare a five-minute speech about an object of art; they would then have to present the speech in front of an expert committee of art critics. (Recall our example of exams and how stressful they can be.) In contrast, the other group's task was just to think about the same object for three minutes.[2]

It is also important to make sure that one's experimental manipulation worked as expected. As mentioned above, the sympathetic nervous system carries anxiety states, and one of the manifestations is increased heart rate, which we typically experience when we feel stressed. Therefore, to assess whether our manipulation was effective, each of our participants wore a heart-rate monitor during the experiment. This allowed us to see whether there was an increase in their heart rates during our anxiety manipulation (preparing the speech) compared to other times. See Figure 18.1(a) for changes in heart rates during the experiment.

Measuring ritualization was more challenging than measuring anxiety. How can we quantify such things as rigidity, repetitiveness, and redundancy and compare ritualization between our two groups? We could have let people wait before giving the speech, observe their behavior, and simply describe with words what they were doing (e.g., "walked back and forth"). However, such an approach would be very imprecise and would introduce a lot of between-participant variation that would be hard to account for in a statistical analysis. Instead, we decided to standardize the performed action by giving participants a specific task: cleaning the artistic object they were supposed to talk about (see Figure 18.1b). But there was one caveat—the object was already clean. Thus, cleaning could serve as a placeholder or platform for expressing participants' ritualization needs. We could have chosen other tasks or objects, but we opted for

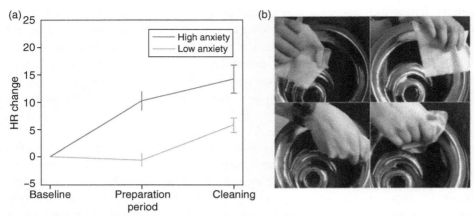

Figure 18.1 (a) Mean change in participants' heart rates during various stages of the experiment. Baseline heart rate (preexperiment) was subtracted from other periods to reflect change in anxiety levels. The mean heart-rate change (with standard errors) shows that our manipulation elicited more anxiety in the high-anxiety condition during the preparation and cleaning periods. (b) An illustration of cleaning patterns. A participant wears ActiGraph accelerometers on his wrists, which capture the hand-movement acceleration that was used to quantify ritualization during cleaning.

cleaning because it is often part of both cultural and OCD rituals (Dulaney & Fiske 1994; Zor et al. 2009). The specific object that we used was circular with small creases, which allowed participants to engage in both variable and ritualized movements while cleaning. (Had we used a square object, all movements would be restricted by its sharp angles and would artificially appear as ritualized.) See Figure 18.1B for an illustration of cleaning patterns on the work of art.

To address the problem of imprecision in observation methodology, we employed accelerometers positioned on participants' wrists to measure various hand-movement characteristics. The isolation and measurement of elementary behavioral expressions was motivated by action-parsing theory, which attempts to describe the ways humans understand actions (Zacks & Swallow 2007; Zacks, Tversky, & Iyer 2001). Human minds divide ongoing actions into smaller units, and this division facilitates an understanding of actions and allows for better prediction of what will happen next. That is, parsing provides constant feedback on whether the smaller action units follow an expected trajectory toward the final goal. For example, *complex scripts* like dressing up are parsed into *behavioral episodes* like putting on pants, which can be further parsed to basic *gestural expressions* such as reaching for the pants with the right hand, lifting the left leg to push it through the pants, and so on. If one of the gestural expressions failed (e.g., pants were not grabbed), the whole complex script would be violated and in need of updating (grab again, more precisely). Such fine-grained parsing is necessary when evaluating the efficacy of actions and their trajectory to the overall goal. Interestingly, when humans lack an understanding of the mechanistic workings behind desired outcomes (as in ritual behavior), they focus on every detail of gestural expression (e.g., a specific finger configuration when throwing rice into the fire). Thus, in the current study, we measured behavioral ritualization at the lowest level of gestural expressions, where the ritual form manifests itself most apparently. Focusing on the characteristics of fine movements allowed us to quantify hand-movement acceleration and examine whether the acceleration patterns exhibited the ritual form.

We used recurrence quantification analysis (RQA), a statistical technique for analyzing the behavior of nonlinear dynamical systems (Marwan et al. 2007; Webber & Zbilut 2005), to assess ritualization in the cleaning task. Put simply, we did not look only at mean acceleration (as in linear statistical approaches), but rather we examined how the acceleration signal evolved over time and measured the signal's rates of recurrence and predictability. RQA is a useful tool for measuring any dynamics, for example, the height of the waves at a beach. Imagine placing a pole in the water at a specific distance from the beach and recording the highest point each wave reached on the pole. After one minute, you could see that wave height is dynamic (it changes over time) but also that wave height recurs in predictable patterns. Now imagine measuring the amplitude of the whole wave (instead of only the peaks) and then comparing it to the amplitudes of all of the other waves during the same minute. The result is a matrix of amplitude points, some of which will be identical; that is, some of them will repeat over time in predictable patterns (see Figure 18.2(a)). This is exactly what RQA measures: how much a signal is recurrent (repetitive) and how much it is deterministic/predictable (rigid in our terms). Figure 18.2(b) illustrates the usage of recurrence plots in the current study (see also Lang et al. (2016) for an application of RQA in a different context). Finally, to quantify redundancy, we measured how much time and how many movements people used while cleaning the art object. After participants finished cleaning, we informed them that they were not selected to give the speech and asked them to fill out a final questionnaire about individual religiosity, age, sex, gender, and perceived anxiety during the study. In summary, we moved from ethnographic observations to a specific experimental hypothesis: we expected that participants in the high-anxiety condition (public speaking) would display more rigid, repetitive, and redundant movements (ritualized behavior) while cleaning an object, compared to participants in the low-anxiety condition.

Nevertheless, what looks like a clear and logical sequence of decisions was actually a product of many discussions and a lot of trial-and-error testing. Although we determined the main contours of our manipulation, manipulation check, and the types of measuring devices at the very beginning of the study, the way we calibrated these elements changed substantially from the first pilot testing to the final data-collection procedure. For example, we first designed our manipulation as a fake TV studio, pretending that we were shooting a video of the participants, which in the high-anxiety condition would later be evaluated by experts, but would only be for our own use in the control condition. This manipulation employed five researchers in total: a cameraman, an assistant, and three evaluators in the other room, connected via a wireless link. The manipulation worked exceedingly well—participants' heart rates went through the roof! However, the entire setup and procedure stressed participants in both the experimental and control

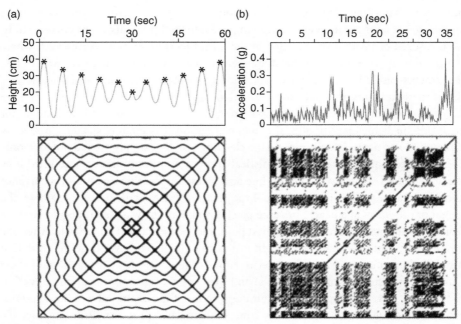

Figure 18.2 (a) A simulated wave height across a one-minute measurement. Asterisks mark the peaks of these imaginary waves, illustrating that wave height is dynamic yet recurs in predictable patterns. Plotting the recurrence of all the points comprising waves (and not only peaks) produces harmonic patterns in the recurrence plot (waves are repeating in a sine-like fashion). (b) Hand-movement acceleration during cleaning. While much more chaotic than the wave example, there are noticeable recurrent patterns in the signal as illustrated by the recurrence plot below the signal. The black dots represent points where the signal repeats itself, and the chunks of black dots represent the predictability of repetitive patterns (rigidity in repetition).

conditions, thus leaving us without the desired contrast between the two groups. From the first pilot test to the final experiment, the procedure changed substantially: we changed the setting, slightly altered the cover story, and excluded the actual speaking. These changes also saved personnel—the final design only required one research assistant, which is important because it minimized variation potentially arising from a complicated procedure and/or having too many cooks in the kitchen. In other words, the more complex an experimental situation, the more fragile this situation will be. In the end, we opted for a simpler design.

Results and Analysis

As expected, we observed higher heart rates among participants in the high-anxiety condition. These participants also reported that they were more anxious than participants in the low-anxiety condition. These results suggest that our manipulation was successful, although there was, of course, individual variation within each condition: some participants in the high-anxiety condition were not petrified by public speaking, while some participants in the low-anxiety condition were quite anxious just from the experimental situation. But overall, the experimental manipulation seems to have worked very well.

In terms of our main variable of interest—ritualized behavior—we observed significant differences between the conditions. Participants in the high-anxiety condition had more recurrent points in their acceleration patterns (they engaged in more repetitiveness) and also displayed more predictable patterns (an index of rigidity). We did not observe any statistical differences in redundancy (time spent cleaning and number of movements used during cleaning). These results largely supported our hypothesis—participants in the high-anxiety condition displayed more rigidity and repetitiveness in their behavior, that is, they differed in two out of three ritual characteristics.

When we examined our results in more detail, two concurrent processes seemed to generate our data: one conscious and one subconscious. Participants who reported being more anxious during the speech preparation/thinking phase (independent of condition) spent more time and engaged in more movements when cleaning the object, but this self-reported anxiety did not predict rigidity and repetitiveness. Those characteristics were, however, predicted by an increase in heart rate during the speech preparation/thinking phase (independent of condition). Thus, ritualization provoked by anxiety seems to be driven by two processes: one at a perceivable level such as the action length, which is more conscious, and one driven by physiological processes at a subconscious level of fine-grained motoric action.

Discussion

Our experimental approach helped us tackle the direction of causality between ritual and anxiety: we found that anxious people performed more ritual-like behavior. This conclusion supports ethnographic observations suggesting that rigidity, repetitiveness, and redundancy may be appealing to people in anxiety-inducing situations. Why might this be so? Ritual actions, be they individual or social, rely upon general psychological proclivities that evaluate the efficacy of possible actions, especially in situations where it is not clear what the person should do in order to meet the goal. Due to its repetitiveness and redundancy, ritualization appears to be helpful under uncertain situations, tapping into intuitive evaluations of efficacy (Legare & Souza 2012). Further formalization of these actions via social convention (i.e., cultural rituals) can amplify the perceived efficacy. For example, anthropologist Roy Rappaport (1999) emphasized the invariable, formal aspects of rituals as one of their most important elements, suggesting that the rigidity of this behavior allows certain types of actions to be stabilized and perpetuated, giving them an aura of eternal efficacy ("it has always been done this way"). Together, the combination of repetitive, redundant, and rigid action may seem the most appealing behavior in situations where people lack control.

This conclusion is compatible with theories of the inner workings of the human brain under anxiogenic situations (Hirsh, Mar, & Peterson 2012). In uncertain and uncontrollable environments, the hierarchical cortical structure tries to minimize errors in predicting future affordances. In other words, the human brain works like a predictive machine, trying to guess what will happen next on several perceptual levels in order to prepare appropriate responses (Clark 2013). When such prediction possibilities are limited (as in uncertain situations), anxiety motivates people to take precautionary actions and decrease the possible prediction errors (e.g., choose the well-lit street over a dark alley). However, this is not always possible, especially in situations where people lack control (recall those missile attacks), and anxiety can become overwhelming; hence, a predictable action that is repeated over and over can help decrease anxiety, despite seeming nonfunctional from a pragmatic perspective. Repeating rigid actions, in other words, can help minimize the prediction errors that arise in the hierarchy of human cortical structures. (For further discussion of this mechanism, see Krátký et al. 2016.)

The ultimate goal of this line of research is to investigate whether ritual behavior actually decreases anxiety. In the study under current discussion, we focused on the first logical part of the prediction: Do people perform more rituals when they are anxious? In order to answer the question of whether or not rituals help decrease anxiety, we will need to design follow-up studies where, for instance, both groups experience an anxiety treatment, such as public speaking, and then the members of one group will perform a ritual while the members of the other will not. We then predict that those in the ritual group will exhibit lower anxiety levels (after the ritual treatment) compared to those in the control group. As for the ritual activity, we need a task that involves predictable and repetitive movements (or verbalizations such as those uttered during prayer), which we can compare with more variable movements. This design could help us answer the *why* question about rituals and anxiety.

Note that in the current study, we measured very simple behavioral gestures, behaviors that are substantially detached from naturally occurring ritual behavior. Our simulation of ritual behavior, and our modelling approach, disentangled the complexities of the real world and allowed us to investigate rituals in a controlled manner. While we believe that we successfully simulated a real-world phenomenon in the lab, the ultimate test would be to perform a similar experiment in naturalistic settings. For example, our group works in Mauritius, where we observe ritual behavior in local Catholic and Hindu populations. We could recruit participants from one of those populations and subject them to the public speaking tasks, and we could measure their heart rate, track their hand movements, and record their speech. After the anxiety treatment, participants could then be asked to perform their rituals or prayers. In comparison with a control group not subjected to public speaking, we would expect to see more ritualization in the anxious group. On the one hand, this approach has the advantage of letting people perform their own habituated rituals, which may manifest the link between rituals and anxiety more effectively. On the other hand, such an approach will also bring a lot of variability, which is minimized under controlled laboratory settings. For example, is there a difference in the usual length of prayer between different traditions? Does one of those traditions comprise more rituals than the other? How frequently, on average, are those rituals performed? Are they performed individually or collectively? These and other questions will be crucial when considering the generalizability of findings from such a study. Moreover, most laboratory studies (including the current one) have been conducted on university students in Western countries (so-called WEIRD populations; see Henrich, Heine, & Norenzayan 2010; Sears, 1986) and thus present a very homogenous sample. In the real world, we will also have to deal with other potential confounding variables such as age, income, socioeconomic status, and so forth. These can be measured and controlled for in statistical models, but they also add more complexity, making it more difficult to interpret the results.

To conclude, there are costs and benefits to both laboratory and field experiments. Ideally, we should strive for the combination of both approaches, moving back and forth between the field and the lab. Only under such methodological collaboration can we be sure that our laboratory simulations represent the real world and our real-world studies are not confounded by unobserved factors. As this chapter hopes to illustrate, we live in exciting times when new methodologies and technologies can help us answer old questions and test classical theories in our disciplines, such as the one by Bronislaw Malinowski (1948/1992).

CHAPTER 19
CAN RITUALS REDUCE STRESS DURING WAR? THE MAGIC OF PSALMS
Richard Sosis

Introduction

In the summer of 2002, I was traveling from Jerusalem to Tzfat in an Israeli taxicab. On the dashboard I noticed a Book of Psalms and, as a meddlesome anthropologist, I asked the driver about it. I was particularly curious because at least by outward appearance he was not religious—he was not wearing a kippah as male religious Jews do in Israel. He responded to my query, "Ah, it's my protection." He added that it made him feel safe driving through areas that were considered dangerous. Our encounter was during the height of the second Palestinian uprising, or Intifada, and concern about terror attacks was palpable everywhere. I asked him what psalms he recited for protection but he shook his head at my foolishness. He did not actually recite psalms; simply having the Book of Psalms on his dashboard was all the protection he needed. And who could argue with him? By his own account he had never been shot at or attacked in his many hours of delivering passengers to their destinations.

While Jewish law does not mandate reciting psalms, many religious Jews regularly do so as a daily spiritual practice, and the Book of Psalms has deep resonance even among secular Jews, such as my cabdriver. For example, the autobiography of Russian refusenik Natan Sharansky (1988) offers an extraordinary account of how the Book of Psalms, which he could barely read, provided hope and sustenance during his imprisonment. Jews throughout the world recite psalms, but it is more common among Israeli than American Jews, and women recite psalms more frequently than men. In Israel, women recite psalms virtually at any time in any place: waiting for an appointment, on a bus, watching children at a playground, at a graveside, in their home, and so forth. Men and women often sway (*shokel*) when they are reciting psalms and chant the words softly, but loud enough to be audible to the reciter. The Talmud provides evidence that Jews have been reciting psalms for protection for much of their history.

The exchange with my cabdriver excited my anthropological imagination. I had observed, in awe and jealousy, Israeli stoicism in the face of constant terror threats; I did not share Israelis' ability to shrug off such threats. Every attack, or even attempted and thwarted attack, increased my stress and paranoia. Obviously, having not grown up in such an environment (I was raised in the safety of American suburbia), I had not developed the fortitude and resilience that most Israelis appear to maintain. But as my encounter with the cabdriver suggested, Israelis evidently had cultural tools, such as carrying around a Book of Psalms, to help them overcome the potential chronic stress they faced from terror attacks. I wondered, what other religious coping strategies did Israelis employ? Were these practices helpful? How did they arise, and who engaged in such practices?

Of Pigeons, Piscivores, and Poker Players: The Uncertainty Hypothesis

In a quirky but classic article entitled " 'Superstition' in the Pigeon," B. F. Skinner (1948) described the results of an experiment in which pigeons, placed inside what we now refer to as a "Skinner box," developed superstitious ritual behaviors in response to an unpredictable feeding schedule. Legend has it that Skinner was so confident in the emergence of such behaviors that he would take a boxed pigeon to his undergraduate lectures at Harvard, dramatically uncover the box at the end of class, and invariably reveal a pigeon engaged in some ritualistic behavioral pattern, presumably in hope of securing food that was in fact being randomly dispersed. Since Skinner's pioneering work, various studies (e.g., Ono 1987; Wagner & Morris 1987) have documented how children and adults in analogous experimental conditions quickly generate novel superstitious practices, or what anthropologists generally refer to as magic.

Years before Skinner's experiments, the anthropologist Bronislaw Malinowski (1925/1954) predicted that individuals would turn toward magic to exercise some control when faced with unpredictable conditions, whereas magic would be absent under conditions of certainty. His insights about magic grew out of his own ethnographic studies in the Trobriand Islands of Papua New Guinea. Malinowski found that Trobriand Islanders employed magic when fishing activities were uncertain or hazardous, but magic was absent when they were simply collecting shellfish or using traps that were reliable.

In recent years, Malinowski's hypothesis has been dubbed the "uncertainty hypothesis" (Burger & Lynn 2005). The uncertainty hypothesis posits that magical rituals increase performers' sense of control, which reduces anxiety, allows individuals to cope with their unpredictable conditions, and successfully enables them to perform the high-risk tasks they face. Researchers have actively explored the emergence of magical rituals and beliefs among diverse populations facing uncontrollable conditions, including gamblers (Bersabé & Martínez Arias 2000), test-taking students (Rudski & Edwards 2007), targets of warfare (Keinan 1994, 2002), golfers (Wright & Erdal 2008), baseball players (Gmelch 2001), track-and-field athletes (Todd & Brown 2003), and various other athletes (Bal et al. 2014; Schippers & Van Lange 2006; Womack 1992).

Malinowski's Trobriand observations and subsequent thesis about magical practices had fascinated me since graduate school because they accorded with my own experiences on Ifaluk, a remote atoll in the Federated States of Micronesia, where I conducted my dissertation research. On Ifaluk, the most unpredictable type of fishing practiced—in terms of returns—was known as torch fishing. An evening of torch fishing begins at dusk with the fishers ritualistically walking in single-file line to their canoes in the center of the lagoon. Each man (only men fish on Ifaluk) carries unlit torches (rolled-up, dried palm fronds), and once everyone is aboard, the men row the sailing canoes beyond the reef to the open ocean waters, where they light several torches. The light from these torches attracts flying fish, which designated men scoop out of the air with hand nets. The flying fish are then used as bait to deep-sea troll for dog-toothed tuna, the largest species of fish they pursue. Fishers generally return when the sun rises. Torch fishing success is highly unpredictable (Sosis 2000, 2001, 2002)—many nights they return with nothing but leftover bait—and fishing at night in the open ocean is risky. Indeed, one man remains ashore all evening as a rescue lookout in case a canoe capsizes. Torch fishing is permeated with magical practices, including food taboos and consultations with the magician, who, using shells, divines the optimal time and location for this fishing activity.

In contrast, rope fishing, by far the most predictable and reliable fishing activity on Ifaluk, has no ritual or magical activity associated with it. To rope fish, men take a fifty-meter rope and adorn it with palm fronds. The fishers then bring the adorned rope to an area of the lagoon, and the fishers create a large circle with the rope. They then dive off their canoes into the lagoon and drag the rope across the lagoon floor. The men swim toward the center of the now decreasing circle, driving the scared fish into this central location, where a large net awaits. The fishers invariably catch hundreds of small reef fish. Successful returns are so predictable that the chief on Ifaluk actually limits the frequency of rope fishing out of concern that fishers will deplete the resources in the lagoon.

As we have seen, Malinowski and others have claimed that magical beliefs and practices reduce anxiety produced by uncertain conditions, thus allowing individuals to focus on and successfully complete a particular high-risk task. If such practices have adaptive significance, it must be shown that they do indeed positively influence task performance. Does the student who clutches her lucky rabbit-foot while taking an exam improve her score? Does bouncing the basketball three times before a foul shot improve the shooter's likelihood of making the basket? Do supplications to God in the foxhole reduce stress and allow the soldier to make clearer decisions, thus increasing his probability of survival? While many scholars assume that magical beliefs and practices must have functional consequences, empirical data supporting such assertions are lacking. (For an exception, see Damisch, Stoberock, & Mussweiler 2010.) Other researchers, with equally sparse data, maintain that magical behaviors are maladaptive, producing no discernable benefits but costing individuals significant time and energy. I was keen to contribute empirical data to this debate and my cabdriver provided just the impetus I needed for doing so.

Psalms for Safety

My cabdriver relied on his Book of Psalms to protect him and deal with the stress of driving through areas where he might be attacked, but he was not an anomaly. Living and working among Israelis, I was attuned to the fact that they did many things to help them cope with the uncertainty of terrorism. I was now anxious to document these practices. Moreover, I wanted to find out if they were efficacious. In other words, did they help individuals deal with the stress of terrorism and enable them to carry out their normal lives?

Methodology

To address these issues, I undertook a study (Sosis 2007) that explored how residents in the northern Israeli town of Tzfat used culturally and religiously defined magical beliefs and practices to cope with the stress of the Second Palestinian Intifada (SPI). Early anthropologists, including Malinowski, carefully distinguished between magic and religion, but later generations realized that these categories of beliefs and behaviors have fuzzy boundaries. Many religious practices have magical qualities, and many magical acts appropriate religious elements. Here, following others, I refer to all of these actions as magico-religious practices.

While throughout their history Israelis have been regularly exposed to threats of terror, in September 2000, which marked the beginning of the SPI, the frequency and severity of attacks began to escalate to new heights. Over the following three years, there were thousands of attempted attacks, including drive-by shootings, stabbings, and suicide bombings. In the SPI's most prolific year, 2002, there were over 450 fatalities, whereas terror-related fatalities never exceeded 100 per year prior to the SPI. Studies by Yechiel Klar and colleagues (1996, 2002) show that Israelis characterize terrorist attacks as both uncontrollable and unpredictable. In commenting on the Israeli experience, psychologist Shabtai Noy notes that "while the expected number of casualties from a terrorist attack is not high, the prolonged effect of the uncertainty of when, where or how an attack will occur can result in disturbance to normal functioning and psychic life, leading to the development of an on-going and pervasive state of generalized anxiety and disruption of life" (2004: 31). Hence, the SPI created conditions of stress and uncertainty where, according to Malinowski's uncertainty hypothesis, magical practices and beliefs were expected to flourish.

Tzfat is located in the Galilee region of northern Israel and has a population of over thirty thousand residents. It is recognized as the home of Jewish mysticism and maintains an eclectic mix of secular and religious Jews who peacefully coexist. Tzfat's scenic and remote setting has not only inspired kabbalists but also attracted artists to the area. An artist colony, which is where I resided with my family during fieldwork, has flourished in Tzfat since 1949. During the SPI, the threat of terrorism was real and constant in Tzfat; however, no attacks ever occurred there. Its relative safety was a significant factor in choosing it as a field site; we lived in Tzfat from June 2002 through August 2003 and then again from May 2005 to September 2006.

Anthropologists often begin their ethnographic studies with open-ended interviews aimed at revealing details about the topic of interest to the researcher. In 2002, following the encounter with my cabdriver, I conducted sixteen such interviews. I learned about a variety of magico-religious practices that people believed could protect them from a terrorist attack, as well as improve the *matzav* (literally, "situation"), as Israelis obliquely referred to the SPI. My interviewees discussed giving to charity, checking the parchment inside phylacteries and *mezuzot* (which hang on the doorframes of Jewish homes), and doing *mitzvot* (good deeds proscribed by Jewish law). They mentioned three practices, however, significantly more than others: reciting psalms, wearing *tziztit* (a garment with fringes worn only by men), and carrying the picture of a *tzaddik* (holy person).

Following these initial open-ended interviews, I developed a survey instrument aimed at finding out how often such practices were employed, who relies on them, and the subjective reasons they do so. Several research assistants and I conducted more than 350 protocol-based interviews at Tzfat's Ministry of the Interior. This office provides passports, visas, birth certificates, national ID cards, and assorted other services. I decided to conduct interviews there because it offered a fairly representative sample of Tzfat residents—everyone needs the office's services occasionally—and the long lines provided a generally willing pool of interviewees.

While my initial open-ended interviews were conducted with men and women, my protocol-based interviews focused exclusively on women. There were two main reasons for this. First, it is a standard finding in trauma literature that women have more significant responses to trauma than men, including higher post-traumatic stress disorder symptom levels following terrorist attacks (Bleich, Gelkopf, & Solomon 2003; Schuster et al. 2001; Silver et al. 2002). Furthermore, Klar et al. (2002) found that Israeli women were more likely to make precautionary changes in response to the SPI than men. Second, the practices I was investigating were folk practices, rituals and beliefs that emerged from the bottom up, so to speak, rather than being rabbinically mandated by Jewish law. Within Orthodox Judaism, women have greater flexibility in ritual practice than men. Orthodox male life is saturated with ritual requirements; their free time should be spent in the study of religious texts or prayer. Thus it is unclear how men could culturally develop additional religious practices in response to terror, as religious duties already consume most of their day. Indeed, my open-ended interviews suggested that in order to improve the *matzav*, men were most commonly increasing the intensity of their prayers and studies, rather than adding new rituals to their daily routines.

Analyses of my protocol-based interviews revealed that reciting psalms was the most common magico-religious practice employed for dealing with the stress of the SPI: in my sample, 83.0 percent of self-defined religious women and 35.7 percent of self-defined secular women were reciting psalms in response to the SPI. Not only was this the most frequently employed practice, but people also believed psalm recitation provided the greatest powers of protection from an attack. Both religious and secular interviewees also believed it to be more effective at improving the terror situation than any other magico-religious practice.

Analyses further revealed that demographic variables such as age, education, ethnicity, and income level did not predict who was reciting psalms. However, experiential variables such as knowing someone who was killed in the SPI, suffering an income loss because of the SPI, or believing that Tzfat would be attacked had a significant impact on whether secular interviewees, but not religious interviewees, were reciting psalms.

Indeed, every secular interviewee in my sample who was reciting psalms believed that Tzfat would be attacked.

The uncertainty hypothesis anticipates that if reciting psalms plays a role in reducing stress and increasing a person's sense of control, it should be negatively correlated with other protective behavioral responses to the SPI, such as being cautious following an attack, and long-term responses like avoiding buses, restaurants, and crowded places. Those who recite psalms are expected to have a greater sense of control and lower anxiety concerning the SPI, and thus to be more comfortable maintaining their daily routine. Analyses showed that this was indeed the case. Among those who believed that Tzfat would be attacked (78.3 percent of the sample), especially for secular interviewees, reciting psalms was a significant negative predictor of short- and long-term precautionary behavioral changes. Women who were reciting psalms were evidently able to continue with their normal lives better than women who were not reciting psalms.

While these results were interesting and supportive of the uncertainty hypothesis, they raised a number of questions for further study. It appears that women who were reciting psalms were better able to cope with the stress of the SPI, but this study did not measure stress levels. Does psalm recitation, as the uncertainty hypothesis would predict, actually reduce anxiety? If so, under what conditions is psalm recitation effective? I sought to answer these questions, and the unfortunate events of the summer of 2006—a war with Hezbollah—provided the conditions that enabled me to further explore psalm recitation among Tzfat women.

Of War and Worship

During the 2006 Lebanon War, which occurred from July 12 to August 14, Tzfat was one of the first places attacked and was subsequently regularly targeted; on most days, dozens of Katyusha rockets landed in Tzfat and the surrounding area. Sirens provided warning when rockets were en route, and most residents who remained in Tzfat would take refuge in bomb shelters upon hearing the sirens. The timing of the attacks was often predictable, whereas the location, even for those launching the Katyushas, was unpredictable.

It has been estimated that over 450,000 Israelis were evacuated from northern Israel during the war (over 900,000 southern Lebanese were displaced), and nearly 3,000 Israelis were treated for shock. Those who left Tzfat primarily did so in the first week of the war, and they settled in central Israel out of reach of the Katyusha rockets. They stayed with friends, family, or in public spaces, including schools, dormitories, community centers, and beaches.

To cope with the stress of the war, women engaged in many of the same magico-religious practices I had documented several years earlier in my study of responses to the SPI. When I asked women why they were engaging in a particular practice, they generally responded that they felt a compulsion "to do something." Most often that compulsion resulted in the recitation of psalms.

For this study (Sosis & Handwerker 2011), I was particularly interested in assessing whether psalm recitation reduced anxiety under tense and uncertain conditions. I decided to team up with one of my colleagues at the University of Connecticut, Penn Handwerker, who had conducted research on anxiety in his own ethnographic field studies. During the 2006 Lebanon War, religious Israeli women from Tzfat all faced stressful conditions. However, the types of stress women encountered largely depended on where they spent the war. Women who remained in Tzfat were primarily concerned with the unpredictable and uncontrollable Katyusha attacks, whereas women who left Tzfat were dealing with the more predictable and mundane stressors of relocation. These contrasts afforded the opportunity to evaluate the efficacy of psalm recitation in reducing anxiety under different circumstances.

In this study, in contrast to my previous work, we interviewed only women who self-identified as Orthodox Jews. Two female research assistants conducted 115 protocol-based interviews between August 1 and August 13, in other words the second half of the war. To measure anxiety, we used a simple mood disorder scale that my coauthor had successfully employed in his own fieldwork. Interviewees were asked, "Since the beginning of the war, how often have you . . ." which was followed by nine questions about their emotional state, such as "felt nervous," "gotten angry quickly," "had difficulty falling asleep at night," and so on. Responses were elicited on a five-point scale (None—Rarely—Sometimes—Regularly—All the time).

Results and Analysis

Of the 115 women we interviewed, 82 left Tzfat during the war and relocated to central Israel. Sixty-three percent of the women in our sample recited psalms daily in response to the war, and the rates of psalm recitation among those who left Tzfat (52 of 82) and those who remained (21 of 33) were virtually identical.

Interviewees were asked, "What has been most stressful since the beginning of the war?" and instructed to list up to three items. While those who left Tzfat and those who remained mentioned many of the same stressors, there are some important differences in the stressors they experienced. Of those who remained in Tzfat, 75.8 percent listed concerns about damage to property (resulting from Katyushas) as one of their most significant sources of anxiety, whereas among those who left Tzfat, only 11.0 percent expressed concerns about property damage. Those who remained were also more likely to be concerned about the loudness of the sirens, conditions of the bomb shelters, and government incompetence. In contrast, 81.7 percent of those who left Tzfat listed at least one challenge of displacement—childcare/occupying children, lack of a schedule, not having their own things, imposing on others—among their primary stressors.

I had naively assumed that those living in a war zone would be more stressed than those who had left the fighting behind, but despite being further from the military conflict, those who left Tzfat had significantly higher anxiety scores than those who remained. There was no significant difference in anxiety levels between those who stayed with family or friends and those who stayed in public spaces. Women reciting psalms during the war scored significantly lower on the anxiety scale than women not reciting psalms. However, the efficacy of psalm recitation was highly dependent on where one experienced the war. Analyses revealed that psalms had no effect on the anxiety of those who left Tzfat but had a significant effect—that is, reduced stress—on those who remained. What could account for this difference? It turns out that this difference is at least partially driven by differential concerns for one's house or apartment. Among those who remained in Tzfat and believed their home would be hit by a rocket—an event completely out of their control—psalms had a significant effect on lowering their anxiety. We found no such effects among those who left Tzfat. One more study in support of Malinowski.

Discussion

Women who remained in Tzfat and those who left expressed equal concern about the safety of friends and family, finances, and the overall uncertainty of everything during the war. However, women who remained were much more stressed about the potential destruction of their property, whereas women who left were much more stressed about issues related to their relocation. The significant difference in concern over the destruction of property is not surprising; women who remained in Tzfat directly experienced the destruction of daily Katyusha attacks, and their lives during the war revolved around the timing and location of attacks. Interestingly, regardless of where they spent the war, women assessed the risk of property destruction equally, but for relocated women this risk was not a primary stressor, as their immediate concerns of dislocation took priority.

Psalm recitation was negatively related to anxiety, but this was highly dependent on location during the war. Psalms were efficacious for women who remained in Tzfat and believed their house would be hit by a rocket, whereas psalms were unrelated to anxiety levels among women who left Tzfat, regardless of their expectation about the destruction of their house.

Consistent with Malinowski's original claims, these results suggest that psalms can reduce anxiety when stressors are unpredictable and uncontrollable. However, psalm recitation does not reduce anxiety when stressors are predictable and controllable. Reciting psalms (our interviewees believed) can protect your house from destruction by a Katyusha, but psalms cannot make the floor space your family is sleeping on grow, keep your children busy, or make your belongings suddenly appear in your new residence. These are all stressors that require action to resolve (moving one's family, enrolling the kids in camp, collecting possessions from the north). There are no actions, however, that could reliably protect one's house from Katyushas. Thus, without instrumental alternatives, psalm recitation is an effective coping strategy, apparently offering a sense of control in otherwise uncontrollable conditions.

Our results raised a number of issues. Two, which were not addressed in our original publication, I will take up here. First, if psalm recitation was ineffective at reducing stress for women who relocated to central Israel, why were they reciting psalms? Specifically, why were 63.4 percent (52 of 82) of the women in our sample who had relocated out of the war zone and faced predictable, solvable stressors turning to psalms? There are undoubtedly various factors involved, but I think the most compelling explanation involves human learning biases and the social nature of psalm recitation for many religious women.

While Jewish women often recite psalms alone, occasionally they will organize themselves to recite psalms in the company of other women in a park, home, or community center. Even during such gatherings, however, psalms are recited individually (in other words, they are not recited in unison). Also, it was not uncommon during the 2006 Lebanon War, as well as the Intifadas, for religious women to ensure that the entire Book of Psalms (150 psalms) was read daily, or even three times daily, by assigning various women five or more psalms to read every day. Thus, for many religious women, social obligation, rather than the stress of unpredictable acts of terror or warfare, was the primary motivation behind their psalm recitations. Conformist learning biases (Henrich 2016), encouraging us to mimic the cultural behaviors of those in our social environment, might explain why some women recited psalms even though the practice was ineffective at reducing stress in their particular situations. Moreover, psalm recitation might serve as a signal of group commitment (Irons 2001; Sosis 2003), indicating to other women that they are part of the religious community. Indeed, understanding psalm recitation as a signal of group commitment might also explain why experiential variables predicted secular women's, but not religious women's, recitation of psalms during the SPI. Secular women do not feel the same social pressures to conform to religious group norms, and they have no need to signal their commitment to a community to which they do not belong.

The second question I wish to consider is why psalm recitation was the most frequently employed magico-religious response to the SPI and 2006 Lebanon War. What distinguishes psalm recitation from other rituals and practices? By way of comparison, let's consider the performance of good deeds (*mitzvot*), such as bringing food to a neighbor or feeding the pets of those who left, in response to terror or war. The comparison is apt because analyses showed that religious interviewees believed that psalm recitation and performing good deeds were equally effective in their ability to improve the *matzav* (situation of the SPI). Over 80 percent of interviewees "really agreed" with the statements that reciting psalms/performing good deeds could improve the *matzav*.

Psalm recitation and good deeds share other similarities as well. Both are manifest because of women's compulsion "to do something" during stressful times, and both lack rigidity in performance but are structured by implicit and explicit social norms. More informative, however, are their differences. Psalm recitation takes the form of a ritual; that is, it is formal, stereotyped, and repetitive. Performing good deeds, on the other hand, is casual and not ritually structured. Likewise, psalm recitation, unlike the performance of good deeds, involves sacred speech. Interestingly, performers do not always comprehend psalms, whereas they fully understand carrying out good deeds, obviously. Although the psalms were composed in Hebrew, the language is archaic and quite challenging for Israelis who have not studied the psalms in detail. Indeed, in Israel the Book of Psalms is often found with modern Hebrew translations accompanying the original text. Many women commented that although they read psalms daily they do not necessarily think about, or even understand, every word they are reciting.

The most noteworthy difference between psalm recitation and performing good deeds is their ability to reduce anxiety. Although interviewees claimed that performing good deeds could improve difficult and stressful conditions, analyses show that these actions had no impact on levels of anxiety. This was true for women who remained in the war zone during the 2006 Lebanon War, as well as those who relocated to central Israel. On reflection these results may seem puzzling because positive psychology informs us that doing nice things for others can lead to happiness. But such an interpretation confuses life satisfaction, the concern of positive psychologists, and the acute stress that women face in the context of war.

Ultimately, psalms are effective as a coping strategy because they increase performers' sense of control. Performing good deeds is not formally structured enough to provide the sense of control that seems essential in engendering power over what objectively are uncontrollable and unpredictable conditions. Psalm recitation, like all rituals (Rappaport 1999), involves bodily movements, speech, formality, stereotypy, repetitiveness, and an opacity that obscures their social functions. These characteristics all contribute to a sense of control that the performer gains. Psalm recitation is an archetypical religious ritual, and our results, as many anthropologists have similarly found, demonstrate the enduring power of ritual.

CHAPTER 20
DOES PRAYING RESEMBLE NORMAL INTERPERSONAL INTERACTION?
Uffe Schjoedt

Introduction

Although Christian prayer takes many forms, praying is generally understood as an attempt to communicate with the divine. In the 2009 study presented here, we asked what communicating with the divine means from a neurocognitive perspective. What happens in the brains of believers when hands are folded and eyes are closed?

The question speaks to our imagination, especially to believers who experience praying to God as feeling different than ordinary cognition. Neuroscientists who share this feeling have spent decades searching for specialized neural substrates of religious experience (e.g., specific brain regions and interconnected brain networks). Researchers have suggested that the felt presence of God is caused by a specific pattern of transient electrical impulses in the temporal lobe (Persinger 1987) and that the transcendental experience of "absolute unitary being" is caused by specific neural mechanisms in the frontoparietal networks (d'Aquili & Newberg 1999). These attempts to map what is unique about religious experience are often termed "neurotheology."

Coming from a secular Scandinavian background, our research team set out to explore the neural substrates of prayer from a slightly different angle. Rather than searching for a universal substrate of religious experience, we assumed, based on conventional cognitive neuroscience, that prayers likely elicit brain processes that correspond to the cognitive content of the specific type of prayer. Thus, we would expect prayers that include verbal content to activate areas of the brain involved with speech production.

Prayer, however, is an incredibly diverse phenomenon. Written prayers are recited in private and in church; personal prayers are practiced silently or spoken at home or at meetings. Some prayers resemble meditation; others are supported by religious paraphernalia such as prayer beads and sacred icons. Some prayers focus on visual content; others on formulaic recitation. The semantic content of prayer is just as diverse, ranging from petitions, thanksgiving, and praise to pleading, anger, and frustration (Geertz 2008). Prayer is far from a uniform type of behavior.

Logically, then, praying likely requires different cognitive processes depending on its form and content, including varying levels of attention, executive processing, reward processing, speech production, visualizing, and mentalizing. Because the brain has evolved for the purpose of solving problems related to survival and reproduction, such basic functions are processed by relatively specialized neural networks and anatomical structures. Neurologists and neuroscientists have mapped these networks and structures in recent decades. We have yet to discover additional machinery specialized for communicating with the divine.

The neuroscientific study of prayer should therefore, at least as a starting point, map the cognitive processes involved in the various types of prayer. At first, this ambition may sound excessively reductionistic and tedious, draining the juicy stuff from a fascinating phenomenon. But the fact is that we know very little, at least from a scientific perspective, about how the brain processes supernatural entities like God. If the brain is designed to deal with the natural environment, what on earth is it doing when it deals with the divine?

Theory

According to Christian theology, God is omnipotent, omnipresent, omniscient, and comprised of the trinity of the Father, the Son, and the Holy Spirit. Conceptualizing abstract entities like the Christian God should demand considerable resources from higher-order cognitive systems involved in abstract thinking such as the attentional and executive networks, which are anatomically associated with specific brain regions.

Christians, however, often report that they picture Jesus when they pray. Picturing the human god, rather than the abstract dogmatic God, makes sense because the brain effortlessly deals with other humans. Engaging in human interaction is natural to most of us and something humans are generally extremely good at. Thus, in a direct conversation with God, Christians may recruit the neurocognitive processes involved in normal interpersonal interaction, rather than those involved in abstract thinking.

Previous studies have identified a distinct network of interrelated brain regions that appears to be centrally involved in social interaction, including the anterior medial prefrontal cortex, the temporoparietal junction (TPJ), and the precuneus (Amodio & Frith 2006; Castelli et al. 2000; Rilling et al. 2004; Schilbach et al. 2008). The *social cognitive* network tends to activate when individuals think about the intentions, beliefs, and desires of other people. Illustratively, in a neuroimaging study in which game players were led to believe that they played against either a computer or a real human, participants activated this network when they believed they were playing against a human opponent (McCabe et al. 2001).

Based on such evidence, we hypothesized that direct conversation with God in improvised personal prayers would recruit the social cognitive network, but we also wanted to illustrate the differences between prayer types. Communicating with God via recitations of written prayers may not recruit regions for social cognition to the same extent, because recitations are less direct and much more formalized. Thus, we examined the neural correlates of improvised personal prayers and the recitation of the Lord's Prayer in a group of devoted Christian practitioners.

Methodology

Functional magnetic resonance imaging (fMRI) was used to measure the blood oxygen level dependent (BOLD) signal, which is related to the brain's blood flow and metabolic activity. fMRI allows the identification of brain regions that are comparably more or less active during various conditions. Because the brain is constantly preoccupied with thinking and solving tasks, even during rest, there is no stable baseline condition against which we can compare any task. Thus, to measure a particular aspect of a task, say, the distinctly religious element of praying, we need a contrast to filter out nonreligious aspects of praying, such as the fact that verbal prayer requires speech production. Thus, we chose our contrast conditions to match the two prayer types on as many aspects as possible except for the religious versus nonreligious distinction, including levels of improvisation and type of speech, in order to capture the neural activities involved in the distinctly religious aspects of praying.

We invited twenty young Danish Christians from a conservative Christian denomination called Inner Mission to perform four different speech acts in a so-called two-by-two factorial design (Figure 20.1). "The Lord's Prayer" (formalized speech) and "personal prayer" (improvised speech) were contrasted with nonreligious counterparts, a "nursery rhyme" (formalized speech) and "making wishes to Santa Claus" (improvised speech). While all participants were confident in God's existence, none believed in Santa Claus. Additionally, we included a simple cognitive task as baseline. The four speech acts plus the baseline were repeated several times (in a semirandomized order) to improve the signal strength and thus to reliably retrieve the neural correlates of each condition.

Results and Analysis

When we tested for common neural substrates across the two prayers in the whole of the brain, we observed no significant effects (when both prayers were contrasted with their nonreligious counterparts).[1] However, it mattered in terms of brain activity if improvised and formalized speech acts were religious or nonreligious (interaction analysis). Our main hypothesis on the relation between social cognition and praying was supported by individual contrasts, which revealed activation of the social cognitive network in

DOMAIN

		Religious	Non-religious
	Formalized	The Lord's Prayer	Nursery rhyme
SPEECH			
	Improvised	Personal prayer	Making wishes to Santa Claus

Figure 20.1 Two-by-two factorial design, domain and speech.

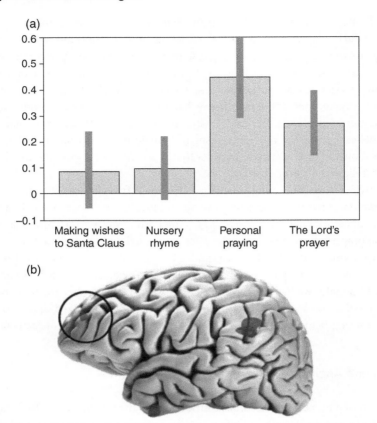

Figure 20.2 (a) Regions significantly more active in "personal prayer" relative to "making wishes to Santa Claus." (b) Effect size analysis of the anterior medial prefrontal cortex (encircled in brain image in "a") in the four conditions relative to baseline (the dark-gray error bars indicate 90 percent confidence intervals, which is an estimate of the accuracy of the observed activations).

"personal prayer" relative to "making wishes to Santa Claus," including regions of the anterior medial prefrontal cortex, the temporoparietal junction, the precuneus, and the temporal pole (see Figure 20.2).

Discussion

The two prayers activated widely different brain regions depending on type. From a neuroscientific perspective, it seems that connecting with God in prayers indeed recruits corresponding brain regions to particular cognitive content. However, our current ability to examine the functional brain may be insufficient for picking up neural processes distinctly associated with divine communication across prayer types. Moreover, specialized neurocognitive processes associated with religious experience may only be present in more extraordinary kinds of experiences. In other words, the fascinating question of whether religious experience correlates with distinct neural processing remains open.

Importantly, we found that personal prayer activates areas associated with social cognition, which supports the assumption that conversations with God in prayer may be comparable to normal interpersonal interaction, at least in terms of underlying neural processing. This finding has influenced at least a couple of intriguing theoretical debates in cognitive science of religion. First, the study has been used to support the popular notion that God beliefs are central in securing moral behavior among anonymous people. The idea, which is sometimes referred to as the *supernatural watcher* hypothesis, claims that humans who feel that a personal god is present become more prosocial. Our study appears to support this idea by showing that God is indeed processed in the social cognitive network (Gervais & Norenzayan 2012). Second, if a personal relationship with God recruits the parts of our brains associated with social cognition, as suggested by our findings, some researchers have argued that people with impaired social cognitive abilities due to autism should have difficulties establishing a personal relationship with God (Norenzayan, Gervais, & Trzesniewski 2012). This idea seems plausible at first, perhaps even logical, but it is disputed (Reddish, Tok, & Kundt 2016); people on the autism spectrum may in fact enjoy the simplicity of gods because gods' intentions and desires tend to be far less ambiguous than those of real human beings. Communicating with God may recruit social cognition, but if God is far easier to process than humans for this system, this would make divine communication less problematic for autistic people (Visuri, 2018).

Both ideas are fascinating, but caution is always advised when neurocognitive evidence is taken as hard evidence for psychologically complex mechanisms. Neuroscience is known for its power to enchant readers with images of spots that light up in the brain. Uninformed scholars tend to overestimate the scientific value of neuroscience interpretations because brain images give the impression of concrete evidence. In reality, the current state of social cognitive neuroscience leaves room for a lot of uncertainty and speculation. Yes, brain maps reveal regions that are likely to be more active in one condition compared to another, but very often knowledge about the function of these regions in a particular task is uncertain at best.

Researchers tend to base their interpretations on insights from previous studies. For example, if a study has demonstrated that a brain region is involved in a social cognitive task, then if this region is active in prayer, prayer may include aspects of social cognition. This logic, which is often referred to as *reverse inference*, is problematic, however. Taking previous insights on functional neuroanatomy into account in interpretations is scientifically sound in many cases, but some studies make unwarranted claims. One way to avoid this problem is to design highly controlled studies that isolate a particular cognitive aspect and then study its neural correlates, but this is not always possible in research on complex cultural phenomena. The level of control required for such analysis would ruin the authenticity of, say, religious practices like prayer. Instead, the solution is to be careful not to make too strong claims about the corresponding cognitive functionality of neural activations, which also means that evidence of this sort should be used with caution.

In our study, a central issue is the interpretation of the so-called social cognitive network. What exactly does it do? The fact that this network was almost exclusively what distinguished personal prayer from making wishes to Santa Claus is intriguing. However, the social cognitive network overlaps with the so-called default network, which has been robustly associated with mind wandering, rest, and thoughts that are not directly related to the outer world. Perhaps the observed activations are simply evidence of minds wandering? Against this interpretation, researchers have shown that even when a social task is more demanding in a contrast analysis, this network tends to be active. Neuroscientists have therefore proposed that the overlap reflects a human predisposition of social cognition as the default mode of cognizing (Schilbach et al. 2008).

Pressed on the specific functionality of each of the implicated regions in prayer, findings become even more uncertain. We expected personal prayer to activate social cognition, so we used standard interpretations from social cognitive neuroscience research to understand our findings, despite the general lack of certainty in social neuroscience. The anterior medial prefrontal cortex, for example, is associated with mentalizing about the intentions of self and others (Amodio & Frith 2006; Gallagher & Frith 2003). There is no way we can be certain that activity in this region in prayer reflects participants' mentalizing efforts, but it is the best model we have based on previous research on other kinds of social interaction. This use of established neuroscience interpretations of region-specific functionality contrasts with the more spectacular kind of interpretations often found in neurotheology. For example, in a study of Carmelite nuns who recalled a prior mystical experience, the brain revealed activity in multiple regions (Beauregaard & Paquette 2006; for a critical review, see Schjoedt 2009). Each region in this study was then interpreted in light of other imaging studies on religious experience. For example, researchers interpreted activations in the temporal lobe as the specific correlate of the felt presence of God, by reference to a highly controversial body of evidence (Persinger 1987).

Regardless of interpretation, our study does not show that relating to God is different from imagining conversations with other persons, despite the observed difference from making wishes to Santa Claus. For example, what if participants were asked to imagine a conversation with a friend, rather than with Santa Claus? A more recent fMRI study on prayer introduced "imagined conversation with a loved one," which elicited overlapping patterns of activity with personal prayer, both in the social cognitive network (Neubauer 2014). This observation certainly adds to the robustness of our original finding, but it also emphasizes the need for further specification of the distinctly religious aspects of prayer in future research.

We need to specify whether we are interested in believers' perception that God is real, that God reciprocates one's prayers, that God is present, or that God is listening. Fascinating neuroscience paradigms from other disciplines could be adapted and used to isolate and test at least some of these aspects of prayer. As enchanting as the brain is, however, brain mapping may not always provide the best testing ground for such questions. Other methods, such as speech analysis of spoken prayer, may allow for higher degrees of control, while alternative measures, such as eye movements in prayer interactions with religious imagery, may get closer to conscious experience and be far less troubled by problems of reverse inference.

At a more general level, some scholars of religion may question whether religious practices like prayer can and should be studied experimentally at all (Batson 1977), especially with neuroimaging technologies that challenge the authenticity of any cultural practice due to its artificial environment (Ladd et al. 2015; Schjoedt 2009). Obviously, prayers that are highly context-dependent cannot be examined in labs, and experiences that are supposed to happen spontaneously are difficult to elicit in experimentally controlled environments (for an attempt, see Beauregard & Paquette 2006), perhaps with the exception of drug-induced experiences, as evidenced in the seminal study by Walter Panhke (1966), which was ethically problematic. Nevertheless, for many Christians, praying is practiced every day and in almost any situation, which makes such prayers ideal for experimental research. Indeed, the participants in our study all felt that they could easily pray inside the brain scanner.

The experimental study of religious experience is still in its infancy. Several attempts now exist either to study religious experience by analogy—that is, to examine phenomena in the lab that resemble cultural experiences in order to understand the cognitive underpinnings of such experiences (Blanke et al. 2014; Deeley et al. 2014)—or to study quasi-religious or spiritual experiences by suggestion and immersive paradigms (Andersen et al. 2014). These are exciting approaches, but if the purpose is to understand the cognitive mechanisms of a particular cultural phenomenon such as personal prayer among young Danish conservative Christians, we need to be able to study this practice in controlled environments.

This, however, may require qualitative research into the meanings and history of the phenomenon, as well as anthropological observations, interviews, and collaboration with the participants. For instance, the 2009 study required several months of fieldwork and active participant observation at missionary houses with lots of informal interviews. This early phase was not only important for the recruitment of participants, it was also essential for the customization of the research design to participants' beliefs and practices. Any attempt to study authentic religious practice in controlled settings will need to carefully adapt the research design to the traditions of a particular group. For example, the nursery rhymes used as contrasts to the Lord's Prayer were of the participants' own choice because we needed to filter out the habitual aspect of recitation. This customization, however, challenges the generalizability of the results to larger populations. In fact, when I'm asked about which population the 2009 study generalizes to, my first impulse is often to say that it may not generalize at all. It is a case study of a particular group's performance of a particular collection of practices that may only make sense to the participants. Whether our findings generalize to other groups of people is for experts on those other groups to evaluate. Yet, Neubauer's replication of our results in a sample of American charismatic Christians (2014) does suggest a degree of generalizability.

In conclusion, the study presented in this chapter revealed important insights on the neurocognitive processing of personal prayer in the young Danish Christian participants. It was the first to examine how the brain processes daily prayers. Our findings have influenced debates on the role of social cognition in religious beliefs and practices. Despite the methodological and theoretical issues discussed above, I still believe the social cognitive interpretation has merit, but I am eager to explore prayer with research designs that enable us to isolate more specific social cognitive aspects of prayer experience. The widespread human attempt to communicate with gods is one of the most incredible and fascinating of all human behaviors. We failed to identify specialized machinery for religious experience, but we did find one possible pathway for processing gods. Direct conversations with God in personal prayer seem to be subserved by systems that evolved to understand other human beings.

CHAPTER 21
HOW ARE RITUALS THOUGHT TO WORK?
Brian Malley

Introduction

If religion is about people's relationship to gods and other superhuman beings, then ritual must be a means of harnessing the gods' powers. One explanation of ritual, the ritual form hypothesis, is a cognitive theory of the underlying logic of ritual as efficacious action, as a way to do things that need to be done, things that cannot be done in any other way. By incorporating the agency of superhuman beings, rituals are able to accomplish unique effects. But these effects vary depending upon the precise way in which the superhuman agency is implicated.

It would be difficult to overstate how surprising this proposal really is. Few scholars would be surprised either by the claim that rituals are thought to have special effects or by the claim that superhuman agents are thought to have special powers. But no one has ever shown how these unsurprising claims could be combined in the form of causal claims about the structure of ritual systems.

Rituals have their special effects because of the ways they enlist the powers of superhuman beings. And the way in which the superhuman being is enlisted makes an important difference to the ritual's efficacy.

Theory

E. Thomas Lawson and Robert N. McCauley initially proposed the ritual form hypothesis in *Rethinking Religion* (1990) then clarified and expanded it in their subsequent *Bringing Ritual to Mind* (McCauley & Lawson 2002).

Lawson and McCauley begin from the premise that the mental representation of religious ritual actions is handled by the same cognitive system that handles the mental representation of everyday actions. They call this system the *action representation system* and provide detailed hypotheses about it in *Rethinking Religion*. The action representation system dictates the logic of ritual action: An action involves an *agent* performing some *act* upon a *patient*. The patient is understood as being changed by the agent's performance of the action. The agent role is filled by some entity—in the natural world, almost always an organism—capable of carrying out goal-driven action. The role of patient may be filled by anything: person, animal, plant, object, event, whatever.

The ritual form hypothesis claims that a person's judgments about a religious ritual's repeatability, reversibility, relative sensory pageantry, and relative emotionality are determined by the role that the *culturally postulated superhuman agent* (CPSA) is thought to play in the ritual's mental representation. A CPSA is any object or being conceived as an agent with unusual powers, powers that go beyond the sorts of effects that normal human beings can achieve via mundane or technical means. The power of the agent makes the ritual work. The transformation of the patient requires a superhuman agent precisely because the transformation is something that cannot otherwise be achieved.

Critical to understanding the ritual form hypothesis is the psychological notion of agency. Agency is one of the earliest developing and fundamental concepts that human beings make use of in interpreting the world. For the ritual form hypothesis, the role of agent functions as a requirement and a variable.

Superhuman agents: Agency required

The requirement is that CPSAs must occupy the agent role. Ritual prescriptions typically specify that only certain persons are eligible to perform the ritual action and that ritual actions must be done in prescribed ways; not just any agent is qualified to perform the ritual, and not just any performance of the requisite action will suffice. Lawson and McCauley's theory of ritual representation represents such requirements in the form of implicated rituals: rituals whose prior efficacious performance is presupposed by the performance of the present ritual.

For example, suppose that Gil, a new convert to Roman Catholicism, wants to be baptized. Babies born into the Roman Catholic faith are usually baptized as infants, but as an adult convert, Gil has never been baptized. Gil knows that not just anyone can baptize him—he cannot simply ask his wife, Jill, to perform the ritual. A Roman Catholic baptism must be carried out by a Roman Catholic priest. So Gil approaches his priest, Will, to baptize him. The action representation system describes the ritual of baptism as in Figure 21.1: an agent performs an action upon a patient.

In Figure 21.1, the focal ritual description is of Will baptizing Gil. Will is qualified to baptize because he is a priest—that is, he has been transformed from a layperson into a priest by a prior ritual, the ritual of ordination. Any ritual in which Will functions as a priest therefore presupposes a prior ritual in which Will was ordained. So the agent

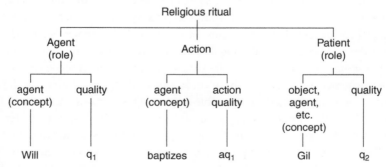

Figure 21.1 Baptism.

in the top ritual, Will, has the property of having been the patient of the prior ritual of ordination.

But it is not enough that Will has gone through the motions of being ordained. His ordination must be valid, and that presupposes a further ritual, in this case that Bill, the priest who ordained Will, was himself ordained. So the ordination of Will presupposes the ordination of Bill, which presupposes that Bill was himself the patient in a prior ritual of ordination. This leads to a representation like that in Figure 21.2.

But was Bill qualified to ordain Will? It becomes evident at this point that any action in which Will acts as a priest must presuppose a long string of other ritual events. At every stage, the actor was qualified to act legitimately only because of his own prior role as a patient. This threatens to turn into an infinite regress unless the chain of authority and power can be ended somehow.

One of Lawson and McCauley's key insights is precisely that this mental representation does not involve an infinite regress. Specifically, they maintain that there will be a mythological explanation of the origin of the ritual, and that this mythological explanation, whatever else it may contain, will include the ultimate anchoring of the ritual in the action of a superhuman being. The chain of ordination must end with the action of a CPSA.

In Roman Catholic theology, the chain ends with the ordination of Peter by Jesus. Jesus is a superhuman being. Doctrinally, he is alleged to be fully human, but he is

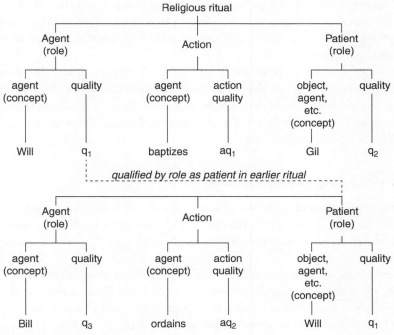

Figure 21.2 Baptism presupposes ordination.

regarded as superhuman in the sense that he is considered capable of actions that no human being can perform. According to Roman Catholic doctrine, Jesus ordains Peter as the first priest (and the first pope) in Matthew 16:13–19 (NRSV):

> Now when Jesus came into the district of Caesarea Philippi, he asked his disciples, "Who do people say that the Son of Man is?" And they said, "Some say John the Baptist, but others Elijah, and still others Jeremiah or one of the prophets." He said to them, "But who do you say that I am?" Simon Peter answered, "You are the Messiah, the Son of the living God." And Jesus answered him, "Blessed are you, Simon son of Jonah! For flesh and blood has not revealed this to you, but my Father in heaven. And I tell you, you are Peter, and on this rock I will build my church, and the gates of Hades will not prevail against it. I will give you the keys of the kingdom of heaven, and whatever you bind on earth will be bound in heaven, and whatever you loose on earth will be loosed in heaven."

Roman Catholic doctrine interprets this passage as the founding of the Christian church and the delegation of sacramental authority to Peter. Roman Catholic believers ultimately regard ordination and baptism as efficacious instruments of grace because they are connected by the church hierarchy and tradition back to this original delegation of salvific authority. The resulting action structure is depicted in Figure 21.3.

In Figure 21.3, we see that Gil's baptism depends upon Will's prior ordination, which depends upon Bill's prior ordination, and that this invokes a chain of ritual connections that ultimately ends in Jesus's ordination of Peter. It is mandatory that, in this ultimate ritual, the superhuman being occupy the agent role. The superhuman being must be the one performing the action. This is why Lawson and McCauley cast their theory in terms of superhuman *agents*.

The ritual form hypothesis entails the claim that all religious rituals are connected to a superhuman agent through the rituals they implicate. This connection, according to Lawson and McCauley, forms the cognitive ground on which participants regard rituals as efficacious. The power of the ritual is ultimately attributed to a superhuman agent, that is, a CPSA in a presupposed ritual.

Types of ritual: Agency as a variable

Once the requirement of superhuman agency is met, the next consideration is how the superhuman agent is implicated. The critical question here is whether the superhuman agent is incorporated through the agent role or through some other role in the top-most, focal ritual.

To appreciate what is at issue here, let's examine some possibilities. In the Roman Catholic ritual of baptism, as depicted in Figure 21.3, the CPSA is implicated through the agent role in the top-most ritual: it is through Will's qualification of being a priest—having been transformed by an ordination ritual—that the connection is made to Jesus.

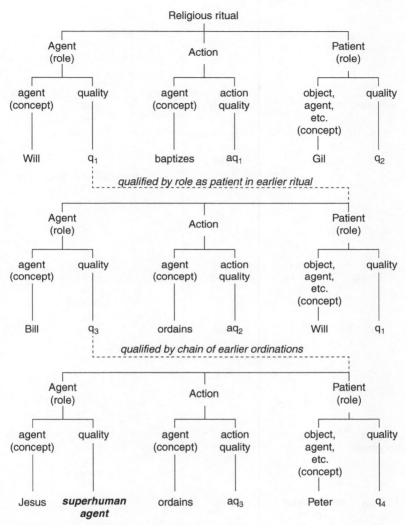

Figure 21.3 Ordination implicates a superhuman agent.

This is an example of a *special agent ritual*, because it is through the special quality of the agent that the superhuman being is implicated.

But there are other ways in which a superhuman being might be implicated. Consider what happens when Jill, also a Roman Catholic, enters a church and blesses herself by dipping her finger into a reservoir of holy water and crossing herself (see Figure 21.4). In the focal ritual, Jill is both agent and patient of the action: she blesses herself. But she is enabled to do this because she makes use of the holy water, water that a priest has previously blessed. Blessing oneself is thus an example of a *special instrument ritual*.

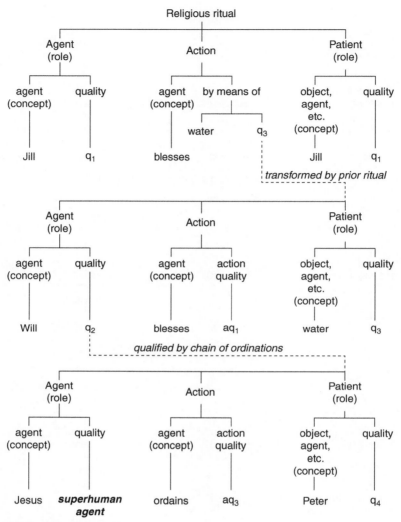

Figure 21.4 Jill blesses herself.

Alternatively, some rituals are *special patient rituals*. In the Roman Catholic Eucharist, the host must be consecrated prior to consumption. The focal act is the consumption of a wafer, but the wafer is not just any bread: it has been subjected to a prior ritual that transforms it from an everyday food into the body of Christ. The structure of this special patient ritual is depicted in Figure 21.5.

Predictions

As noted earlier, what makes the ritual form hypothesis a causal hypothesis is its contention that the role played by superhuman agents in a ritual's structure description

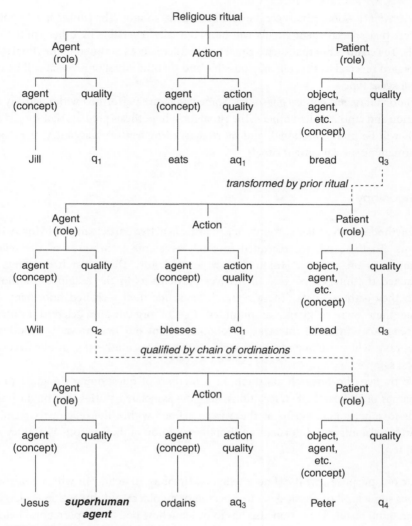

Figure 21.5 Jill takes the Eucharist.

determines participants' judgments about the ritual's repeatability, reversibility, emotionality, and sensory pageantry. Although other scholars have made observations about these aspects of ritual, none prior to Lawson and McCauley have proposed a causal explanation for them. Let's examine each of these predictions.

Repeatability. Some rituals, such as the Lord's Supper, must be periodically repeated in order to be continually effective. It is as if the effects wear off after a certain time. Other rituals, such as baptism, can be performed on a particular patient just once and remain effective forever after. It is as if their effects are superpermanent. The ritual form hypothesis predicts that special agent rituals will have these superpermanent effects and will not need to be repeated.

Reversibility. Some rituals can be undone; others cannot. The ritual form hypothesis predicts that special agent rituals will be potentially reversible by other special agent rituals. The claim is not that such a ritual reversal actually exists but that the ritual system will regard reversal as theoretically possible and that the ritual of reversal will be of the special agent type.

Emotionality and sensory pageantry. Some rituals are performed with relatively more attention and emotion than others. The ritual form hypothesis predicts that special agent rituals will be more emotional, and more marked by sensory pageantry, than special instrument or special patient rituals.

Methodology

Our method was to gather accounts of rituals from active participants in living religious systems. To this end, we recruited research assistants from three of the religious communities on campus: Hindu, Jewish, and Islamic. The research assistants who conducted the interviews were themselves participants in the religious tradition for which they gathered data. These research assistants then recruited informants from among their own religious communities. Use of organization-selected informants and religiously involved interviewers doubtless bent our data toward orthodoxy or orthopraxy, which we hoped would increase the representativeness of our necessarily modest samples.

We trained the research assistants in a method of questioning designed to elicit the names of rituals, their descriptions, and any associated stories that might link the rituals to superhuman agents as these were defined within the religious system. Our research assistants gave informants a simplified version of the Lawson–McCauley ritual definition:

> For our purposes, we'll define a religious ritual as an action in which someone does some kind of physical act to a person or an object and this action evokes an unnatural result. The action also has to be somehow tied to a supernatural being, either the person who is performing the action, the object being used to perform the action, or the thing that the action is being performed on. This action has to be religiously motivated.

We thus characterized ritual in accordance with the ritual form hypothesis as an action, implicating a superhuman agent, in which someone or something is transformed. The research assistants asked each informant what actions in their religion might be rituals by this definition.

The informants then described each of the rituals, both the procedures themselves and the connections between the ritual forms and the tradition's superhuman agents. We reserved for ourselves the ultimate determination of whether a ritual was a special agent ritual, because there was no practical way to explain the nuances of the ritual form hypothesis to our informants. Follow-up questions ascertained whether informants regarded the ritual as reversible, repeatable, relatively emotional, and involving relatively high sensory pageantry for the patient.

Our method allowed both that informants would report different sets of rituals and that they would have different understandings of the rituals' characteristics. From ethnographic literature, we knew that rituals are often only loosely standardized, and we wanted our method to allow for this variability in understanding.

Results and Analysis

Hinduism

We received responses from seven Hindus: five male and two female. All but one described themselves as devout and said that their religion was important to their identity. They attended the temple monthly or annually, and prayed daily. The Hindu responses concerned the thread ceremony, the wedding ceremony, abhishekam, aarthi, and raksha bandhan (descriptions below).

The thread ceremony (upanayanam or munja). Six informants described this coming-of-age ritual for Brahman males in which a priest ties a thread (*poonul*) across the chest of a pubescent, unmarried male. Informants disagreed as to whether the ceremony gave the boy the power to chant Vedic verses, conveyed the rights and responsibilities of being an adult Brahman, or merely signified the attainment of manhood. Because the ceremony required a priest and it was clear that the informants considered a priest to be a special class of individual, we classified the thread ceremony as a *special agent ritual*. Our informants indicated that the thread ceremony is not repeatable, not reversible, and relatively high in emotionality and sensory pageantry.

The wedding ceremony. Although the wedding ceremony varies considerably from place to place, the descriptions we received from four informants shared the common characteristics that a priest conducts the wedding with the aim of changing the social status of the two individuals being married. Because of the role of the priest, we classified the wedding as a *special agent ritual*. Our informants said that the wedding ceremony is not repeatable, not reversible, and relatively high in emotionality and sensory pageantry.

Abhishekam. Abhishekam is the ritual washing of a god, performed at the beginning of a *puja*, a worship festival. The worshipper reads verses invoking the god to enter into the idol and then pours a mixture of certain liquids over the idol. Our informants said that the actions symbolize cleaning and providing refreshment to the god, as an element of welcoming the god into the household as an honored guest. Because believers perform abhishekam upon a deity, we classified it as a *special patient ritual*. Our informants judged that abhishekam is repeatable, not reversible, and moderate in emotionality and sensory pageantry.

Aarthi. In the aarthi ritual, participants show a lighted candle to pictures of gods by circling it clockwise around the picture/deity. Believers interpret this as an act of

Table 21.1 Summary of results from Hindu informants.

Ritual	Special	Repeatable	Reversible	Emotional	Sensory pageantry
Thread	Agent	No	No*	High	High
Wedding	Agent	No	No*	High	High
Abhishekam	Patient	Yes	No	Medium	Medium
Aarthi	Patient	Yes	No	High	Medium
Raksha bandhan	Instrument	Yes	No	Mixed	Medium

thanksgiving. Because they perform the aarthi upon the deity, we classified it a *special patient ritual*. Our informants described the aarthi as repeatable, not reversible, relatively high in emotionality, but with only moderate sensory pageantry.

Raksha bandhan. Three informants mentioned the ritual of raksha bandhan, in which a sister ties a special string (rakhi) onto her brother's wrist in exchange for money or gifts. The string is purported to protect the brother from evil. Because the rakhi is special—not just an ordinary string—we classify this as a *special instrument ritual*, though our informants were uncertain as to what exactly made the rakhi special. Our informants indicated that the raksha bandhan is repeatable, is not reversible, and has only moderate sensory pageantry. Our informants' ratings of the emotionality of the raksha bandhan were widely discrepant.

Overall. Informants also mentioned fire walking, janmastami (a celebration of Krishna's birthday), animal sacrifice, and other rituals, but we could not include them because of the low frequency with which they were reported. Table 21.1 summarizes the overall results. In addition, we would note that our informants disagreed as to whether the raksha bandhan was an emotionally salient ritual.

Judaism

We received data from seven Jewish informants: four female and three male. All described themselves as devoted to the tradition and indicated that Judaism was very important to their identity. They discussed multiple rituals, as described below.

Bris. In the bris, a *mohel*, a religious circumcision specialist, circumcises an eight-day-old male child. (Some bris prescriptions suggest that the child's father may carry out the procedure, but delegation to a mohel is customary or, according to some informants, mandatory.) The circumcision establishes the distinctive Jewish covenant between the male child and God. Informants were uncertain as to the procedure by which a person becomes a mohel but seemed to regard mohels as a special class of person, uniquely eligible to carry out the bris. The tradition of the bris extends, in Jewish mythology, back to Abraham, who was the agent of the first circumcisions (including his own). We therefore interpret the bris as a *special agent ritual*.

Our informants agreed that the ritual was not repeatable on the same patient; most agreed that the ritual was not even potentially reversible. Informants rated the bris low in emotionality for the patient, whom they said did not even feel it, but several informants suggested that the ritual is high in emotionality for the parents. Informants gave widely varying judgments about its sensory pageantry.

Bar/Bat mitzvah. In this rite of passage, a thirteen-year-old boy (*bar mitzvah*) or twelve-year-old girl (*bat mitzvah*) goes before a congregation and says a blessing over the Torah reading. The bar/bat mitzvah is thereby established as an adult, with all the rights and responsibilities attendant thereto. Because the transformation of the young person is accomplished by utterance of the ritually prescribed blessing, we interpret the bar/bat mitzvah as a *special instrument ritual*. Our informants described the bar/bat mitzvah as not repeatable, not reversible, and relatively high in emotionality and sensory pageantry.

Wedding. In the wedding ritual, the couple stands under a canopy held up by four poles and recites seven blessings. Attendance of at least ten religious Jews is required. The couple then drinks wine and smashes a glass or plate. We interpret the wedding as a *special instrument ritual*, in that the bride and groom perform all actions, and it is their own status that they transform. Although it is customary for a rabbi to be present, he is not an agent in the ritual. Our informants described the wedding ceremony as not repeatable, not reversible, and relatively high in emotionality and sensory pageantry.

Mikvah. The mikvah is a pool of fresh, moving water used for ritual cleansing. The water is blessed, and a person completely submerges herself or himself in it. Any adults can go to the mikvah, and this form of cleansing is required before some ceremonies. Married women also go to the mikvah twelve or fourteen days after the start of their menstrual period; a woman is not permitted to have sex with her husband from the beginning of her menstrual period until she has completed the mikvah. Because the water seems to be instrumental in the ritual purification of a person and no special characteristic is required of the agent or patient, we regard the mikvah as a *special instrument ritual*. Our informants indicated that the mikvah is repeatable, not reversible, and involves little emotionality or sensory pageantry.

Conversion. In conversion, a non-Jew studies Judaism and Jewish law. The potential convert then goes before a court of religious Jews, including at least one rabbi, who decide if he or she may become Jewish. If the panel approves the conversion, the non-Jew goes to a ritual bath (*mikvah*; see above) and is completely immersed in water in the presence of the panel of Jews. If the non-Jew is male, he must also be circumcised. The new convert is then given a new, Jewish name. Because of the role of rabbis in the training, evaluation, and naming (and the role of the mohel in circumcision), we interpret conversion as a *special agent ritual*. Our informants rated conversion as not repeatable but disagreed about its reversibility. They thought it highly emotional but lacking sensory pageantry.

Burning chametz. In preparation for Passover, an eight-day period when Jews are not permitted to eat leavened food, Jewish people clean their homes completely. First, they remove all the leavened and leavening products (*chametz*) from the home and clean everything to eliminate any traces of food. Then they place six pieces of chametz in areas where they generally store leavened products. They sweep up these six pieces with a feather and dustpan, then burn them. Because God directly prescribed the removal of chametz through Moses, we regard the removal of chametz as a *special instrument ritual*. Our informants said that burning chametz is repeatable, is not reversible, and involves little emotionality or sensory pageantry.

Lighting Shabbat candles. On Friday night just before sunset, Jewish people light and bless two candles. This ends the normal work week and begins Shabbat (the Sabbath). These candles are allowed to burn out naturally. The lighting of the Shabbat candle is a *special instrument ritual*, because it establishes the beginning of the Sabbath. Our informants indicated that the lighting of the Shabbat candle is repeatable, not reversible, and low in emotionality or sensory pageantry.

Havadalah. On Saturday night just after sunset, a three-wicked candle is lit, a spice box is passed around, and the candle is extinguished by putting it into a glass of wine. This ends Shabbat and starts the week. Havadalah is a *special instrument ritual*, on the same grounds that the lighting of the Shabbat candle is so interpreted. Our informants rated Havadalah as repeatable, not reversible, and low in emotionality, but with moderate sensory pageantry.

Mezuzah. This rectangular-shaped box holding a handwritten scroll of a section of the Torah (Deut. 6.4–9; 11.13) is placed at a forty-five-degree angle on the doorpost of the house. This makes the home kosher and allows a Jewish person to live there. The mezuzah is a *special instrument ritual*, because the use of the Torah implicates a special agent. Our informants judged that the mezuzah is not repeatable, is reversible, and is low in emotionality and sensory pageantry.

Overall. A few informants mentioned other rituals—the wearing of a kind of shawl (the tallit), the ordination of rabbis, the naming of babies, and so forth—but with such low frequency that we could not include them. Table 21.2 summarizes the overall results.

Table 21.2 Summary of results from Jewish informants.

Ritual	Special	Repeatable	Reversible	Emotional	Sensory pageantry
Bris	Agent	No	No*	Low	Mixed
Bar/Bat mitzvah	Instrument	No	No	High	High
Wedding	Instrument	No*	No	High	High
Mikvah	Instrument	Yes	No	Low	Low
Conversion	Agent	No*	Mixed	High	Low
Burning chametz	Instrument	Yes	No	Low	Low
Lighting Shabbat candle	Instrument	Yes	No	Low	Low
Havadalah	Instrument	Yes	No	Low	Medium
Mezuzah	Instrument	No*	Yes*	Low	Low

Islam

We interviewed eight Muslim students: three males and five females. All described themselves as devout and said that their faith was very important to their identity. They discussed marriage, divorce, hajj, and wuduu, as described below.

Marriage. Informants described marriage as the union of two people, usually done in the presence of an imam, a religious leader. The ritual involves reading from the Qur'an. The marriage officially takes place when the imam asks the husband and wife to sign the marriage contract in his presence. Witnesses are usually present as well. Our informants seemed to think of marriage as something that an imam does to a willing and eligible couple, rather than as something the couple does for themselves. This contrasts with the understanding of marriage usually derived from Islamic law but seems to accord fairly well with actual practice. Certainly, our informants regarded an imam as necessary for an efficacious wedding. We therefore interpret marriage as a *special agent ritual.* Our informants said that the marriage ritual was not repeatable, that it was reversible, and that it was high in emotionality and sensory pageantry.

Divorce. Informants were not as sure about the ritualistic description of divorce, but they agreed that it is done with an imam, can reverse a lifetime marriage, and renders a husband and wife as strangers (two separate entities after they had been unified in marriage). The specification of divorce procedures in Islamic law describes a ritual in which a man utters formulaic words at specified times in the presence of certain kinds of witnesses. Our informants, however, described an imam as being necessary for the procedure and seemed to regard the divorce as something the imam did. We therefore conclude that, whatever the actual Islamic legal procedure, our informants considered divorce a *special agent ritual.* Our informants said that the divorce ritual was not repeatable and that it was reversible. They rated divorce high in emotionality but disagreed about its degree of sensory pageantry.

Hajj. Informants described the hajj as the visit to the Kaaba, something that Muslims are required to do. Many said that it did not necessarily require an imam but that people usually go in groups that are led by an imam. An imam also conducts the prayer there. Muhammad modeled the visit to the Kaaba, and the actions are focused around the Kaaba, which forms the focal object of the pilgrimage. We therefore interpret the hajj as a *special patient ritual.* Informants agreed that the pilgrimage was repeatable. All informants but one regarded it as irreversible. Informants rated it high in emotionality and sensory pageantry.

Wuduu. Wuduu is the washing that is done before prayer (and whenever one must be clean for a religious act, i.e., reading the Qur'an). It involves washing certain body parts while saying a prescribed set of intentions. Though it is physically only a washing (cleansing of specific body parts), believers consider it to cleanse the entire body and the soul. Wuduu is a *special instrument ritual,* because the special agent is implicated through the example of Muhammad using water. Informants agreed that wuduu is repeatable, not reversible, and medium in emotionality and sensory pageantry.

Overall. Individual informants also mentioned other religious acts—baby initiation, putting a Qur'an under a child's pillow for protection from jinn, tasbeeh, and so

Table 21.3 Summary of results from Muslim informants.

Ritual	Special	Repeatable	Reversible	Emotional	Sensory pageantry
Marriage	Agent	No	Yes	High	High
Divorce	Agent	No	Yes	High	Mixed
Hajj	Patient	Yes	No	High	High
Wuduu	Instrument	Yes	No	Medium	Medium

forth—as rituals, but these were mentioned so infrequently that we could not include them. Table 21.3 summarizes the overall results.

The results for repeatability and reversibility support the Lawson–McCauley predictions, but the Lawson–McCauley predictions for sensory pageantry are not especially confirmed: sensory pageantry surrounds the hajj, a special patient ritual.

Table 21.4 reports the overall results for repeatability and reversibility.

Discussion

The ritual form hypothesis predicted the repeatability and reversibility of the rituals we examined at levels well above what would be predicted by chance. Moreover, the exceptions are largely of a single type: life-course rituals. (The other exception—the mezuzah—remains anomalous.) The success of the Lawson–McCauley hypothesis in predicting participants' judgments about repeatability and reversibility is striking.

The predictions about the relatively heightened sensory pageantry and emotionality of special agent rituals are also largely borne out. Table 21.5 compares, for each tradition, the emotionality of each special agent ritual with each special instrument or special patient ritual.

Systematic comparison shows that the ritual form hypothesis's predictions for emotionality are statistically significant. The predictions for sensory pageantry are also accurate, though falling slightly short of the conventional standard of $p < .05$. For those who are unfamiliar with statistics, the p-value indicates the probability, between 0 and 1, that a given result will occur simply as a part of chance variation, on the assumption that the distribution of results is statistically normal. The conventional limit for "statistical significance"—that is, the likelihood that the results are *not* due to chance—is $p \leq .05$. A p-value less than .05 means that there is an estimated 1-in-20 chance that the results are simply coincidental. There is nothing special about a p-value of .05; in fact, many large studies use the higher standard of $p \leq .005$, meaning that a result is considered statistically significant only if there is an estimated 1-in-200 chance of the results being due to chance. The sensory pageantry predictions are confirmed with a p-value of .076, meaning that the results we found would be expected to occur simply by chance 1 out of 14 times. This evidence is not as strong as the rest of our results, but it is noteworthy.

Table 21.4 Overall interview results for repeatability and reversibility.

Ritual	Special	Repeatable?	Reversible?
Hinduism			
Thread	Agent	No	No*
Wedding	Agent	No	No*
Abhishekam	Patient	Yes	No
Aarthi	Patient	Yes	No
Raksha bandhan	Instrument	Yes	No
Judaism			
Bris	Agent	No	No*
Bar/Bat mitzvah	Instrument	No	No
Wedding	Instrument	No*	No
Mikvah	Instrument	Yes	No
Conversion	Agent	No*	Mixed
Burning chametz	Instrument	Yes	No
Lighting Shabbat candle	Instrument	Yes	No
Havadalah	Instrument	Yes	No
Mezuzah	Instrument	No*	Yes*
Islam			
Marriage	Agent	No	Yes
Divorce	Agent	No	Yes
Hajj	Patient	Yes	No
Wuduu	Instrument	Yes	No
Accuracy		**15 of 18** **$p = .004$**	**13 of 17** **$p = .025$**

It is worth noting too that the correlation between emotionality and sensory pageantry ($r = 0.66$) suggests that Lawson and McCauley are substantially justified in using sensory pageantry as a proxy for emotionality in their theory.

Our research did, however, raise one serious difficulty for the ritual form hypothesis: very often, our informants indicated that they *did not know* how a ritual implicated a superhuman agent. This poses a significant challenge because the hypothesis alleges that people use precisely this information to produce their judgments about the repeatability, reversibility, and relative centrality of a ritual. Our informants indicated that they did not have the one key piece of knowledge that, according to the ritual form hypothesis, forms the basis for their judgments.

Table 21.5 Comparison of emotionality and sensory pageantry between special agent and other rituals.

	Special agent ritual	vs.	Special instrument/ patient ritual	Emotionality prediction fit?	Sensory pageantry prediction fit?
Hindu	Thread	vs.	Abhishekam	Yes	Yes
			Aarthi	No	Yes
			Raksha bandhan	Yes	Yes
	Wedding	vs.	Abhishekam	Yes	Yes
			Aarthi	—	Yes
			Raksha bandhan	Yes	Yes
Judaism	Bris	vs.	Bar/Bat mitzvah	No	No
			Wedding	No	No
			Mikvah	Yes	Yes
			Burning chametz	Yes	Yes
			Lighting Shabbat candles	Yes	Yes
			Havadalah	Yes	Yes
			Mezuzah	Yes	Yes
	Conversion	vs.	Bar/Bat mitzvah	Yes	No
			Wedding	Yes	No
			Mikvah	Yes	Yes
			Burning chametz	Yes	Yes
			Lighting Shabbat candles	Yes	No
			Havadalah	Yes	No
			Mezuzah	Yes	Yes
Islam	Marriage	vs.	Hajj	No	Yes
			Wuduu	Yes	Yes
	Divorce	vs.	Hajj	No	No
			Wuduu	Yes	No
	Accuracy			**18 of 23** $p = .003$	**16 of 24** $p = .076$

Now it is evident that we humans have only very incomplete or distorted introspective access to most of our cognitive processes. In principle, informants' inability to describe their own mental representations is not particularly surprising for a cognitive theory. Yet, given that information about a ritual form's connection to a superhuman agent is—and must be—culturally transmitted, it is hard to see how it could be transmitted in anything other than an explicit fashion, and we think it unlikely that this bit of information— if genuinely crucial to ritual understanding—had been forgotten. Thus the ritual form hypothesis presupposes that in many cases, people have more information than they actually do.

It is possible that what Lawson and McCauley have proposed is not a model of ordinary folks' ritual representations but a model of ritual *expertise*. (We consider this possibility despite the fact that Lawson and McCauley contrast the folk knowledge modeled in their theory with that of experts [1990: 134]—this is not an interpretation they intend.) In this scenario, the ritual experts would be the ones with all the relevant knowledge, and they would determine a ritual's repeatability, reversibility, and so forth. Our informants, none of whom were ritual experts, would then be merely echoing the repeatability and reversibility determinations made by others. This is an area for further research.

The ritual form hypothesis has clearly identified some important factors in the structure of religious rituals. The significant ability of this model to predict practitioners' intuitions on the basis of a ritual's mythology is remarkable and reveals a previously unanticipated kind of connection between myth and ritual. Myth has long been viewed as a kind of charter for ritual, but until Lawson and McCauley's work, this relation was conceived in only the most general sense. Lawson and McCauley have shown that present-day ritual practices are still understood, at least formally, as the ongoing work of the gods.

CHAPTER 22
HOW DO HUMANS PROCESS RITUALIZED ACTIONS?
Jesper Sørensen and Kristoffer L. Nielbo

Introduction

Ritual is an enigma. Despite the fact that people in all cultures and all historical periods engage in ritual, psychologists, anthropologists, and scholars of religion have failed to reach a consensus about what exactly constitutes ritualized behavior and how we can explain its universal presence. Still, the student of religion might reasonably ask, What is the buzz about? Is ritual not merely the behavioral expression of religious beliefs? Even if this approach has some truth to it—ritual is often explicitly connected to specific beliefs—the devil is in the detail. As we shall see, the relationship between beliefs and ritual actions is not quite as straightforward as we tend to believe intuitively. At this point, it suffices to point to the fact that people performing a particular ritual are not necessarily in agreement about what beliefs should motivate its performance, and neither do participants always refer to explicitly held beliefs when asked about their underlying motivations.

This disparity between the actions observed, their purported underlying beliefs, and the apparent strangeness of most rituals is, of course, what makes ritual something in need of a scientific explanation. Space does not permit a thorough discussion of the more-than-a-century-long and intricate history of the research on ritual. Instead we merely wish to outline two broadly conceived approaches that, each in their own manner, have influenced the development of ritual studies and therefore form a background to the experiments described below. One way to establish the link between beliefs and behavior is to highlight the former as determining the latter. Hence, the intellectualist and evolutionist anthropologists of the late nineteenth and early twentieth centuries argued that ritual should be understood as inherently rational actions based on flawed and ultimately childish beliefs about the world, beliefs that are typical at primitive stages of cultural evolution. They further argued that the apparent irrationality of ritual behaviors dissipates once the underlying beliefs motivating them are made clear. For instance, throwing water into the air in order to attract rain might seem irrational, but it is a rational action if it is informed by an underlying belief in the invisible correspondence between all expressions of water and the ability of one to attract the other. Even if these early anthropologists argued that magical and religious rituals are distinct types of ritual, both were argued to be explicable as instrumental and rational expressions of underlying belief: in the case of magic, participants believe that entities in the world are connected and able to influence each other in a lawful manner (e.g., between an effigy, such as a doll, and a person), even though these connections really rest upon the misapplication of associative principles (as when you associate a walnut with a brain due to likeness); in the case of religion, participants believe that the world is governed by powerful beings that must be appeased through worship, even though, according to this approach, this is merely an analogical projection of human agency onto the world (understanding events in the world as caused by powerful agents, just like humans can produce changes in the world). (See Tylor 1871 and Frazer 1911 for typical examples of this approach.)

Whereas the intellectualists thus understand ritual quite literally and focus on its instrumental dimension, that is, what performers believe it accomplishes, the symbolists have an altogether different approach. Symbolists understand ritual not as a flawed instrumental behavior but as exactly symbolic—as expressing a nonapparent meaning that the cultural analyst must unveil. Symbolists come in several varieties from psychoanalysts to sociologists, depending on the preferred bedrock of symbolic analysis. With its insistence on the social function of ritual activity, the sociological variety has been particularly influential among anthropologists and scholars of religion alike. In short, sociologically inclined symbolists argue that rituals enable participants to engage with and reconfirm central aspects of their society—be those power, gender, age, or authority—through indirect, symbolic means. Ritual thus constitutes a specific type of behavior that serves particular functions in relation to society, for instance bolstering social coherence or mending social fissures (e.g., when social disputes are solved by means of joint ritual action symbolically addressing the conflict). And this is the case even if this inherent meaning of the ritual is unclear or completely unknown to the participants. (See Douglas 1966; Durkheim 1995 [1912]; Radcliffe-Brown 1952; and Turner 1967 for examples of this approach.)

A common feature of the intellectualist and symbolist approaches is the underlying assumption that the observable strangeness of actions in many rituals dissolves when the observer uncovers either the explicit beliefs motivating their performance or the underlying symbolic system they arguably express. In short, ritual becomes meaningful only if we know its cultural milieu, that is, the social context and symbolic system prevalent in a given setting. And, indeed, we must pay attention to both the explicit reasons that participants give for performing rituals and how ritual relates to explicitly held beliefs, and to the symbols found in any given ritual and how these relate to more general symbolic structures. Emphasizing these aspects, however, often entails a concurrent disregard of what is in most need of an explanation: why ritual behavior seems so strange to begin with. In fact, both approaches end up dissolving the phenomena they set out to explain, by reducing ritual either to flawed instrumental behavior or to just another type of symbolic communication. They both end up in an explanatory dead end. Even though the intellectualists rightly point to the instrumental aspects of ritual, that is, the fact that people often use ritual to attain particular goals, they fail to explain why people who otherwise achieve their goals through ordinary, functional actions suddenly resort in some cases to ritualized actions. The symbolists, on the other hand, recognize that ritual constitutes a special type of behavior, but by asserting its essentially symbolic nature, they effectively recategorize ritual not as a type of action but as a mode of communication, in the most extreme cases as some sort of immaterial text waiting to be deciphered. They thereby disregard the many features that contradict the communicative model: the inherent inability of participants and analysts to agree on what counts as symbolic and what the symbols actually mean, as well as the intrinsic difficulty in establishing who is in fact communicating with whom. Thus if ritual is a type of symbolic communication, it is a very particular kind that fails to live up to the standards required for successful communication in other domains of life.

Theory

Researchers raised points of criticism similar to those just mentioned and presented alternative approaches from various points during the 1970s and 1980s. Dan Sperber (1975) criticized attempts to unlock ritual meaning through a "symbolic key" as an essentially "cryptological" approach (i.e., that rituals consist in symbolic codes that one needs a special knowledge to decipher) that misconstrues ritual as a message to be deciphered. Instead, he argued, ritual and other types of symbolism should be understood as culturally successful methods used to elicit certain types of cognitive processing—in fact, a ritual's very obscurity (technically described as its "semantic underdetermination") is a crucial component of its cognitive function. Ritual does not mean anything in itself but will, in some cases, generate the construction of meaning by participants. Later, Frits Staal (1979) argued that rituals were intrinsically meaningless, that they should be construed as "pure activity without meaning or goal" (p. 9), and that the important aspects of rituals rest in their formal structure and participants' focus on correct execution. He argued that rituals were similar to grammar and, building upon linguist Noam Chomsky's absolute distinction between grammar (rules) and semantics (meaning) in the domain of language, Staal paved the way for a renewed focus on the formal or, one could say, surface characteristics of ritual. About the same time, anthropologist Roy Rappaport made a critical contribution to the future study of ritual. In his seminal paper, "The Obvious Aspects of Ritual" (1979, expanded in Rappaport 1999), he stressed the importance of explaining the distinguishing features of ritual itself, that is, what make rituals different from other types of actions. Linking human ritualization to ritual displays among animals, he pointed to characteristics such as invariance and rigidity, and the prevalence of redundancy and iteration—in short, the formal features that make ritual distinct. Only when we have explained the role and effect of these will we be able to reach a better understanding of rituals' potential function in society.

This formal turn in the study of ritual was the point of departure for cognitive approaches to ritual, two of which are particularly relevant for the experiment presented below. In 1990, E. Thomas Lawson and Robert N. McCauley published *Rethinking Religion*. Inspired by Chomsky, Sperber, and Staal, the authors presented an ambitious theory that linked a formal model of the cognitive competences underlying individuals' judgments of ritual form on the one hand—that is, the degree to which a ritual is deemed "acceptable" by performers and observers—and culturally transmitted, religious ideas on the other. What is of particular relevance in this context is the proposal that religious ritual action, like other types of actions, is processed by a cognitive system designed to deal with ordinary actions. This so-called action representation system traces who is doing what to whom when observing or engaging in an action. Lawson and McCauley argued that religious ritual is characterized by the insertion of superhuman agents—gods, spirits, ancestors, and so on—into the action representation system either as the (more or less) direct agent of the action (e.g., in baptism) or as the patient or target of the action (e.g., in sacrifice).

This was a crucial step forward as it emphasized the fact that ritual is a type of action processed by a cognitive system with particular structures and constraints. However, while Lawson and McCauley's theory addressed the structural relations between religious rituals as well as their connections to conceptual structure, it left the question of ritualization itself unanswered. Boyer and Liénard (2007, 2008; Liénard and Boyer 2008) and Sørensen (2007b) directly addressed this, proposing somewhat similar models of how ritualization influences cognitive processing, and in the following we shall explain some of the basic components of human action representation according to these models.

Inspired by a number of studies of action processing in cognitive psychology, we can model action processing as a hierarchical system in which individual action elements are chunked into basic-level action gestalts (i.e., prototypical sub-actions such a "gripping," "lifting," or "turning") that, in turn, are integrated into representations of larger action sequences specified by an overarching intention (e.g., drinking coffee). For instance, imagine you want to go to the baker to buy bread. This high-level goal specifies a long series of actions, chunked into action gestalts such as getting into your car, turning the ignition, putting the car into gear, backing out from the driveway, driving on the road, parking, and so on. Whereas each sub-action is specified by your intention (you *want* to start the car, etc.), they are all causally specified by the overarching intention of buying bread. Alternatively you could take your bike, which would specify a different sequence of actions. In any case, the complete action can be described as going to the baker to get bread, and this illustrates the human ability to represent actions by an overarching intention and thereby provide a way to judge the success or failure of the action. The example further illustrates that the system extends both downward, toward more fine-grained actions (you need to put your hand in your pocket to grab the key), as well as upward to even more overarching goals (you buy bread to satisfy hunger—if the baker is closed you need to find another way to satisfy your hunger).

At this point we should emphasize two things. First, the action hierarchy is integrated both in terms of intentions (overarching goals specify underlying actions) and causal structure (you need to find your car keys prior to igniting the car). Second, actions at all levels are evaluated by an error-monitoring system that activates when information from the senses does not fit the current model. On a fine level this means that you update your internal model, for instance when the car starts, and that directs your expectations to a number of relevant and causally related sub-actions (getting the car into gear, pressing the gas pedal, etc.). In this case, the error signal leads you to update where you are in the action sequence that will take you to your ultimate goal. However, stronger error signals arise in cases where information violates expectations to the overarching intention of the action sequence. Thus, if your car starts smoothly, you pay no further attention to the fact that you turned the ignition. If the car fails to start, however, you must repeat the action and, if failure persists, either give up your overarching intention to buy bread or change the underlying action sequence into another one that will allow you to reach your goal (e.g., get your bike out from the garage).

All this may seem like an overly technical way to describe the banal observation that our actions depend on each other and are determined by our goals. This model, however, allows us to make a number of inferences that subsequently enable the investigation of some of the characteristic features that distinguish ritual from ordinary actions. First, the hierarchical nature of the action system entails that we constantly form predictions of both our own and other peoples' actions based on models of overarching intentions. When I turn the ignition of the car, I expect the car to start. And if you know I want to buy bread at the baker, you will not be surprised to hear the car start. This is in line with recent neurocognitive theorizing about predictive processing that argues that predictions minimize cognitive load, as we only need to pay attention to sub-actions when these *fail* to produce the expected result, such as when the car fails to start (For discussion, see Clark 2013).

Second, we will expect that our attention drifts toward the highest level in the system that is able to successfully predict the underlying actions. We process information by extracting the most relevant overarching intention, and we therefore only pay attention to the underlying action structures if we are prompted to by other considerations. Thus, initially it does not matter how you get to the baker, as long as there is bread on the table. However, if you are late, clarifying that you had to take the bike is relevant as it explains your delay.

Now, our model of ritual is based on the assumption that a number of the features described above as automatic aspects of ordinary or functional action processing are violated when performing or observing ritual action. First, no causal structure seems to connect the intentions motivating participants' ritual performance and the concrete actions they perform. These intentions only relate to the overarching level of actually performing the whole ritual sequence (e.g., the Catholic Eucharist) but not to the distinct sub-actions the ritual is composed of (e.g., kneeling, receiving bread). There is no way the uninformed observer or participant can guess what actions will be performed, solely based on knowledge of the intentions, nor can the intentions be inferred based on observation of the actions. There are simply no obvious causal relations between the actions performed and their purported effect. This was, of course, what led the symbolists to focus on the symbolic nature of ritual action in the first place, but rather than focus on how interpretations change over time or what the ritual might mean, we focus our attention on *why* rituals violate these expectations and what these violations entail in terms of cognitive processing.

Second, in contrast to ordinary action sequences in which sub-actions are causally codependent (I need to insert the key before igniting the car), ritual sub-actions show much fewer causal dependencies. The correct ritual sequence is decided upon by reference to tradition, rather than by reference to how one action causally enables another. For instance, participants kneel before receiving bread in the Eucharist, but this is specified by tradition and not by any causal necessity (it is perfectly possible to eat bread without kneeling). Third, in contrast to going to the baker, the success of a ritual cannot be evaluated by reference to any perceivable effect on the world but only by the degree to which ritual performance conforms to preconceived ideas about how it should be performed. When you drink a glass of water, the action is completed when your thirst is quenched. In contrast, it is impossible to empirically decide when you have eaten enough consecrated bread to receive grace (is a crumb sufficient?), and therefore tradition takes over and guides our evaluation by reference to more or less explicit norms. Thus, neither participants nor observers can form causal schemas linking the individual sub-actions to the purported ritual goal.

Methodology

Experiment 1: Segmentation of nonfunctional actions

But how do we test whether these ideas and predictions about the effect of ritual on human action processing are on the right track? How do we attain relevant data? Fortunately, a line of research into so-called event segmentation had already paved a way (see Newtson & Engquist 1976; Wilder 1978; Zacks, Tversky, & Iyer 2001). In short, event segmentation studies investigate how humans parse, that is, subdivide, actions into meaningful chunks at different levels of the action hierarchy. Researchers asked participants to parse an observed action by pressing a key every time a new action began. Further, they asked participants to do this at coarse, intermediate, and fine levels. So, imagine you watch a movie of someone making coffee before going out to mow the lawn. If you are told to parse at the most coarse level, you are likely to press only once, at the point when the person shifts from making coffee to mowing the lawn. If you are asked to parse at an intermediate level, you will press more often, as you distinguish between putting coffee in the grinder, filling the kettle, turning on the stove, and so on. And finally, if you are asked to parse at a fine level, you will increase the number of times you press even more as you distinguish between gripping the kettle's handle, lifting your hand, moving the kettle to the water faucet, turning on the water, and so on. Results from these studies show that participants agreed on (a) intra-level boundaries, that is, participants segmented actions similarly within coarse and fine levels; and (b) inter-level boundaries, such that fine-level boundaries represented subsets of coarse-level boundaries; for example, participants agreed that gripping the kettle and turning on the water faucet are subsets of making coffee, while putting gas in the lawn mower and starting the ignition are subsets of mowing the lawn. These findings offer strong support for the hierarchical nature of human action perception.

However, as we wanted to investigate the difference between ordinary, functional actions (like making coffee) and ritualized, nonfunctional actions, we needed to change aspects of the experimental paradigm, that is, how the experiment is constructed. Whereas previous studies used coarse-, intermediate-, and fine-level parsing as *independent* variables (the variable manipulated by the experimenter, as he or she asked participants to perform the task on a particular level), we aimed to test how ritualization affects the level on which participants spontaneously parse actions. As described above, we argue that in rituals it is hard to integrate sub-actions into coherent causal models. At any point in the ritual, it is therefore difficult to predict what comes next as no causal structure will guide such predictions. We therefore expected that participants would parse observed nonfunctional actions at a finer level than functional actions. Thus, level of parsing, measured as the number of partitions into which participants divide an observed action sequence, is the *dependent* variable in our experiments.

In order to test our prediction, two things followed naturally. First, the study had to be within subject (the same participant parsing both functional and nonfunctional actions), as individuals might differ on the level at which they prefer to parse an observed action. Second, we had to balance stimuli, that is, we needed to construct stimuli that contained the same number of sub-actions in both the functional and the nonfunctional conditions. Initially, we did this by filming sixteen functional action sequences, and thereafter we made sixteen nonfunctional equivalents, thus ending up with thirty-two 30-second film clips as our stimuli. For instance, we shot a film of an actor who made a cup of instant coffee following a detailed script containing both necessary and unnecessary parts. Next we counted exactly how many sub-actions the sequence contained. Then we shot the nonfunctional counterpart by adding three features that previous studies have claimed to be characteristic of ritualized behavior: redundancy (e.g., repetition), rigidity (e.g., rigid movements), and goal demotion (e.g., removing goal). In order to ensure that both actions contained an equal number of sub-actions, we removed an unnecessary part every time we added a "ritualized" part, and we further controlled that the numbers were indeed balanced by having an expert group with no knowledge of the hypotheses segment all films.

We were now ready to run our experiment. We enrolled twenty-three undergraduate students from Aarhus University in Denmark. We asked them to watch the films (shown on a monitor in a randomized order) and to segment (by pressing a key) the actions observed in a manner they found meaningful. We further emphasized that there was no correct way to do so. The results showed that participants did indeed spontaneously parse the nonfunctional actions on a finer scale than their functional equivalent. Our experiment thus supported our initial hypothesis that ritual actions lead people to segment on a finer level in the action hierarchy. As is the case with all experimental findings, however, we had to critically reflect upon whether this support for our hypothesis could be an artifact, that is, if our results were produced by some uncontrolled-for aspect of our experimental manipulation and had really nothing to do with our initial hypothesis. A candidate for such "noise" arose early on: our manipulation was based on film shots of functional actions that were known to participants prior to the experiments, in contrast to shots of nonfunctional actions that none of the participants had ever seen before. Could it be that our result was based on some sort of novelty effect?

Experiment 2: Segmentation of goal-demoted actions

In order to control for a potential novelty effect, we devised a new segmentation experiment. Results from Experiment 1 suggested that goal demotion (the lack of intuitive connections between actions performed and the purported result) was enough to make participants increase segmentation rate, that is, segment actions into finer details. We therefore made a new set of stimuli consisting of 20-second film clips of six functional action sequences, as well as six goal-demoted transformations of these. In order to avoid a novelty affect, this time we used unfamiliar functional actions, such as assembling a tattoo machine or setting up a mandolin. Thus both the functional actions and their nonfunctional counterparts were equally novel for participants. We first shot the six 20-second films of the functional actions. We then had expert parsers, with no knowledge of the hypotheses motivating the study, segment the films at a fine level. We chose a fine level, as the films were of relatively short duration and we wanted as many sub-actions identified as possible. Based on these results, we identified the relevant sub-actions and then randomized the sequence in order to create a nonfunctional script. We then shot the six nonfunctional equivalents, which consisted of the same sub-actions as the functional actions but in a random order leading to no functional end-state.

Further, we wanted to see whether familiarization would have an effect on segmentation rate. We presumed that even nonfunctional actions that are familiar to participants or observers, such as many cultural rituals, would lead to participants segmenting the familiarized films at a coarser level. We therefore familiarized participants with half of the stimuli set, three functional and three nonfunctional films, by showing these six films three times each in a randomized order before asking participants to segment all twelve film clips in the same manner as in Experiment 1. As in the first experiment, we used a within-subject design (meaning that all participants would segment all films), and the experiment had two conditions: functional versus nonfunctional and familiarized versus nonfamiliarized.

The results once again supported the hypothesis that participants would segment ritualized actions, operationalized as observation of nonfunctional action sequences, at a finer, more detailed level of action representation in contrast to functional actions. Surprisingly, familiarization had no effect.

Discussion

So what have we learned from these studies? Of course, one can question the extent to which our operationalization succeeds in measuring ritual behavior. Would it not be better to have people parse real rituals? In an ideal world, yes. However, such enhanced ecological validity (i.e., more directly matching the conditions we really aim to explain) would come at a price, as it would be very hard to construct equivalent and balanced functional actions. Further, using real-world rituals would raise all sorts of questions concerning participants' prior knowledge and conceptions of both in-group and out-group, or familiar and unfamiliar, ritual. In our operationalization, participants were unaware that we investigated ritual behavior, and any of their preconceptions about ritual thus did not influence our results.

One major concern should be raised, however. Why did familiarization not influence participants' segmentation? If we accept that our study does indeed say something about how people process ritual actions, the results entail that prior knowledge of a ritual does not influence people's partitioning of the action. This raises a number of possible points. First, if we presume our method (showing an action three times) is a valid mode of familiarizing participants, it could be that the human partitioning system is purely perceptual and that prior conceptual knowledge has no impact on the processing of actions perceived. So, just as visual illusions persist even when we know they are just illusions, the cognitive systems responsible for processing action might function independently of our conceptual knowledge about these actions. In light of recent models of predictive processing in the brain, we find this to be a highly unlikely possibility. Theories of predictive processing argue that higher-level models guide expectations to lower-level input, and thus an absolute distinction between low-level perceptual systems and high-level conceptual knowledge must be abandoned. A more likely possibility is that goal-demoted actions, that is, causally incoherent action sequences, are very hard to encode in memory, and it would take much stronger and longer exposure to such actions to have an effect on actual processing. Translated into real-world situations, this means that ritual action sequences take longer to learn and demand more executive control to perform than functional actions. In short, the formation of stable schematic representations of a ritual action sequence is more cumbersome, as it can only be done by means of rote learning. This interpretation is supported by both anecdotal and ethnographic evidence. Thus, while preparing for the second experiment, it took much longer to shoot the films containing nonfunctional actions than their functional counterparts, as nothing but rote learning could guide the actor in his performance. This is in line with ethnographic field-observations that learning correct ritual performance is hard work that demands investment of both time and cognitive resources. Using a computational approach (i.e., simulating exposure to nonfunctional actions in neural networks in a computer), in a subsequent study we modeled the effect that prolonged exposure to the action sequence as well as knowledge about the "meaning" of actions had on the networks' ability to correctly predict subsequent actions. Thereby we were able to simulate how extensive rote learning and prior conceptual knowledge lowered segmentation rate, indicating that the neural networks gradually increased their ability to integrate nonfunctional actions in overarching schemas. These models are partially supported in a later behavioral study that utilized verbal narration to enhance learning (Nielbo, Schjødt, & Sørensen 2013).

Given that one accepts how we operationalized ritualized behavior in order to study it in the lab, we can conclude that the two experiments support the hypothesis that ritualized behavior is processed at a finer/lower level in the action-processing hierarchy. When actions cannot be causally related, it is more difficult to integrate them into overarching schemas by means of intuitive causal inferences. This, in turn, impedes the prediction of subsequent actions, forcing the cognitive system to focus attention on the individual sub-actions or gestures in order to extract their potential pragmatic significance. It is next to impossible to predict what will follow next in a ritual sequence unless you know the ritual by rote. A number of theoretical propositions follow naturally from this observation.

First, redirecting cognitive attention to the gestural level, that is, to the finer details of the physical actions themselves, might help explain representations of efficacy or "magic" associated with ritual. More than a hundred years ago, Frazer pointed to the fact that magical rituals achieve their perceived effect by exploiting possible associative connections of gestures, such as similarity (e.g., piercing a doll to harm an enemy) and contagion (e.g., burning a person's hair to harm him or her) (Frazer 1911). Elsewhere, Sørensen (2007a) has proposed that rituals are efficient ways to evoke such associative relations in the heads of both ritual participants and observers. These associations link ritual sub-actions to specific goals. Thus, even though no causal models relate a doll with a person or a hair with the person to whom it used to belong, establishing such relations of similarity and contagion seem to be a readily available secondary cognitive strategy that is automatically activated when a person engages in or observes ritual actions and, thereby, connects these to events outside the ritual itself. (For experimental evidence, see Nemeroff & Rozin 1994; Subbotsky 2014, 2011.)

Second, redirecting attention to the gestural level of processing is a costly affair in terms of cognitive resources. Just as speaking (or worse, texting) on your mobile phone demands attention and thus should not be done while you are driving a car, focusing attention to the concrete actions performed in a ritual sequence will necessarily take away attention that could be used for other purposes. Together with our colleagues, we have argued that ritualization is one among several methods used to deplete cognitive resources in the executive network in the brain. In short, participating in or even observing ritual action will inhibit both symbolic processing (e.g., what the action means) and memory of the event, which are not part of the specified ritual sequence (i.e., what *actually* happened). This interpretation obviously supports the critical points raised against symbolist accounts of ritual mentioned at the beginning of this chapter. However, another less incompatible interpretation is possible: that redirecting attention to the minute details in fact enables already established, culturally diffused interpretations to stand unquestioned, and that it further facilitates the construction of collective (and potentially false) memory subsequent to ritual performance (Schjoedt et al. 2013). According to this approach, the cognitive effects of ritualized action lead to an understanding of ritual as a cultural technology that promotes adherence to already established authoritative symbolic models, as well as aligning participants' experience of what really took place.

CHAPTER 23
DID RITUALIZED HUMAN SACRIFICE HELP BUILD AND SUSTAIN SOCIAL INEQUALITY?

Joseph Watts, Oliver Sheehan, Quentin Atkinson,
Joseph Bulbulia, and Russell Gray

Introduction

Human sacrifice was surprisingly common in early human societies. In ancient Egypt, the bodies of pharaohs were buried with human sacrifices, who were believed to assist in the pharaoh's afterlife. In Europe, mutilated bodies from thousands of years ago are regularly uncovered alongside ritual artifacts. In Central America, Aztec priests extracted the beating hearts of sacrificial victims and then rolled their corpses down temple stairs. Today, references to human sacrifice can still be found in the Bible, Quran, Torah, and Vedas. Why was something as gory and costly as human sacrifice so common in human history?

Scholars have often argued that human sacrifice occurred because it served some kind of function. Some argue that human sacrifice was a form of social catharsis that allowed communities to release their built-up resentments and animosity (Girard et al. 1987). Others argue that leaders used human sacrifice to justify politically motivated wars by claiming that the gods demanded sacrificial victims from enemy groups (Price 1978). It has even been suggested that human sacrifice, when combined with cannibalism, was a way of overcoming protein shortages in harsh environments (Harner 1977).

In this study we decided to test the Social Control Hypothesis of human sacrifice. According to this hypothesis, social elites, such as priests and chiefs, used human sacrifice to control social underclasses (Carrasco 1999; Turner & Turner 1999). Social elites were able to use human sacrifice as a tool for social control because they could claim that gods demanded violent and gory human sacrifices, and then they could use human sacrifices to punish rebels and terrorize populations into obedience. The Social Control Hypothesis doesn't claim that this is the only reason that human sacrifices occurred, but suggests that human sacrifice could have contributed to the growth and maintenance of social hierarchies in human history. Over time, these early hierarchical societies evolved into the kinds of large, complex societies we live in today (Flannery & Marcus 2012).

While the Social Control Hypothesis was inspired by archeological and historical records of human sacrifice in North and Central American cultures (Carrasco 1999; del Castillo 2008; Turner & Turner 1999), it could apply generally across cultures. To test the generality of the Social Control Hypothesis, we used cross-cultural comparative methods to test how human sacrifice coevolved with social inequality across ninety-three Austronesian cultures.

Methodology

Sample

The Austronesian-speaking peoples were some of the greatest ocean explorers in human history. Thousands of years before the Viking sagas, Austronesians began their great expansion from Taiwan out into the Pacific Ocean (Gray, Drummond, & Greenhill 2009). They settled as far west as Madagascar, as far south as Aotearoa (New Zealand), and as far east as Rapa Nui (Easter Island). This is an area covering over half the world's longitude and a third of its latitude.

Austronesian cultures are described as a "natural experiment" for testing theories about cultural evolution because of their cultural diversity and relative isolation from the rest of the world (Diamond 1997; Goodenough 1957). At the time of European contact they had developed social systems ranging from egalitarian, family-based communities to hierarchically organized kingdoms (Watts et al. 2015b). The different kinds of supernatural agents they worshipped included the spirits of recently deceased ancestors, nature spirits, and remote creator gods. Ritual practices included community songs and dances, tattooing, piercings, and scarification, as well as sacrifices. Things that were sacrificed included discarded coconut husks, first harvests of crops, and the lives of humans. This diversity makes Austronesian cultures an ideal test case for studying how religious and social systems coevolved in early human societies.

Variables

For each culture in our study, we recorded the presence or absence of human sacrifice. The term "human sacrifice" refers to the ritualized slaughter of humans, motivated or justified by supernatural belief (Bremmer 2007). In many cases human sacrifice is believed to please gods, and in return the gods provide the community with benefits. These benefits include things like success in war, plentiful harvests, or the end of harsh weather. Human sacrifice was coded as present if there was evidence that members of the culture practiced the ritual killing of human beings, in a nonmilitary context, for the sole or primary purpose of pleasing or appeasing a supernatural agent. Deaths that occurred during raids on enemy groups, or nonritual murders that resulted from interpersonal conflicts, were not considered to be human sacrifice. Human sacrifice was coded as absent if ethnographic sources explicitly stated that human sacrifice was not practiced, or if there was no evidence of human sacrifice from a substantial description of the culture's religious practices.

We were interested in how human sacrifice coevolved with different kinds of social inequality (also known as social stratification). To do this we created a variable on the presence or absence of "general social inequality" a well as a variable on the presence or absence of "high social inequality." Cultures were coded as having high social inequality if they had class systems with pronounced differences in wealth and/or status and if these class systems were strictly inherited over generations. This means that high social inequality includes things like ruling noble lineages or heritable slave castes where people were stuck with the social standing that they were born into. Cultures were coded as having general social inequality if they had class systems that were associated with differences in wealth and/or status and these differences *tended* to be inherited over generations. This means that general inequality includes both high social inequality as well as less severe forms of inequality where people could change their social class if they were particularly talented or worked hard.

The data we collected on these Austronesian cultures was based on how these cultures were at the time of first contact with Europeans and is part of the Pulotu database (www.pulotu.com) (Watts et al. 2015b). We are interested in studying how Austronesian cultures were before the introduction of major world religions such as Christianity, Islam, Hinduism, and Buddhism. We gathered information from historical documents such as ethnographies, missionary records, and the descriptions of early explorers. Today none of these cultures still practices human sacrifice, and their social systems have changed substantially.

Cross-cultural studies and Galton's Problem

Comparative cross-cultural studies have the potential to reveal broad patterns in human cultures, but they also involve challenges. One of these challenges is due to the fact that cultures are related to each other through common ancestry and the borrowing of traits between them (Mace & Pagel 1994). This means that in cross-cultural studies, some cultural traits will tend to cluster together not because they are causally related to one another but instead because the cultures with those traits are related to one another. For example, today the United States, South Africa, New Zealand, and Australia all have a democratic political system and a fondness for beer. The reason these countries share these traits isn't because democratic political systems are causally related to a fondness for beer. Instead, it is because these countries inherited them from a common ancestor, Great Britain. The difficulty of telling if traits tend to cluster together because of "historical" relationships or if they cluster together because of a causal relationship between the variables has come to be known as Galton's Problem (Tylor 1889). For the first half of the twentieth century, many anthropologists found Galton's Problem so formidable that many simply gave up on the cross-cultural comparative method entirely (Naroll 1961).

Phylogenetic comparative methods

In recent years scientists have developed ways of addressing Galton's Problem by creating a range of "Phylogenetic Comparative Methods" (Mace & Holden 2005; Mace, Jordan, & Holden 2003). What these methods have in common is that they include comparative cross-cultural data and a family tree (also known as a phylogeny) that represents the ancestry of the cultural groups. Cultures that are "sisters" on a tree share a recent common ancestor, and cultures that are further away from each other on the tree are more distantly related to one another in history. Because Phylogenetic Comparative Methods take into account the common ancestry of cultures, they provide a principled way of addressing Galton's Problem. These methods have been used in the social sciences to study the evolution of kinship systems (Fortunato & Jordan 2010), means of subsistence (Holden & Mace 2003; Jordan 2013), political hierarchies (Currie et al. 2010), and language (Atkinson et al. 2008) across a large number of cultures.

In this study we used a Phylogenetic Comparative Method called Pagel's Discrete (Pagel 1994). This method includes two variables, and each variable is simply coded as present or absent (also known as dummy or binary coding). This method works by testing how millions of different possible models of evolution fit the data we observed (Pagel & Meade 2006). In each of these different models, the rates at which each trait evolves can vary (rates are represented as arrows in Figure 23.1). For example, Figure 23.1 shows an independent model where cultures are more likely to gain social inequality than they are to lose social inequality. We can then use statistical methods to identify the best fitting models of evolution.

To test whether human sacrifice and social inequality have coevolved we can test whether independent or dependent models of evolution best fit our data (Pagel &

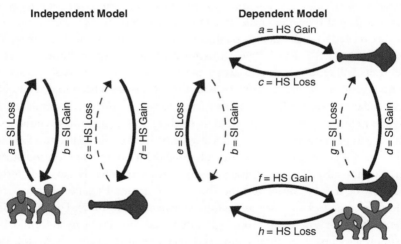

Figure 23.1 Possible models of dependent and independent models of trait evolution. Arrows represent the rate at which human sacrifice (HS) and social inequality (SI) are gained and lost by cultures. The club icon indicates the presence of human sacrifice and the human-figures icon represents social inequality. In an independent model of evolution, the rate at which one trait is gained or lost is independent of the state of the other trait. In a dependent model of evolution, the rate at which a culture gains or loses one trait depends on the state of the other trait. In this example, cultures gain social inequality at a higher rate when human sacrifice is present than if it is absent (*rate d* is greater than *rate b*).

Meade 2006). In an independent model the chance of a culture gaining or losing one trait is independent of the state of the other trait (Figure 23.1). In this case, the chance of a culture gaining or losing social inequality is the same for cultures with and without human sacrifice. If the evolutionary histories of human sacrifice and social inequality are unrelated, then we expect our analyses to favor independent models of evolution. In a dependent model, the rate at which a trait is gained or lost can depend on the state of the other trait (Figure 23.1). In this case, cultures can be more likely to gain social inequality if they have human sacrifice than if they lack human sacrifice. If the evolutionary histories of human sacrifice and social inequality are related to one another, we expect our analyses to favor dependent models of evolution.

One of the advantages that Pagel's Discrete has over other comparative methods is that it doesn't just tell us whether two traits are associated with one another; it can also get at the nature of the causal relationship between them. The reason that we can get at the causal relationship between the traits is that dependent models of evolution can tell us whether one trait tends to facilitate or inhibit the other. For example, if cultures with human sacrifice are more likely to go on to develop social inequality, then we would expect our dependent model to show us that *rate d* (the rate at which cultures with human sacrifice gain social inequality) is greater than *rate b* (the rate at which cultures without human sacrifice gain social inequality). This means that we can tell whether human sacrifice is associated with social inequality because cultures with social inequality are more likely to gain human sacrifice, or because cultures with human sacrifice are more likely to gain social inequality.

Hypotheses

The Social Control Hypothesis makes three predictions about the relationship between social inequality and human sacrifice. First, it predicts that we will find evidence for the coevolution of human sacrifice and social inequality. Therefore, we should expect to find support for dependent models of evolution over independent models of evolution. Second, we expect to find that cultures with human sacrifice are more likely to develop social inequality than cultures without human sacrifice. Therefore, the best-fitting dependent models should show that cultures with human sacrifice gain social inequality at a higher rate (*rate d* in the dependent model of Figure 23.1) than cultures without human sacrifice gain social inequality (*rate b* in the dependent model of Figure 23.1). Third, we expect to find that once social inequality has arisen, human sacrifice helps to maintain it. This means that the best-fitting dependent models should show that cultures with human sacrifice lose social inequality at a lower rate (*rate g* in the dependent model of Figure 23.1) than cultures without human sacrifice (*rate e* in the dependent model of Figure 23.1).

Results and Analysis

When we first examined our data we found that human sacrifice was remarkably common in early Austronesian cultures. Almost one half (43 percent) of the cultures we studied were documented as having practiced human sacrifice. While only 25 percent of egalitarian cultures practiced human sacrifice, 48 percent of cultures with general social inequality performed human sacrifice and 67 percent of cultures with high social inequality performed human sacrifice. This suggests that there is some kind of association between social inequality and human sacrifice (Figure 23.2).

While the association between human sacrifice and social inequality is interesting, it doesn't address Galton's Problem and it doesn't tell us much about the causal relationship between these traits. Instead of human sacrifice helping to build and sustain social inequality, it could be that human sacrifice is just a side effect of more unequal societies. We used Pagel's Discrete to test whether the relationship between human sacrifice and social inequality holds after addressing Galton's Problem and to test between the different causal explanations for the relationship between social inequality and human sacrifice.

In this study we tested how human sacrifice coevolved with both general social inequality as well as high social inequality. The results of our first analyses on general social inequality showed that dependent models best explain the evolutionary history of human sacrifice and general social inequality. This provides evidence that human sacrifice coevolved with social inequality in Austronesia, but on its own it does not tell us about the nature of this coevolution. To understand precisely how human sacrifice coevolved with social inequality, we examined the rates of change in the best-fitting dependent models. In these models (summarized in Figure 23.3) cultures with human sacrifice were less likely to lose social inequality than those without human sacrifice

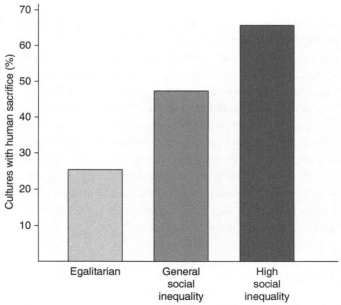

Figure 23.2 The prevalence of human sacrifice across cultures with different levels of social inequality. As social inequality increases, so too does human sacrifice.

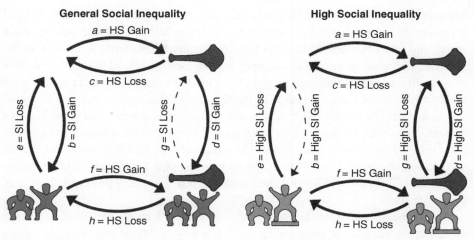

Figure 23.3 Summary of our results on the coevolution of human sacrifice with general social inequality and high social inequality. The best-fitting model of general social inequality shows that cultures with human sacrifice are less likely to lose general social inequality than cultures without human sacrifice (*rate g* is lower than *rate e*). The model of high social inequality shows that cultures with human sacrifice are more likely to gain high social inequality than those without (*rate d* is higher than *rate b*).

(*rate g* is lower than *rate e*). However, we found no evidence that human sacrifice made it more likely for egalitarian cultures to gain social inequality (*rate b* is close to *rate d*). This suggests that human sacrifice functioned to stabilize social inequality once it had arisen but provides no evidence that human sacrifice affected whether egalitarian cultures developed social inequality in the first place.

Next we looked at how human sacrifice coevolved with high social inequality. We found that dependent models of evolution also best explain the evolutionary history of human sacrifice and high social inequality. This indicates that human sacrifice has coevolved with high social inequality. In the best-fitting dependent models (summarized in Figure 23.3), cultures with human sacrifice were more likely to gain high social inequality than cultures without human sacrifice (*rate d* is higher than *rate b*). However, we found no evidence that ritualized human sacrifice helped sustain high social inequality once it had emerged (*rate e* is close to *rate g*). This provides evidence that human sacrifice helped cultures gain high social inequality, but that human sacrifice did not necessarily function to stabilize high social inequality once it had arisen.

Discussion

Our results show that human sacrifice helped to build and sustain some forms of social inequality in human history. Human sacrifice occurred in almost half of the cultures we studied, and the effects of human sacrifice depended on the level of social inequality found in a society. In egalitarian societies, human sacrifice was relatively scarce and while human sacrifice did not help egalitarian societies to develop social inequality, once social inequality emerged, human sacrifice helped to maintain it. This suggests that in order for human sacrifice to be used as a means of social control, there must first be social elites to exploit it. We also found that human sacrifice occurred in the majority of cultures with high social inequality and helped to build, but not sustain, high social inequality. This suggests that human sacrifice helped to build the most unequal societies in Austronesia. The reason that we find no evidence of human sacrifice stabilizing high social inequality may be that high social inequality was rarely lost in the early history of Austronesian cultures, providing little power to detect this particular effect.

In Austronesian cultures, human sacrifice was called for on a variety of occasions, including the funerals of chiefs, inauguration of new buildings and boats, to ensure plentiful harvests, to avoid natural disasters, and to restore balance after the breach of social taboos. The means of death were equally varied and included being crushed under a newly built canoe, buried at the foundations of a building, bludgeoning, strangulation, drowning, burning, stabbing, and being rolled off a roof and then decapitated (Beatty 1992; Burt 1994; Kamakau 1964). One pattern that emerges throughout these descriptions is that human sacrifice tended to be orchestrated by social elites and the victims tended to be of low social status, such as slaves. This can be seen in Figure 23.4, a drawing by the

Figure 23.4 Illustration of human sacrifice in Hawaii by the French explorer Jacques Arago, 1819.

French explorer Jacques Arago (1822) depicting a Hawaiian chief overseeing a human sacrifice.

While human sacrifice was justified as necessary to appease or please supernatural agents, in practice it often served the interests of social elites. In Hawaii, undermining the sacred authority of the king was a serious matter:

> *The transgressor must be put to death, then, in person or through a substitute. But this execution must take a form that permits the reaffirmation of the existing relationship between the social hierarchy and the gods that are its principal foundation. As a result, the transgressor will be consecrated to the gods, and his sacrifice will at once reconstitute these gods and the social hierarchy that rests upon them.* (Valeri 1985)

However, if the person that broke the rule was wealthy, they could simply substitute one of their slaves' lives for their own. In these cases the rules and beliefs around human sacrifice blatantly support social hierarchies and elites (Bulbulia et al. 2017).

However, even in cultures where the rules didn't so obviously favor social hierarchies, elites generally got to choose who the sacrifice victims were. We know from ethnographic descriptions that these victims were often "persons who had incurred the displeasure of the king" (Metraux 1940). In these kinds of social environments it was certainly worth staying on the good side of the elites! While there are many factors that help build and sustain social inequality, human sacrifice may be a particularly effective means of maintaining and building social control because it minimizes the potential of retaliation by eliminating the victim and shifts the agent believed to be ultimately responsible to the realm of the supernatural.

A major reason that human sacrifice could be used as a form of social control was because of the overlap between religious and political authority in early Austronesian societies. Political and religious leaders were often one and the same, had strong ties, or came from the same lineage. This created an environment in which the upper classes of society had substantial influence over religious systems and, over time, could shape religious systems toward their own ends. For example, the people of Bugotu in the Solomon Islands believed that the gods demanded food sacrifices, but for the food to make its way to the gods it first had to be eaten by the high priest (Bogesi 1948). In other cultures, such as Tonga, political leaders claimed to have descended from the gods and have a privileged ability to communicate with them (Cummins 1977). The use of ritualized human sacrifice as a means of social control highlights the dangers of unchecked religious and social authority in the hands of social elites.

Future research

Future research is needed to understand the role of human sacrifice across a broader range of social environments. The functionality of a trait depends on the environment in which is occurs. Here we have shown that human sacrifice helped build and sustain social inequality in cultures without the kinds of formalized policing and political institutions found in modern societies. We caution that this does not necessarily mean that human sacrifice would have these effects across more egalitarian societies or in modern societies that have more subtle ways to maintain social inequality.

A question we leave open for future research is whether ritualized human sacrifice is functional for the cultural group generally, or just social elites. Whether human sacrifice provided an overall benefit or cost to social groups likely depends on the effects of social inequality in early human societies. While social inequality generally provides a benefit to social elites, its broader effects on early human societies are less clear. One possibility is that social inequality is functional for the social group generally because it provides a form of social coordination and enables larger and more efficient societies to form. Another possibility is that social inequality only benefited social elites and was maladaptive at the group level because it increased conflict within communities.

Conclusion

Religion has long been proposed to play a functional role in society (Coulanges 1877; Durkheim 1915) and is commonly claimed to underpin morality. Recent evolutionary theories of religion have focused on the potential of prosocial and moral religious beliefs to increase cooperation (Norenzayan et al. 2014; Watts et al. 2015a). Our findings suggest that religious rituals also played a darker role in the evolution of modern complex societies. In traditional Austronesian cultures there was substantial religious and political overlap, and ritualized human sacrifice may have been co-opted by elites as a divinely sanctioned means of social control (Bellah 2011; Cronk 1994; Marx & Engels 1975). The approach adopted in this paper demonstrates how combining computational phylogenetic methods and historical cultural data can be used to test theories about major transitions in human social organization. Unpalatable as it might be, our results suggest that ritual killing helped humans transition from the small egalitarian groups of our ancestors to the large, complex societies we live in today.

NOTES

Chapter 2

1. In the 1990s, talk about the virtues and vices of "political correctness" and all things "PC" was abuzz on university campuses. The use of the terms "theologically correct" and "theological correctness" (TC) in this paper was a self-conscious play on political correctness. To be "theologically correct" is to espouse the beliefs that orthodoxy demands, whether someone has deep understanding of the claim or can use it to explain, predict, or generate inferences. "Theological correctness" is the gap between a person's stated theology and the religious concept used on the fly to think (Barrett 1999).

2. Here is how Uncomp was described: "The year is 4093 A.D. Uncomp is a super-computer, which was built by the United Nations to help keep peace and do good in the world. Uncomp is a system of pairs of microscopic disks: one a sensor and one an effector. The sensor disk of each pair gives Uncomp abilities roughly similar to hearing, seeing, smelling, tasting, and feeling even when an object is not in direct contact with the sensors. The sensors also perceive heat, electric, and chemical activity with great sensitivity. Uncomp can use these capabilities to understand what a person does even without seeing or hearing them. Uncomp can even track the electric activity of the brain and thus read minds. The effector disks make use of electromagnetic and antigravity emissions to act on the world. These effectors enable Uncomp to move anything without touching it or being near it. Uncomp can even effect how people think and feel. These pairs of disks cover every square centimeter of the earth and so no information escapes processing. The disks do not move. Uncomp has no other components. The disks are electrically linked with any other part of the system at any time. Uncomp has no central processor and so is not anywhere in particular. Uncomp has been given a program for ethics and a program for emotions as well, which run in the entire network at once. Uncomp runs independently all the time and can perform many different functions in many different places at the same time. Uncomp can retrieve information from many different places simultaneously." (Barrett & Keil 1996)

3. I suspect the fourth story of the set, concerning a mountain pass in Europe and some goats, is the guiltiest. It actually includes language of God being "at a narrow, rocky, mountain pass." Though an all-present God may be "at" a location just as oxygen or the atmosphere could be said to be "at a narrow, rocky, mountain pass," such specification seems to violate the rules of good storytelling: you don't include facts that are obviously true. Hence, mentioning that God is present in a place may encourage anthropomorphic thought. I encourage researchers to drop this story from the set, and this story was not part of Barrett and Keil (1996), Study 3.

Chapter 3

1. Because it was technically possible to just press a single button all the time (or answer in a patterned fashion), we included the distractor questions to test whether or not people were actually paying attention and to make sure that all questions had "no" responses. The

distractor questions ranged from trivia you would hear in a pub quiz to bizarre questions that were difficult to understand. Our distractor questions took participants a lot longer to answer, which gave us confidence that participants were paying attention to all the questions in the experiments.

2. While one of our reviewers worried that it was a bit too much like "Noah's ark" or the "Ark of the Covenant" and therefore may make people think about religion, we used it simply because an "ark" is a big boat and was the name of a ship in a science fiction television series in the 1970s. One way to check our results is to replicate our study and extend it by comparing the "Ark" with an alien species of the same kind but with a different name.

3. Logarithms are ways to find out how many times you need to multiply a certain number to get another number. Logarithms have various bases. So, the "base 10" logarithm of 100 is 2. So, $\log_{10}(100) = 2$, $\log_{10}(1,000) = 3$, $\log_{10}(10,000) = 4$, and so on. Each time we add a zero to the target number, the answer increases by 1. Think of this like a rate of increase. We used the natural logarithm, which uses "Euler's number," which is around 2.72 (often looks like $\log_e$ or "ln" for "logarithmus naturali"). In our study, if someone took 6,232 milliseconds to answer a question, this transformation converts it into 8.74 ($\log_e(6,232) \approx 8.74$). If they took 1,000 milliseconds, the number becomes around 6.91. This condenses values to more manageable units (and makes graphs easier to understand). Transformations like this are very common. As long as every value gets transformed the same way, you don't confuse the transformed data with the raw data, and you're transparent about what you did, these transformations can help interpret results.

4. Note that participants could technically answer before the recordings of the questions were finished playing. The program we used would therefore create negative response speed values. There are no natural logarithms to negative numbers, so we added 1,000 milliseconds to each response time and log-transformed those values.

5. A confidence interval is a range of probable values based around some value (in our case, the mean). It is standard practice to report 95 percent confidence intervals, though this 95 percent level is arbitrary and fairly strict. What it means is that if we reran our study many times and again calculated the same confidence intervals of the mean, 95 percent of the intervals would contain the true mean. In other words, if we calculated the 95 percent confidence interval of the mean in 100 studies, 95 of them would contain the true mean. So, if we calculated, instead, the 80 percent confidence interval, 80 of the studies would contain the true mean, and so on. When you see confidence intervals like this, it helps to remind yourself that they represent a range of ranges. Understood in this light, just because two intervals overlap doesn't mean what they're measuring aren't completely different, and likewise, just because two intervals don't overlap doesn't necessarily mean the target variables are. Rather than absolutely, think probabilistically. Typically, p-values often accompany such intervals as an index of the magnitude of difference, and this often encourages the imposition of discrete conclusions based on continuous phenomena (see the next note for why this is misleading).

6. In the case of comparing two things, the p-value is a number that indicates the probability that a result—or a more extreme result—would happen if there were no real differences between whatever one is looking at. When comparing things statistically, by convention, researchers and readers tend to look for p-values that are smaller than .05 and call those things "statistically significantly different." If you find a "statistically significant difference" between two things, it really means that if the two things were actually the same on average, the probability of getting your reported differences is less than 5 percent. Put differently, if you run a test of differences and your p-value is .85, that means that there's an 85 percent chance that you'd get your results if there really are no differences. In our original paper, we

reported that "there were no significant differences between response times to non-strategic questions and strategic questions" with some statistics to show this for the Ark study (Purzycki et al. 2012: 861). Note, however, that the conclusion that they are not different is probably too strong, particularly as this determination is based on a p-value being greater than .05 (another arbitrary cutoff; see the previous note). In the case of the differences between moral and nonmoral information for the Ark questions, the p-value was .13 (and moral questions were answered more quickly than nonmoral questions). So, *if there really are no differences* between response times to moral and nonmoral questions for the Ark (our "null hypothesis"), there is only a 13 percent chance of getting our results (or the more extreme possibilities). That sounds pretty low! In other words, it's fairly *un*likely that we'd get our results if there really were no differences! This is a bit unintuitive, which is part of the reason why there are movements toward avoiding reliance on or even reporting p-values and instead paying more attention to effect sizes (e.g., Cumming 2012). Their "levels of significance" are arbitrary, and relying on them will often lead to missing out on important details. So, contrary to what we emphasized, it's probably better to say that the Ark did, in fact, lead people to respond more quickly to moral questions! Indeed, throughout the original article, we noted many instances of there being "no significant differences" or "no significant effects" based on similarly weak criteria and arbitrary conventions. This is also why replicating studies is very important.

7.   See the previous note.

8.   See note 5.

Chapter 5

1.   As a hearty, starchy root vegetable, cassava is one of the most important sources of calories in the traditional iTaukei (see the following note) diet. On islands further east, people keep taro (a special variant called *dalo ni tana*) and *kumara* (sweet potato) gardens for such emergencies. However, Yasawans cannot fall back on such emergency crops because taro requires wet, swampy conditions and Yasawa's arid landscape can support only limited cultivation. Yasawans rely more on wild yams in such times of need.

2.   The word iTaukei in Standard Fijian translates to "owner" and connotes a person to whom the land belongs but also who belongs to the land.

3.   Because traditional iTaukei society is patrilineal (traces clan membership through the father; iTaukei Fijians also trace the mother's side with a separate concept of *vasu*), most people move to where the husband is *kai* (where the husband's father's clan comes from).

4.   *Yavusa* can extend beyond a single village, and a single village can have more than one *yavusa*. However, in Yasawa, villages tend to consist of only one *yavusa*.

5.   Elsewhere in Fiji, Bible God is also referred to as *Kalou dina*, or "true God." While the phrase *Kalou dina* is understood in Yasawa, the term is not often used locally. "True God" also connotes the Christian God's higher status above the *Kalou-vu* in the sociospiritual hierarchy. The *Kalou dina* takes care of the universe, and the *Kalou-vu* take care of local matters.

6.   Though *Kalou-vu* mostly focus on village life, they are sometimes believed to see and affect people in their lineage (therefore under their influence) from afar.

7.   For a more in-depth explanation of the statistical measures, including regression analyses, that led to the overview of results shown here, please see McNamara et al. (2016) and McNamara and Henrich (2017).

Chapter 7

1. In this particular study, we drew upon the online database maintained by the National Palace Museum in Taipei, Taiwan (http://210.69.170.100/s25/index.htm).

2. Using the online database maintained by the Chinese University of Hong Kong (http://bamboo.lib.cuhk.edu.hk/). The Guodian corpus was chosen because of the ease of accessing and searching it online.

3. In addition to the standard, common words for the body in classical Chinese, *xing* 形, *shen* 身, and *ti* 體, we also included *li* 力 ("physical strength," one instance in the late Warring States period) and *qi* 氣 (when used in the sense of physiological energy) as references to the "body."

4. *Mencius* 4:A:19, where physically taking care of one's parents is characterized as "merely caring for their mouths and limbs" (*yang kouti* 養口體). This arguably expresses a coordination rather than a contrast.

5. Note that, for the purposes of the final analysis, content codes 13–15 (all referring to various aspects of what one might term "higher cognition") were collapsed into one code.

6. See, for instance, the critique of our study in *Cognitive Science* by Klein & Klein (2011).

7. One prominent exception, as Luther Martin has observed (personal communication), has been the work of biblical scholars, who since the nineteenth century have used concordances (and more recently electronic databases) to perform word-count studies aimed at, for instance, distinguishing between "genuine" Pauline letters and the deutero-Pauline literature.

8. The coding of primate behavior is notoriously difficult and subject to individual bias or, as was apparently the case in the lab of Marc Hauser at Harvard, active fraud. For the Hauser lab controversy, see Johnson (2012).

Chapter 9

1. Among other things.

2. Something that can be studied scientifically.

3. One's individual development; as opposed to phylogenesis, which is defined as the evolution of a species.

4. Folk sciences (sometimes also called naïve sciences) refer to more or less innate inferences about the functioning of the biological world (folk biology—cows cannot fly as they do not have wings) or the physical world (folk physics—an object cannot levitate as it violates the laws of gravity) or the mental functioning of other minds (folk psychology—we cannot read others' minds). They are present and manifested roughly at the same age in one's development and therefore are seen as a result of evolutionary adaptation of our cognitive processes.

5. Memory decay refers to the amount of forgetting that occurs between the initial presentation of a to-be-learned material and its subsequent recall.

6. In cognitive psychological research, it has been shown that information that stands out from other information (von Restorff's effect), is bizarre (the bizarreness effect), or simply violates our predictions and inferences (the expectation-violation effect) results in greater memory, mostly due to deeper encoding. Therefore, these effects demonstrate a preponderance of evidence that our cognitive system is designed to retain any violations to expectations.

7. Bayesian statistics deems cognitive (as well as artificial) systems as operating based on probabilities of prior inferences and hypotheses (also called "priors") that are changed as the

system accumulates evidence or counterevidence according to probabilistic rules of inference (called as "posterior beliefs").

8. By epidemiology of beliefs, the author refers to the causes as well as the distribution of beliefs. For instance, one believes in a god because the idea of God has some characteristics or content that makes it interesting, that is, attractive, to our human cognitive system.

Chapter 11

1. The *Chronicle*'s measure of charitable giving, on the one hand, correlates with Pew's measure of religiosity ($r = .53$, $p < .001$) and the importance of religion ($r = .56$, $p < .001$). CAF America's measures of charitable giving, on the other hand, do not correlate with either religiosity ($r = .016$, $p = .91$) or importance of religion ($r = -.10$, $p = .46$). Finally, murder rates reported by the FBI correlate with both religiosity ($r = .53$, $p < .001$) and importance of religion ($r = .67$, $p < .001$).

Chapter 12

1. This particular SDM was programmed using a software called AnyLogic (AnyLogic Company 2015). A personal learning edition is available free for students. We encourage all interested people (particularly students) to download our model and the software, manipulate it, and change it. Such experimentation could produce significant results that can supplement (or even critique) the model as we programmed it. Many journals, such as the *Journal of Cognition and Culture*; *Religion, Brain, and Behavior*; and the *Journal for the Cognitive Science of Religion*, have published models of religion such as this and welcome the submission of critiques and revisions.

Chapter 18

1. That is, an observation of people's behavior in their natural environment, often performed by anthropologists.
2. We could have opted for using different methods, e.g., mild electric shocks, stimulation by random white noise, or carbon dioxide inhalation. (These are all standardized methods for inducing anxiety.) Practicality and ethical concerns were the main factors leading our decisions.

Chapter 20

1. We did perform a region-of-interest (ROI) analysis of the caudate nucleus (dorsal striatum) to examine if prayer stimulates the dopaminergic system, which among other functions serves as a reward system involved in habitual behaviors. Release of dopamine in this system is associated with reward experience and a pleasurable mood state. In this hypothesis-driven ROI analysis, we found a main effect across prayer types that was mainly driven by activity in the caudate nucleus during recitation of the Lord's Prayer (Schjoedt et al. 2008).

REFERENCES

Chapter 1

Bering, J. M., & Parker, B. D. (2006). Children's attributions of intentions to an invisible agent. *Developmental Psychology, 42,* 253–62.

Bloom, P. (2007). Religion is natural. *Developmental Science, 10,* 147–51.

Burns, J. K. (2004). An evolutionary theory of schizophrenia: Cortical connectivity, metarepresentation, and the social brain. *Behavioral and Brain Sciences, 27,* 831–55.

Gendler, T. S. (2008). Alief and belief. *The Journal of Philosophy, 105,* 634–63.

Heywood, B. T., & Bering, J. M. (2014). "Meant to be": How religious beliefs and cultural religiosity affect the implicit bias to think teleologically. *Religion, Brain & Behavior, 4,* 183–201.

Humphrey, N. K. (1976). The social function of intellect. In P. P. G. Bateson & R. A. Hinde (Eds.), *Growing points in ethology* (pp. 303–17). Cambridge, UK: Cambridge University Press.

Newman, G. E., Keil, F. C., Kuhlmeier, V. A., & Wynn, K. (2010). Early understandings of the link between agents and order. *Proceedings of the National Academy of Sciences, 107,* 17140–45.

Perner, J., & Howes, D. (1992). "He Thinks He Knows": And more developmental evidence against the simulation (role taking) theory. *Mind & Language, 7,* 72–86.

Piazza, J., Bering, J. M., & Ingram, G. (2011). "Princess Alice is watching you": Children's belief in an invisible person inhibits cheating. *Journal of Experimental Child Psychology, 109,* 311–20.

Woolley, J. D., Boerger, E. A., & Markman, A. B. (2004). A visit from the Candy Witch: Factors influencing young children's belief in a novel fantastical being. *Developmental Science, 7,* 456–68.

Chapter 2

Astuti, R., & Harris, P. L. (2008). Understanding morality and the life of the ancestors in rural Madagascar. *Cognitive Science, 32,* 713–40. doi:10.1080/03640210802066907.

Barrett, J. L. (1998). Cognitive constraints on Hindu concepts of the divine. *Journal for the Scientific Study of Religion, 37,* 608–19.

Barrett, J. L. (1999). Theological correctness: Cognitive constraint and the study of religion. *Method and Theory in the Study of Religion, 11,* 325–39.

Barrett, J. L. (2011). *Cognitive science, religion, and theology: From human minds to divine minds.* West Conshohocken, PA: Templeton Press.

Barrett, J. L. (2012). *Born believers: The science of children's religious belief.* New York: Free Press.

Barrett, J. L., & Keil, F. C. (1996). Anthropomorphism and god concepts: Conceptualizing a non-natural entity. *Cognitive Psychology, 31,* 219–47. doi:10.1006/cogp.1996.0017.

Barrett, J. L., & VanOrman, B. (1996). The effects of image use in worship on god concepts. *Journal of Psychology and Christianity, 15*(1), 38–45.

Bek, J., & Lock, S. (2011). Afterlife beliefs: Category specificity and sensitivity to biological priming. *Religion, Brain & Behavior, 1*(1), 5–17.

References

Boyer, P. (1992). Explaining religious ideas: Elements of a cognitive approach. *Numen*, *39*, 27–35.

Boyer, P. (1994). *The naturalness of religious ideas: A cognitive theory of religion*. Berkeley, CA: University of California Press.

Bransford, John D., & McCarrell, Nancy S. A sketch of a cognitive approach to comprehension: Some thoughts about understanding what it means to comprehend. In Walter Weimer & David Palermo (Eds.), *Cognition and the symbolic processes* (pp. 189–229). New York: Lawrence Erlbaum, 1974.

Chilcott, T., & Paloutzian, R. F. (2016). Relations between Gauḍīya Vaiṣṇava devotional practices and implicit and explicit anthropomorphic reasoning about Kṛṣṇa. *Journal of Cognition and Culture*, *16*(1–2), 107–21. doi:10.1163/15685373-12342170.

Cohen, E., & Barrett, J. L. (2008). Conceptualising possession trance: Ethnographic and experimental evidence. *Ethos*, *36*(2), 246–67.

Gregory, J. P., & Greenway, T. S. (2017). Is there a window of opportunity for religiosity? Children and adolescents preferentially recall religious-type cultural representations, but older adults do not. *Religion, Brain & Behavior*, *7*, 98–116. doi:10.1080/2153599X.2016.1196234.

Guthrie, S. E. (1980). A cognitive theory of religion. *Current Anthropology*, *21*, 181–203.

Guthrie, S. E. (1993). *Faces in the clouds: A new theory of religion*. New York: Oxford University Press.

Keil, F. C. (1979). *Semantic and conceptual development*. Cambridge, MA: Harvard University Press.

Keil, F. C. (1989). *Concepts, kinds and conceptual development*. Cambridge, MA: MIT Press.

Knight, N. & Astuti, R. (2008). Some problems with property ascription. *Journal of the Royal Anthropological Institute*, *14*, 142–58. doi:10.1111/j.1467-9655.2008.00498.x.

McCauley, R. N. (2011). *Why religion is natural and science is not*. New York: Oxford University Press.

Slone, D. J. (2004). *Theological incorrectness: Why religious people believe what they shouldn't*. New York: Oxford University Press.

Sperber, D. (1985). Anthropology and psychology: Towards an epidemiology of representations. *Man*, *20*, 73–89.

Chapter 3

Atkinson, Q. D., & Bourrat, P. (2011). Beliefs about God, the afterlife and morality support the role of supernatural policing in human cooperation. *Evolution and Human Behavior*, *32*(1), 41–9. doi:10.1016/j.evolhumbehav.2010.07.008.

Barber, N. (2011). A cross-national test of the uncertainty hypothesis of religious belief. *Cross-Cultural Research*, *45*(3), 318–33. doi:10.1177/1069397111402465.

Baron-Cohen, S. (1995). *Mindblindness: An essay on autism and theory of mind*. Cambridge: MIT Press.

Barrett, J. L. (2008). Why Santa Claus is not a God. *Journal of Cognition and Culture*, *8*, 149–61. doi:10.1163/156770908X289251.

Barrett, J. L., & Keil, F. C. (1996). Conceptualizing a nonnatural entity: Anthropomorphism in god concepts. *Cognitive Psychology*, *31*(3), 219–47.

Boyer, P. (2001). *Religion explained: The evolutionary origins of religious thought*. New York: Basic Books.

Bulbulia, J., Sosis, R., Harris, E., Genet, R., Genet, C., & Wyman, K. (Eds.) (2008). *The evolution of religion: Studies, theories, & critiques*. Santa Margarita, CA: Collins Foundation Press.

Cumming, G. (2012). *Understanding the new statistics: Effect sizes, confidence intervals, and meta-analysis.* New York: Routledge.

Dennett, D. C. (1987). *The intentional stance.* Cambridge: MIT Press.

Gray, H. M., Gray, K., & Wegner, D. M. (2007). Dimensions of mind perception. *Science, 315*(5812), 619–19. doi:10.1126/science.1134475.

Gray, K., Young, L., & Waytz, A. (2012). Mind perception is the essence of morality. *Psychological Inquiry, 23*(2), 101–24. doi:10.1080/1047840X.2012.651387.

Greenwald, A. G., McGhee, D. E., & Schwartz, J. L. K. (1998). Measuring individual differences in implicit cognition: The implicit association test. *Journal of Personality and Social Psychology, 74*(6), 1464–80. doi:10.1037/0022-3514.74.6.1464.

Guthrie, S. E. (1980). A cognitive theory of religion. *Current Anthropology, 21*(2), 181–203. doi:10.1086/202429.

Guthrie, S. E. (1995). *Faces in the clouds: A new theory of religion.* New York: Oxford University Press.

Henrich, J., Heine, S. J., & Norenzayan, A. (2010). The weirdest people in the world? *Behavioral and Brain Sciences, 33*(2–3), 61–83. doi:10.1017/S0140525X0999152X.

Inzlicht, M., Tullett, A. M., & Good, M. (2011). The need to believe: A neuroscience account of religion as a motivated process. *Religion, Brain & Behavior, 1*(3), 192–212. doi:10.1080/21535 99X.2011.647849.

Johnson, D. D. P. (2005). God's punishment and public goods: A test of the supernatural punishment hypothesis in 186 world cultures. *Human Nature, 16*(4), 410–46. doi:10.1007/s12110-005-1017-0.

Norenzayan, A. (2013). *Big gods: How religion transformed cooperation and conflict.* Princeton, NJ: Princeton University Press.

Norenzayan, A., Gervais, W. M., & Trzesniewski, K. H. (2012). Mentalizing deficits constrain belief in a personal god. *PLOS One, 7*(5), e36880. doi:10.1371/journal.pone.0036880.

Orwell, G. [1949] (2003). *Nineteen Eighty-Four.* New York: Plume.

Purzycki, B. G. (2013). The minds of gods: A comparative study of supernatural agency. *Cognition, 129*(1), 163–79. doi:10.1016/j.cognition.2013.06.010.

Purzycki, B. G. (2016). The evolution of gods' minds in the Tyva Republic. *Current Anthropology, 57*(S13), S88–S104.

Purzycki, B. G., Apicella, C., Atkinson, Q. D., Cohen, E., McNamara, R. A., Willard, A. K., ... & Henrich, J. (2016). Moralistic gods, supernatural punishment and the expansion of human sociality. *Nature, 530*(7590), 327–30. doi:10.1038/nature16980.

Purzycki, B. G., Finkel, D. N., Shaver, J., Wales, N., Cohen, A. B., & Sosis, R. (2012). What does God know? Supernatural agents' access to socially strategic and non-strategic information. *Cognitive Science, 36*(5), 846–69. doi:10.1111/j.1551-6709.2012.01242.x.

Purzycki, B. G., & McNamara, R. A. (2016). An ecological theory of gods' minds. In H. De Cruz & R. Nichols (Eds.), *Cognitive science of religion and its philosophical implications* (pp. 143–67). New York: Continuum.

Purzycki, B. G., & Sosis, R. (2011). Our gods: Variation in supernatural minds. In U. J. Frey, C. Störmer, & K. P. Willführ (Eds.), *Essential building blocks of human nature* (pp. 77–93). Berlin, Heidelberg: Springer. Retrieved May 30, 2017 from http://link.springer.com/chapter/10.1007/978-3-642-13968-0_5.

Reddish, P., Tok, P., & Kundt, R. (2016). Religious cognition and behaviour in autism: The role of mentalizing. *International Journal for the Psychology of Religion, 26*(2), 95–112. doi:10.1080/1 0508619.2014.1003518.

Roes, F. L., & Raymond, M. (2003). Belief in moralizing gods. *Evolution and Human Behavior, 24*(2), 126–35. doi:10.1016/S1090-5138(02)00134-4.

References

Schloss, J. P., & Murray, M. J. (2011). Evolutionary accounts of belief in supernatural punishment: A critical review. *Religion, Brain and Behavior, 1*(1), 46–99. doi:10.1080/2153599X.2011.558707.

Sears, D. O. (1986). College sophomores in the laboratory: Influences of a narrow data base on social psychology's view of human nature. *Journal of Personality and Social Psychology, 51*(3), 515–30. doi:10.1037/0022-3514.51.3.515.

Shariff, A. F., Purzycki, B. G., & Sosis, R. (2014). Religions as cultural solutions to social living. In A. Cohen (Ed.), *Culture reexamined: Broadening our understanding of social and evolutionary influences* (pp. 217–38). Washington, DC: American Psychological Association.

Snarey, J. (1996). The natural environment's impact upon religious ethics: A cross-cultural study. *Journal for the Scientific Study of Religion, 35*(2), 85–96. doi:10.2307/1387077.

Stark, R. (2001). Gods, rituals, and the moral order. *Journal for the Scientific Study of Religion, 40*(4), 619–36.

Wallace, A. F. C. (1966). *Religion: An anthropological view.* New York: McGraw-Hill.

Willard, A. K., & Norenzayan, A. (2013). Cognitive biases explain religious belief, paranormal belief, and belief in life's purpose. *Cognition, 129*(2), 379–91. doi:10.1016/j.cognition.2013.07.016.

Chapter 4

Barrett, J. L., & Richert, R. A. (2003). Anthropomorphism or preparedness? Exploring children's god concepts. *Review of Religious Research, 44*(3), 300–12.

Barrett, J. L., Richert, R. A., & Driesenga, A. (2001). God's beliefs versus mother's: The development of nonhuman agent concepts. *Child Development, 2*(1), 50–65.

Dennett, D. C. (1978). Three kinds of intentional psychology. In Robert J. Stainton (Ed.), *Perspectives in the philosophy of language: A concise anthology* (pp. 163–86). Peterborough, Ontario: Broadview Press.

Knight, N., Sousa, P., Barrett, J. L., & Atran, S. (2004). Children's attributions of beliefs to humans and god: Cross-cultural evidence. *Cognitive Science, 28*(1), 117–26. doi:10.1016/j.cogsci.2003.09.002.

Lane, J. D., Wellman, H. M., & Evans, E. M. (2010). Children's understanding of ordinary and extraordinary minds. *Child Development, 81*(5), 1475–89. doi:10.1111/j.1467-8624.2010.01486.x.

Lane, J. D., Wellman, H. M., & Evans, E. M. (2012). Sociocultural input facilitates children's developing understanding of extraordinary minds. *Child Development, 83*(3), 1007–21. doi:10.1111/j.1467-8624.2012.01741.x.

Perner, J., Leekam, S. R., & Wimmer, H. (1987). Three-year-olds' difficulty with false belief: The case for a conceptual deficit. *British Journal of Developmental Psychology, 5*(2), 125–37.

Piaget, J. (1960). *The child's conception of the world.* Paterson, NJ: Littlefield, Adams.

Piaget, J. (1969). *The psychology of the child.* New York: Basic Books.

Purzycki, B. G. (2013). The minds of gods: A comparative study of supernatural agency. *Cognition, 129*(1), 163–79. doi:10.1016/j.cognition.2013.06.010.

Purzycki, B. G., Finkel, D. N., Shaver, J., Wales, N., Cohen, A. B., & Sosis, R. (2012). What does god know? Supernatural agents' access to socially strategic and non-strategic information. *Cognitive Science, 36*(5), 846–69. doi:10.1111/j.1551-6709.2012.01242.x.

Wellman, H. M., & Bartsch, K. (1988). Young children's reasoning about beliefs. *Cognition, 30*(3), 239–77.

Wellman, H. M., & Woolley, J. D. (1990). From simple desires to ordinary beliefs: The early development of everyday psychology. *Cognition, 35*(3), 245–75.

Wimmer, H., & Perner, J. (1983). Beliefs about beliefs: Representation and constraining function of wrong beliefs in young children's understanding of deception. *Cognition, 13*(1), 103–28.

Chapter 5

Abramson, A. (2000). Bounding the unbounded: Ancestral land and jural relations in the interior of Eastern Fiji. In A. Abramson & D. Theodossopoulos (Eds.), *Land, law and environment: Mythical land, legal boundaries* (pp. 191–210). London: Pluto Press.

Atkinson, Q. D., & Bourrat, P. (2011). Beliefs about God, the afterlife and morality support the role of supernatural policing in human cooperation. *Evolution and Human Behavior, 32*(1), 41–9. doi:10.1016/j.evolhumbehav.2010.07.008.

Bering, J. M. (2002). Intuitive conceptions of dead agents' minds: The natural foundations of afterlife beliefs as phenomenological boundary. *Journal of Cognition and Culture, 2*(4), 263–308.

Botero, C. A., Gardner, B., Kirby, K. R., Bulbulia, J., Gavin, M. C., & Gray, R. D. (2014). The ecology of religious beliefs. *Proceedings of the National Academy of Sciences, 111*(47), 16784–89. doi:10.1073/pnas.1408701111.

Boyer, P. (2001). *Religion explained: The evolutionary origins of religious thought.* New York: Basic Books.

Brison, K. J. (2007). The empire strikes back: Pentecostalism in Fiji. *Ethnology, 46*(1), 21–39. doi:10.2307/20456609?ref=search- gateway:b92a740076d0eced0755432ccca09a88.

De Weerdt, J., & Dercon, S. (2006). Risk-sharing networks and insurance against illness. *Journal of Development Economics, 81*(2), 337–356. doi:10.1016/j.jdeveco.2005.06.009.

Farrelly, T., & Vudiniabola, A. T. (2013). Kerekere and indigenous social entrepreneurship. *SITES: Journal of Social Anthropology and Cultural Studies, 10*(2), 1–29.

Fincher, C. L., & Thornhill, R. (2012). Parasite-stress promotes in-group assortative sociality: The cases of strong family ties and heightened religiosity. *Behavioral and Brain Sciences, 39*(2–3), 155–60.

France, P. (1969). *The charter of the land: Custom and colonization in Fiji.* Melbourne, Australia: Oxford University Press.

Gelfand, M. J., Nishii, L. H., & Raver, J. L. (2006). On the nature and importance of cultural tightness-looseness. *The Journal of Applied Psychology, 91*(6), 1225–44. doi:10.1037/0021-9010.91.6.1225.

Gervais, M. M. (2013). *Structures of sentiment: Mapping the affective bases of social relationships in Yasawa, Fiji.* University of California, Los Angeles. Retrieved August 28, 2018 from https://escholarship.org/uc/item/79d936s0.

Gervais, W. M., Shariff, A. F. A., & Norenzayan, A. (2011). Do you believe in atheists? Distrust is central to anti-atheist prejudice. *Journal of Personality and Social Psychology, 101*(6), 1189–206. doi:10.1037/a0025882.

Henrich, J., Ensminger, J., McElreath, R., Barr, A., Barrett, C., Bolyanatz, A., ... & Ziker, J. (2010). Markets, religion, community size, and the evolution of fairness and punishment. *Science, 327*(5972), 1480–84. doi:10.1126/science.1182238.

Hruschka, D. J., Efferson, C., Jiang, T., Falletta-Cowden, A., Sigurdsson, S., McNamara, R. A., ... & Henrich, J. (2014). Impartial institutions, pathogen stress and the expanding social network. *Human Nature, 25*(4), 567–79. doi:10.1007/s12110-014-9217-0.

Johnson, D. D. P. (2009). The error of God: Error management theory, religion, and the evolution of cooperation. In S. A. Levin (Ed.), *Games, groups, and the global good* (pp. 169–80). Berlin: Springer Physica-Verlag.

Johnson, D. D. P., & Bering, J. M. (2006). Hand of God, mind of man: Punishment and cognition in the evolution of cooperation. *Evolutionary Psychology, 4*, 219–33.

References

doi:10.1177/147470490600400119. Retrieved from http://www.epjournal.net/filestore/ep04219233.pdf.

Jolly, M. (1992). Custom and the way of the land: Past and present in Vanuatu and Fiji. *Oceania, 62*(4), 330–54. doi:10.2307/40332509?ref=no-x- route:f2ab9f6c084a36e78650fd5cce7cca91.

Katz, R. (1999). *The straight path of the spirit: Ancestral wisdom and healing traditions in Fiji.* Rochester, VT: Park Street Press.

McNamara, R. A., & Henrich, J. (2016). Kin and kinship psychology both influence cooperative coordination in Yasawa, Fiji. *Evolution and Human Behavior, 38*(2), 197–207. http://doi.org/10.1016/j.evolhumbehav.2016.09.004.

McNamara, R. A., & Henrich, J. (2017). Jesus vs. the ancestors: How specific religious beliefs shape prosociality on Yasawa Island, Fiji. *Religion, Brain & Behavior, 39*(2), 1–20. doi:10.1080/2153599X.2016.1267030.

McNamara, R. A., Norenzayan, A., & Henrich, J. (2016). Supernatural punishment, in-group biases, and material insecurity: Experiments and ethnography from Yasawa, Fiji. *Religion, Brain & Behavior, 6*(1), 34–55.

Nayacakalou, R. R. (1955). The Fijian system of kinship and marriage: Part I. *Journal of the Polynesian Society, 64*(1), 44–55.

Nayacakalou, R. R. (1957). The Fijian system of kinship and marriage: Part II. *Journal of the Polynesian Society, 66*(1), 44–59.

Newland, L. (2004). Turning the spirits into witchcraft: Pentecostalism in Fijian villages. *Oceania, 75*(1), 1–18. doi:10.2307/40331952?ref=no-x- route:8803096ac68e19ac17557a7b1b4f42f7.

Norenzayan, A., Shariff, A. F. A., Gervais, W. M., Willard, A. K., McNamara, R. A., Slingerland, E., & Henrich, J. (2015). The cultural evolution of prosocial religions. *Behavioral and Brain Sciences, 39*, e1. doi:10.1017/S0140525X14001356.

Peoples, H. C., & Marlowe, F. W. (2012). Subsistence and the evolution of religion. *Human Nature, 23*(3), 253–69. doi:10.1007/s12110-012-9148-6.

Purzycki, B. G. (2013). The minds of gods: A comparative study of supernatural agency. *Cognition, 129*(1), 163–79. doi:10.1016/j.cognition.2013.06.010.

Purzycki, B. G., Apicella, C., Atkinson, Q. D., Cohen, E., McNamara, R. A., Willard, A. K., ... & Henrich, J. (2016). Moralistic gods, supernatural punishment and the expansion of human sociality. *Nature, 530*(7590), 327–30. doi:10.1038/nature16980.

Purzycki, B. G., & Arakchaa, T. (2013). Ritual behavior and trust in the Tyva Republic. *Current Anthropology, 54*(3), 381–8. doi:10.1086/670526.

Purzycki, B. G., Finkel, D. N., Shaver, J., Wales, N., Cohen, A. B., & Sosis, R. H. (2012). What does God know? Supernatural agents' access to socially strategic and non- strategic information. *Cognitive Science, 36*(5), 846–69. doi:10.1111/j.1551-6709.2012.01242.x.

Purzycki, B. G., Henrich, J., Apicella, C., Atkinson, Q. D., Baimel, A., Cohen, E., ... & Norenzayan, A. (2017). The evolution of religion and morality: A synthesis of ethnographic and experimental evidence from eight societies. *Religion, Brain & Behavior, 1*(7), 1–32. doi:10.1080/2153599X.2016.1267027.

Purzycki, B. G., & McNamara, R. A. (2016). An ecological theory of gods' minds. In H. De Cruz & R. Nichols (Eds.), *Advances in religion, cognitive science, and experimental philosophy* (pp. 143–69). New York: Bloomsbury Academic.

Purzycki, B. G., & Sosis, R. H. (2011). Our gods: Variation in supernatural minds. In U. J. Frey, Störmer, C., & Willführ, K. P. (Eds.), *Essential building blocks of human nature: The frontiers collection* (pp. 77–93). Berlin: Springer. doi:10.1007/978-3-642-13968-0_5.

Roes, F. L., & Raymond, M. (2003). Belief in moralizing gods. *Evolution and Human Behavior, 24*(2), 126–135. doi:10.1016/S1090-5138(02)00134-4.

Rubenstein, D. I., & Wrangham, R. W. (Eds.) (1986). *Ecological aspects of social evolution.* Princeton, NJ: Princeton University Press.

Ryle, J. (2010). *My God, my land: Interwoven paths of Christianity and tradition in Fiji.* Burlington, VT: Ashgate.

Schloss, J. P., & Murray, M. J. (2011). Evolutionary accounts of belief in supernatural punishment: A critical review. *Religion, Brain & Behavior, 1*(1), 46–99. doi:10.1080/2153599X.2011.558707.

Schlossberg, M. (1998). Kerekere, hierarchy and planning in Fiji: Why cultural understanding should be a prerequisite to international planning. In H. Dandekar (Ed.), *City, space and globalization: An international perspective* (pp. 225–31). Ann Arbor: University of Michigan Press.

Shariff, A. F. A., & Norenzayan, A. (2011). Mean gods make good people: Different views of god predict cheating behavior. *International Journal for the Psychology of Religion, 21*(2), 85–96. doi:10.1080/10508619.2011.556990.

Sosis, R. H. (2005). Does religion promote trust? The role of signaling, reputation, and punishment. *Interdisciplinary Journal of Research on Religion, 1*, 1–30.

Srebrnik, H. (2002). Ethnicity, religion, and the issue of aboriginality in a small island state: Why does Fiji flounder? *Round Table, 364*, 187–210.

Tan, J. H. W., & Vogel, C. (2008). Religion and trust: An experimental study. *Journal of Economic Psychology, 29*(6), 832–48. doi:10.1016/j.joep.2008.03.002.

Tomlinson, M. (2009). *In God's image: The metaculture of Fijian Christianity.* Los Angeles: University of California Press.

United Nations (2014, July 10). World's population increasingly urban with more than half living in urban areas. United Nations Department of Economic and Social Affairs. Retrieved July 27, 2017, from http://www.un.org/en/development/desa/news/population/world-urbanization-prospects- 2014.html.

Watts, J., Greenhill, S. J., & Lieberman, M. D. (2015). Broad supernatural punishment but not moralizing high gods precede the evolution of political complexity in Austronesia. *Proceedings of the Royal Society B: Biological Sciences, 282*, 1–7.

Willard, A. K., & McNamara, R. A. (2016). The minds of god(s) and humans: Differences in mind perception in Fiji and Canada. Unpublished manuscript.

Williksen-Bakker, S. (1990). Vanua—a symbol with many ramifications in Fijian culture. *Ethnos, 55*(3), 232–47. doi:10.1080/00141844.1990.9981416.

Chapter 6

Astuti, R., & Harris, P. L. (2008). Understanding mortality and the life of ancestors in rural Madagascar. *Cognitive Science, 32*, 713–40. doi:10.1080/03640210802066907.

Bering, J. M. (2002). Intuitive conceptions of dead agents' minds: The natural foundations of afterlife beliefs as phenomenological boundary. *Journal of Cognition and Culture, 2*, 263–308. doi:10.1163/15685370260441008.

Bering, J. M. (2006). The folk psychology of souls. *Behavioral and Brain Sciences, 29*, 453–62. doi:10.1017/S0140525X06009101.

Bering, J. M., & Bjorklund, D. F. (2004). The natural emergence of reasoning about the afterlife as a developmental regularity. *Developmental Psychology, 40*(2), 217–33. doi:10.1037/0012-1649.40.2.217.

Bloom, P. (2004). *Descartes' baby: How the science of child development explains what makes us human.* New York: Basic Books.

Bloom, P. (2007). Religion is natural. *Developmental Science, 10*, 147–51. doi:10.1111/j.1467-7687.2007.00577.x.

Emmons, N. A., & Kelemen, D. (2014). The development of children's prelife reasoning: Evidence from two cultures. *Child Development, 85*(4), 1617–33. doi:10.1111/cdev.12220.

References

Emmons, N. A., & Kelemen, D. (2015). I've got a feeling: Urban and indigenous children's beliefs about early life mentality. *Journal of Experimental Child Psychology, 138*, 106–25. doi:10.1016/j.jecp.2015.05.001.

Gelman, S. A. (2003). *The essential child: Origins of essentialism in everyday thought*. Oxford, UK: Oxford University Press.

Hodge, K. M. (2008). Descartes' mistake: How afterlife beliefs challenge the assumption that humans are intuitive Cartesian substance dualists. *Journal of Cognition and Culture, 8*, 387–415. doi:10.1163/156853708X358236.

Hodge, K. M. (2011). On imagining the afterlife. *Journal of Cognition and Culture, 11*, 367–89. doi:10.1163/156853711X591305.

Kahneman, D. (2011). *Thinking, fast and slow*. New York: Farrar, Straus, and Giroux.

Lindeman, L., Riekki, T, & Svedholm-Hakkinen, A. M. (2015). Individual differences in conceptions of soul, mind, and body. *Journal of Individual Differences, 36*(3), 157–62. doi:10.1027/1614-0001/a000167.

McCauley, R. (2011). *Why religion is natural and science is not*. New York: Oxford University Press.

McConnel, K. A., & Edman, L. R. O. (2013a, May). *The theological correctness effect in online and offline processing tasks*. Poster presented at annual Midwestern Psychological Association Conference, Chicago, IL.

McConnel, K. A., & Edman, L. R. O. (2013b, November). *The relationship between practiced naturalness and theological correctness*. Paper presented at annual Society for the Scientific Study of Religion Conference, Boston, MA.

Richert, R. A., & Harris, P. L. (2006). The ghost in my body: Children's developing concept of the soul. *Journal of Cognition and Culture, 6*, 409–27. doi:10.1163/156853706778554913.

Richert, R. A., & Harris, P. L. (2008). Dualism revisited: Body vs. mind vs. soul. *Journal of Cognition & Culture, 8*, 99–115. doi:10.1163/156770908X289224.

Richert, R. A., & Smith, E. I. (2012). The essence of soul concepts: How soul concepts influence ethical reasoning across religious affiliation. *Religion, Brain & Behavior, 2*(2), 161–76. doi:10.1080/2153599X.2012.683702.

Roazzi, M., Nyhof, M., & Johnson, C. (2013) Mind, soul and spirit: Conceptions of immaterial identity in different cultures. *International Journal for the Psychology of Religion, 23*(1), 75–86, doi:10.1080/10508619.2013.735504.

Watson-Jones, R. E., Busch, J. T. A., Harris, P. L., & Legare, C. H. (2016). Does the body survive death? Cultural variation in beliefs about life everlasting. *Cognitive Science, 41*, 455–76. doi:10.1111/cogs.12430.

Chapter 7

Geaney, J. (2002). *On the epistemology of the senses in early Chinese thought*. Honolulu: University of Hawaii Press.

Johnson, C. (2012, September 5). Ex-Harvard scientist fabricated, manipulated data, report says. *Boston Globe*.

Jullien, F. (2007). *Vital nourishment: Departing from happiness*. Translated by Arthur Goldhammer. New York: Zone Books.

Klein, E., & Klein, C. (2011). Did the Chinese have a change of heart? *Cognitive Science, 36*, 179–82.

Slingerland, E., & Chudek, M. (2011a). The challenges of qualitatively coding ancient texts. *Cognitive Science, 36*, 183–6.

Slingerland, E., & Chudek, M. (2011b). The prevalence of mind-body dualism in early China. *Cognitive Science, 35*, 997–1007.

Slingerland, E., Nichols, R., Nielbo, K., & Logan, C. (2017). The distant reading of religious texts: A "big data" approach to mind-body concepts in early China. *Journal of the American Academy of Religion, 85*(4), 985–1016.

Chapter 8

Barrett, J. L. (1998). Cognitive constraints on Hindu concepts of the divine. *Journal for the Scientific Study of Religion, 37*(4), 608–19.

Barrett, J. L. (1999). Theological correctness: Cognitive constraint and the study of religion. *Method and Theory in the Study of Religion, 37*, 608–19.

Barrett, J. L., & Keil, F. C. (1996). Anthropomorphism and God concepts: Conceptualizing a non-natural entity. *Cognitive Psychology, 31*, 219–47.

Bering, J. M. (2002). Intuitive conceptions of dead agent's minds: The natural foundations of afterlife beliefs as a phenomenological boundary. *Journal of Cognition and Culture, 2*, 262–308.

Bloom, P. (2004). *Descartes' baby: How child development explains what makes us human.* London: William Heinemann.

Dundas, P. (2002). *The Jains.* New York: Routledge.

Gobbini, A. I., Leibenluft, E., Santiago, N., & Haxby, J. V. (2004). Social and emotional attachment in the neural representation of faces. *Neuroimage, 22*, 1628–35.

Haraldsson, E., & Samararatne, G. (1999). Children who speak of memories of a previous life as a Buddhist monk: Three new cases. *Journal of the Society for Psychical Research, 63*, 268–91.

Klein, S. B., & Nichols, S. (2012). Memory and the sense of personal identity. *Mind, 121*(483), 677–702.

Matlock, J. G., & Mills, A. (1994). A trait index to North American Indian and Inuit reincarnation beliefs. In A. Mills & R. Sobodin (Eds.), *Amerindian rebirth: Reincarnation belief among North American Indians and Inuit* (pp. 299–356). Toronto, Canada: University of Toronto Press.

Obeyesekere, G. (2002). *Imagining karma: Ethical transformation in Amerindian, Buddhist, and Greek rebirth.* London: University of California Press.

Pyysiäinen, I. (2004). Intuitive and explicit in religious thought. *Journal of Cognition and Culture, 4*, 123–50.

Reid, T. ([1785] 1969). *Essays on the intellectual powers of man.* Cambridge, MA: MIT Press.

Ronch, J. L. (1996). Mourning and grief in late life Alzheimer's dementia: Revisiting the vanishing self. *American Journal of Alzheimer's Disease and Other Dementias, 11*, 25–8.

Sacks, O. (1970). *The man who mistook his wife for a hat.* New York: Harper.

Slone, J. (2007). *Theological incorrectness: Why religious people believe what they shouldn't.* New York: Oxford University Press.

White, C. (2015). Establishing personal identity in reincarnation: Minds and bodies reconsidered. *Journal of Cognition and Culture, 15*, 402–29.

White, C. (2016a). The cognitive foundations of reincarnation. *Method and Theory in the Study of Religion, 28*(3), 1–23.

White, C. (2016b). Cross-cultural similarities in reasoning about personal continuity in reincarnation: Evidence from South India. *Religion, Brain & Behavior, 6*(2), 130–53.

White, C., Kelly, B., & Nichols, S. (2015). Remembering past lives: Intuitions about memory and personal identity in reincarnation. In H. Cruz & R. Nichols (Eds.), *The cognitive science of religion and its philosophical implications* (pp. 169–96). London: Bloomsbury Academic.

White, C., Sousa, P., & Berniunas, R. (2014). Psychological essentialism in selecting the 14th Dalai Lama: An alternative account. *Journal of Cognition and Culture, 14*(1–2), 157–8.

References

Chapter 9

Atran, S. (2002). *In gods we trust*. Oxford, UK: Oxford University Press.

Barrett, J. L. (2004). *Why would anyone believe in God?* Lanham, MD: Alta Mira Press.

Barrett, J. L., & Nyhof, M. (2001). Spreading non-natural concepts. *Journal of Cognition & Culture, 1*, 69–100.

Boyd, R., & Richerson, P. J. (1985). *Culture and the evolutionary process*. Chicago, IL: University of Chicago Press.

Boyer, P. (1994). *The naturalness of religious ideas*. Berkeley: University of California Press.

Boyer, P. (2001). *Religion explained*. New York: Basic Books.

Dawkins, R. (1976). *The selfish gene*. Oxford: Oxford University Press.

Gervais, W. M., & Henrich, J. (2010). The Zeus problem: Why representational content biases cannot explain faith in gods. *Journal of Cognition and Culture, 10*, 383–9.

Norenzayan, A., & Atran, S. (2004). *Cognitive and emotional processes in the cultural transmission of natural and nonnatural beliefs*. In M. Schaller & C. Crandall (Eds.), *The psychological foundations of culture* (pp. 149–69). Hillsdale, NJ: Lawrence Erlbaum Associates.

Norenzayan, A., Atran, S., Faulkner, J., & Schaller, M. (2006). Memory and mystery: The cultural selection of minimally counterintuitive narratives. *Cognitive Science, 30*, 531–53.

Porubanova, M. (2015). MCI theory: Can MCI theory alone explain the abundance of religious ideas? *Religion, Brain & Behavior, 6*(3), 262–4. doi:10.1080/2153599X.2015.1015046.

Porubanova, M., & Shaver, J. (2017). Minimal counterintuitiveness revisited, again: The role of emotional valence in memory for conceptual incongruity. In L. Martin & D. Wiebe (Eds.), *Religion explained? The cognitive science of religion after 25 years* (pp. 123–32). London: Bloomsbury Press.

Purzycki, B., & Willard, A. (2015). MCI theory: A critical discussion. *Religion, Brain & Behavior, 6*(3), 207–48. doi:10.1080/2153599X.2015.1024915.

Sperber, D. (1996). *Explaining culture: A naturalistic approach*. Cambridge, MA: Blackwell.

Summerfield, C., & de Lange, F. P. (2014). Expectation in perceptual decision making: Neural and computational mechanisms. *Nature Reviews Neuroscience, 15*, 745–56.

Chapter 10

Atran, S. (2002). *In gods we trust: The evolutionary landscape of religion*. New York: Oxford University Press.

Barrett, J. L., & Nyhof, M. A. (2001). Spreading non-natural concepts: The role of intuitive conceptual structures in memory and transmission of cultural materials. *Journal of Cognition and Culture, 1*, 69–100.

Bartlett, F. C. (1932). *Remembering: A study in experimental and social psychology*. Cambridge: Cambridge University Press.

Boyer, P., & Ramble, C. (2001). Cognitive templates for religious concepts: Cross-cultural evidence for recall of counterintuitive representations. *Cognitive Science, 25*, 535–64.

Bruner, J. (1990). *Acts of meaning*. Cambridge, MA: Harvard University Press.

Cavicchi, E. (2003). Experiences with the magnetism of conducting loops: Historical instruments, experimental replications, and productive confusions. *American Journal of Physics, 71*(2), 156–67.

Dunbar, K. N. & Fugelsang, J. A. (2005). Causal thinking in science: How scientists and students interpret the unexpected. In M. E. Gorman, R. D. Tweney, D. C. Gooding, & A. P. Kincannon (Eds.), *Scientific and technological thinking* (pp. 57–80). Mahwah, NJ: Lawrence Erlbaum Associates.

Durmysheva, Y., & Kozbelt, A. (2004). The creativity of invented alien creatures: The role of invariants. In K. Forbus, D. Gentner, & T. Regier (Eds.), *Proceedings of the 26th Annual Conference of the Cognitive Science Society* (p. 1554). Mahwah, NJ: Lawrence Erlbaum Associates.

Gonce, L., Upal, M. A., Slone, D. J., & Tweney, R. D. (2006). Role of context in the recall of counterintuitive concepts. *Journal of Cognition & Culture, 6*(3–4), 521–47.

Lawson, E. T. & McCauley, R. N. (1990). *Rethinking religion: Connecting cognition and culture.* Cambridge: Cambridge University Press.

McCauley, R. N. (2000). The naturalness of religion and the unnaturalness of science. In F. C. Keil & R. A. Wilson (Eds.), *Explanation and cognition* (pp. 61–86). Cambridge, MA: MIT Press.

McCauley, R. N., & Whitehouse, H. (2005). New frontiers in the cognitive science of religion. *Journal of Cognition and Culture, 5*, 1–13.

Murphy, G. L., & Medin, D. L. (1985). The role of theories in conceptual coherence. *Psychological Review, 92*, 289–316.

Norenzayan, A., & Atran, A. (2004). Cognitive and emotional processes in the cultural transmission of natural and nonnatural beliefs. In M. Schaller & C. Crandall (Eds.), *The psychological foundations of culture* (pp. 149–69). Hillsdale, NJ: Lawrence Erlbaum Associates.

Perkins, D. N. (1981). *The mind's best work.* Cambridge, MA: Harvard University Press.

Piaget, J. (1958/1977). Equilibration processes in the psychobiological development of the child. In H. E. Gruber & J. J. Vonèche (Eds.), *The essential Piaget: An interpretive reference and guide* (pp. 832–7). New York: Basic Books.

Slone, D. J. (2004). *Theological incorrectness: Why religious people believe what they shouldn't.* New York: Oxford University Press.

Tweney, R. D., Doherty, M. E., & Mynatt, C. R. (Eds.) (1981). *On scientific thinking.* New York: Columbia University Press.

Tweney, R. D., Mears, R. P., & Spitzmüller, C. (2005). Replicating the practices of discovery: Michael Faraday and the interaction of gold and light. In M. Gorman, R. D. Tweney, D. Gooding, & A. Kincannon (Eds.), *Scientific and technological thinking* (pp. 137–58). Mahwah, NJ: Lawrence Erlbaum Associates.

Upal, M. A., Gonce, L., Slone, D. J., & Tweney, R. D. (2007) Contextualizing counterintuitiveness: How context affects comprehension and memorability of counterintuitive concepts. *Cognitive Science, 31*(3), 415–39.

Ward, T. B. (1994). Structured imagination: The role of conceptual structure in exemplar generation. *Cognitive Psychology, 27*, 1–40.

Ward, T. B., Patterson, M. J., & Sifonis, C. M. (2004). The role of specificity and abstraction in creative idea generation. *Creativity Research Journal, 16*(1), 1–9.

Chapter 11

Ahmed, A. M. (2009). Are religious people more prosocial? A quasi-experimental study with *Madrasah* pupils in a rural community in India. *Journal for the Scientific Study of Religion, 48*(2), 368–74. doi:10.1111/j.1468-5906.2009.01452.x.

Ahmed, A. M., & Salas, O. (2008). In the back of your mind: Subliminal influences of religious concepts on prosocial behavior. *Working Papers in Economics, 331*, 1–25.

Ahmed, A. M., & Salas, O. (2013). Religious context and prosociality: An experimental study from Valparaíso, Chile. *Journal for the Scientific Study of Religion, 52*(3), 627–37.

Aveyard, M. E. (2014). A call to honesty: Extending religious priming of moral behavior to Middle Eastern Muslims. Edited by James Coyne. *PLOS One, 9*(7), e99447. doi:10.1371/journal.pone.0099447.

References

Bargh, J. A., Chen, M., & Burrows, L. (1996). Automaticity of social behavior: Direct effects of trait construct and stereotype activation on action. *Journal of Personality and Social Psychology, 71*(2), 230.

Bateson, M., Nettle, D., & Roberts, G. (2006). Cues of being watched enhance cooperation in a real-world setting. *Biology Letters, 2*(3), 412. doi:10.1098/rsbl.2006.0509.

Batson, C. D., Oleson, K. C., & Weeks, J. L. (1989). Religious prosocial motivation: Is it altruistic or egoistic? *Journal of Personality and Social Psychology, 57*(5), 873–84.

Brenner, P. S. (2011). Exceptional behavior or exceptional identity?: Overreporting of church attendance in the U.S. *Public Opinion Quarterly, 75*(1), 19–41. doi:10.1093/poq/nfq068.

CAF America (2017). *World Giving Index 2017*.

Chaves, M. (2010). Rain dances in the dry season: Overcoming the religious congruence fallacy. *Journal for the Scientific Study of Religion, 49*, 1–14.

Christopher, A. J. (1992). Ethnicity, community and the census in Mauritius, 1830–1990. *Geographical Journal, 158*, 57–64.

Chronicle of Philanthropy (2014). *How America gives*. Washington, DC: Chronicle of Philanthropy.

Darley, J. M., & Batson, C. D. (1973). "From Jerusalem to Jericho": A study of situational and dispositional variables in helping behavior. *Journal of Personality and Social Psychology, 27*(1), 100–8. doi:10.1037/h0034449.

Duhaime, E. P. (2015). Is the call to prayer a call to cooperate? A field experiment on the impact of religious salience on prosocial behavior. *Judgment and Decision Making, 10*(6), 593–6.

Eckel, C. C., & Grossman, P. J. (2004). Giving to secular causes by the religious and nonreligious: An experimental test of the responsiveness of giving to subsidies. *Ethnography, 33*(2), 271–89. doi:10.1177/0899764004263423.

Edelman, B. (2009). Red light states: Who buys online adult entertainment? *Journal of Economic Perspectives, 23*(1), 209–20. doi:10.1257/089533009797614117.

Eriksen, T. H. (1988). *Communicating cultural differences and identity*. Oslo: University of Oslo Occasional Papers in Social Anthropology.

Friedrichs, R. W. (1960). Alter versus ego: An exploratory assessment of altruism. *American Sociological Review, 25*(4), 496–508.

Furrow, J., King, P. E., & White, K. (2004). Religion and positive youth development: Identity, meaning, and prosocial concerns. *Applied Developmental Science, 8*(1), 17–26. doi:10.1207/S1532480XADS0801_3.

Galen, L. W. (2012). Does religious belief promote prosociality? A critical examination. *Psychological Bulletin, 138*(5), 876–906. doi:10.1037/a0028251.

Gervais, W. M., Shariff, A. F., & Norenzayan, A. (2011). Do you believe in atheists? Distrust is central to anti-atheist prejudice. *Journal of Personality and Social Psychology, 101*(6), 1189–206. doi:10.1037/a0025882.

Gervais, W. M., Xygalatas, D., McKay, R. T., van Elk, M., Buchtel, E. E., Aveyard, M., ... & Bulbulia, J. (2017). Global evidence of extreme intuitive moral prejudice against atheists. *Nature Publishing Group, 1*(August), 1–5. doi:10.1038/s41562-017-0151.

Goldfried, J., & Miner, M. (2002). Quest religion and the problem of limited compassion. *Journal for the Scientific Study of Religion, 41*(4), 685–95.

Grønbjerg, K. A., & B Never. (2004). The role of religious networks and other factors in types of volunteer work. *Nonprofit Management and Leadership, 14*(3), 263–89.

Grossman, P. J., & Parrett, M. B. (2011). Religion and prosocial behaviour: A field test. *Applied Economics Letters, 18*(6), 523–6. doi:10.1080/13504851003761798.

Gurven, M., & Winking, J. (2008). Collective action in action: Prosocial behavior in and out of the laboratory. *American Anthropologist, 110*(2), 179–90.

Guthrie, S. E. (1995). *Faces in the clouds: A new theory of religion.* New York: Oxford University Press.

Haley, K. J., & Fessler, D. M. T. (2005). Nobody's watching? Subtle cues affect generosity in an anonymous economic game. *Evolution and Human Behavior, 26,* 245–56.

Johnson, D. D. P., & Bering, J. M. (2006). Hand of God, mind of man: Punishment and cognition in the evolution of cooperation. *Evolutionary Psychology, 4*(2), 9–233.

Koenig, L. B., McGue, M., Krueger, R. F., & Bouchard, T. J. (2007). Religiousness, antisocial behavior, and altruism: Genetic and environmental mediation. *Journal of Personality, 75*(2), 265–90. doi:10.1111/j.1467-6494.2007.00439.x.

Krátký, J., McGraw, J. J., Xygalatas, D., Mitkidis, P., & Reddish, P. (2016). It depends who is watching you: 3-D agent cues increase fairness. Edited by Tom Verguts. *PLOS One, 11*(2), e0148845–e01488411. doi:10.1371/journal.pone.0148845.

Lang, M., Mitkidis, P., Kundt, R., Nichols, A., Krajčíková, L., & Xygalatas, D. (2016). Music as a sacred cue? Effects of religious music on moral behavior. *Frontiers in Psychology, 7*(110), 323–33. doi:10.3389/fpsyg.2016.00814.

Malhotra, D. (2010). (When) are religious people nicer? Religious salience and the "Sunday effect" on pro-social behavior. *Judgment and Decision Making, 5*(2), 138–43.

Mazar, N., Amir, O., & Ariely, D. (2008). The dishonesty of honest people: A theory of self-concept maintenance. *Journal of Marketing Research, 45*(6), 633–44.

McKay, R., Efferson, C., Whitehouse, H., & Fehr, E. (2011). Wrath of God: Religious primes and punishment. *Proceedings of the Royal Society B: Biological Sciences, 278*(1713), 1858–63.

Miyazaki, Y. (2017). Being watched by anthropomorphized objects affects charitable donation in religious people. *Japanese Psychological Research, 59*(3), 221–9. doi:10.1111/jpr.12158.

Norenzayan, A., & Shariff, A. F. (2008). The origin and evolution of religious prosociality. *Science, 322,* 58–62.

Orbell, J., Goldman, M., Mulford, M., & Dawes, R. (1992). Religion, context, and constraint toward strangers. *Rationality and Society, 4*(3), 291–307. doi:10.1177/1043463192004003004.

Ostrom, E., Gardner, R., & Walker, J. (1994). *Rules, games, and common-pool resources.* Ann Arbor: University of Michigan Press.

Pazhoohi, F., Pinho, M., & Arantes, J. (2017). Effect of religious day on prosocial behavior: A field study. *International Journal for the Psychology of Religion, 10*(March): 1–8. doi:10.1080/10508 619.2017.1301742.

Pew Research Center (2016). How religious is your state?

Pichon, I., Boccato, G., & Saroglou, V. (2007). Nonconscious influences of religion on prosociality: A priming study. *European Journal of Social Psychology, 37,* 1032–45.

Purzycki, B. G., Apicella, C., Atkinson, Q. D., Cohen, E., McNamara, R. A., Willard, A. K., ... & Henrich, J. (2016). Moralistic gods, supernatural punishment and the expansion of human sociality. *Nature, 530,* 327–30. doi:10.1038/nature16980.

Randolph-Seng, B., & Nielsen, M. E. (2007). Honesty: One effect of primed religious representations. *International Journal for the Psychology of Religion, 17*(4), 303–15.

Randolph-Seng, B., & Nielsen, M. E. (2008). Is God really watching you? A response to Shariff and Norenzayan (2007). *International Journal for the Psychology of Religion, 18*(2), 119–22. doi:10.1080/10508610701879373.

Roes, F. L., & Raymond, M. (2003). Belief in moralizing gods. *Evolution and Human Behavior, 24*(2), 126–35.

Saroglou, V., Delpierre, V., & Dernelle, R. (2004). Values and religiosity: A meta-analysis of studies using Schwartz's model. *Personality and Individual Differences, 37*(4), 721–34. doi:10.1016/j.paid.2003.10.005.

References

Saroglou, V., Pichon, I., & Trompette, L. (2005). Prosocial behavior and religion: New evidence based on projective measures and peer ratings. *Journal for the Scientific Study of Religion, 44*, 323–48.

Shariff, A. F., & Norenzayan, A. (2007). God is watching you. *Psychological Science, 18*(9), 803–809.

Shariff, A. F., Willard, A. K., Andersen, T., & Norenzayan, A. (2015). Religious priming: A meta-analysis with a focus on prosociality. *Personality and Social Psychology Review, 20*, 1–22. doi:10.1177/1088868314568811.

Sosis, R., & Ruffle, B. J. (2003). Religious ritual and cooperation: Testing for a relationship on Israeli religious and secular kibbutzim. *Current Anthropology, 44*(5), 713–22.

Stegmueller, D., Scheepers, P., Rossteutscher, S., & de Jong, E. (2012). Support for redistribution in western Europe: Assessing the role of religion. *European Sociological Review, 28*(4), 482–97. doi:10.1093/esr/jcr011.

Tan, J., & Vogel, C. (2008). Religion and trust: An experimental study. *Journal of Economic Psychology, 29*(6), 832–48.

US Department of Justice (2017). FBI uniform crime report for 2016.

Ware, J., & Dethmer, J. (2009). The trust project. Rebuilding trust one nancial professional at a time. White paper, 1–16.

Xygalatas, D. 2012. Effects of religious setting on cooperative behavior: A case study from Mauritius. *Religion, Brain & Behavior, 3*(2), 91–102. doi:10.1080/2153599X.2012.724547.

Xygalatas, D. (2013). Přenos Laboratoře Do Terénu: Využití Smíšených Metod Během Terénního Studia Náboženství (Bringing the lab into the field: Using mixed methods to study religion in the wild). *Sociální Studia, 10*(2), 15–25.

Xygalatas, D., Klocová, E. K., Cigán, J., Kundt, R., Maňo, P., Kotherová, S., ... & Kanovsky, M. (2016). Location, location, location: Effects of cross-religious primes on prosocial behavior. *International Journal for the Psychology of Religion, 26*(4), 304–19. doi:10.1080/10508619.201 5.1097287.

Xygalatas, D., Kotherová, S., Maňo, P., Kundt, R., Cigán, J., Klocová, E. K., & Lang, M. (2017). Big gods in small places: The Random Allocation Game in Mauritius. *Religion, Brain & Behavior, 10*(1), 1–19. doi:10.1080/2153599X.2016.1267033.

Xygalatas, D., & Lang, M. (2016). Prosociality and religion. In N. K. Clements (Ed.), *Mental religion* (pp. 119–33). Farmington Hills, MI: Macmillan.

Xygalatas, D., Mitkidis, P., Fischer, R., Reddish, P., Skewes, J., Geertz, A. W., ... & Bulbulia, J. (2013). Extreme rituals promote prosociality. *Psychological Science, 24*(8), 1602–5. doi: 10.1177/0956797612472910.

Chapter 12

AnyLogic Company (2015). AnyLogic Professional 7.3. St. Petersburg, Russia: AnyLogic Company. Retrieved from http://www.anylogic.com/. Accessed September 10, 2015.

Braxton, D. M., Upal, M. A., & Nielbo, K. L. (2012). Computing religion: A new tool in the multilevel analysis of religion. *Method & Theory in the Study of Religion, 24*(3), 267–90. doi:10.1163/157006812X635709.

Gelfand, M. J., Raver, J. L., Nishii, L., Leslie, L. M., Lun, J., Lim, B. C., ... Yamaguchi, S. (2011). Differences between tight and loose cultures: A 33-nation study. *Science, 332*, 1101–4. doi:10.1126/science.1197754.

Kahn, K., & Noble, H. (2010). The BehaviourComposer 2.0: A web-based tool for composing NetLogo code fragments. In *Constructionism 2010* (pp. 1–14). Brussels, Belgium: Institute for Computer Sciences, Social-Informatics and Telecommunications Engineering. Retrieved from https://docs.google.com/viewer?a=v&pid=sites&srcid=ZGVmYXVsdGRvbWFpbnxtb2RlbGxpbmc0YWxscHJvamVjdHxneneDoxZDhmOGI5NjViMzhkZjA.

Kelley, D. M. (1986). *Why conservative churches are growing* (ROSE edition). Macon, GA: Mercer University Press.

Lane, J. E. (2013). Method, theory, and multi-agent artificial intelligence: Creating computer models of complex social interaction. *Journal for the Cognitive Science of Religion*, 1(2), 161–80.

Mort, J., Fux, M., & Lawson, E. T. (2015). Rethinking Conventional Wisdom: Ecological Effects on Potential Danger Preoccupation Salience. *Human Ecology*, 43(4), 589–99. doi:10.1007/s10745-015-9774-9.

Norenzayan, A., Dar-nimrod, I., Hansen, I. G., & Proulx, T. (2009). Mortality salience and religion: divergent effects on the defense of cultural worldviews for the religious and the non-religious. *European Journal of Social Psychology*, 39(1), 101–13. doi:10.1002/ejsp.482.

Poulter, P., Jackson, J., Jong, J., Bluemke, M., & Morgenroth, L. (2016). Testing the causal relationship between implicit religiosity and death anxiety. *Religion, Brain & Behavior*, 6(2), in press.

Pyszczynski, T. A., Greenberg, J., & Solomon, S. (2003). *In the wake of 9/11: The psychology of terror*. Washington, DC: American Psychological Association.

Railsback, S. F., & Grimm, V. (2011). *Agent-based and individual-based modeling: A practical introduction*. Princeton, NJ: Princeton University Press.

Shults, F. L. (2014). *Theology after the birth of God: Atheist conceptions in cognition and culture*. New York: Palgrave Macmillan.

Sibley, C. G., & Bulbulia, J. (2012). Faith after an earthquake: a longitudinal study of religion and perceived health before and after the 2011 Christchurch New Zealand Earthquake. *PLOS One*, 7(12), e49648. doi:10.1371/journal.pone.0049648.

Siegel, E. (2013). *Predictive analytics: The power to predict who will click, buy, lie, or die*. Hoboken, NJ: Wiley & Sons.

Smith, J. Z. (2004). *Relating religion: Essays in the study of religion*. Chicago, IL: University of Chicago Press.

Vail, K. E., Arndt, J., & Abdollahi, A. (2012). Exploring the existential function of religion and supernatural agent beliefs among Christians, Muslims, atheists, and agnostics. *Personality & Social Psychology Bulletin*, 38(10), 1288–300. doi:10.1177/0146167212449361.

Vail, K. E., Rothschild, Z. K., Weise, D. R., Solomon, S., Pyszczynski, T., & Greenberg, J. (2010). A terror management analysis of the psychological functions of religion. *Personality and Social Psychology Review*, 14(1), 84–94.

Wilensky, U. (1999). *Netlogo*. Evanston, IL: Center for Connected Learning and Computer-Based Modeling. Retrieved from http://ccl.northwestern.edu/netlogo/. Accessed September 10, 2015.

Yilmaz, L. (Ed.). (2015). *Concepts and methodologies for modeling and simulation*. New York: Springer.

Chapter 13

Ahmed, A. M., & Salas, O. (2011). Implicit influences of Christian religious representations on dictator and prisoner's dilemma game decisions. *Journal of Socio-Economics*, 40, 242–6.

Boehm, C. (2008) Purposive social selection and the evolution of human altruism. *Cross-Cultural Research*, 42, 319–52.

Brenner, P. S. (2011). Exceptional behavior or exceptional identity? Overreporting of church attendance in the US. *Public Opinion Quarterly*, 75(1), 19–41.

References

Brooks, A. C. (2003). Religious faith and charitable giving. *Policy Review, 121*, 39–50.

Brooks, A. C. (2006). *Who really cares: The surprising truth about compassionate conservatism.* New York: Basic Books.

Cox, D., Jones, R. P., & Navarro-Rivera, J. (2014). I know what you did last Sunday: Measuring social desirability bias in self-reported religious behavior, belief, and identity. *Public Religion Research Institute, 2*, 57–58.

Dunbar, R. I. (1993). Coevolution of neocortical size, group size and language in humans. *Behavioral and Brain Sciences, 16*(4), 681–94.

Gervais, W. M., & Najle, M. B. (2017). How many atheists are there? *Social Psychological and Personality Science, 9*, 3–10. doi:10.1177/1948550617707015.

Gervais, W. M., Xygalatas, D., McKay, R. T., van Elk, M., Buchtel, E. E., Aveyard, M., ... & Bulbulia, J. (2017) Global evidence of extreme intuitive moral prejudice against atheists. *Nature Human Behaviour, 1*, article number 0151.

Gomes, C. M., & McCullough, M. E. (2015). The effects of implicit religious primes on dictator game allocations: A preregistered replication experiment. *Journal of Experimental Psychology: General, 144*, e94–e104.

Hamilton, W. D. (1963). The evolution of altruistic behavior. *American Naturalist, 97*(896), 354–6.

Henrich, J., Ensminger, J., McElreath, R., Barr, A., Barrett, C., Bolyanatz, A., ... & Ziker, J. (2010) Markets, religion, community size, and the evolution of fairness and punishment. *Science, 327*, 1480–4.

Hoffman, E., McCabe, K., Shachat, K., & Smith, V. (1994). Preferences, property rights and anonymity in bargaining games. *Games and Economic Behavior, 7*, 346–80.

Johnson, M. K., Rowatt, W. C., & LaBouff, J. (2010). Priming Christian religious concepts increases racial prejudice. *Social Psychological and Personality Science, 1*(2), 119–26.

Kahneman, D. (2012, September 26). A proposal to deal with questions about priming effects. Retrieved from http://www.nature.com/polopoly_fs/7.6716.1349271308!/suppinfoFile/Kahneman%20Letter.pdf.

LaBouff, J. P., Rowatt, W. C., Johnson, M. K., & Finkle, C. (2012). Differences in attitudes toward outgroups in religious and nonreligious contexts in a multinational sample: A situational context priming study. *International Journal for the Psychology of Religion, 22*(1), 1–9.

Laurin, K., Shariff, A. F., Henrich, J., & Kay, A. (2012). Outsourcing punishment to god: Beliefs in divine control reduce earthly punishment. *Proceedings of the Royal Society B: Biological Sciences, 279*(1741), 3272–81.

Norenzayan, A. (2013) *Big gods: How religion transformed cooperation and conflict.* Princeton, NJ: Princeton University Press.

Norenzayan, A., & Shariff, A. F. (2008) The origin and evolution of religious prosociality. *Science, 322*(5898), 58–62.

Norenzayan, A., Shariff, A. F., Gervais, W. M., Willard, A.K., McNamara, R., Slingerland, E. & Henrich, J. (2016). The cultural evolution of prosocial religions. *Behavioral and Brain Sciences, 39*, 1–65.

Paulhus, D. L. (1984). Two-component models of socially desirable responding. *Journal of Personality and Social Psychology, 46*(3), 598.

Pew Research Center (2017). A growing share of Americans say it's not necessary to believe in God to be moral. Retrieved from http://www.pewresearch.org/fact-tank/2017/10/16/a-growing-share-of-americans-say-its-not-necessary-to-believe-in-god-to-be-moral/.

Pichon, I., Boccato, G., & Saroglou, V. (2007). Nonconscious influences of religion on prosociality: A priming study. *European Journal of Social Psychology, 37*(5), 1032–45.

Purzycki, B. G., Apicella, C., Atkinson, Q. D., Cohen, E., McNamara, R. A., Willard, A. K., ... & Henrich, J. (2016). Moralistic gods, supernatural punishment and the expansion of human sociality. *Nature, 530*(7590), 327–30.

Rand, D. G., Dreber, A., Haque, O. S., Kane, R. J., Nowak, M. A., & Coakley, S. (2013). Religious motivations for cooperation: an experimental investigation using explicit primes. *Religion, Brain & Behavior, 4*(1), 31–48.

Randolph-Seng, B., & Nielsen, M. E. (2007) Honesty: One effect of primed religious representations. *International Journal for the Psychology of Religion, 17*(4), 303–15.

Roes, F. L., & Raymond, M. (2003). Belief in moralizing gods. *Evolution and Human Behavior, 24,* 126–35.

Sagioglou, C., & Forstmann, M. (2013). Activating Christian religious concepts increases intolerance of ambiguity and judgment certainty. *Journal of Experimental Social Psychology, 49,* 933–9.

Saroglou, V., Corneille, O., & Van Cappellen, P. (2009). "Speak, Lord, your servant is listening": Religious priming activates submissive thoughts and behaviors. *International Journal for the Psychology of Religion, 19*(3), 143–54.

Sasaki, J. Y., Kim, H. S., Mojaverian, T., Kelley, L. D., Park, I. Y., & Janušonis, S. (2013). Religion priming differentially increases prosocial behavior among variants of the dopamine D4 receptor (DRD4) gene. *Social cognitive and affective neuroscience, 8*(2), 209–15.

Shariff, A. F., & Norenzayan, A. (2007). God is watching you: Supernatural agent concepts increase prosocial behavior in an anonymous economic game. *Psychological Science, 18,* 803–9.

Shariff, A. F., & Norenzayan, A. (2011). Mean gods make good people. *International Journal for the Psychology of Religion,* 21, 85–96.

Shariff, A. F., Norenzayan, A., & Henrich, J. (2009). The birth of high gods: How the cultural evolution of supernatural policing agents influenced the emergence of complex, cooperative human societies, paving the way for civilization. In M. Schaller, A. Norenzayan, S. Heine, T. Yamagishi, & T. Kameda (Eds.), *Evolution, culture and the human mind* (pp. 117–36). Hoboken, NJ: Lawrence Erlbaum and Associates.

Shariff, A. F., & Rhemtulla, M. (2012). Divergent effects of heaven and hell beliefs on national crime. *PLOS One, 7*(6), e39048.

Shariff, A. F., Willard, A. K., Andersen, T., & Norenzayan, A. (2016). Religious priming: A meta-analysis with a focus on prosociality. *Personality and Social Psychology Review, 20*(1), 27–48.

Simmons, J. P., Nelson, L. D., & Simonsohn, U. (2011). False-positive psychology: Undisclosed flexibility in data collection and analysis allows presenting anything as significant. *Psychological Science, 22*(11), 1359–66.

Snarey, J. (1996) The natural environment's impact upon religious ethics: A cross-cultural study. *Journal for the Scientific Study of Religion, 80,* 85–96.

Srull, T. K., & Wyer, R. S., Jr. (1979). The role of category accessibility in the interpretation of information about persons: Some determinants and implications. *Journal of Personality and Social Psychology, 37,* 1660–72.

Swanson, G. E. (1960) *The Birth of the Gods.* Ann Arbor: University of Michigan Press.

Trivers, R. L. (1971). The evolution of reciprocal altruism. *Quarterly Review of Biology, 46*(1), 35–57.

Van Cappellen, P., Corneille, O., Cols, S., & Saroglou, V. (2011). Beyond mere compliance to authoritative figures: Religious priming increases conformity to informational influence among submissive people. *International Journal for the Psychology of Religion, 21*(2), 97–105.

Weingarten, E., Chen, Q., McAdams, M., Yi, J., Hepler, J., & Albarracín, D. (2016). From primed concepts to action: A meta-analysis of the behavioral effects of incidentally presented words. *Psychological Bulletin, 142*(5), 472.

White, C. J. M., Kelly, J. M., Shariff, A. F., & Norenzayan, A. (2017). Reminders of God and Karma reduce believers' selfishness in anonymous dictator games. Unpublished manuscript, University of British Columbia.

References

Yilmaz, O., & Bahçekapili, H. G. (2016). Supernatural and secular monitors promote human cooperation only if they remind of punishment. *Evolution and Human Behavior, 37*, 79–84.

Chapter 14

Ahmed, A. M., & Salas, O. (2011). Implicit influences of Christian religious representations on dictator and prisoner's dilemma game decisions. *Journal of Socio-Economics, 40*(3), 242–6.

Botero, C. A., Gardner, B., Kirby, K. R., Bulbulia, J., Gavin, M. C., & Gray, R. D. (2014). The ecology of religious beliefs. *Proceedings of the National Academy of Sciences, 111*(47), 16784–9.

Boyd, R., & Richerson, P. J. (2005). *Not by genes alone: How culture transformed human evolution*. Chicago, IL: University of Chicago Press.

Fehr, E., & Gächter, S. (2000). Cooperation and punishment in public goods experiments. *American Economic Review, 90*, 980–94.

Fehr, E., & Gächter, S. (2002). Altruistic punishment in humans. *Nature, 415*(6868), 137–40.

Gray, K., & Wegner, D. M. (2010). Blaming God for our pain: Human suffering and the divine mind. *Personality and Social Psychology Review, 14*(1), 7–16.

Heine, S. J., Proulx, T., & Vohs, K. D. (2006). The meaning maintenance model: On the coherence of social motivations. *Personality and Social Psychology Review, 10*(2), 88–110.

Henrich, J., Ensminger, J., McElreath, R., Barr, A., Barrett, C., Bolyanatz, A., ... & Ziker, J. (2010). Markets, religion, community size, and the evolution of fairness and punishment. *Science, 327*, 1480–4.

Higgins, E. T. (1996). Knowledge activation: Accessibility, applicability, and salience. In E. T. Higgins & A.W. Kruglanski (Eds.), *Social psychology: Handbook of basic principles* (pp. 133–68). New York: Guilford.

Hughes, K. A. (2006). Justice expenditure and employment in the United States, 2003. *Bureau of Justice Statistics, NCJ212260*. US Department of Justice, Washington, DC.

Johnson, D. D. P., & Krüger, O. (2004). Supernatural punishment and the evolution of cooperation. *Political Theology*, 5, 159–76.

Kelemen, D. (2004). Are children "intuitive theists"? Reasoning about purpose and design in nature. *Psychological Science, 15*(5), 295–301.

Krupka, E., & Weber, R. (2013). Identifying social norms using coordination games: Why does dictator game sharing vary? *Journal of the European Economic association, 11*, 495–524.

Lerner, M. J. (1980). The belief in a just world. In *The belief in a just world: A fundamental delusion* (pp. 9–30). Boston, MA: Springer US.

Molden, D. C. (2014). Understanding priming effects in social psychology: What is "social priming" and how does it occur? *Social Cognition, 32*(Supplement), 1–11.

Norenzayan, A. (2016). Theodiversity. *Annual Review of Psychology, 67*, 21.1–21.24.

Norenzayan, A., Shariff, A. F., Gervais, W. M., Willard, A. K., McNamara, R. A., Slingerland, E., & Henrich, J. (2016). The cultural evolution of prosocial religions. *Behavioral and Brain Sciences, 39*, e1.

Pinker, S. (2011). *The better angels of our nature: Why violence has declined* (Vol. 75). New York: Viking.

Purzycki, B. G., Apicella, C., Atkinson, Q. D., Cohen, E., McNamara, R. A., Willard, A. K., ... & Henrich, J. (2016). Moralistic gods, supernatural punishment and the expansion of human sociality. *Nature, 530*, 327–30.

Randolph-Seng, B., & Nielsen, M. E. (2007). Honesty: One effect of primed religious representations. *International Journal for the Psychology of Religion, 17*(4), 303–15.

Shariff, A. F., & Norenzayan, A. (2007). God is watching you: Priming God concepts increases prosocial behavior in an anonymous economic game. *Psychological Science, 18*(9), 803–809.

Shariff, A. F., & Rhemtulla, M. (2012). Divergent effects of beliefs in heaven and hell on national crime rates. *PLOS One*, *7*(6), e39048.

Simmons, J. P., Nelson, L. D., & Simonsohn, U. (2011). False-positive psychology: Undisclosed flexibility in data collection and analysis allows presenting anything as significant. *Psychological Science*, *22*(11), 1359–66.

Snarey, J. (1996). The natural environment's impact upon religious ethics: A cross-cultural study. *Journal for the Scientific Study of Religion*, 85–96.

Wason, P. C. (1960). On the failure to eliminate hypotheses in a conceptual task. *Quarterly journal of experimental psychology*, *12*(3), 129–40.

White, C. J. M., Kelly, J. M., Shariff, A. F. & Norenzayan, A. (2017). God is still watching: Reminders of God and Karma both increase prosociality. Manuscript in preparation.

Wilson, D. S. (2002). *Darwin's cathedral: Evolution, religion, and the nature of society*. Chicago, IL: University of Chicago Press.

Yilmaz, O., & Bahçekapili, H. G. (2016). Supernatural and secular monitors promote human cooperation only if they remind of punishment. *Evolution and Human Behavior*, *37*(1), 79–84.

Chapter 15

Ahmed, A. M., & Salas, O. (2011). Implicit influences of Christian religious representations on dictator and prisoner's dilemma game decisions. *Journal of Socio-Economics*, *40*(3), 242–6.

Alcorta, C. S., & Sosis, R. (2005). Ritual, emotion, and sacred symbols. *Human Nature*, *16*(4), 323–59.

Berman, E. (2009). *Radical, religious, and violent: The new economics of terrorism*. Cambridge, MA: MIT Press.

Bulbulia, J., & Mahoney, A. (2008). Religious solidarity: The hand grenade experiment. *Journal of Cognition and Culture*, *8*(3), 295–320.

Fishman, A. (1994). Religious socialism and economic success on the orthodox kibbutz. *Journal of Institutional and Theoretical Economics*, *150*(4), 763–8.

Fishman, A., & Goldschmidt, Y. (1990). The orthodox kibbutzim and economic success. *Journal for the Scientific Study of Religion*, *29*, 505–11.

Graham, J., & Haidt, J. (2010). Beyond beliefs: Religions bind individuals into moral communities. *Personality and Social Psychology Review*, *14*(1), 140–50.

Hall, D. L., Cohen, A. B., Meyer, K. K., Varley, A. H., & Brewer, G. A. (2015). Costly signaling increases trust, even across religious affiliations. *Psychological Science*, *26*(9), 1368–376.

Irons, W. (1996). In our own self-image: The evolution of morality, deception, and religion. *Skeptic*, *4*(2), 50–61.

Irons, W. (2001). Religion as a hard-to-fake sign of commitment. In R. Nesse (Ed.), *Evolution and the capacity for commitment* (pp. 292–309). New York: Russell Sage Foundation.

Johnson, D. (2016). *God is watching you: How the fear of God makes us human*. New York: Oxford University Press.

Malhotra, D. K. (2010). (When) are religious people nicer? Religious salience and the "Sunday effect" on pro-social behavior. *Judgment and Decision Making*, *5*(2), 138–43.

McCullough, M. E., Swartwout, P., Shaver, J. H., Carter, E. C., & Sosis, R. (2016). Christian religious badges instill trust in Christian and non-Christian perceivers. *Psychology of Religion and Spirituality*, *8*(2), 149–63.

Norenzayan, A. (2013). *Big gods: How religion transformed cooperation and conflict*. Princeton, NJ: Princeton University Press.

Norenzayan, A., Shariff, A. F., Gervais, W. M., Willard, A. K., McNamara, R. A., Slingerland, E., & Henrich, J. (2016). The cultural evolution of prosocial religions. *Behavioral and Brain Sciences*, *39*, 1–19.

References

Oved, I. (1988). *Two hundred years of American communes*. New Brunswick, London: Transaction Books.

Power, E. A. (2017). Discerning devotion: Testing the signaling theory of religion. *Evolution and Human Behavior, 38*(1), 82–91.

Purzycki, B. G., Apicella, C., Atkinson, Q. D., Cohen, E., McNamara, R. A., Willard, A. K., ... & Henrich, J. (2016). Moralistic gods, supernatural punishment and the expansion of human sociality. *Nature, 530*(7590), 327–30.

Purzycki, B. G., Henrich, J., Apicella, C., Atkinson, Q. D., Baimel, A., Cohen, E., ... & Norenzayan, A. (2018). The evolution of religion and morality: A synthesis of ethnographic and experimental evidence from eight societies. *Religion, Brain & Behavior, 8*(2), 101–132.

Purzycki, B. G., & Sosis, R. (2009). The religious system as adaptive: Cognitive flexibility, public displays, and acceptance. In E. Voland & W. Schiefenhovel (Eds.), *The biological evolution of religious mind and behavior* (pp. 243–56). Berlin, Heidelberg: Springer.

Purzycki, B. G., & Sosis, R. (2013). The extended religious phenotype and the adaptive coupling of ritual and belief. *Israel Journal of Ecology & Evolution, 59*(2), 99–108.

Ruffle, B. J., & Sosis, R. (2006). Cooperation and the in-group-out-group bias: A field test on Israeli kibbutz members and city residents. *Journal of Economic Behavior & Organization, 60*(2), 147–63.

Ruffle, B. J., & Sosis, R. (2007). Does it pay to pray? Costly ritual and cooperation. *BE Journal of Economic Analysis & Policy, 7*(1), 1–35 (Article 18).

Ruffle, B. J., & Sosis, R. (2010). Do religious contexts elicit more trust and altruism? An experiment on Facebook.

Shaver, J., Divietro, S., Lang, M., & Sosis, R. (2018). Costs do not explain trust among secular groups. *Journal of Cognition and Culture, 18*, 180–204.

Soler, M. (2012). Costly signaling, ritual and cooperation: Evidence from Candomblé, an Afro-Brazilian religion. *Evolution and Human Behavior, 33*(4), 346–56.

Sosis, R. (2000). Religion and intragroup cooperation: Preliminary results of a comparative analysis of utopian communities. *Cross-Cultural Research, 34*(1), 70–87.

Sosis, R. (2003). Why aren't we all Hutterites? Costly signaling theory and religious behavior. *Human Nature, 14*(2), 91–127.

Sosis, R. (2016). Religions as complex adaptive systems. In N. Clements (Ed.), *MacMillan Interdisciplinary Handbooks on Religion. Mental Religion: The Brain, Cognition, and Culture* (pp. 219–36). Farmington Hills, MI: Macmillan.

Sosis, R., & Bressler, E. R. (2003). Cooperation and commune longevity: A test of the costly signaling theory of religion. *Cross-cultural Research, 37*(2), 211–39.

Sosis, R., Kress, H. C., & Boster, J. S. (2007). Scars for war: Evaluating alternative signaling explanations for cross-cultural variance in ritual costs. *Evolution and Human Behavior, 28*(4), 234–47.

Sosis, R., & Ruffle, B. J. (2003). Religious ritual and cooperation: Testing for a relationship on Israeli religious and secular kibbutzim. *Current Anthropology, 44*(5), 713–22.

Sosis, R., & Ruffle, B. J. (2004). Ideology, religion, and the evolution of cooperation: Field experiments on Israeli kibbutzim. *Research in Economic Anthropology, 23*, 89–117.

Tan, J. H., & Vogel, C. (2008). Religion and trust: An experimental study. *Journal of Economic Psychology, 29*(6), 832–48.

Chapter 16

Aronson, E., & Mills, J. (1959). The effect of severity of initiation on liking for a group. *Journal of Abnormal and Social Psychology, 59*(2), 177–81.

Atran, S., & Henrich, J. (2010). The evolution of religion: How cognitive by-products, adaptive learning heuristics, ritual displays, and group competition generate deep commitments to prosocial religions. *Biological Theory, 5*(1), 18–30.

Bastian, B., Jetten, J., & Ferris, L. J. (2014). Pain as social glue: Shared pain increases cooperation. *Psychological Science, 25*(11), 2079–85. doi:10.1177/0956797614545886.

Bem, D. J. (1967). Self-perception: An alternative interpretation of cognitive dissonance phenomena. *Psychological Review, 74*(3), 183–200.

Choi, J. K., & Bowles, S. (2007). The coevolution of parochial altruism and war. *Science, 318*(5850), 636–40. doi:10.1126/science.1144237.

Clingingsmith, D., Khwaja, A. I., & Kremer, M. (2009). Estimating the impact of the Hajj: Religion and tolerance in Islam's global gathering. *Quarterly Journal of Economics, 124*(3), 1133–70.

Diamond, J., & Robinson, J. A. (2012). *Natural experiments of history*. Cambridge, MA: Harvard University Press.

Durkheim, É. (1915). *The elementary forms of the religious life*. London: George Allen & Unwin.

Festinger, L. (1962). *A theory of cognitive dissonance*. Stanford, CA: Stanford University Press.

Fischer, R., Xygalatas, D., Mitkidis, P., Reddish, P., Tok, P., Konvalinka, I., & Bulbulia, J. (2014). The fire-walker's high: Affect and physiological responses in an extreme collective ritual. Edited by B. Bastian. *PLOS One, 9*(2), e88355. doi:10.1371/journal.pone.0088355.

Fisher, R. J. (1993). Social desirability bias and the validity of indirect questioning. *Journal of Consumer Research, 20*(2), 303–15. doi:10.1086/209351.

Gaertner, S. L., Dovidio, J. F., Rust, M. C., Nier, J. A., Banker, B. S., Ward, C. M., ... & Houlette, M. (1999). Reducing intergroup bias: Elements of intergroup cooperation. *Journal of Personality and Social Psychology, 76*(3), 388–402.

Gerard, H. B., & Mathewson, G. C. (1966). The effects of severity of initiation on liking for a group: A replication. *Journal of Experimental Social Psychology, 2*(3), 278–87.

Ginges, J., Hansen, I., & Norenzayan, A. (2009). Religion and support for suicide attacks. *Psychological Science, 20*(2), 224–30.

Henrich, J. (2009). The evolution of costly displays, cooperation and religion: Credibility enhancing displays and their implications for cultural evolution. *Evolution and Human Behavior, 30*(4), 244–60. doi:10.1016/j.evolhumbehav.2009.03.005.

Henrich, J., Heine, S. J., & Norenzayan, A. (2010). The weirdest people in the world?. *Behavioral and Brain Sciences, 33*(2–3), 61–83. doi:10.1017/S0140525X0999152X.

Hornsey, M., & Hogg, M. (2000). Assimilation and diversity: An integrative model of subgroup relations. *Personality and Social Psychology Review, 4*(2), 143–56. doi:10.1207/S15327957PSPR0402_03.

Konvalinka, I., Xygalatas, D., Bulbulia, J., Schjoedt, U., Jegindø, E-M. E., Wallot, S., ... & Roepstorff, A. (2011). Synchronized arousal between performers and related spectators in a fire-walking ritual. *Proceedings of the National Academy of Sciences of the United States of America, 108*(20), 8514–19. doi:10.1073/pnas.1016955108.

Manusov, V. L. (2005). *The sourcebook of nonverbal measures: Going beyond words*. New York: Routledge.

Norenzayan, A., & Shariff, A. F. (2008). The origin and evolution of religious prosociality. *Science, 322*, 58–62.

Norton, M. I., Ariely, D., & Mochon, D. (2012). The IKEA effect: When labor leads to love. *Journal of Consumer Psychology, 22*(3), 453–60.

Olivola, C. Y., & Shafir, E. (2011). The martyrdom effect: When pain and effort increase prosocial contributions. *Journal of Behavioral Decision Making, 26*(1), 91–105. doi:10.1002/bdm.767.

Power, E. A. (2017a). Discerning devotion: Testing the signaling theory of religion. *Evolution and Human Behavior, 38*(1), 82–91. doi:10.1016/j.evolhumbehav.2016.07.003.

Power, E. A. (2017b). Social support networks and religiosity in rural South India. *Nature Human Behavior, 1*(3), 1–6.

References

Schjoedt, U., Sørensen, J., Nielbo, K.L., Xygalatas, D., Mitkidis, P., & Bulbulia, J. (2013). Cognitive resource depletion in religious interactions. *Religion, Brain & Behavior, 3*(1), 39–55. doi:10.10 80/2153599X.2012.736714.

Shariff, A. F., & Norenzayan, A. (2007). God is watching you. *Psychological Science, 18*(9), 803–9.

Snodgrass, J. G., Most, D. E., & Upadhyay, C. (2017). Religious ritual is good medicine for indigenous Indian conservation refugees: Implications for global mental health. *Current Anthropology, 58*, 257–84. doi:10.1086/691212.

Sosis, R. (2000). Costly signaling and torch fishing on Ifaluk Atoll. *Evolution and Human Behavior, 21*(4), 223–244.

Sosis, R. (2003). Why aren't we all Hutterites? *Human Nature, 14*(2), 91–127.

Sosis, R., & Bressler, E.R. (2003). Cooperation and commune longevity: A test of the costly signaling theory of religion. *Cross-Cultural Research, 37*(2), 211.

Sosis, R., & Ruffle, B. J. (2003). Religious ritual and cooperation: Testing for a relationship on Israeli religious and secular kibbutzim. *Current Anthropology, 44*(5), 713–22.

Tajfel, H., Billig, M. G., & Bundy, R. P. (2005). Social categorization and intergroup behavior. *European Journal of Social Psychology, 1*(2), 149–78.

Tewari, S., Khan, S., Hopkins, N., Srinivasan, N., & Reicher, S. (2012). Participation in mass gatherings can benefit well-being: Longitudinal and control data from a North Indian Hindu pilgrimage event. Edited by P. Holme. *PLOS One, 7*(10), e47291. doi:10.1371/journal. pone.0047291.t001.

Whitehouse, H. (1992). Memorable religions: Transmission, codification and change in divergent Melanesian contexts. *Man, 27*(4), 777–97.

Whitehouse, H., & Lanman, J. A. (2014). The ties that bind us. *Current Anthropology, 55*(6), 674–95. doi:10.1086/678698.

Xygalatas, D. (2012). *The burning saints*. London: Equinox.

Xygalatas, D. (2013). Přenos laboratoře do terénu: Využití smíšených metod během terénního studia náboženství. *Sociální Studia, 10*(2), 15–25.

Xygalatas, D., Klocová, E.K., Cigán, J., Kundt, R., Maňo, P., Kotherová, S., ... & Kanovsky, M. (2016). Location, location, location: Effects of cross-religious primes on prosocial behavior. *International Journal for the Psychology of Religion, 26*(4), 304–19. doi:10.1080/10508619.201 5.1097287.

Xygalatas, D., Konvalinka, I., Roepstorff, A., & Bulbulia, J. (2011). Quantifying collective effervescence heart-rate dynamics at a fire-walking ritual. *Communicative & Integrative Biology, 4*(6), 735–38.

Xygalatas, D., Kotherová, S., Maňo, P., Kundt, R., Cigán, J., Klocová, E.K., & Lang, M. (2017). Big gods in small places: The random allocation game in Mauritius. *Religion, Brain & Behavior, 10*(1), 1–19. doi:10.1080/2153599X.2016.1267033.

Xygalatas, D., & Martin, L. (2016). Prosociality and religion. In N. K. Clements (Ed.), *Mental Religion* (pp. 119–33). Farmington Hills, MI: Macmillan Reference USA.

Xygalatas, D., Mitkidis, P., Fischer, R., Reddish, P., Skewes, J., Geertz, A. W., ... & Bulbulia, J. (2013). Extreme rituals promote prosociality. *Psychological Science, 24*(8), 1602–5. doi:10.1177/0956797612472910.

Xygalatas, D., & Schjoedt, U. (2013). Autobiographical memory in a fire-walking ritual. *Journal of Cognition and Culture, 13*, 1–16. doi:10.1163/15685373-12342081.

Chapter 17

Daniels, J. P., & von der Ruhr, M. (2010). Trust in others: Does religion matter? *Review of Social Economy, 68*(2), 163–86.

Johansson-Stenman, O., Mahmud, M., & Martinsson, P. (2009). Trust and religion: Experimental evidence from rural Bangladesh. *Economica, 76*, 462–85.

Pew Research Center (2010). *Millennials: A portrait of generation next.* Retrieved from http://www.pewsocialtrends.org/files/2010/10/millennials-confident-connected-open-to-change.pdf. Accessed August 8, 2014.

Raiya, H. A., Pargament, K. I., Mahoney, A., & Trevino, K. (2008). When Muslims are perceived as a religious threat: Examining the connection between desecration, religious coping, and anti-Muslim attitudes. *Basic and Applied Social Psychology, 30*, 311–25.

Sosis, R. (2005). Does religion promote trust? The role of signaling, reputation, and punishment. *Interdisciplinary Journal of Research on Religion, 1*, 1–30.

Sosis, R., & Alcorta, C. (2003). Signaling, solidarity, and the sacred: The evolution of religious behavior. *Evolutionary Anthropology, 12*, 264–74.

Strabac, Z., & Listhaug, O. (2008). Anti-Muslim prejudice in Europe: A multilevel analysis of survey data from 30 countries. *Social Science Research, 37*(1), 268–86.

Tajfel, H., & Turner, J. C. (1979). An integrative theory of intergroup conflict. In W. G. Austin & S. Worchel (Eds.), *Social psychology of intergroup relations* (pp. 33–47). Monterey, CA: Brooks-Cole.

Tversky, A., & Kahneman, D. (1983). Extension versus intuitive reasoning: The conjunction fallacy in probability judgment. *Psychological Review, 90*, 293–315.

Chapter 18

Boyer, P., & Liénard, P. (2006). Why ritualized behavior? Precaution systems and action parsing in developmental, pathological and cultural rituals. *Behavioral and Brain Sciences, 29*, 1–56.

Clark, A. (2013). Whatever next? Predictive brains, situated agents, and the future of cognitive science. *The Behavioral and Brain Sciences, 36*(3), 181–204.

Dulaney, S., & Fiske, A. (1994). Cultural rituals and obsessive-compulsive disorder: Is there a common psychological mechanism? *Ethos, 22*(3), 243–83.

Eilam, D., Izhar, R., & Mort, J. (2011). Threat detection: Behavioral practices in animals and humans. *Neuroscience and Biobehavioral Reviews, 35*(4), 999–1006.

Eilam, D., Zor, R., Szechtman, H., & Hermesh, H. (2006). Rituals, stereotypy and compulsive behavior in animals and humans. *Neuroscience & Biobehavioral Reviews, 30*(4), 456–71.

Felson, R., & Gmelch, G. (1979). Uncertainty and the use of magic. *Current Anthropology, 20*(3), 587–89.

Henrich, J., Heine, S. J., & Norenzayan, A. (2010). The weirdest people in the world? *Behavioral and Brain Sciences, 33*(2–3), 61–135.

Hirsh, J., Mar, R. A., & Peterson, J. B. (2012). Psychological entropy: A framework for understanding uncertainty-related anxiety. *Psychological Review, 119*(2), 304–20.

Keinan, G. (1994). Effects of stress and tolerance of ambiguity on magical thinking. *Journal of Personality and Social Psychology, 67*(1), 48–55.

Krátký, J., Lang, M., Shaver, J. H., Jerotijević, D., & Xygalatas, D. (2016). Anxiety and ritualization: Can attention discriminate compulsion from routine? *Communicative & Integrative Biology, 9*(3), e1174799.

Lang, M., Bahna, V., Shaver, J. H., Reddish, P., & Xygalatas, D. (2017). Sync to link: Endorphin-mediated synchrony effects on cooperation. *Biological Psychology, 127*, 191–7.

Lang, M., Krátký, J., Shaver, J. H., Jerotijević, D., & Xygalatas, D. (2015). Effects of anxiety on spontaneous ritualized behavior. *Current Biology, 25*(14), 1892–7.

Lang, M., Shaw, D. J., Reddish, P., Wallot, S., Mitkidis, P., & Xygalatas, D. (2016). Lost in the rhythm: Effects of rhythm on subsequent interpersonal coordination. *Cognitive Science, 40*(7), 1797–815.

References

Legare, C. H., & Souza, A. L. (2012). Evaluating ritual efficacy: Evidence from the supernatural. *Cognition, 124*(1), 1–15.

Liénard, P., & Boyer, P. (2006). Whence collective rituals? A cultural selection model of ritualized behavior. *American Anthropologist, 108*(4), 814–27.

Malinowski, B. (1948/1992). *Magic, science and religion and other essays.* Long Grove, IL: Waveland Press.

Marwan, N., Romano, M. C., Thiel, M., & Kurths, J. (2007). Recurrence plots for the analysis of complex systems. *Physics Reports, 438*(5–6), 237–329. doi:10.1016/j.physrep.2006.11.001.

Rappaport, R. (1999). *Ritual and religion in the making of humanity.* Cambridge: Cambridge University Press.

Schippers, M., & Van Lange, P. (2006). The psychological benefits of superstitious rituals in top sport: A study among top sportspersons. *Journal of Applied Social Psychology, 36*(10), 2532–53.

Sears, D. O. (1986). College sophomores in the laboratory: Influences of a narrow data base on social psychology' s view of human nature. *Journal of Personality and Social Psychology, 51*(3), 515–30.

Sosis, R., & Handwerker, W. P. (2011). Psalms and coping with uncertainty: Religious Israeli women's responses to the 2006 Lebanon war. *American Anthropologist, 113*(1), 40–55.

Webber, C. L., & Zbilut, J. P. (2005). Recurrence quantification analysis of nonlinear dynamical aystems. In M. Riley & G. Van Orden (Eds.), *Tutorials in contemporary nonlinear methods for the behavioral sciences* (pp. 26–94). Arlington, VA: National Science Foundation.

Xygalatas, D., & Lang, M. (2017). Religion and prosociality. In N. Clements (Ed.), *Macmillan interdisciplinary handbooks. Religion: Mental religion* (pp. 119–33). Farmington Hills, MI: Macmillan Reference USA.

Zacks, J., & Swallow, K. (2007). Event segmentation. *Current Directions in Psychological Science, 16*(2), 80–4.

Zacks, J. M., Tversky, B., & Iyer, G. (2001). Perceiving, remembering, and communicating structure in events. *Journal of Experimental Psychology. General, 130*(1), 29–58.

Zor, R., Keren, H., Hermesh, H., Szechtman, H., Mort, J., & Eilam, D. (2009). Obsessive-compulsive disorder: A disorder of pessimal (non-functional) motor behavior. *Acta Psychiatrica Scandinavica, 120*(4), 288–98.

Chapter 19

Bal, B. S., Singh, D., Badwal, K. K., & Dhaliwal, G. S. (2014). Superstitions behavior and decision making in collegiate athletes: An illogical phenomenon. *Advances in Physical Education, 4*(1), 1–5.

Bersabé, R., & Martínez Arias, R. (2000). Superstition in gambling. *Psychology in Spain, 4*, 28–34.

Bleich, A., Gelkopf, M., & Solomon, Z. (2003). Exposure to terrorism, stress-related mental health symptoms, and coping behaviors among a nationally representative sample in Israel *Journal of the American Medical Association, 290*, 612–20.

Burger, J., & A. Lynn. (2005). Superstitious behavior among American and Japanese professional baseball players. *Basic and Applied Social Psychology, 27*, 71–6.

Damisch, L., Stoberock, B., & Mussweiler, T. (2010). Keep your fingers crossed! How superstition improves performance. *Psychological Science, 21*(7), 1014–20.

Gmelch, G. (2001). *Inside pitch.* Washington, DC: Smithsonian Institution Press.

Henrich, J. (2016). *The secret of our success.* Princeton, NJ: Princeton University Press.

Irons, W. (2001). Religion as a hard-to-fake sign of commitment. In R. Nesse (Ed.), *Evolution and the capacity for commitment* (pp. 292–309). New York: Russell Sage Foundation.

Keinan, G. (1994). Effects of stress and tolerance of ambiguity on magical thinking. *Journal of Personality and Social Psychology, 67*, 48–55.

Keinan, G. (2002). The effects of stress and desire for control on superstitious behavior. *Personality and Social Psychology Bulletin, 28*, 102–8.

Klar, Y., Medding, A., & Sarel, D. (1996). Nonunique invulnerability: Singular versus distributional probabilities and unrealistic optimism in comparative risk judgments. *Organizational Behavior and Human Decision Processes, 67*, 229–45.

Klar, Y., Zakay, D., & Shavrit, K. (2002). "If I don't get blown up…": Realism in face of terrorism in an Israeli nationwide sample. *Risk Decision and Policy, 7*, 203–19.

Malinowski, B. (1954). *Magic, science, and religion.* Garden City, NY: Doubleday Anchor Books.

Noy, S. (2004). Minimizing casualties in biological and chemical threats (war and terrorism): The importance of information to the public in a prevention program. *Prehospital and Disaster Medicine, 19*, 29–36.

Ono, K. (1987). Superstitious behavior in humans. *Journal of the Experimental Analysis of Behavior, 47*, 261–71.

Rappaport, R. (1999). *Ritual and religion in the making of humanity.* New York: Cambridge University Press.

Rudski, J. M., & Edwards, A. (2007). Malinowski goes to college: Factors influencing students' use of ritual and superstition. *Journal of General Psychology, 134*, 389–403.

Schippers, M. C., & Van Lange, P. A. M. (2006). The psychological benefits of superstitious rituals in top sport: A study among top sportspersons. *Journal of Applied Social Psychology, 36*, 2532–53.

Schuster, M. A., Stein, B. D., Jaycox, L. H., Collins, R. L., Marshall, G. N., Elliott, M. N., … & Berry, S. H. (2001). A national survey of stress reactions after the September 11, 2001, terrorist attacks. *New England Journal of Medicine, 345*, 1507–12.

Sharansky, N. (1988). *Fear no evil.* New York: Random House.

Silver, R., Holman, E., McIntosh, D., Poulin, M., & Gil-Rivas, V. (2002). Nationwide longitudinal study of psychological responses to September 11. *Journal of the American Medical Association, 288*, 1235–44.

Skinner, B.F. (1948). "Superstition" in the pigeon. *Journal of Experimental Psychology, 38*, 168–72.

Sosis, R. (2000). Costly signaling and torch fishing on Ifaluk Atoll. *Evolution and Human Behavior, 21*, 223–44.

Sosis, R. (2001). Sharing, consumption, and patch choice on Ifaluk Atoll. *Human Nature, 12*, 221–45.

Sosis, R. (2002). Patch choice decisions on Ifaluk Atoll. *American Anthropologist, 104*, 583–598.

Sosis, R. (2003). Why aren't we all Hutterites? Costly signaling theory and religious behavior. *Human Nature, 14*, 91–127.

Sosis, R. (2007). Psalms for safety: Magico-religious responses to threats of terror. *Current Anthropology, 48*, 903–11.

Sosis, R., and Handwerker, P. (2011). Psalms and coping with uncertainty: Israeli women's responses to the 2006 Lebanon War. *American Anthropologist, 113*, 40–55.

Todd, M., & Brown, C. (2003). Characteristics associated with superstitious behavior in track and field athletes: Are there NCAA divisional level differences? *Journal of Sport Behavior, 26*, 168–87.

Wagner, G. A., & Morris, E. K. (1987). "Superstitious" behavior in children. *Psychological Record, 37*, 471–88.

Womack, M. (1992). Why athletes need ritual: A study of magic among professional athletes. In S. J. Hoffman (Ed.), *Sport and Religion* (pp. 191–202). Champaign, IL: Human Kinetics.

Wright, P. B., & Erdal, K. J. (2008). Sport superstition as a function of skill level and task difficulty. *Journal of Sport Behavior, 31*, 187–99.

References

Chapter 20

Amodio, D. M., & Frith, C. D. (2006). Meeting of minds: The medial frontal cortex and social cognition. *Nature, 7*, 268–77.

Andersen, M., Schjoedt, U., Nielbo, K. L., & Sørensen, J. (2014). Mystical experience in the lab. *Method & Theory in the Study of Religion, 26*(3), 217–45.

Batson, C. D. (1977). Experimentation in psychology of religion: An impossible dream. *Journal for the Scientific Study of Religion, 16*, 413–18.

Beauregard, M., & Paquette, V. (2006). Neural correlates of a mystical experience in Carmelite nuns. *Neuroscience letters, 405*(3), 186–90.

Blanke, O., Pozeg, P., Hara, M., Heydrich, L., Serino, A., Yamamoto, A., ... & Arzy, S. (2014). Neurological and robot-controlled induction of an apparition. *Current Biology, 24*(22), 2681–86.

Castelli, F., Happe, F., Frith, U., & Frith, C. (2000). Movement and mind: A functional imaging study of perception and interpretation of complex intentional movement patterns. *NeuroImage, 12*, 314–25.

d'Aquili, E. G., & Newberg, A. B. (1999). *The mystical mind*. Minneapolis: Fortress Press.

Gallagher, H. L., & Frith, C. D. (2003). Functional imaging of "theory of mind." *Trends in Cognitive Sciences, 7*, 77–83.

Geertz, Armin W. (2008). Comparing prayer: On science, universals, and the human condition. In W. Braun & R. T. McCutcheon (Eds.), *Introducing religion: Essays in honor of Jonathan Z. Smith* (pp. 113–39). London & Oakville: Equinox.

Gervais, W. M., & Norenzayan, A. (2012). Like a camera in the sky? Thinking about God increases public self-awareness and socially desirable responding. *Journal of Experimental Social Psychology, 48*(1), 298–302.

Ladd, K. L., Cook, C. A., Foreman, K. M., & Ritter, E. A. (2015). Neuroimaging of prayer: Questions of validity. *Psychology of Religion and Spirituality, 7*(2), 100.

McCabe, K., Houser, D., Ryan, L., Smith, V., & Trouard, T. (2001). A functional imaging study of cooperation in two-person reciprocal exchange. *Proceedings of the National Academy of Sciences, 98*, 11832–5.

Neubauer, R. L. (2014). Prayer as an interpersonal relationship: A neuroimaging study. *Religion, Brain & Behavior, 4*(2), 92–103.

Norenzayan, A., Gervais, W. M., & Trzesniewski, K. H. (2012). Mentalizing deficits constrain belief in a personal God. *PLOS One, 7*(5), e36880.

Pahnke, W. N. (1966). Drugs and mysticism. *International Journal of Parapsychology, 8*(2), 295–313.

Persinger, M. A. (1987). *Neuropsychological bases of God beliefs*. New York: Praeger.

Reddish, P., Tok, P., & Kundt, R. (2016). Religious cognition and behaviour in autism: The role of mentalizing. *The International Journal for the Psychology of Religion, 26*(2), 95–112.

Rilling, K. J., Sanfey, G. A., Aronson, A. J., Nystrom, L. E., & Cohen, J. D. (2004). The neural correlates of theory of mind within interpersonal interactions. *NeuroImage, 22*, 1694–1703.

Schilbach, L., Eickhoff, S. B., Rotarska-Jagiela, A., Fink, G. R., & Vogeley, K. (2008). Minds at rest? Social cognition as the default mode of cognizing and its putative relationship to the "default system" of the brain. *Consciousness and Cognition, 17*, 457–67.

Schjoedt, U. (2009). The religious brain: A general introduction to the experimental neuroscience of religion. *Method & Theory in the Study of Religion, 21*(3), 310–39.

Schjoedt, U., Stødkilde-Jørgensen, H., Geertz, A. W., & Roepstorff, A. (2008). Rewarding prayers. *Neuroscience letters, 443*(3), 165–8.

Visuri, I. (2018). Rethinking autism, theism and atheism: Bodiless agents and imaginary realities. *Archive for the Psychology of Religion, 1*, 1–31.

Chapter 21

Lawson, E. T., & McCauley, R. N. (1990). *Rethinking religion: Connecting cognition and culture.* Cambridge: Cambridge University Press.

McCauley, R. N., & Lawson, E. T. (2002). *Bringing ritual to mind: Psychological foundations of cultural forms.* Cambridge: Cambridge University Press.

Chapter 22

Boyer, P., & Liénard, P. (2007). Precaution systems and ritualized behavior. *Behavioral and Brain Sciences, 29,* 595–660. doi:10.1017/S0140525X06009575.

Boyer, P., & Liénard, P. (2008). Ritual behavior in obsessive and normal individuals: Moderating anxiety and reorganizing the flow of action. *Current Directions in Psychological Science, 17*(4), 291–4. doi:10.1111/j.1467-8721.2008.00592.x.

Clark, A. (2013). Whatever next? Predictive brains, situated agents, and the future of cognitive science. *Behavioral and Brain Sciences, 36*(3), 181–204. doi:10.1017/S0140525X12000477.

Douglas, M. (1966). *Purity and danger.* London: Burns & Oates.

Durkheim, É. (1995 [1912]). *Elementary forms of the religious life.* Translated by Karen Fields. New York: Free Press.

Frazer, J. G. (1911). *The golden bough; Study of magic and religion* (3rd edn.). London: MacMillan.

Lawson, E. T., & McCauley, R. N. (1990). *Rethinking religion: Connecting cognition and culture.* Cambridge: Cambridge University Press.

Liénard, P., & Boyer, P. (2008). Whence collective rituals? A cultural selection model of ritualized behavior. *American Anthropologist, 108*(4), 814–27. doi:10.1525/aa.2006.108.4.814.

Nemeroff, C., & Rozin, P. (1994). The contagion concept in adult thinking in the United States: Transmission of germs and of interpersonal influence. *Ethos, 22*(2), 158–86.

Newtson, D., & Engquist, G. (1976). The perceptual organization of ongoing behavior. *Journal of Experimental Social Psychology, 12,* 436–50.

Nielbo, K. L., Schjødt, U., & Sørensen, J. (2013). Hierarchical organization of segmentation in non-functional action sequences. *Journal for the Cognitive Science of Religion, 1*(1), 71–97. doi:10.1558/jcsr.v1i1.71.

Radcliffe-Brown, A. R. (1952). *Structure and function in primitive society. Essays and addresses.* Glencoe: Free Press.

Rappaport, R. A. (1979). *Ecology, meaning, and religion.* Berkeley, CA: North Atlantic Books.

Rappaport, R. A. (1999). *Ritual and religion in the making of humanity.* Cambridge: Cambridge University Press.

Schjoedt, U., Sørensen, J., Nielbo, K. L., Xygalatas, D., Mitkidis, D., & Bulbulia, J. (2013). The resource model and the principle of predictive coding: A framework for analyzing proximate effects of ritual. *Religion, Brain & Behavior, 3*(1), 79–86. doi:10.1080/2153599X.2012.745447.

Sørensen, J. (2007a). *A cognitive theory of magic.* Walnut Creek: AltaMira Press.

Sørensen, J. (2007b). Acts that work: A cognitive approach to ritual agency. *Method & Theory in the Study of Religion, 19*(3–4), 281–300.

Sperber, D. (1975). *Rethinking symbolism.* Cambridge: Cambridge University Press.

Staal, F. (1979). The meaninglessness of ritual. *Numen, 26*(1), 2–22. doi: org/10.1163/156852779X00244.

Subbotsky, E. (2014). The belief in magic in the age of science. *SAGE Open, 4,* 1–17. doi:10.1177/2158244014521433.

References

Subbotsky, E. (2011). The ghost in the machine: Why and how the belief in magic survives in the rational mind. *Human Development, 54*(3), 126–43. doi:10.1159/000329129.

Turner, V. (1967). *The forest of symbols*. London: Cornell University Press.

Tylor, E. B. (1871). *Primitive culture: Researches into the development of mythology, philosophy, religion, art and custom*. London: John Murray.

Wilder, D. A. (1978). Effect of predictability on units of perception and attribution. *Personality and Social Psychology Bulletin, 4*(2), 281–4.

Zacks, J. M., Tversky, B., & Iyer, G. (2001). Perceiving, remembering, and communicating structure in events. *Journal of Experimental Psychology: General, 130*(1), 29–58.

Chapter 23

Arago, J. É. V. (1822). *Promenade autour du monde pendant les années 1817, 1818, 1819 et 1820, sur les corvettes du roi l'Uranié et la Physicienne commandées par M. Freycinet: avec Atlas de 26 planches Dessinées par l'auteur* (Vol. 2). Paris: Leblanc.

Atkinson, Q. D., Meade, A., Venditti, C., Greenhill, S. J., & Pagel, M. (2008). Languages evolve in punctuational bursts. *Science, 319*, 588.

Beatty, A. (1992). *Society and exchange in Nias*. Oxford: Claredon Press.

Bellah, R. N. (2011). *Religion in human evolution: From the paleolithic to the axial age*. Cambridge, MA: Harvard University Press.

Bogesi, G. (1948). Santa Isabel, Solomon Islands. *Oceania, 18*(4), 208–32.

Bremmer, J. N. (2007). *The strange world of human sacrifice*. Leuven: Peeters.

Bulbulia, J., Fraser, G., Watts, J., Shaver, J. H., & Gray, R. D. (2017). Can honest signaling theory clarify religion's role in the evolution of social inequality? *Religion, Brain & Behavior, 7*(4), 285–9.

Burt, B. (1994). *Tradition and Christianity: The colonial transformation of a Solomon Islands society*. Chur: Harwood Academic.

Carrasco, D. (1999). *City of sacrifice*. Boston: Beacon Press.

Coulanges, F. (1877). *The ancient city: A study of religion, laws, and institutions of Greece and Rome*. Boston: Lee and Shepard.

Cronk, L. (1994). Evolutionary theories of morality and the manipulative use of signals. *Zygon, 29*(1), 81–101.

Cummins, H. G., 1977. Tongan Society at the time of European Contact. In N. Rutherford (Ed.), *Friendly islands: A history of Tonga* (pp. 63–89). Melbourne: Oxford University Press.

Currie, T. E., Greenhill, S. J., Gray, R. D., Hasegawa, T., & Mace, R. (2010). Rise and fall of political complexity in island South-East Asia and the Pacific. *Nature, 467*(7317), 801–4.

del Castillo, B. D. (2008). *The history of the conquest of New Spain*. Edited by D. Carrasco. Albuquerque: University of New Mexico Press.

Diamond, J. (1997). *Guns, germs, and steel: The fates of human societies*. New York: W. W. Norton.

Durkheim, E. (1915). *The elementary forms of the religious life*. London: Allen & Unwin.

Flannery, K., & Marcus, J. (2012). *The creation of inequality: How our prehistroic ancestors set the stage for monarchy, slavery, and empire*. Cambridge, MA: Harvard University Press.

Fortunato, L., & Jordan, F. (2010). Your place or mine? A phylogenetic comparative analysis of marital residence in Indo-European and Austronesian societies. *Philosophical Transactions of the Royal Society B: Biological Sciences, 365*(1559), 3913–22.

Girard, R., Hamerton-Kelly, R. G., Burkert, W., & Smith, J. Z. (1987). *Violent origins: Walter Burkert, René Girard & Jonathan Z. Smith on ritual killing and cultural formation*. Palo Alto, CA: Stanford University Press.

Goodenough, W. H. (1957). Oceania and the problem of controls in the study of cultural and human evolution. *Journal of the Polynesian Society, 66*(2), 146–55.

Gray, R. D., Drummond, A. J., & Greenhill, S. J. (2009). Language phylogenies reveal expansion pulses and pauses in Pacific settlement. *Science, 323*(5913), 479–83.

Harner, M. (1977). The ecological basis for Aztec sacrifice.*American Ethnologist, 4*(1), 117–35.

Holden, C. J., & Mace, R. (2003). Spread of cattle led to the loss of matrilineal descent in Africa: A coevolutionary analysis. *Proceedings of the Royal Society B: Biological Sciences, 270*(1532), 2425–33.

Jordan, F. M. (2013). Comparative phylogenetic methods and the study of pattern and process in kinship. In P. McConvell, I. Keen, & R. Hendery (Eds.), *Kinship systems: Change and reconstruction* (pp. 43–58). Salt Lake City: University of Utah Press.

Kamakau, S. M. (1964). *Ka Po'E Kahiko: The people of old.* Honolulu: Bernice P. Bishop Museum.

Mace, R., & Holden, C. J. (2005). A phylogenetic approach to cultural evolution. *Trends in Ecology & Evolution, 20*(3), 116–21.

Mace, R., Jordan, F. M., & Holden, C. J. (2003). Testing evolutionary hypotheses about human biological adaptation using cross-cultural comparison. *Comparative Biochemistry and Physiology, 1*(136), 85–94.

Mace, R., & Pagel, M. (1994). The comparative method in anthropology. *Current Anthropology, 35*(5), 549–64.

Marx, K., & Engels, F. (1975). *Karl Marx and Friedrich Engels: Collected works.* New York: International Publishers.

Metraux, A. (1940). *Ethnology of Easter Island.* Honolulu: Bernice P. Bishop Museum.

Naroll, R. (1961). Two solutions to Galton's Problem. *Philosophy of Science, 28*(1), 15–39.

Norenzayan, A., Shariff, A. F., Gervais, W.M., Willard, A. K., McNamara, R. A., Slingerland, E., & Henrich, J. (2014). The cultural evolution of prosocial religions. *Behavioral and Brain Sciences, 39*, 1–86.

Pagel, M. (1994). Detecting correlated evolution on phylogenies: A general method for the comparative analysis of discrete characters. *Proceedings of the Royal Society B: Biological Sciences, 255*(1342), 37–45.

Pagel, M., & Meade, A. (2006). Bayesian analysis of correlated evolution of discrete characters by reversible-jump Markov chain Monte Carlo. *American Naturalist, 167*(6), 808–25.

Price, B. J. (1978). Demystification, enriddlement, and Aztec cannibalism: A materialist rejoinder to Harner. *American Ethnologist, 5*(1), 98–115.

Turner, C. G., & Turner, J. A. (1999). *Man corn: Cannibalism and violence in the prehistroic American southwest.* Salt Lake City: University of Utah Press.

Tylor, E. B. (1889). On a method of investigating the development of institutions: Applied to laws of marriage and descent. *Journal of the Anthropological Institute of Great Britain and Ireland, 18*, 245–72.

Valeri, V. (1985). *Kingship and sacrifice: Ritual and society in ancient Hawaii.* Chicago: University of Chicago Press.

Watts, J., Greenhill, S. J., Atkinson, Q. D., Currie, T. E., Bulbulia, J., & Gray, R. D. (2015a). Broad supernatural punishment but not moralising high gods precede the evolution of political complexity in Austronesia. *Proceedings of the Royal Society B: Biological Sciences, 282*(1804), 20142556.

Watts, J., Sheehan, O., Greehill, S. J., Gomes-Ng, S., Atkinson, Q. D., Bulbulia, J., & Gray, R. D. (2015b). Pulotu: Database of Austronesian supernatural beliefs and practices. *PLOS One, 10*(9), e0136783.

INDEX

Index

euthanasia 59
Evans, E. M. 38
evolutionary biology 125
evolutionary history 27, 243, 244, 245
evolution of religion 155, 156, 161, 162, 242–3
expectation violation, and memory 94–5, 96–7, 98, 99, 100, 109, 233, 252 n.6 (Ch 9)

face blindness 75
facial features 76, 85, 86
fairness 54, 119
fallible human 36
false beliefs 13, 33–8
false memory 16
familiarization 236–7
family 1, 7, 42, 43, 45, 49, 54, 57, 76, 78, 160, 173, 179, 181, 200
family-based prosociality 133
Fantaghiro (Italian fairy tale series) 94
Faraday, Michael 110
favoritism 48, 50, 51, 54
fear 18, 124, 145
fire-walking 163, 165
flying cow concept 103, 252 n.4(Ch 9)
folk dualism 63–73, 66, 68
folk psychology 33 *see also* theory of mind
folk sciences 96, 108, 252 n.4 (Ch 9)
forgiveness 46, 51, 113
free will 152
friends 43, 77, 179, 198, 200, 208
fundamentalism 124, 130
Fux, M. 132

Galton's Problem 241, 242, 244
Geaney, Jane 69, 70
Gelman, Susan 55
genetic evolution 133
Gervais, W. M. 100
gestural expressions 186–7
ghosts 7, 24, 26, 102
goal-demoted actions 236, 237
goal demotion 235–6
God concepts 17, 138
    acquisition of 33–4
    anthropomorphism *see* anthropomorphism
    measurement of 15–24
    multiplicity of 23
God(s)
    and abundance 93
    agency *see* agency, agents
    anthropomorphization of *see* anthropomorphism
    in Christian theology 204
    communicating with 203–4, 206, 207
    depiction of 15
    direct conversation with 204, 207, 210

emotions of 102
and goodness 133–43
as humanlike 16, 17, 19, 20, 21, 23
minds of 26
non-human properties 20
personal relationship with 204, 206–7, 211
and prayers *see* praying, prayers
punitive aspects 143, 146, 147, 152–3
and social regulation 27
special characteristics of 36
surveillance 41–54, 145–53
visibility of 18
good deeds, performance of 197, 201, 202
goodness, god's role in 133–43
government 25, 26, 28
Greek fraternities 157
Grimm, V. 131
group commitment, signals of 155, 157, 201
group identity 173–4
Gulf War 182
Guodian corpus 64, 252 n.2 (Ch 7)
Guthrie, Stewart 3, 16, 17

habitual behavior 87, 190, 209, 253
hajj 223, 224, 225, 226
Halal dietary 177, 178
hallucinations 13
hand-movement acceleration 186–8, 189
Handwerker, Penn 199
Han Dynasty 71
happenings, reasons for 12
hard-to-fake signals of group commitments, religion as 156, 157
Harris, P. L. 59, 60, 62
Hauser lab controversy 252 n.8
Havadalah 222, 225, 226
hazard precaution theory 126
hazards, and religion 124, 125, 128, 131, 132
healing, and rituals 172
Heidegger, Martin 181
Henrich, J. 100
heuristics 90
high-anxiety condition 186, 187, 188, 189
high-arousal ritual 163, 169
higher cognition 64, 67, 68, 72, 252 n.5 (Ch 7)
higher power, connection to 57, 58
Hinduism 115, 165–6, 190, 218, 219–20, 225, 240
    aarthi ritual 219–20
    abhishekam ritual 219
    raksha bandhan festival 220
    thread ceremony (upanayanam or munja) 219
    wedding ceremony 219
Hodge, K. M. 60
homophobia 62
honesty 143, 173

Index

Index

Religious Kibbutz Movement Federation 158
religious leaders 113, 159, 161, 223, 247
religious prime 119, 120, 121, 136, 137, 139, 142, 143
Rethinking Religion (Lawson and McCauley) 211, 231
reverse inference 207, 209
Riekki, T. 60
rite of passage 221
ritualization 93, 182, 184, 185, 186, 187, 189, 190, 229–38
ritualized actions, processing of 229–38
ritual killing *see* human sacrifice
ritual meaning 231
rituals 26, 42, 56, 161, 163–72, 211–27
   and anxiety 125, 181–91, 190
   collective performance 158, 164
   daily rituals 78
   display among animals 231
   engagement in 127, 128, 129
   healing powers of 172
   high-intensity 164, 167, 170–1
   human sacrifice, and social inequality 239–48
   mental representations 211–12, 213
   mythological explanation of the origin of 213
   and prosocial behavior 166
   ritualized actions, processing of 229–38
   as signals of commitment 156, 160, 172
   and social cohesion 163–72
   and stress during war 193–202
   superstition 194
Roazzi, M. 60
"Robbers" story 111–12
rope fishing 195
Ruffle, Bradley 158

Sabbath 158, 160, 222
   lighting Shabbat candles 160, 222, 225, 226
Sacks, Oliver 75
sacrifice 145, 232
   of animals 220
   of humans 239–48
sacrificial victims 239, 246, 247
salience 147–8, 150, 152
   manipulation 147–8, 153
   mortality salience 124, 125, 128, 130, 131–2
Santa Claus 28, 205, 206, 208
scarcity, and formation of social structure 42
science 71, 110
second-order theory of mind 13
Second Palestinian Intifada (SPI) 193, 196, 201
secular institutions 138–40, 146
secularism 134–5, 137–40, 156–7, 161, 197–8, 201
secular kibbutzim 159, 160, 162
secular prime 116, 118, 139
secular punishment 27

seeing meaningful signs in natural events 5–14
self 54, 62, 64, 79, 82, 133, 173, 174
self-deceptive enhancement 135
selfishness 149
self-reports 116, 135, 164, 168, 169, 171, 178, 180, 184, 189
semantic underdetermination 231
sensory pageantry, ritual as 211, 217–26
sexism 62
Sharansky, Natan 193
shen (physical body, self) 64, 66, 72, 252 n.3 (Ch 7)
Sifonis, C. M. 109
signaling theories of religion 155–62, 173–80
similarity perspective 33–9
Simmons, J. P. 141, 142
Simonsohn, U. 141
simulated agents *see* computer simulation
Skinner, B. F. 194
slaves 241, 246–7
Slingerland, E. 71, 73
Smith, Erin 59
Smith, J. Z. 125
social behavior 26, 54, 115, 121
social cognition 6, 55, 204, 205–6, 207–8, 210
social cohesion, and rituals 163–72
social construction 3
social desirability issue 135, 164
social elites 239, 246, 247, 248
social hierarchies 239, 247
social inequality, and human sacrifice 239–48
social structures, formation of 42
sociographic prudery (SP) 125, 127
solidarity 157, 158, 161, 163
sorcery 45, 46
Sørensen, Jesper 232, 238
soul 55–62
   essentialism 55–6, 61–2
   influence of culture on the concept of 61
   and intuitive mind–body dualism 60
soul spirituality 58
South Africa 132, 241
South Asia 76, 89, 90
special agent rituals 215, 217–19, 220, 221, 222, 223–4, 226
special patient rituals 216, 220, 223, 224, 225
speech production 203, 205, 208
Spelke, Elizabeth 15
Sperber, Dan 17, 94, 231
spirits 26, 31, 54, 60, 240
spiritualists 60
spirit worship 115
Spitzmüller, C. 110
"Spring Day" story 107, 112
Staal, Frits 231
stem cell research 57, 58, 59

Index